Vulcan's Hammer

V-Force Projects and Weapons Since 1945

Vulcan's Hammer

V-Force Projects and Weapons Since 1945

Chris Gibson

HIKOKI
PUBLICATIONS

'What stands out above all is that compared with the Americans we try to do this kind of thing on a shoestring. They may be lavish but we have overdone carefulness. It is frightening that in future these troubles should be tackled by management that are responsible to several different countries at once.'

Richard Chilver, Deputy Secretary, Ministry of Defence, 1961

To Paul Henney,
who only saw the draft.

First published in 2011 by
Hikoki Publications Ltd
1a Ringway Trading Est
Shadowmoss Rd
Manchester
M22 5LH
England

Email: enquiries@crecy.co.uk
www.crecy.co.uk

Reprinted 2013

© Chris Gibson 2011

Colour drawings: © Adrian Mann 2011
Line drawings: © Chris Gibson 2011

Layout by Russell Strong

ISBN 9 781902 109176

Printing in China through World Print

Half-title page: Deep inside Soviet airspace, the return stage of an Avro WRD TRM-3 radar reconnaissance drone separates from the radar carrier at the end of its run. The upper stage will return to base with recordings of radar imagery. *Adrian Mann*

Title page, upper: Aircraft of the V-Force. Avro Vulcan XA892 leads this vic from the A&AEE, trailed by the Handley Page Victor XA919 to port and the Vickers Valiant WZ373 to starboard. *Via Terry Panopalis*

Title page, lower: The Two-Stage Aircraft. A Blue Steel on its loading trolley on display with its Vulcan carrier. *Author's Collection*

Contents

Avro Vulcan XA903 retracts its undercarriage on departure from Avro's Woodford Aerodrome on a Blue Steel trials flight.
Via Kev Darling

I have nothing but admiration for the staff, mainly volunteers, at the archives that hold the information that made this book possible. Thankfully not all organisations see their history as an encumbrance; BAE Systems takes a particularly benevolent view of their heritage and maintain archives at Brooklands, Warton and Woodford all of which are staffed by knowledgeable former employees. The RAF Museum at Hendon is an invaluable source of information while the National Archives at Kew is a treasure trove of material and, as the location of many an 'aero-palaeontology' find, is the Burgess Shale of aviation historical research.

Vulcan's Hammer would not have been possible without the help and patience of a wide range of people, none of whom I can thank enough. Top of the patience list is my wife Kirsten whose encouragement and help has been invaluable. Neil Lewis edited and made *Vulcan's Hammer* possible while Adrian Mann brought the various paper planes to life with his illustrations. Russ Strong, who designed and laid out *Vulcan's Hammer*, deserves special thanks for turning a stack of images and a text file into the book you now hold.

Tony Buttler and Phil Butler have provided much assistance and advice not to mention keeping me on the straight and narrow. Special thanks are reserved for Gordon Leith and Peter Elliot at the RAF Museum who have an uncanny knack of finding very interesting material. Professor John Allen was kind enough to allow access to his archive material on the Avro Weapons Research Division while information on Avro aircraft projects came from George Jenks, David Fildes and the volunteers at Avro Heritage at BAE Woodford. The new material on the English Electric P.10 was furnished by Tony Wilson and the volunteers at the North West Heritage Group at BAE Warton. Telling the story of the VC10 pofflers and the Vickers supersonic bomber was made possible by the sterling work of Albert Kitchenside, Chris Farara and Jack Fuller from the Brooklands Museum. Harry Fraser-Mitchell of the Handley Page Association provided invaluable information on the Victor and HP's fascinating laminar flow control work. Brian Burnell's relentless research into unravelling Britain's nuclear weapons deserves wider recognition, while Richard Moore helped place these in their political framework.

To gain an insight into the use of Blue Steel, John Saxon provided interesting recollections of testing at Woomera while the fascinating information on the servicing and preparation of Blue Steel, particularly from the 'liney's' point of view, was furnished through the 617 Squadron Association who put me in touch with Dave Moore, Mike Hines and Rob Gilvary.

While not directly involved with the research and writing of *Vulcan's Hammer*, it could not have been completed without practical help from Bobbie Alexander, Bob Thornton, David Howe and the drilling team of the Forties Field.

A Hawker Siddeley Dynamics, formerly Avro Weapons Research Division, Blue Steel stand-off weapon rests on a trolley before loading on an Avro Vulcan. *Via Terry Panopalis*

'He had once conceived the thought of writing The Life Of Oliver Cromwell...He at length laid aside this scheme, on discovering that all that can be told of him is already in print; and that it is impracticable to procure any authentick (sic) information in addition to what the world is already possessed of.'

James Boswell on Dr Johnson

Dr Johnson's musings on a work about the life of Cromwell are relevant to many subjects in the first decade of the Twenty First Century. In the field of aviation literature the Avro Vulcan springs to mind immediately as one such topic, being the subject matter of books ranging from general histories, pilots' experiences and ultimately, a workshop manual. The Vulcan and its stablemates, Victor and Valiant, deserve the volume of coverage they have attracted and have become an enduring feature of British aviation publishing.

Readers must bear in mind that these aircraft were developed for a reason: to carry the United Kingdom's nuclear deterrent and as the V-Force; they did so from 1956 until replaced by the Polaris system in 1969. The shape of that airborne deterrent changed over the years from a large free-fall bomb to a sleek missile, Blue Steel, which has been described as the most complex vehicle ever built in Britain. The Blue Steel missile installed under a Vulcan, as close to the public face of the deterrent as can be imagined, was but a solitary example of the tremendous amount of work that was carried out behind closed doors. While *Vulcan's Hammer* is about the British efforts, the American Skybolt missile must be examined. Hailed as the saviour of the V-Force, it was shot from under Bomber Command by a US President and his sceptical Secretary of Defense. Skybolt formed the basis of a number of design studies for aircraft to carry it on continuous air

The size of the Soviet Union is apparent in this map of the Earth. The relative coverage of British Skybolt and Polaris missiles from their proposed launch areas are superimposed. In reality, only Polaris provided optimum targeting. Modified from Wikicommons.

Key to the illustration:

------ Extent of Skybolt coverage from a launch point at 200nm stand-off.

——— Limit of Polaris coverage from selected launch points. Area within boundary is outside Polaris range.

alert and its cancellation triggered a 'flap' in Whitehall and a plethora of stop-gaps.

There were more than just threats and counter-threats to influence the development of the British deterrent. Economics has never played a great role in the written history of the V-Force or the story of postwar British aviation; however it is impossible to ignore the economic and political factors that affected this story. The policy-makers and the decisions made by them have been vilified by many in the field of aviation history, despite the reasoning behind many of the decisions having rarely been examined nor have the economic conditions influencing these decisions been discussed.

The economic problems that began in 2008 ushered in what the media referred to as 'a new Age of Austerity' in the United Kingdom. The use of the adjective 'new' informed the public that a similar situation had arisen before: in the decade following the Second World War. It was in this era that the V-Force had its origins. Such was the economic turmoil of these times that the cost of what became the V-bombers placed a drain on the British economy, so much so that alternatives were sought.

These alternatives, such as unmanned bombers, were doubly attractive because they were both cheap, expendable and could use all their fuel for the long mission to the Soviet heartland. Geographical distance had not been a great hindrance to the western Allies in their prosecution of the war against Germany, but was a factor in the USAAF's bomber offensive against Japan. However, the distances involved in any attack on the Soviet Union, a country whose extent defies description, posed the same problem to the Air Staff as it had to Hitler and Napoleon. The Soviet Union covered one sixth of the Earth's land surface, eleven time zones and extended across forty six degrees of longitude and forty degrees of latitude. If that fails to impress, consider that the Soviet Union was two-and-a-half times larger than the United States. Added to that were the Warsaw Pact countries, the satellite states of Eastern Europe that acted as a buffer between the Soviet Union and the countries of the North Atlantic Treaty Organisation (NATO). Any force that intended attacking the Soviet Union required equipment with sufficient range to cross the vast tracts of land that form the Russian landscape.

Even if the range of bombers and missiles was sufficient to attack targets in the depths of Russia, knowledge of these targets was sparse. Even the location of major cities, the so-called closed cities such as Chelyabinsk-65 (now called Ozersk) or Krasnoyarsk-26 associated with the production of plutonium, was unknown. Therefore some means of locating and identifying targets was required in the form of reconnaissance aircraft, which on seeing the opportunity, the Air Staff promptly reconfigured as a bomber.

With the targets identified there was also the need to navigate to that target and deliver a weapon. The navigational aids developed for the bomber offensive on the Third Reich lacked the range for use over Russia so a new suite of navigational aids was required.

The weapons themselves had to be developed from scratch after the Truman Administration passed the Atomic Energy Act of 1946 (McMahon Act) that forbade foreign involvement in nuclear weapons development and the release of nuclear technology. The United Kingdom's Atomic Weapons Research Establishment embarked on an audacious programme to develop a bomb with 'a bloody Union Jack on top of it' and had by 1957 demonstrated that they were a force to be reckoned with. However such devices are of no use on a test site; it must be turned into a weapon which requires a means of delivery. While the recent opening up of archive material under the Freedom of Information Act 2000 has helped researchers in the aviation and military history fields, material relating to nuclear weapons can still be retained under Section 3(4) of that act. The answers to numerous questions on the UK deterrent lie within such retained material.

Vulcan's Hammer examines Avro's Weapons Research Division efforts to meet changing threats, from within and without, over the decade of Blue Steel development and their attempts to interest unsympathetic ministries in improved equipment.

Vulcan's Hammer is not about V-Force operations, squadron histories, development trials or operations. Look elsewhere for details of individual aircraft and their histories. *Vulcan's Hammer* is about how British deterrent policies changed, how this influenced weapons development and how Britain's engineers and scientists strove to fill the Air Staff's requirements. *Vulcan's Hammer* examines how Britain's engineers and scientists met the economic, geographical, political and technological challenges they faced from 1945 until 1963. They attempted this by using some of the most interesting technologies that came out of the mid-Twentieth Century, details of which languish in archives around the country.

Chris Gibson, Washington, 2011.

1 The Alternative V-Force

A Bristol RA.6 target marker sets off on a reconnaissance mission into Soviet territory.
Adrian Mann

'The only answer to an atomic bomb on London will be an atomic bomb on another great city.' – Clement Attlee, British Prime Minister, August 1945.

Torn between harsh economic reality and the desire to remain at the top table, the British Government saw nuclear weapons and their delivery systems as the only way forward. Denied American atomic weapons knowhow, the British embarked on an atomic bomb programme and development of a means of delivery. These became Blue Danube and the V-bombers that were brought into service at great cost. Such costs, in the Age of Austerity, prompted analysis of other delivery systems that could have formed an alternative V-Force.

In 1945 the United Kingdom emerged from a six-year war that had almost bankrupted the nation. The populace had elected a Labour Government, led by Clement Attlee, on the basis of building a welfare state with education and health care for all. Attlee had been Churchill's deputy throughout the war, a member of a coalition government that had steered the country through the strife-torn early Forties.

Attlee was a reformer on social issues, but on Imperial and military matters Attlee was of the old school. On hearing of the use of the atomic bombs on Japanese cities, he opined that the 'only answer to an atomic bomb on London will be an atomic bomb on another great city.' As such Attlee was the father of

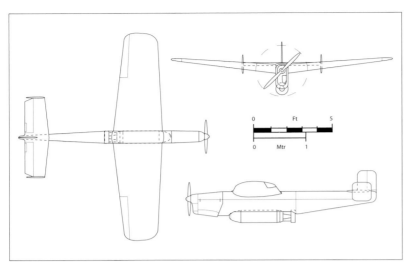

The Miles Hoop-La was a very early attempt to produce a cheap, expendable bomb-delivery system. In 1942 the RAE considered a jet-propelled weapon a better proposition. The Germans came to a similar conclusion and produced the V-1.

of carrying a 10,000 lb (4,535kg) bomb at 500kts (926km/h) at an altitude of 55,000ft (16,763m). This would ultimately lead to the Vulcan and Victor bombers but these projects were still under development. In the light of this the Air Ministry examined alternatives to the B.35/46 types that would provide equivalent capability for a fraction of the cost.

Two options were examined: The unmanned expendable bomber and the Minimum Conventional Bomber. Both were designed around the need to carry a 10,000 lb (4,535kg) payload, which was the weight specified for the 'special' bomb under development to meet OR.1001.

Britain's experience with unmanned bombers dated back to the Larynx, (Long-range gun with Lynx engine) a catapult launched aircraft used for ship-to-ship bombardment that carried a 250 lb (113.4kg) warhead. Larynx was flight tested from HMS *Stronghold* and in 1927 a series of flights in Iraq examined its use in the long range bombardment role. Larynx used a fairly uncomplicated gyro control system to maintain a preset course. By 1929 the trials had shown that the Larynx was an interesting but not particularly effective weapon.

By 1940 the RAF had discovered to its cost that daylight bombing was hazardous and night bombing was haphazard and dangerous. Both saw high casualty rates that were unsustainable in aircrew and airframes. The solution to the haphazard nature of night bombing was a series of bombing aids based around radio technology. These would only become practicable with the development of the cavity magnetron and the centimetric radar in the shape of the H2S ground-mapping set. Until then the RAF could only mount piecemeal operations with mixed results and high loss rates. Such high loss rates were not only at the hands of the Germans, but also that 'unforeseen enemy'; the hill tops of Britain that exacted a heavy toll on aircrew under training.

Influenced by the low accuracy of Bomber Command's raids and the possibility of crew shortages, Miles Aircraft were confident that they could reduce the losses in manpower. They sought to develop a small unmanned bomb-carrying aircraft that could allow attacks on a city-sized target from bases in Britain. Called Hoop-La, Miles designed a small monoplane powered by a de Havilland Gipsy Major engine that could carry a 1,000 lb (453.5kg) bomb. Launched from ramps aligned on the target and with an odometer to count the range Hoop-la was to fly along a bearing and on reaching the desired range, cut the engine. Miles envisaged

deterrence and saw that deterrence would be the future of warfare between major states.

Attlee and his government, having the day after Nagasaki set up the GEN75 committee to develop a nuclear capability, were intent on Britain maintaining its world power status. The atom bomb was of little use without a delivery system and the Air Ministry's plans for a nuclear strike force was going to be very expensive and there were many other Government departments with plans for the country's finances.

Unfortunately the finances were short, leading to the esteemed economist John Maynard Keynes being dispatched to Washington, cap-in-hand to the American government for a loan. One interesting but little known fact about the economics of postwar Britain is the use of Marshall Plan money. The European Recovery Plan was enacted by the US Government to help rebuild the economic foundations of a war-ravaged Europe and was named after US Secretary of State George Marshall. From 1948 until 1952 a sum of approximately thirteen billion dollars was given to help European countries assist in their recovery. Britain received $3,297 million from the programme, more than any other country. Much of this British money went up in smoke, as it remained in the US to pay for tobacco that was seen as a morale booster in Britain where rationing was still in place.

Deterrence was seen as the cheapest way to avoid warfare but in itself would cost a fortune. Not only would the weapon and carrier be expensive but the infrastructure to maintain the deterrent force would need major investment. One outcome of the economic crisis was the examination of alternatives to the bomber projects drawn up to meet Specification B.35/46 (OR.229) for a four-engine bomber capable launching mass attacks on German cities, but the Air Ministry would not sanction such barbarous activity and Hoop-La fell by the wayside. Within a year and after the devastating raid on Coventry, the Air Ministry adopted the doctrine of area bombing of cities.

While Miles were investigating Hoop-La, the Royal Aircraft Establishment (RAE) turned their attention to a small aircraft powered by a novel invention called a turbojet that could carry a 250 lb (113.4kg) bomb load for 300nm (556km) at 400mph (644km/h). This aircraft, with a 10ft (3.05m) wingspan would have weighed in at 680 lb (308kg) making it very cheap to produce if a suitable turbojet had been available. In 1940 no such engine was available, so the RAE dropped the work.

The year 1943 saw another bout of RAE interest in the unmanned bomber, possibly prompted by the increasingly alarming intelligence that was becoming available on German developments in the field. The RAE carried out a series of parametric studies to investigate the possibilities of using alternative engines to power a pilotless bomber. The basic requirement was for a range of 150nm (278km) at 5,000ft (1,524m) with an all-up-weight of 8,000 lb. The studies looked at turbojet, ramjet and liquid rocket power and observed that all three would require catapult launch with rocket boost motors for the climb to 5,000ft (1,524m). The jet showed most promise, with a weapons load of 4,000 lb (1,814kg) at a speed of 400mph (644km/h), the ramjet could carry 3,000 lb (1,360.5kg) at 500mph (805km/h) while the liquid rocket, in the early stages of development at the Rocket Propulsion Establishment (RPE) at Westcott, could only manage 900 lb (408kg) at 400mph (644km/h), with a launch weight of 9,500 lb (4,308kg).

The study concluded that the jet engine was best but most expensive. Within six months Allied air forces had attained air superiority over Western Europe, so yet again the expendable bomber withered on the vine.

The expendable bomber had been examined as a solution to the high costs in manpower and material that accompanied offensive operations

Early Blue Moon configurations. The ramjet variants were non-starters while the turbojet-powered versions, with a payload of 5 x 1,000 lb bombs were incapable of carrying the British atomic bomb.

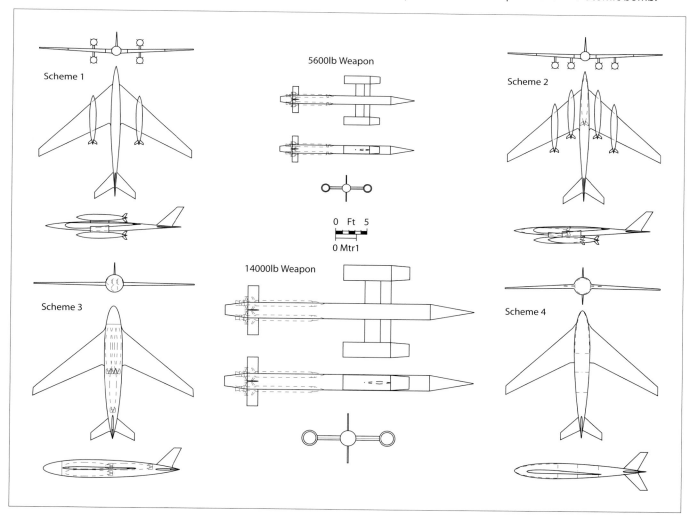

Scheme 1

Scheme 2

Scheme 3

Scheme 4

5600lb Weapon

14000lb Weapon

0 Ft 5

0 Mtr 1

over enemy territory and it was to the expendable bomber that the Air Staff and Air Ministry turned in the straitened economic times of the early 1950s.

Ramjets were all the rage for design studies in the late 1940s and for the long-range expendable bomber appeared to offer speeds and altitudes that would make the weapon invulnerable. Dated May 1950, Technical Memo GW (Guided Weapon) 116 outlined a large ramjet-powered missile to carry a 5,000 lb (2,268kg) warhead a distance of 400nm (741km) at Mach 2 at an altitude of 45,000ft (13,716m). The missile carried a 30in (76cm) ramjet at the end of each rectangular wing and was boosted to Mach 1.5 by a massive rocket motor, almost as large as the missile itself. A version to carry a 2,000 lb (907kg) warhead would have used an 18in (46cm) ramjet. Weights, excluding the boosts, of the missiles were estimated at 14,000 lb (6,350kg) and 5,600 lb (2,540kg) respectively. Two factors scuppered the plans for a ramjet missile. Firstly there were no rocket motors or engines with sufficient thrust to boost the weapon and secondly, the National Gas Turbine Establishment (NGTE) were having enough trouble developing a 6in (15cm) ramjet never mind a large one. It would take a visit to America to provide the key information that would allow Bristol Engines to make large ramjets, so the ramjet expendable bomber was put aside.

The Royal Aircraft Establishment at Farnborough in January 1951 produced Technical Memorandum, Armament, No.1213 in which they examined a series of less ambitious unmanned bombers, Schemes 1 to 3 to carry four or five 1,000 lb (454kg) conventional bombs. These were either the British 1,000 lb, MC, HA/HS (high-altitude/high-speed), or the US naval low-drag bomb, both of which were capable of penetrating 2ft (0.6m) of reinforced concrete. Being an armament paper, the memo did not discuss the propulsion or guidance systems, so no information on engines was supplied. Various combinations of internal and external carriage configurations were examined and these included over and underwing pylons with the overwing stores fired off the pylon by a rocket motor in the tail. Internal carriage required flip-out tailfins and the high drag of external carriage made this the preferred method.

A larger 5,000 lb (2,268kg) bomb was proposed, Scheme 4, and this was to form the forward fuselage, with radar and guidance equipment in the rear portion. The wings of Scheme 4 were intended to be released on reaching the target to allow the fuselage to plummet onto the target. These studies went on to form the basis of an unmanned bomber to carry a much bigger and more powerful weapon – The Special Bomb.

Crewless Expendable Bomber

The Air Ministry was of the opinion that performance on a par with, if not in excess of the B.35/48 types could be achieved by the simple expedient of dispensing with the crew and their associated equipment. To this end in April 1949 a series of draft requirements was issued that would be formalised in OR.203. Issue 1 of this requirement was the supersonic ramjet-powered missile described above that was far beyond the state of the art in 1949. Issue 2 was much more realistic and formed the basis of the design studies in Tech. Memo. 1213. For the Special Weapon a far grander project was required.

What the Air Staff sought was an expendable aircraft capable of carrying 10,000 lb of bombs at 500kts. Air- and ground-launched

The four versions of Blue Moon that the RAE became most interested in. The early A and B lacked the flexibility of the later C and D models that could swap their payloads, thus allowing for developments in weapons.

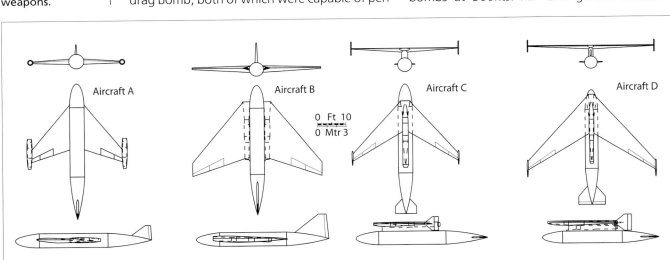

Aircraft A   Aircraft B   0 Ft 10 / 0 Mtr 3   Aircraft C   Aircraft D

versions were examined with a range of 1,670nm (3,093km) which was sufficient to carry a bomb load to Moscow. During the studies that arose from this requirement a number of observations were made including that a pilotless aircraft would be lighter and smaller for the same, if not better, height over target and radius of action. This better performance and with economy its raison d'être, the expendable bomber ensured the best chance of an aircraft carrying an expensive 'Special Store' reaching its target without interception by flak or fighters.

As the studies came under the aegis of the Ministry of Supply (MoS) they were assigned a rainbow code, Blue Moon. Four configurations were examined, A to D, and given the time that the studies were carried out, made the most allowance for the great unknown of the time – the size of the Special Store. Despite the requirement stating that the atomic bomb should weigh no more than 10,000 lb (4,534kg) and have a diameter of 5ft (1.5m), the shape was open to conjecture. All these uncertainties led to the adoption of two basic configurations whereby the weapon was either integrated with the airframe or installed in a large aerodynamic pod.

Aircraft A and B were mid-winged with the special store housed within the fuselage. The A type featured Rolls-Royce Avon turbojets fitted in wingtip nacelles while the B carried its Avons in the wing roots. Each installation had its pros and cons, with the Type B being less susceptible to asymmetric thrust at a critical point in the flight such as take-off. The prospect of a Type A cartwheeling across the airfield with an armed nuclear weapon aboard was not one the Air Staff relished. On the other hand, the wingtip engines made air launch of the Type A much easier than Type B. This is the earliest proposal for an air-launched, nuclear-armed stand-off weapon found in British records. Although no carrier aircraft is identified that would be capable of carrying the 24,500 lb (11,113kg) Aircraft A, carriage by a modified Vulcan might have been feasible. When air-launched the Blue Moon was to be carried up to 36,000ft (10,973m) and once 30 miles (48km) from its take-off base, released by the carrier aircraft. The advantage of this technique was that it avoided the high fuel consumption of the take-off and climb and thus allowed maximum range to be gained from the fuel on the missile.

Integrated stores produced a somewhat inflexible weapon system, so Types C and D were designed around a detachable pod that

A USAF Martin MGM-1 Matador takes off from its zero-length launcher. The Matador had similar capabilities to the putative Blue Moon. *USAF*

would allow weapons upgrades and the facility of swapping the major components around should either become unserviceable. Wings, engines and controls were housed in a detachable structure that could be bolted onto a large pod holding the weapon and most of the fuel. This allowed new pods to be attached, providing for future developments and the ability to fit a manned pod that was to carry controls and a pilot to allow deployment of the aircraft prior to fitting the warhead.

Britain's Snark

The USAAF had by 1946 decided that a pilotless aircraft was a viable means for carrying a nuclear weapon to the Soviet Union. In that year Northrop embarked on development of the MX-775 project and by 1953 the MX-775 had been developed by Northrop as the SM-62 Snark. British expendable bombers could be described as sharing the same niche as the Snark (and its US Navy equivalent, the Regulus) and like the Americans, the British realised that a subsonic aircraft would be vulnerable to defences. In parallel to the subsonic Snark programme, North American Aviation (NAA) began development of a supersonic unmanned bomber (or in modern parlance, a cruise missile, but the difference is an exercise in semantics) under the designation MX-770.

NAA designed a two-stage system that utilised an XLR-71 rocket engine to boost the missile to a speed of Mach 3 where its Wright XRJ-47 ramjets could operate, at which point the booster was jettisoned. The project spawned an X-plane in the shape of the X-10 and eventually this system gained the designation XB-64 and the name 'Navaho'. With a cruising speed of Mach 3 and a ceiling in excess of 80,000ft (24,382m), Navaho was a very

Another equivalent of the Blue Moon studies was Northrop's SM-62 Snark seen here at high altitude. Powered by a Pratt & Whitney J-57 turbojet, the Snark had intercontinental range and in the early 1950s such types would have carried the US deterrent to the Soviet Union. *Author's Collection*

The bulk of the Snark and the large boost rocket motors it required for launch can be seen in this image. Blue Moon would have been just as large, if not larger due to the size of British warheads. *Author's Collection*

advanced and complex system, but by the mid 1950s such weapons were on a cusp. The ballistic missile was beginning to show promise and boasted an invulnerability that an air-breathing system could never have demonstrated.

Meanwhile in Britain, the subsonic expendable bombers had lost out to the V-bombers. However, there was the question of what should follow on from the V-bombers and like the Americans, the Air Staff considered a supersonic expendable bomber with performance in the same class as the Navaho. There were two Mach 2+ projects ongoing in the United Kingdom in the mid 1950s. The first was the OR.330 reconnaissance aircraft to meet Spec. R.156 and the second was Bristol's Type 188 to meet experimental requirement ER.134, intended to support the OR.330 programme.

The OR.330 tender process reached a climax in mid 1955 when Avro were contracted to develop their Type 730. Unfortunately, the Avro 730 was very much a compromise as a proposal from English Electric Aviation at Warton had shown much promise and was the Air Staff's choice on technical grounds. Warton's P.10 was, in comparison, a radical departure from the mainstream designs tendered by the other companies. A more detailed description of the P.10 and the pros and cons of the other OR.330 proposals is available in Chapter Two. Suffice to say, two aspects of the P.10 attracted the Air Staff's attention: its Mach 3 performance and radar cross-section, which was 1/15th that of the Avro 730.

When the Air Staff's thoughts turned to a supersonic flying bomb, Warton's P.10 with its compact design, Mach 3 speed and high ceiling which combined with the small radar signature was considered an ideal basis for a missile. Although the documents in the National Archives mention a P.10B expendable bomber, the English Electric design study for the P.10B in North West Heritage Group archive at Warton is a manned aircraft and the archive holds no record of such an expendable bomber type. The P.10B that English Electric actually drew up is described in a separate chapter, as is the P.10D stand-off weapon.

Perhaps the Air Staff carried out some freelance design studies of their own and the Air Staff's description of the 'P.10B' expendable bomber contains the following information. Equipped to meet OR.330, the P.10 would have had an AUW of around 124,000 lb (56,235kg), speed of Mach 3 and an unrefuelled range of 5,000nm at 70-80,000ft (21,335-24,382m).

When configured as a missile with a 4,500 lb (2,040kg) warhead and 1,000 lb (454kg) of guidance equipment, the AUW would have been almost halved, with a take-off weight of about 60,000 lb (27,211kg), excluding the boost rocket motors.

Guidance systems

Despite the Air Staff's high hopes for Blue Moon, its Achilles Heel was its guidance system. The RAF had honed its navigation and targeting systems in the skies over Western Europe, but the Soviet Union was a different matter. Radio navigation aids such as Oboe were accurate at distances of 250nm (463km) from the base stations while Gee could stretch to 400nm (741km). The maximum useable range of radio aids was increased to 1,200nm (2,222km) by the introduction of LORAN (LOng RAnge Navigation) that was an American development of Gee.

The distances involved in attacking the Soviet Union called for a novel approach. Radio navigation systems could be given extra range by the use of repeater aircraft orbiting on the borders but this would require more support aircraft and would still be limited in range. The Air Staff had high hopes for 'Auto-Astro' which was a star tracker system that located the aircraft position by tracking various stars. The MoS had two systems under development: Orange Tartan which was capable of operation in daylight and Blue Sapphire that could only work at night. However there was concern about the ability of Orange Tartan to operate on eastbound flights during northern Russia's long hours of summer daylight.

Perhaps the most surprising idea, at least in the early 21st Century, was a radio beacon called Blue Sugar which was developed by the TRE to meet OR.3514. Airborne forces had encountered a similar problem, with parachute forces being scattered widely across their objective. The solution was a radio beacon such as Rebecca that was dropped by pathfinder forces allowing the following main force to be deployed close to its target. The Air Staff hoped that a similar Blue Sugar beacon could be deployed at or close to a target in the Soviet Union, allowing the inbound force to home in on it and attack. In fact the Staff were informed that such air-dropped beacons could provide an bombing accuracy of 300 yards (274m) from an aircraft flying at a height of 45,000ft (13,716m) and a speed of 600kts (1,111km/h). These beacons were to be deployed by a pathfinder force or by 'agents' within the country. Blue Moon could use this technique and in 1952 there were also high hopes of modifying the Blue Boar guided bomb to home in on such a beacon. One problem was that the vast distances of the Soviet Union meant that one beacon on the target was far from sufficient and a series of Blue Sugar beacons would have been required, laid along the line of attack.

The beacon homing systems were considered only because there was no other method of providing accurate navigation without resorting to a human navigator. In 1947, a development programme began at the TRE that would have provided a breakthrough in autonomous navigation: Blue Sapphire. To navigate with accuracy three items of information are required: the elevation of the Sun or other celestial body above the horizon, the time and an ephemeris (an almanac that provides the positions of celestial bodies at certain times). Navigators have used these to plot their positions since the 18th Century, when an accurate chronometer became available.

In Blue Sapphire the TRE sought to automate this process by using an automatic sextant comprising a photoelectric cell and telescope to track a star and generate readings for a mechanical calculator. This would send its position data to the control system and make course adjustments. Blue Sapphire could only operate at night which restricted its use in the deterrent role, so the TRE developed a daylight version called Orange Tartan that could track stars such as Polaris in daylight. Daylight capability would have allowed any system thus equipped to navigate to a target anywhere on

Earth with no external input other than specific stars to steer by.

The Blue Moon was to take off from a trolley under the control of a ground-based observer using radio control. Once airborne the navigation system would switch to using Orange Tartan astronavigation and fly to its target. Sounds plausible enough, but there was the small matter of the Soviet air defences. Blue Moon was to carry no defensive armament as its operating altitude was deemed to be beyond that of Soviet fighters, although it could have been fitted with a variety of countermeasures. These included a 'jinker' that made the aircraft take evasive action for the last 400nm (740km) of the flight; however this required extra fuel, so a tail warning device was used to initiate jinking only when required. Window dispensers, triggered by nearby shell bursts were to be fitted to counter radar-directed anti-aircraft fire. A further counter to anti-aircraft fire was Indigo Miller, a device to trigger proximity-fuzed shells before they came within lethal range. By the mid-1950s ballistic missiles were showing potential, so OR.203 and Blue Moon were cancelled in favour of OR.1139, a ballistic missile that bore the codename Blue Streak.

The Minimum Conventional Bomber

As mentioned above, there was another alternative to the B.35/46 bombers and also intended as a cheaper means of deterrence. Called the Minimum Conventional Bomber (MCB) it could be described as a bare-bones bomb carrier, the aim of the study was '…to permit accurate bombing independent of automatic terminal guidance.'

In the 1940s 'conventional' referred to a manned bomber rather than its role, which was to carry the OR.1001 Special Store in a semi-recessed installation. The Air Staff's view was that by reducing the crew and dispensing with life support systems and ejection seats the MCB could provide the same, if not better, performance than B.35/46 in a smaller airframe. The basic configuration was a tailless, swept-wing jet with a vestigial fuselage. The two crew were housed in the nose, with the H2S radar scanner behind the unpressurised cockpit. Power was provided by a pair of Conway bypass turbofans in the rear fuselage. The members of the MCB study group became quite pedantic in their quest for minimum weight. They were vehemently opposed to adding any form of fuselage

The Minimum Conventional Bomber combined the low cost of the Blue Moon with the accuracy of the manned bomber. The Blue Danube bomb could be replaced by a bomb carrier with HE bombs. Unlike Blue Moon, the MCB could be used for non-atomic roles.

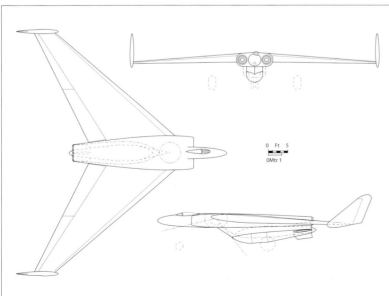

0 Ft 5
0Mtr 1

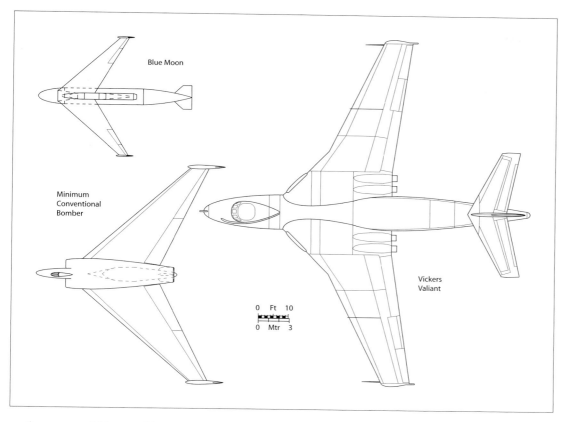

In an era of austerity, cost was proportional to size so the attraction of Blue Moon is evident. The Minimum Conventional Bomber combined the accuracy of a manually-navigated bomber with the low cost of the expendable Blue Moon.

as the space within would encourage designers to fill the available space with heavy items. Undercarriage came under scrutiny at an early stage and the decision was made to provide landing gear but to take off using a boosted trolley.

The advantages the Air Staff saw in the MCB were that a smaller, lighter aircraft would be cheaper for the same performance as B.35/46, and at half the weight can have greater height over target with a greater radius of action. The MCB could achieve all these with less stress on runways and might even be a better carrier air-craft for 'winged bombs'. The reduction in crew would ease the pressure on crew training facilities. The only drawback the Air Staff saw was that the MCB would have been much less flexible than the B.35/46 types, despite being required to carry the same bombing and navigation systems as B.35/46.

In the end the Air Staff and Air Ministry opted for aircraft now familiar as the Valiant, Victor and Vulcan. The alternatives, where viable, were scuppered mainly by the RAF's desire to keep the manned bomber but also by the sheer size of the atomic bombs themselves.

The Alternative V-Force – leading particulars

Type	Length	Span	Diameter	Weight	Propulsion	Speed	Range
Martin Matador	39ft 6in	28ft 7in	4ft 6in	12,000 lb	J33 t/jet	Mach 0.9	608nm
Northrop Snark	67ft 2in	42ft 3in	5ft	48,150 lb	J57 t/jet	Mach 0.9	5,500nm
Blue Moon A	48ft	32ft	5ft 2in	24,500 lb	2 x Avon	Mach 0.9	4,000nm
Blue Moon B	48ft	45ft 5in	5ft 2in	22,700 lb	2 x Avon	Mach 0.9	4,000nm
Blue Moon C	48ft	37ft 6in	5ft 2in	25,800 lb	2 x Avon	Mach 0.9	4,000nm
Blue Moon D	48ft	51ft	5ft 2in	27,700 lb	2 x Avon	Mach 0.9	4,000nm
Blue Moon 1	37ft 6in	15ft	2ft 6in	14,000 lb	2 x ramjet	Mach 2	500nm
Blue Moon 2	36ft	9ft	1ft 6in	5,600 lb	2 x ramjet	Mach 2	500nm
Minimum Conventional Bomber	66ft	75ft	n/a	59,000 lb	2 x Conway	Mach 0.8	Radius of action = 2,500nm

2 The Sons of Vulcan

Vulcan begat two sons, Caeculus and Cacus. Caeculus could ignite and extinguish fires at will, but the smoke from these fires had rendered him blind. Cacus was a monster who breathed fire and consumed human flesh.

Early 1961 – An Avro Type 730 releases its P.18Z payload on a test flight over the Woomera range. The P.18Z was one of a number of supersonic missiles studied by Avro's Weapons Research Department. *Adrian Mann*

Having opted for the V-Bombers, there was a need to identify potential targets and prepare the radar maps for any offensive action. The pace of aviation technology was such that a supersonic reconnaissance aircraft was possible and eventually that might even form the basis of a bomber. While a number of types were considered only three were deemed suitable for reconnaissance and that later conversion to the bomber role. Also of interest are the reconnaissance drones suggested as a less hazardous reconnaissance method.

There can be no over-emphasis of the size of the Soviet Union and it, and its Imperial forebear, had relied on that vastness and climate for defence against invaders from the west. 'General Winter' had seen off Napoleon and Hitler, whose forces had been drawn into the depths of the Russian landmass where, hastened by the severe weather of Russian winters, they had suffered defeat.

To navigate across this vastness required maps and in the case of the Soviet Union, these were neither accurate nor readily available, being classified and even deliberately misleading. The German armed forces had attempted to map the Soviet Union prior to launching Operation Barbarossa in 1941, but such were the changes made to Soviet industry in wartime by the 'crossing of the Urals' that these German maps were rendered useless by the war's end.

To carry out an attack on targets in Russia, the USAF (as the USAAF had become in 1947) and Bomber Command needed knowledge of their locations. Added to this was the uncertainty created by the secret or closed cities that the Soviet Government had established to produce its weapons and nuclear technology. Vastness was a double-edged sword; if a large geographic feature such as a closed city could be hidden, an aircraft, even a large one, could operate with impunity particularly when faced with 1950s Soviet air defences. These were considered to be on a par with Britain's in 1940 and comprised fighters operating under ground-controlled interception directions. Soviet interceptors lacked the range to reach the operating altitude of the attacking bombers and would remain so until the arrival of the MiG-19 (NATO reporting name: *Farmer*).

Almost immediately after the war, the USAAF and RAF commenced reconnaissance flights over Russian territory. Having cancelled specialist long-range reconnaissance aircraft designed for the Pacific War, such as the Republic F-12 Rainbow, wartime types such as the Boeing RB-29/F-13 and Convair RB-36D were deployed. Fitted with arrays of cameras, these attempted to acquire photographic images of possible targets. As defences improved, experiments were conducted involving the Convair GRB-36D as carriers for smaller reconnaissance aircraft such as the Republic RF-84K that were to fly into areas denied to a large, slow bomber. Over the years, as Soviet fighters and radar systems improved, aircraft with higher performance such as North American RB-45C Tornado and the English Electric Canberra replaced the ageing bombers.

In the 1950s radar bombing aids were becoming the primary means of targeting and bomb aiming, so obtaining images of the target's response to radar was required. This mission involved filming the display of a radar-equipped aircraft as it flew over the target, with the results issued to bomber crews to allow them to recognise the target on their own radar displays on a bombing run. By 1949 it had become obvious that the pace of advance in aerospace would make the contemporary reconnaissance types such as the Canberra (modified B.2 and the later PR.3) obsolete sooner rather than later. There was a need for a long-range photo and radar reconnaissance aircraft that could also mark targets or deploy the Blue Sugar beacons that were under development.

The Bristol Aeroplane Co in May 1950 proposed such an aircraft to locate and act as pathfinder for the main force. The RA.4 was a

51,380 lb (23,302kg) AUW single-seat twin-engined type with a mid-mounted wing swept at 45°. Powered by a pair of 50% scaled Bristol Olympus turbojets (4,400 lbf/19.6kN static thrust) it was to be capable of cruising at 505 knots (935km/h) at an altitude of 42,000ft (12,802m) carrying a pilot and 1,200 lb (544kg) of droppable stores for a distance of 7,000nm (12,964km). This range was deceptive as it equated to a mission profile comprising a cruise of 2,500nm (4,630km), a descent to 5,000ft (1,524m) to perform a twenty minute target search or marking operation and on completion of the task, a climb to 40,000ft (12,192m) for the return to base.

The RA.4 had a thin (8.5% chord thickness) swept wing that carried no high-lift devices and therefore had a very high wing loading of 96 lb/ft² (465kg/m²) and needed the thrust of ten 9in (23cm) rocket motors to reach its 224 knot (415kph) take-off speed. Correspondingly, the RA.4's landing speed was in the region of 160 knots (296km/h). The RA.4's wing loading was so high that a revised version with reduced wing loading called the RA.6 was drawn up with a net wing area of 490ft² (45.5m²) as opposed to 475ft² (44.1m²) on the RA.4.

For a target marking or beacon dropping mission the aircraft would take off loaded with

At the end of the Second World War the Americans cancelled their long-range reconnaissance aircraft such as the handsome Republic F-12 Rainbow. Fast and high-flying, the Rainbow carried its own film lab for in-flight processing. Its capabilities could have been put to good use in the Cold War. *Author's Collection*

Types such as the Boeing B-50 Superfortress, here seen with long-range tanks, carried out reconnaissance over the Soviet satellite states and borders. Deep penetration missions became increasingly perilous. *Author's Collection*

Bristol Aircraft's RA.4 and RA.6 would have performed reconnaissance, pathfinding and target marking duties for the V-Force. These types benefited from advanced aerodynamics and represent the cutting edge of British high-speed, long-range design in the early 1950s.

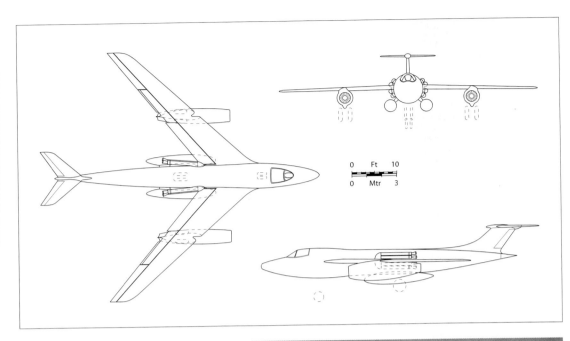

Convair B-36 Peacemakers over the American Mid West. The B-36 was until the mid 1950s the only aircraft in the western air force inventory with the range to reach targets in the Soviet Union. Their reconnaissance missions became untenable as the Fifties progressed, prompting a need for dedicated types such as the U-2 and Bristol RA.6. *USAF*

In response to the requirement OR.285/Spec. B104D for a target marker aircraft, Vickers developed the Valiant B.2. Unfortunately information on where those targets were posed a problem. *Author's Collection*

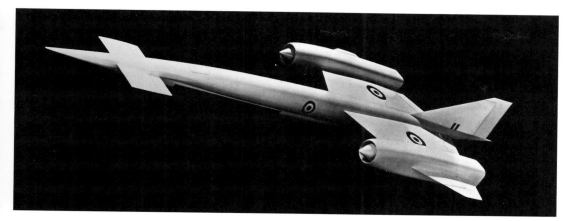

Avro's Type 730 reconnaissance aircraft was to be converted to a bomber under RB.156. Avro proposed shortening the Red Drover antenna and fitting a bomb bay for a 15ft bomb.
BAE Systems/ Avro Heritage

1,000 lb (453kg) of markers and 216 lb (98kg) of flares, or a radio beacon. After dropping the RATO motors on take-off, the fuel in the drop tanks was used first in the climb and the tanks jettisoned. Entering a cruise climb to 42,000ft (12,802m) the RA.4 continued at high altitude until, on entering the target area, it commenced a rapid descent to 5,000ft (1,524m) to hunt for the target, with 20 minutes being available for searching. The target markers would have been dropped in a shallow dive before the aircraft climbed back up to 40,000ft (12,192m) for the return to base.

For a reconnaissance mission it would carry two drop tanks, camera and photoflashes and would follow the same mission profile without the descent to mark the target and consequently would have the full 7,000nm (11,265km) still air range.

The RA.4 and RA.6 were unarmed and depended on speed, altitude plus its tail warning radar and proximity fuze detonation equipment for protection. The single pilot was installed in a pressurised cockpit that could, in the event of an emergency, be jettisoned in its entirety to escape at high altitude or the pilot could use an ejection seat at lower levels.

Bristol also proposed a larger version with an AUW of 73,000 lb (33,106kg) powered by the Armstrong Siddeley Sapphire turbojet (8,300 lb/ 36.9kN). This was designed to cruise at 44,000ft (19,955m) and carry an extra 2,700 lb (1,224kg) of mission equipment or stores.

Caeculus – the Little Blind Son

The pace of aerospace development mentioned above caught up with Bristol's swept-wing designs and speeds of 505kts (935km/h) and altitudes under 50,000ft (15,240m) were soon eclipsed by Soviet fighters such as the MiG-15 *Fagot* and MiG-17 *Fresco* that could reach such speeds and altitudes. These interceptors, plus

the Soviets' work on surface-to-air guided weapons gave the Air Staff grave concern about the survival prospects of subsonic bombers such as the Vulcan and Victor.

Operations Research Department OR.16 in August 1953 issued a paper called 'Pattern of the Future Offensive'. The document indicated a need for a replacement for the V-bombers, (later to become Operational Requirement OR.336) in the early 1960s but also indicated a more pressing need for a reconnaissance platform, specified as R.156, to provide target information. Both roles could be filled by the same basic airframe but to develop it as a bomber would add two years to the in-service date of both types. Therefore, in April 1954 and in the light of the lack of reconnaissance capability, the bomber to meet OR.336 was put into abeyance and the decision was made to develop the new reconnaissance aircraft to meet OR.330 and provide target information for the V-bombers armed with stand-off weapons in the 1960s. The Air Staff requirements branch advised that thirty reconnaissance aircraft were needed and a draft of what would become OR.330 was sent to the Ministry of Supply in July 1954.

An early proposal for the Avro 730. This carries a stand-off weapon on a ventral pylon. The Red Drover radar would be fitted in the fuselage fairings.
Via David Fildes, Avro Heritage

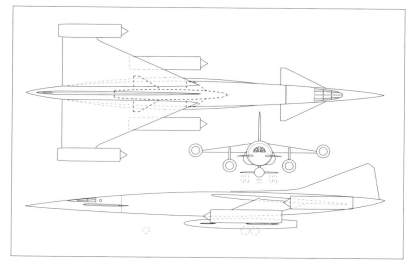

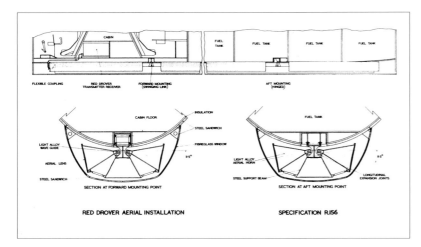

RED DROVER AERIAL INSTALLATION   SPECIFICATION R.156

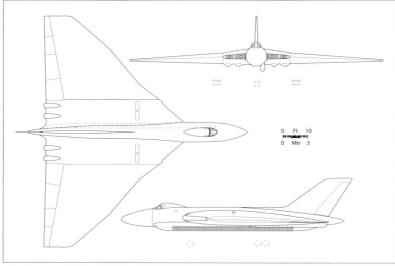

The requirement and attendant specification R.156 called for a supersonic high-altitude reconnaissance aircraft to be in service around 1960 and capable of flying more than 4,000nm (7,408km) at 60,000ft (18,288m) at a speed of Mach 2.5 carrying its primary reconnaissance sensor, the Red Drover radar.

Red Drover was an X–band, later J-band, ground mapping radar that used a pair of 50ft (15.2m) antenna arranged along the lower fuselage sides, what would become known as a sideways-looking airborne radar (SLAR). These long antennae looked downwards and to the side of the aircraft's ground track, but were blind to a swathe of terrain twenty miles (32.2km) wide beneath the aircraft's track. R.156 was to use radar rather than optical sensors and with no direct means of looking out of their aircraft, the crew were blind to what passed below them. One half of a Red Drover was to commence flight trials on a modified Vulcan in 1957. For these trials a single antenna was mounted in a long fairing that stretched from just aft of the crew entry door along the lower fuselage and terminated just forward of the wing trailing edge.

Two versions of Red Drover were developed, one by EMI and used on the Avro 730 and another by Vickers themselves for their SP4. The Vickers Red Drover antennae used two back-to-back parabolic reflectors 50ft (15.2m) long mounted on a central beam. Either side of the central beam, directed inwards onto each

Top: Cross-section of EMI's Type 800 radar to meet the OR.3579. This sideways-looking airborne radar (SLAR) was to provide radar reconnaissance pictures for the V-Force.
BAE Systems/ Avro Heritage

Above: As a flying testbed, Avro proposed fitting a Vulcan trials aircraft with a 'half' Red Drover radar for trials. The size of the antenna is evident.
Via David Fildes, Avro Heritage

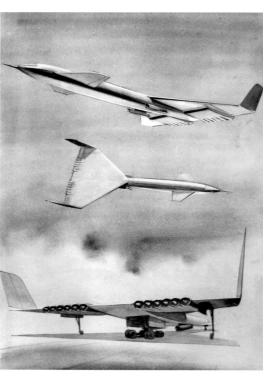

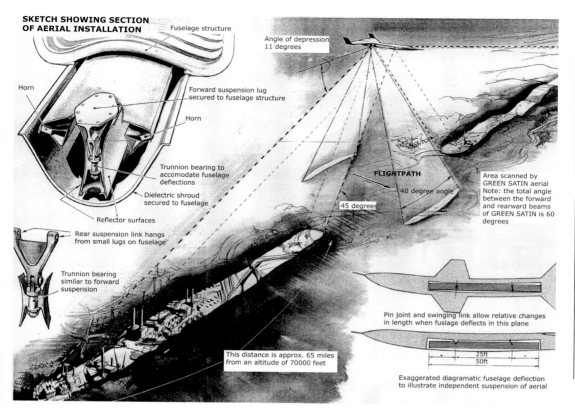

SKETCH SHOWING SECTION OF AERIAL INSTALLATION

Fuselage structure

Angle of depression 11 degrees

Horn

Forward suspension lug secured to fuselage structure

Horn

Trunnion bearing to accomodate fuselage deflections

FLIGHTPATH

Dielectric shroud secured to fuselage

40 degree angle

Area scanned by GREEN SATIN aerial Note: the total angle between the forward and rearward beams of GREEN SATIN is 60 degrees

Reflector surfaces

45 degrees

Rear suspension link hangs from small lugs on fuselage

Trunnion bearing similar to forward suspension

This distance is approx. 65 miles from an altitude of 70000 feet

Pin joint and swinging link allow relative changes in length when fuslage deflects in this plane

25ft

50ft

Exaggerated diagramatic fuselage deflection to illustrate independent suspension of aerial

Opposite page, bottom left: Vickers' SP4 certainly looked the part. This version was fitted with 14 RB.121 engines to propel it to the required Mach 2. *BAE Systems/ Brooklands Museum*

Opposite page, bottom right: This version of the Vickers SP4 was fitted with six large turbojets such as the DH Gyron. The engine changes were intended to allow the SP4 to meet R.156. *BAE Systems/ Brooklands Museum*

reflector at an angle, was a 50ft (15.2m) long horn transmitter/receiver. This meant that the reflectors could be mounted to allow for movement of the aircraft structure. EMI's Red Drover for the Avro Type 730 lacked the central reflector and used larger transmit/receive horns directed outwards and downwards. The whole antenna assembly was mounted to allow for movement rather than just the reflector. The Vickers version may have been a more compact installation, but could a 50ft (15.2m) long radar be described as compact?

The intention of Red Drover was to prepare radar maps of routes into the Soviet Union and allow the V-Force to follow these predetermined tracks, by day or night, with great accuracy on their own radars. As a navigation aid to the OR.330 types it was essentially a very refined form of dead reckoning as the V-bombers used H2S radars that would provide a different radar image to the SLAR. The Air Staff intended that later versions of the V-bombers such as the Victor Phase 3 would have had their own SLAR in the rear fuselage.

The Ministry accepted tenders from Avro Aircraft, English Electric Aviation, Handley Page Aircraft and Vickers. Shorts and Saunders-Roe (Saro) submitted studies but the Shorts tender, the PD.12, was considered more of a fall-back design, playing a similar role in the OR.330/R.156 process to that of that company's SA.4 Sperrin

played in the OR.239/B.14/46 V-bomber development. Therefore Shorts did not submit its PD.12 as a formal tender. Saro's design was the P.188, which came in two versions, one with 16 RB.121 turbojets, eight in each wingtip engine pod. Another version used a RB.122 in each wingtip pod with two mounted on the upper fuselage ahead of the tail surfaces. Neither of these went further than initial drawings and Saunders-Roe did not tender for the OR.330 contest.

Of the four tenders taken most seriously by the Ministry and Air Staff only two, the Avro Type 730 and the English Electric P.10 met the speed and range requirements. Handley Page's HP.100 failed to meet the required range while Vickers' Type SP.4 met neither the speed nor range. Only the P.10 used cockpit glazing, the others relying

Above: Vickers' own electronics department created its own radar to meet OR.3579 Red Drover. The differences from the EMI radar, specifically a back-to-back reflector can be seen in this diagram from a Vickers brochure. *BAE Systems/ Brooklands Museum*

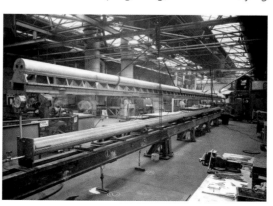

Left: This jig was used to manufacture the antenna components for the EMI Type 800 Red Drover radar. Again the length of the antenna is obvious. *BAE Systems/ Avro Heritage*

This diagram from the Vickers SP4 brochure shows the crew stations and cockpit layout. The pilot used a periscope to view the world through the nose undercarriage bay. *BAE Systems/ Brooklands Museum*

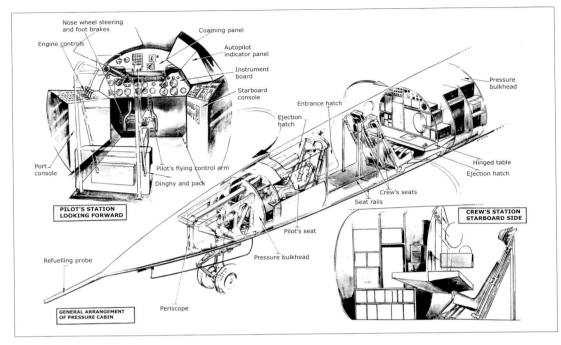

Vickers took a separate approach to the bomber aircraft with this six-engined canard. This may have been to meet OR.336 or perhaps a later tactical requirement carrying Red Beard.

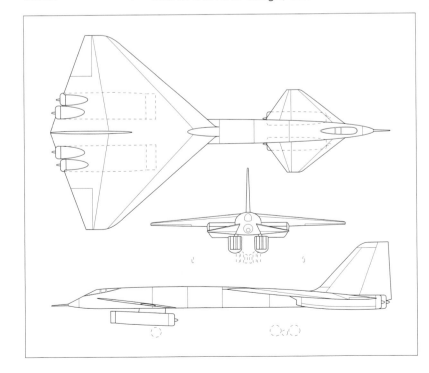

on periscopes for the pilot to use on take-off and landing. The Avro 730's periscope extended upward from the top of the cockpit, whereas the Vickers SP.4 periscope's objective lens was in the nose undercarriage bay allowing the pilot to see only when the wheels were down.

The Air Staff were particularly taken with English Electric's P.10 that possessed a ceiling in excess of 70,000ft (21,336m) and speed of Mach 3 thanks to an innovative integrated ram-jet wing. It also had a radar signature 1/15th that of the Avro design, thanks no doubt to its smaller airframe and two turbojets buried in the wing roots. Unfortunately the integrated ram-jets would take time to develop and the Air Staff were sceptical of English Electric's claim that it would only take one year longer than the competing Avro design. In response to this, English Electric examined fitting the P.10 with conventional Bristol Engines axisymetric podded ram-jets and drew up the P.10C, described below.

The winner was the Avro Type 730. It met the range, speed and timescale guidelines laid out in R.156 and Avro were awarded the contract in 1955.

Cacus – the Fire-Breathing Son

Meantime, although put on a back-burner, the supersonic bomber was still on the Air Staff's wish list. The Air Staff were well aware that the ballistic missile was the future, but wished to continue development of a V-bomber replacement until such time that the ballistic missile could be proven. In the RAE's technical Note Aero.2353 issued in December 1954, Messrs Lawlor and Griggs described the use of the OR.330 reconnaissance aircraft as a bomber. The note concluded that semi-recessed carriage of a 12,000 lb (5,442kg) weapon would incur an 8% reduction in range and a 1,500ft (457m) decrease in cruising height. The weapon was to be cylindrical and flat-nosed to produce high drag, thus slowing the bomb, allowing the aircraft to escape its blast on detonation.

To stabilise the bomb, three fins were to be fitted, two protruding into the airstream and the third being retracted into the bomb casing. The diameter was almost the same as the aircraft and so would have to be installed semi-recessed in an enlarged reconnaissance equipment bay between the radar antennae and would require fore and aft fairings to smooth the airflow around the bomb. Fortunately these could be used to carry fuel and be dropped at the same time as the bomb. Exposed to the airflow of a Mach 2.5 flight, the bomb casing would heat up, so some form of cooling would also have been required.

Meanwhile Avro had carried out their own design studies into modifying the original Type 730 into a bomber. At this point it must be pointed out that the design teams were supplied with scant details of the 'Special Weapon' called Blue Rosette, merely length and diameter. Diameter was based on the size of the physics package of the Green Bamboo warhead which was a 45in (114cm) diameter sphere.

Avro examined three options, named after the type of weapon they were intended to carry as the '15ft internally carried', '25ft internally carried' and '50ft externally carried stand-off bomb'. The Air Staff's thinking was that the length of the Red Drover antenna should be maintained or the changes to it kept to a minimum; however the Air Staff agreed that as development progressed, the antenna could be shortened to 35ft (10.7m). While the shorter antenna might not possess the resolution required for reconnaissance, it would be sufficient for bombing. This shorter antenna would allow a bomb to be installed ahead of the 730's main undercarriage bay at the expense of 1,645 Imperial gallons (7,478 litres) of fuel.

The great unknown was how to deliver a weapon from the cosseted temperature-controlled environment of the weapons bay into the hostile conditions of the Mach 2.5 airstream. Avro took a different tack from that of English Electric (of which more later) and relied on a sequence of rapid events to minimise the airframe's exposure to the effects of a gaping hole at supersonic speeds.

Conventional clamshell weapons bay doors were not feasible so the bay was to be closed and sealed by a one-piece fairing that would be jettisoned as the bomb was ejected. Above the fairing, the bomb was mounted under a second panel that was shaped to fill the bomb bay after the weapon was released. The bomb and the panel were mounted on an explosive ejection gun that fired to launch the bomb downwards through the bomb bay door, with four pinions on the second panel that engaged into four racks at

the corners of the door, thus sealing the panel.

On toggling the bomb release, the ejector gun would have fired and pushed the bomb and panel downwards, which pushed off the external fairing and as the bomb shot into the airstream it pulled the internal door down to seal off the bomb bay.

The Air Staff's thinking was based on a minimum of changes to the Type 730 whereas Avro were prepared to make major changes to accommodate the bomber role. The 25ft internally-carried bomb required a radical redesign of the Type 730 to maintain the minimum length 35ft (10.7m) Red Drover antenna. The original bicycle/outrigger undercarriage was to be replaced by a new tricycle undercarriage with the four-wheel main gear that retracted into streamlined nacelles located mid-span under the wings. The volume of fuel held in the fuselage was reduced by 420 Imp gal (1,909 litres) while an additional 820 Imp gal (3,728 litres) in the fore and aft sections of the undercarriage nacelles produced a net gain in fuel capacity of 400gal (1,818 litres).

The RAE examined the conversion of the R.156/OR.330 reconnaissance aircraft to the bombing role. Of course none of the subsequent bids had the necessary fuselage shape to house a weapons bay.

Avro proposed shortening the Red Drover radar antennas and fitting a '15ft bomb' between the radar and the undercarriage bay.

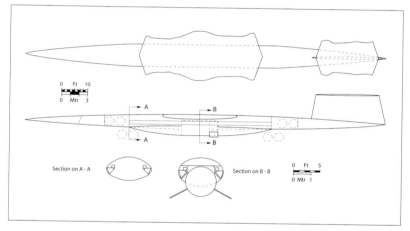

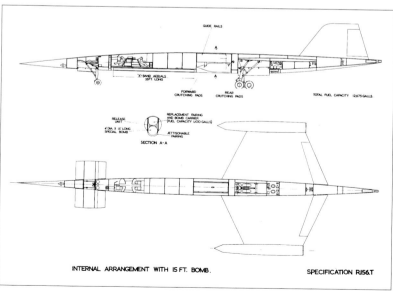

INTERNAL ARRANGEMENT WITH 15 FT. BOMB.   SPECIFICATION R156T

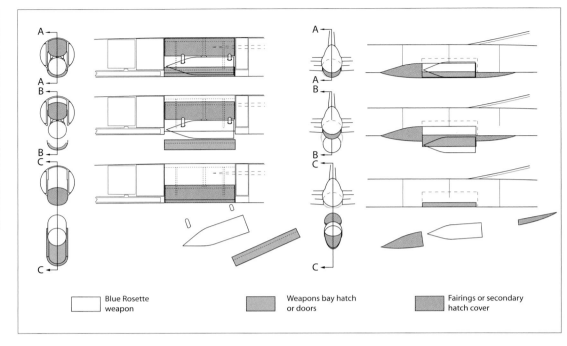

Releasing a weapon from a bomb bay at Mach 2 posed major problems to the engineers and aerodynamicists. Avro's solution was to fire the bomb out of the bay aperture, rapidly followed by a hatch that closed the bay. English Electric used clamshell doors and fairings on the P.10.

| | Blue Rosette weapon | | Weapons bay hatch or doors | | Fairings or secondary hatch cover |

Ejection of the 25ft weapon was along similar lines to the 15ft weapon, with a secondary hatch installed above the bomb. Obviously this would be larger and was slightly inclined to the aircraft datum to avoid the need to modify the forward main spar where it passed through the fuselage.

The new undercarriage arrangement for the 25ft bomb opened up the possibility of an externally-carried stand-off bomb. The initial designs for this were for a 50ft (15.2m) long winged bomb, such as the P37Z/SBM-1 carried under the fuselage of the Type 730. Structurally, the carriage of an external store posed a lesser challenge than the internal bay, which now

held a fuel tank and when combined with the undercarriage nacelle tanks, increased capacity by 2,600gal (11,820 litres).

The P37Z weighed in at 18,000 lb (8,165kg) and followed the soon to be standard canard delta with ventral fin configuration. It was to be powered by an Armstrong Siddeley PR.9 twin-chamber rocket engine that was the immediate predecessor of the Stentor. This engine was capable of powering the P37Z to cruise at Mach 7.8 and 93,000ft (28,346m) and have a range of 650nm (1,204km). Its trajectory involved launch at 60,000ft and Mach 2.5, boost climb to 93,000ft and Mach 7.8 under the power of the 26,000 lbf (115.6kN) main chamber then cruise on the 4,000 lbf (17.8kN) small chamber. On burn out the missile would then glide and decelerate to Mach 2.5 at 75,000ft (22,860m) to the target, perform a bunt and dive onto the target. An alternative weapon could have been the P18Z/SBM-4, a handsome delta with end-plate fins. With a length of 50ft (15.2m) and a span of 14ft (4.3m) and powered by a DH Spectre rocket engine, rated at 8,000 lbf (35.6kN) per chamber for the boost phase and throttled to 2,000 lbf (8.9kN) for the cruise, the P18Z weighed 14,500 lb (6,577kg) and was intended to have a range of 1,000nm (1,852km) and cruise at 100,000ft (30,480m) at Mach 6.

In effect the Air Staff could have their supersonic bomber sooner, at the expense of some performance, if it was based on the OR.330 aircraft. As a result of this, the Air Staff decided that the winner of the tender process should be capable of conversion to a bombing role. In the

While the 15ft bomb required minimal changes, the 25ft bomb required major modifications. These included moving the main undercarriage to underwing pods. *BAE Systems/ Avro Heritage*

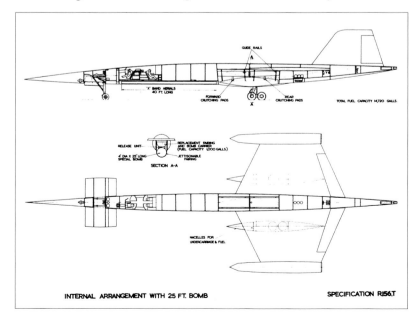

INTERNAL ARRANGEMENT WITH 25 FT. BOMB   SPECIFICATION R156.T

end all this discussion of roles and delays in the tender process did nothing but produce further delays. This resulted in the reconnaissance type being delayed to such an extent that the reconnaissance and bomber roles should be merged to bridge the gap between the V-bombers and the OR.336 type that was in limbo. In short the reconnaissance bomber would become the V-bombers' replacement.

Therefore a revised OR.330 Issue 2 with a bombing capability as its primary role in a reversal of its previous requirement was submitted on 4th January 1956 to the MoS, who produced specification RB.156D in May 1956 and Avro were charged with development of a complete weapons system. This was called the '1965 Medium Bomber System' and fairly rapidly Air Commodore Evans, Director of the OR branch ordered that the '1965' was to be deleted as it failed to indicate that the RAF '…badly require the system in 1962.' It was also pointed out by Air Vice-Marshal Jordan, Director General, Operations, that if the system could be set in place quickly, there was a possibility that a saving could be made by avoiding '…considerable unnecessary expenditure on Victors and Vulcans.'

The MoS maintained control of four of the components of the system: the Red Drover navigation radar and bombing system, the Blue Rosette weapon, the Armstrong Siddeley P.176 engines and the electronic warfare suite. The amendments to R.156 included a reduction in the length of the Red Drover antenna to 35ft (10.7m), thanks to the change to J-band. That allowed a bomb to be carried and a reduction in range to 3,500nm (6,482km) reflected the increased payload and drag penalty incurred from the semi-recessed Blue Rosette. In the pure reconnaissance role, the Blue Rosette was to be substituted by a camera pack.

Within six months of issuing RB.156 Issue 2, the Air Staff took a hard look at the burgeoning Soviet air defence systems. It was becoming apparent that not only were the V-bombers at the mercy of the Soviets, but by 1965 the OR.330 aircraft would be incapable of operating in defended air space. Another factor was that '…more certain methods of delivering nuclear weapons were expected to be available in the same timescale.' and this convinced the Air Staff that OR.330 was not a viable deterrent carrier. They advised that OR.330 be cancelled and the Minister of Defence, Duncan Sandys, was informed of this by the Secretary of State for Air on 27th February 1957. It wasn't Sandys who took the decision to cancel the Avro Type 730; he acted on the advice of the experts in the field.

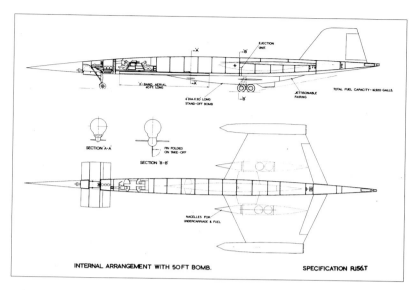

INTERNAL ARRANGEMENT WITH 50FT BOMB. SPECIFICATION RJ56T

The reasons for cancellation

The Air Staff were concerned that the Avro 730 would be vulnerable to SAGWs with conventional warheads and later, nuclear warheads and thus be unable to complete its mission. Low-altitude penetration had gained favour in the face of improved Soviet SAGW systems, which also precluded the Avro 730's use as a supplement to the Medium Range Ballistic Missile (Blue Streak). The argument that the Avro 730 could be used in the limited war role was also dismissed as the Canberra replacement could perform that role better. The conclusion was that the MRBM should be supplemented by a low-altitude strike aircraft – TSR.2. The deep penetration mission was impractical for a large aircraft such as the Avro 730, but the V-bombers with the Long Range Guided Bomb (what became the OR.1149 stand-off missile) would provide a credible deterrent.

Not Just High and Fast – Decoyed and Spoofed Too

In the immediate postwar era the RAF had greater experience and expertise in radar and electronic warfare than their American allies. This was due, according to Squadron Leader Poole of the Operational Requirements Branch OR.18B, to the Americans '…not having come up against it in World War Two to the same extent as the British.' The V-bombers had been fitted with an extensive and evolving electronic warfare suite to protect them from interception on their penetration missions. The R.156/OR.330 would be no different, despite its much higher speed and altitude.

Having opted to move the undercarriage of the R156, Avro sought to fit larger weapons such as the 50ft stand-off bomb. The missile had a flat top to facilitate carriage of such a long weapon under the fuselage. *BAE Systems/ Avro Heritage*

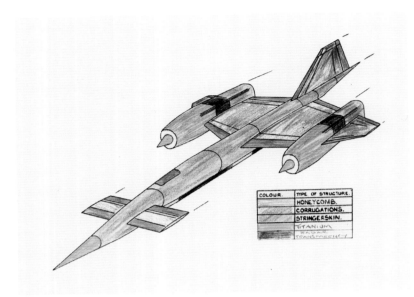

COLOUR.	TYPE OF STRUCTURE.
	HONEYCOMB.
	CORRUGATIONS.
	STRINGER SKIN.
	TITANIUM.
	RADAR TRANSPARENCY

No computer graphics in 1955, only coloured pencils. This Avro diagram shows the variety of materials used on the Type 730. Note the relatively minor use of titanium at key points.
BAE Systems/ Avro Heritage

Avro's Type 734 'free-running' drone that would have accompanied the Type 730 into Soviet Airspace.

A full suite of infrared (IR) and radar counter-measures were planned for the aircraft, no doubt derived from those being developed for the V-Force aircraft. Against air defence surveillance and interception systems 'radar camouflage', what is now called stealth or low-observable technology, was desired: 'The development of a lightweight radio-absorbent material able to withstand the high skin temperatures encountered in supersonic flight would be most valuable in this context'. Such radar-absorbent materials called DX1 and DS2 had been tested on a Radar Research Establishment Boulton Paul Balliol between 1951 and 56 and an English Electric Canberra flew with DX3 in 1959. While these were not heat-resistant to the extent required for OR.330, they did demonstrate that radar camouflage was possible.

Window (now called chaff) would be used against surveillance radars and the Americans had demonstrated its use by supersonic aircraft; it could be ejected from the aircraft by small rockets or cartridges. It was also suggested that the 'window cloud could be illuminated to provide false Doppler information'. in the hope that it

confused velocity discriminators and forced the Soviets to change their interception methods.

IR countermeasures on an aircraft that would have become very hot from kinetic heating could have been problematic. The OR.330 aircraft of whatever type would have been an airborne infrared beacon that would have drawn the attention of any heat-seeking missile or sensor for miles around. The main sources of IR radiation would be the hot metal around the jet pipes and the skin of the airframe, particularly the leading edges and nosecone.

In a 1950s era turbojet, there was not much that could be done about the signature apart from switching it off. That is precisely what was on the cards as an IR countermeasure on the Type 730. It had been calculated that the 'cessation of thrust by judicious cutting of the engines' was the best way to reduce the IR signature of the aircraft. By studying the effect on skin and jet pipe temperature of an abrupt cessation of thrust it was discovered that from a cruise at Mach 2.5 the speed dropped to Mach 2.22 in thirty seconds after cutting the engines and Mach 1.96 in 60 seconds. There would also be a reduction in temperature of 250-300°C (482-572°F) at the jet pipe, working temperature around 680°C (1,256°F), and 100°C (212°F) on the skin, normally 160-200°C (320-392°F) over that 60 seconds. This method depended heavily on early warning of an incoming missile as the 20 seconds warning that would be received from the onboard systems would not provide enough time for the airframe or engine to cool to an extent where the missile lost its lock. The Air Staff suggested that some means of extending the warning period be obtained and if not, the technique was a waste of time.

A more profitable practice would have been the ejection of 'alternative sources of radiation' into the airstream to draw away the incoming missile — what are now called flares. Unfortunately unless the 'distracting radiation' was 'sufficiently far removed from the aircraft to ensure that the latter would be well outside the range of the warhead' this would also be fruitless. Concern was also voiced about the method's utility against SAMs with nuclear warheads.

The above techniques could be combined with evasive manoeuvres including zoom climbs to 87,000ft (26,517m) to evade missiles and fighters. This of course led to a reduction in speed; fortunately much of the loss could be regained in the return to the 65,000ft (19,812m) cruise altitude.

Towed decoys have become fairly common on modern aircraft, with the first use of the

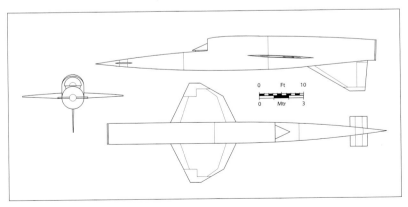

Marconi Ariel towed decoy on the BAe Nimrod MR.2s during the 1991 Gulf War and later became standard fit on the Eurofighter Typhoon. Back in the mid 1950s such decoys were mooted for the Type 730 and were intended as a foil for both heat-seeking and radar-guided missiles. The main drawback was the need to tow the decoy at a distance that would take the aircraft out of the lethal radius of a nuclear explosion. While this could be possible the 'intolerable performance penalties upon the aircraft and, in addition, power and cooling requirements would make it an impracticable proposition.'

Free-running decoys were another matter. The OR.330 aircraft could accommodate a single air-launched decoy, '…which would have a range of 200-300nm and, consequently the cover provided by this means would be very limited.' There was a longer-ranged decoy called the Avro Type 734 (described in the section on reconnaissance drones) that would be air-launched from Vulcans and accompany the Type 730 into hostile air space. Another possibility was to launch the decoys from the ground and in January 1957 the surface-launched variant of the stand-off bomb under development to meet OR.1159 was proposed and the Air Staff were keen for reasons other than bomber support: 'As a possible means of expending the enemy's stock of nuclear warheads they might be most worthwhile.'

There is no doubt that the OR.330/RB.156 type would have become vulnerable to Soviet defences by the mid-1960s if not before. Once Sputnik was beeping its way along above the Earth, the writing was on the wall for the free-fall bomber, no matter how fast it might be.

P.10 – Quite Interesting

Avro and English Electric were only serious contenders. P.10 most technically interesting. – RAE comment on the P.10, 2/3/59

Quantum leap is an over-used description in the world of technology. However, in a century of British aircraft development, one type stands out as a quantum leap. That aircraft originated from a little-known aircraft builder based in northwest England. In fact a company that, apart from a few seaplanes, had until 1945 been producing other companies' aircraft. From its Samlesbury works at Preston in Lancashire, the English Electric Company Ltd (EECo) produced over 700 Handley Page Hampden and 2,000 Handley Page Halifax bombers, built under the shadow factory scheme during

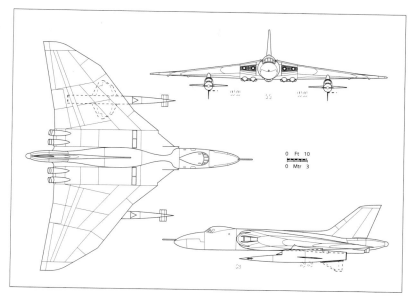

the Second World War. EECo moved into the jet age by building 1,300 de Havilland Vampire fighters. When the English Electric parent company acquired the aero engine company D Napier and Son in 1942, this gave English Electric access to advanced aero-engines. English Electric was also involved with guided weapons from the onset of such work in 1949 with the Red Shoes SAM.

In April 1945 Sir George Nelson, the chairman of English Electric announced that the company would move into the aircraft design and development field. This was the first public disclosure of a long-held intention. W E W 'Teddy' Petter had been hired from Westland Aircraft as Chief Engineer of the new English Electric design team in July 1944. Petter's first design was to meet B.3/45 and the resulting Canberra first flew in 1949. Petter's next project was the P.1, for which Petter drew up the original layout, though turning it into the Lightning interceptor was the work of A E Ellison and F W Page. Petter left English Electric in 1950 to pursue his ideas for lightweight fighters, namely the Folland Midge.

When the requirement for a medium bomber arose, English Electric bid for the contract and in April 1947 Petter drew up a graceful six-engined high-wing design for B.35/46. The initial proposal was powered by Napier axial turbojets and weighed in at 84,000 lb (38,095kg) but it failed meet the range requirements. A larger study was drawn up with a redesigned wing that had its angle of sweep increased to 30° rather than 20° and a kinked trailing edge. This was 25% larger with an all-up-weight of 111,000 lb (50,340kg) and its Rolls-Royce Avon turbojets housed within the

> The Type 734 was to be carried in pairs by Vulcans operating in the radio countermeasures and bomber support role. The 734s carried up to 1,500 lb of RCM equipment, more than the Type 730.

Escorted by two English Electric P.10E, a P.10 reconnaissance-bomber delivers a 'Special Store'. Could this spherical bomb have been an answer to the problem of weapons tumbling on release?
Adrian Mann

swept inboard section of the its high wing. The Air Ministry were keen that English Electric concentrated on developing the much-needed Canberra for the RAF, so requested that they drop out of the running. The specification was ultimately met with the Vickers Valiant.

This may have prompted English Electric to separate their development and projects operations so a Future Projects Department was set up in late 1947, headed by Raymond Creasey. When the requirement for a supersonic reconnaissance aircraft was issued as OR.330/R.156 in 1954, the Future Projects Department rose to the challenge. Perhaps English Electric's industrial diversity made this possible, but their tender for OR.330/R.156 was very advanced for its time and without a doubt would have led to the

most advanced aircraft in the world. Based on the Air Staff's requirement, Creasey and chief project engineer B O 'Ollie' Heath and the future projects team produced a design, the P.10, which exceeded the requirement in many ways.

What made the P.10 so advanced was its mixture of radical configuration, innovative solutions to operational problems and novel powerplant. Its canard configuration comprised low-mounted trapezoidal wings with a pair of highly swept all-moving foreplanes. Also capable of differential movement for roll control, these were mounted high on the needle-like fuselage just aft of the cockpit. The fuselage cross-section was pear-shaped and merged into a large tailfin that extended almost halfway along the length of the fuselage. The tail fin's

English Electric bid for the B.35/46 requirement with their high-speed medium bomber. The urgent need for the Canberra put paid to any work by English Electric on B.35/46.
BAE Systems/ North West Heritage Group

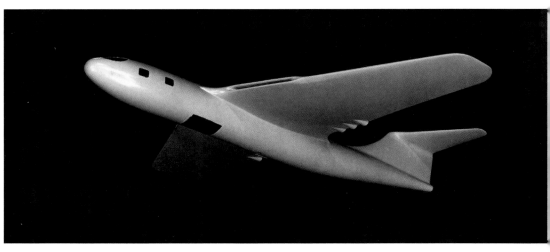

size was dictated by the need to maintain lateral stability at high Mach Numbers. Unlike the Avro 730, the pilot was accommodated in a raised cockpit and enjoyed good visibility over the long nose through a glazed canopy. The observer's position was below and forward of the cockpit with portholes on the fuselage sides to view the outside world.

What dictated the configuration was the need to carry the R.156's raison d'être: the Red Drover sideways-looking airborne radar being developed by EMI to meet OR.3579. The antenna for this X-band radar ran all along each side of the lower fuselage and to achieve the required resolution for mapping targets, an antenna length of 50ft (15.2m) was required. Red Drover forced a long fuselage on the designers and to improve the aircraft's rotation on take-off, the canard was the preferred configuration for the P.10 and the other contenders. With their background in the electronics industry, English Electric's design team were convinced that the radar antenna could be smaller and perform just as effectively. This conviction was no doubt fostered by English Electric's wider field of expertise in electronics and the design team believed that by the time the P.10 entered service in 1960, Ku-band or a Q-band radar would be preferred and would allow a smaller, 35ft (10.7m) antenna to be utilised. This belief in future systems also prompted Heath and his team to reduce the P.10's crew to two, contrary to the complement of pilot and two observers laid out in the requirement. Again, the potential of future developments in systems automation was stated for this change, but English Electric had a further reason.

Back in 1954 English Electric were of the opinion that an aircraft cruising at Mach 3 at 70,000ft (21,336m) had no need for a pilot therefore 'The pilot would be completely unoccupied during the cruise phase and therefore liable to suffer fatigue through boredom.' The piloting activity would be '…limited to occasional adjustments or emergency operations.' so could have a secondary role as observer. This would require the pilot to be in the glazed upper section of the cockpit when the aircraft was taking off, landing or refuelling in flight, but could be lowered into the fuselage for the bulk of the mission, attending to reconnaissance equipment.

The pilot's ejection seat was mounted on rails that allowed the seat to translate to the upper or lower position, maintaining the same angle to the ejection seat gun. English Electric

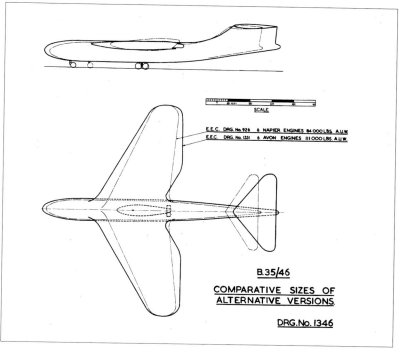

B.35/46
COMPARATIVE SIZES OF ALTERNATIVE VERSIONS.
DRG. No. 1346

E.E.C. DRG. No. 926   6 NAPIER ENGINES 84 000 LBS. A.U.W.
E.E.C. DRG. No. 1331 6 AVON ENGINES 111 000 LBS. A.U.W.

was granted a patent for this system that had duplicated control columns to allow the pilot to fly the aircraft from either position. Interestingly the control column for the lower station was a side-stick on the pilot's right, something that would not be seen until the General Dynamics YF-16 of 1974. Rudder control pedals were not duplicated as the rudder was hardly used in the cruise with adjustment made by differential thrust from the ramjets and roll control via the foreplanes. The flight instruments were mounted on a tilting panel that allowed the pilot to view them from the upper or lower position.

English Electric's B35/46 was a handsome, if conventional design that was discontinued to ensure that Warton kept working on Canberra development. *BAE Systems/ North West Heritage Group*

P.10 as bid for OR.330/R.156. It was thought to be too advanced and therefore had potential for delay. The Air Staff thought it a very interesting design. *BAE Systems/ North West Heritage Group*

31

To prevent pilot boredom on a long reconnaissance flight and reduce crew numbers, EECo's Ollie Heath proposed a moving pilot's seat that moved from the cockpit once the cruise was established. The pilot could carry out reconnaissance tasks and use secondary controls to make minor adjustments to the flight path. The seat and pilot would return to the cockpit for approach and landing.

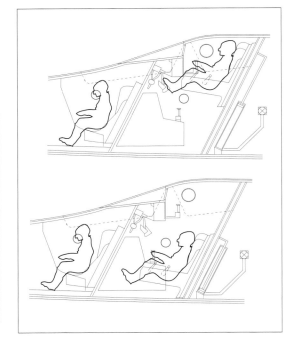

Comparison of Vickers SP.4, powered by no less than 16 RB.121 turbojets arranged along the trailing edge, and the EECo P10. The P.10 would have benefited from technological advances if these had worked as advertised.

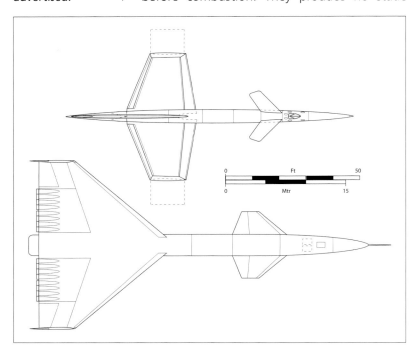

One major benefit of these changes was the reduction in size of the overall airframe, which was almost a third smaller than its Avro, Handley Page and Vickers competitors. With two crew and a smaller radar, the more compact P.10 could gain much from a propulsion system that in the mid Fifties appeared to be on the brink of taking the aviation world by storm: the ramjet.

Usually associated with guided weapons, ramjets work best at supersonic flight speeds and rely on forward velocity plus intake and diffuser shaping to compress the incoming air before combustion. They produce no static thrust so to work efficiently a ramjet requires boosting to high speeds before it will produce sufficient thrust to accelerate the aircraft. Missiles can use solid rocket motors to provide that boost, but this would not be viable for an aircraft the size of a P.10. Therefore a pair of turbojets were used to allow the aircraft to take off and accelerate to a speed where the ramjets could provide thrust and to provide an additional push through the transonic region of the flight envelope.

English Electric's P.10 was not unique in its use of ramjets and turbojets in what has become known as a combination engine, whereby ramjets and turbojets that share a common intake but with separate jet pipes are used to propel an aircraft from a standing start to Mach 3. This should not be confused with a turbo-ramjet that uses common intake and jet pipe. What was unique in the case of the P.10 was the combination engine integrated into the wing itself with a series of Napier ramjet burners arranged spanwise within the upper and lower surfaces of the wing. The turbojets, a pair of Rolls-Royce RB.123 with reheat, were installed in the wing root/fuselage interface. The RB.123 was rated at 10,250 lbf (45.6kN) static thrust and 16,700 lbf (74.3kN) with reheat. The turbojets also drove generators to provide the electrical power for the radar and systems and continued to drive the generators in the cruise by cutting the fuel supply and allowing them to windmill.

The leading and trailing edges of the wing were open, leading to the term 'split wing' being used to describe it in Air Staff documents. Just inside the leading edge opening that served as the intake was a raised area that performed a dual role: firstly as an intake diffuser providing compression for incoming air and secondly as a fuel tank. Fuel also served to cool the wing surfaces as it was pumped from fuselage tanks to the ramjets. Additional fuel was carried in stub wings attached to the wingtips. These had an aerofoil profile suited to subsonic flight and were used to carry fuel for the takeoff and climb portions of the flight but jettisoned before the P.10 reached transonic speed. At the trailing edge, the opening held a similar 'ramp' that could be raised and lowered to act as a variable area nozzle.

In the cruise the outboard portions of this variable nozzle could also provide roll control for the P.10, with the foreplanes providing pitch control. At the trailing edge root of each wing was a Rolls-Royce RB.123 turbojet fed by the same intake in the leading edge as the ramjets.

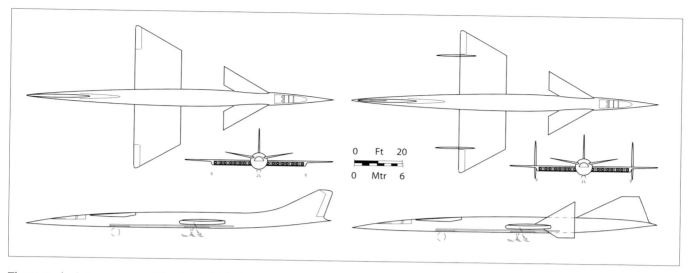

These turbojets were used in the initial phases of the flight and produced thrust in the sub-sonic regime where the ramjets are less efficient up to a speed of Mach 1.2.

This was such a radical rethink of aircraft design that Ollie Heath and his colleague Raymond Creasey were granted patents on the P.10, specifically for the canard configuration with the foreplane behind the cockpit and the translating pilot's seat and dual controls.

The P.10 lost out to the Avro 730 in the OR.330/R.156 tender contest, but the Air Staff were rightly intrigued by the P.10. They saw that it had a lot of potential and quite probably opted for the Avro 730 on the basis that it would be available well before the P.10 and used proven technology. Oddly enough the Air Staff and Air Ministry thought the P.10 'quite interesting' and considered the possibility of continuing its funding as a research aircraft.

While the split-wing combination engine version of the P.10 has become fairly well-known, English Electric proposed a few other variants with alternative powerplant or configurations. In January 1955 Ollie Heath drew up a very sleek P.10 variant powered by 16 RB.121 turbojets (as used on the Handley Page and Vickers proposals for OR.330) housed within the inner two-thirds of the split wing. The constant-chord inner wing stops abruptly at two-thirds span with the outer third of the wing formed into a small 60° delta. The canard fore-planes had a planform reminiscent of the Lightning mainplanes. This aircraft was 124ft (37.8m) long with a 61ft 5in (18.7m) wingspan. The original drawing shows a small swept tail-fin, but the drawing has been modified and shows a trapezoidal fin with greater chord and additional fins on the wings at the two-thirds span position on each wing.

The crew (probably two but the number isn't clear) were seated in the extreme nose under a glazed, faired-in canopy. The drawing shows a Red Drover radar antenna along the lower fuselage flank and this appears to be the 50ft (15.2m) X-band radar. This P.10 (there is no suffix, but may be the P.10A) must have been intended for trolley launch as the under carriage comprised a nose-wheel with a large retractable skid for the main undercarriage. Smaller outrigger skids retract into the wing just outboard of the split wing.

The P.10B dates from March 1955 and was a different bird indeed. The swept canard configuration was retained albeit with a completely

Lateral stability has always been a problem for high-speed aircraft, latterly resolved by fold-down outer wing panels. For this P.10 variant, additional side area was to be provided by fins on the wings just outboard of the engine housings.

ENGLISH ELECTRIC P 10b

950 SQ FT.

180 SQ FT.

15'
25'
30'
100'

18'
30.5'
20'
50'

0   10   20 FT

B.O.H
18-3-55

The EECo P.10B from March 1955 may have formed the basis of an expendable bomber. While no details are available, the skid undercarriage and lack of turbojets suggests a trolley launch.
BAE Systems/ North West Heritage Group

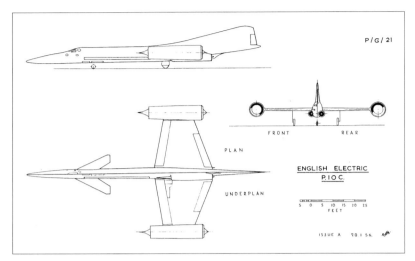

P/G/21

FRONT   REAR

PLAN

ENGLISH ELECTRIC
P.10.C.

UNDERPLAN

5 0 5 10 15 20 25
FEET

ISSUE A   20.1.56.

Massive ramjets dominate the P.10C study from January 1956. No such ramjet was available at this time, when the largest practicable ramjet had a diameter of 18in. *BAE Systems/ North West Heritage Group*

A California Air National Guard Convair F-106 Delta Dart launches a Douglas AIR-2 Genie inert training round. The EECo P10E long-range fighter would have filled a similar air defence and escort role. *Via Kev Darling*

different planform, with a straight leading edge and a reverse-tapered trailing edge. The wing featured the integrated ramjet with twelve ramjet burners arranged within the wings structure. The drawing shows no turbojet engines, which with the skid undercarriage, suggests a trolley launch, but the turbojets may be housed entirely within the wing roots and not visible on the drawing.

The P.10B is shown fitted with wingtip tanks which in addition to increasing the fuel capacity acted as end plates to smooth out the tip vortices and reduce drag, which was also one reason the initial Avro 730 configuration carried its engines on the wingtips. The P.10B's tailfin comprised a long sweeping curve as the leading edge that curved over to a short, almost vertical trailing edge with the fin faired into the rear fuselage. The fin leading edge starts at a point almost halfway along the circular cross-section fuselage. Again, the 50ft (15.2m) Red Drover antennae were fitted in the lower fuselage. The P.10B also sports a bulged ventral fairing that matched those shown as scrap views of the bomber variant in the brochure.

By late January 1956 the shape of the P.10 to R.156 had evolved with its now familiar broad, faired-in fin and pear-shaped cross-section fuselage with the 30ft Red Drover antennae. What made the P.10C stand out were the massive 60in (152cm) diameter ramjets on each wingtip. The date of January 1956 is interesting because in a letter later that year Stanley Hooker of Bristol Engines told the MoS that Bristol Engines would not be able to participate in turborocket research because of commitments to work on the ramjet for English Electric's P.10. It was assumed that this referred to the integrated/split-wing ramjet, but perhaps actually related to work on the axisymetric ramjet shown on the P.10C. If so this project was given the Bristol Ramjet Department designation RP.10

The P.10C is also of interest because, as a straightforward re-winging of the P.10 as bid, it shows the position of the two RB.123 turbojets under the rear fuselage. There is a problem with the P.10C, an impracticality of the type that crops up time and again with design studies: the ramjets. With a diameter of 60in (152cm), they are far larger than any ramjet Bristol Engines had on the drawing board at the time. Perhaps Bristol Engines were contemplating such a ramjet, but it is also possible that, with some degree of knowledge on ramjets, Ollie Heath scaled up a ramjet (whose thrust is proportional to its intake capture area) to match the thrust required for the P.10.

There was one role that the Air Staff were most interested in applying the P.10's innovations to: a long-range fighter. Warton's proposal was called the P.10E and was very much a different animal to the preceding design studies. At only 80ft (24.4m) long the P.10E was the shortest of the manned P.10 variants. The two crew sat in tandem cockpits under separate canopies. Installed in the nose was an air interception (AI) radar with a 36in (91cm) dish, possibly an AI.23 as fitted to the Lightning. In the Lightning this type of radar was used to bring the aircraft to an intercept position where the IR seeking AAMs such as Firestreak or Red Top could be launched. On the P.10E fighter, a pair of missiles were to be housed side-by-side in a 10ft (3m) long weapons bay in the lower fuselage. These appear to be the Douglas AIR-2 Genie, an unguided weapon with a 1.5Kt warhead. Also known as Ding-Dong, this weapon was also proposed as armament for the Lightning with the designation RP3 applied. The P.10E would have fitted into a similar long-range interceptor role that the Americans filled by developing the Convair F-102 Delta Dagger and F-106 Delta Dart.

What made the P.10E stand out in the series of studies was a new integrated propulsion system in the wings. The planform of the 44ft (13.4m) span wings was a simple rectangle with a curved end that housed the retractable outrigger for the bicycle undercarriage. The outrigger housing also carried a small delta wing surface. The propulsion system was the subject of Patent Number 2956759 and comprised ramjet burners and turbojets arranged alternately across the wing's span, with four of each engine type to a wing. This arrangement allowed the airflow to be equalised throughout the flight regime and reduce intake losses.

When Issue 2 of OR.330 was issued with the specification RB.156 in 1956, the requirement was raised to turn the reconnaissance aircraft into a bomber. This posed many problems to the design teams as the techniques for delivering a free-fall weapon from a supersonic aircraft were in their infancy. Despite being instructed not to provide for a bombing role in their bids, all the OR.330 contenders had, as would be expected, looked into conversion of their aircraft to the bombing role. This was not a simple matter of hanging bombs on pylons, as the aircraft was to be a strategic bomber capable of delivering a nuclear weapon on a target 4,000nm (7,408km) from base and that nuclear weapon would be very large.

A further problem with nuclear weapons carriage was that the complex innards required cosseting at a controlled temperature. The heat generated by Mach 2.5 flight, with 220°C (428°F) expected on the wing leading edges, would have played havoc with the intricate bomb equipment. Therefore internal stowage

of the weapon was a necessity and the dual problem of a large diameter bomb and narrow fuselage set the designers a thorny dilemma. In 1954. The British nuclear weapon was massive, Blue Danube was 62in (158cm) in diameter and with a total length of 24ft (7.4m) there would be no prospect of installing that in an Avro 730 or EECo P.10. Then there was the small matter of the sideways-looking radar antenna along the fuselage flanks.

The antenna length was reduced from 52ft (15.9m) to 50ft (15.2m) and ultimately to 35ft (10.7m) on the Avro 730 and on the P.10 the 35ft aerial was shortened to 30ft (9.1m). This allowed the Avro designers to fit a 15ft (4.6m) bomb bay between the antennae and the main undercarriage bay. EECo crafted a similar sized weapons bay between the main spar and the antennae and so the attention turned to the stores likely to be carried.

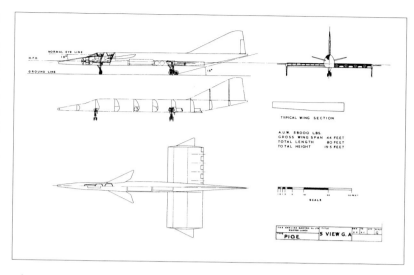

The P.10E, showing its air interception radar and bay for two air-to-air missiles. This version could have become a long-range escort or air defence aircraft, something the RAF only acquired with the Tornado ADV in 1986. *BAE Systems/ North West Heritage Group*

The missile in front of this USAF Convair F-106 Delta Dart is a Douglas AIR-2 Genie. Armed with a 1.5kt warhead, the compact Genie with a diameter of 17.5in (44cm) exemplifies the difference in size of US and UK warheads in the mid 1950s. *USAF*

The Tumbling Bomb

Britain has produced a number of specialised free-fall weapons: the 8,000 lb (3,629kg) Blockbuster or Cookie, the 22,000 lb (9,979kg) Grand Slam earthquake bomb and, of course, the 9,250 lb (4,196kg) Upkeep bouncing bomb. These had been developed to attack specific targets: urban areas, fortified or strongly-built structures and dams respectively. Each posed a particular problem to the carrier aircraft either by their size or need for specialised delivery tactics.

With the advent of the V-bombers a new problem arose in the delivery of large stores from an aircraft flying at high subsonic speed. As outlined above, the size of the V-bombers' weapons bay had been governed by the dimensions of the Special Weapon to meet OR.1001. The carriage of atomic bombs dated back to the Fat Man and Little Boy of 1945. At one point the layout of the Boeing B-29 Superfortress bomb bay was deemed unsuitable to carry these new weapons, so the Avro Lancaster was considered. On hearing of this plan, General Leslie Groves, the head of the Manhattan Project, was not unsurprisingly somewhat aggrieved, so much so that a programme, *Silverplate*, was initiated in October 1943 to modify B-29s as the first nuclear bomber.

Prior to developing the Blue Danube weapon, the RAF, RAE and AWRE were concerned about the stability of bomb casings when dropped at high speed. A series of trials called 'Emulsion' were conducted to evaluate bomb shapes based on the Tallboy and fitted with different fin configurations. The Emulsion tests were conducted in the United States with a borrowed USAF Boeing B-29, the only aircraft available that could reach the altitude of 35,000ft (10,668m) and speed of 350kts (648kph) to emulate the performance of forth-coming jet bombers. Emulsion showed that the casing was most stable when the span of the tail fins was 1.4 times that of the bomb casing. Ultimately Blue Danube was fitted with fins 1.6 times the diameter of the casing, and this forced the use of retractable fins to allow internal carriage on the V-bombers.

A decade later, OR.330 Issue 2 posed a similar problem to the design teams who worked on the modification of an Avro 730 radar reconnaissance aircraft into a supersonic bomber. The store intended for the OR.330 aircraft was to meet OR.1144 and involved a casing called Blue Rosette and a warhead called Green Bamboo. Since OR.330 Issue 2 called for an aircraft that could carry out reconnaissance and bombing with minimal change, some compromise was necessary. The sideways-looking X-band radar required a long antenna along each side of the fuselage and these, plus the location of the Avro 730's single-bogie main undercarriage, enforced a limit on Blue Rosette's length of 12ft (3.7m). AWRE advised that the Green Bamboo warhead would need a casing with a maximum diameter of 4ft 2in (1.3m) and since they were not intended as bombers, the OR.330 types all shared a narrow fuselage that meant a semi-recessed installation for Blue Rosette would be necessary.

These dimension limits produced a casing with a low length-to-diameter ratio that would cause instability as soon as the weapon was released and cause dispersion that affected bombing accuracy. The traditional way to counter this was adding fins to the store or using parachutes or retro rockets to slow and stabilise the bomb. Messrs Lawler and Griggs of the RAE in December 1954 issued Technical Note Aero 2353 that examined possible use of the reconnaissance aircraft as a bomber. The scheme involved a store carried semi-recessed

A 192 Squadron Washington at RAF Watton in the mid 1950s. In the immediate postwar era only the provision of US-surplus Boeing B-29s kept the RAF in the strategic bombing business. WW346 was a B-29 variant used to support sigint/elint around the Soviet borders.
Author's Collection

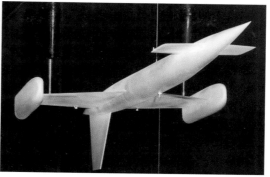

This wind tunnel model of the Avro 730 shows the slim fuselage that was not ideal for carrying the large nuclear weapons that Britain had developed by 1956. *BAE Systems/ Avro Heritage*

in a bay between the bicycle undercarriage and the Red Drover aerials of a generic supersonic aircraft. The cylindrical store, that had the stated dimensions of Blue Rosette, was fitted with aerodynamic fairings fore and aft that could carry fuel with the entire assembly stretching 50ft (15.2m) along the aircraft's underside. The weapon was fitted with a trio of stabilising fins at the rear; however due to volume restrictions within the weapons bay, the single vertical fin had to be made fully retractable. While this was a neat installation Lawler and Griggs' generic aircraft featured a fuselage with a flat elliptical section that allowed a bay to be installed between the radar antennae. In reality none of the OR.330 designs studies featured such a fuselage profile; a narrow/deep cross-section was the norm.

Blue Rosette would be released into the hostile aerodynamic environment of Mach 2.5 at 60,000ft (18,288m). Supersonic release of freefall weapons from a ventral weapons bay has been a thorn in the side of the bomber designer since the 1950s and the problem was never really solved. Designers opted for external carriage on ejection racks or rearwards deployment from a tunnel between the engines as in the North American A-3 Vigilante and apart from these there is no example of a bomber capable of weapons release from a conventional bomb bay at speeds in excess of Mach 2.

In a June 1956 progress report the RAE proposed using the inherent instability of Blue Rosette by imparting a rotation on the bomb that would average out, with respect to the trajectory, the aerodynamic forces causing dispersion. This was seen as a possible solution to dispersion, despite misgivings about the effect the rotation would have on fuzing, having encountered problems with the barometric fuses of Blue Danube being affected by supersonic flow over its surface.

While these discussions were under way, the aircraft designers were tasked with converting their OR.330 proposals into a bomber. Consider

the position of aircraft designers on the very margins of the compartmentalised security world of nuclear weapons development. The designers, whether they were at Warton, Weybridge or Woodford, would be presented with the dimensions listed above, a weight and the term 'Tumbling Bomb'. What would they come up with? Perhaps a clue lies in a drawing cabinet in the North West Heritage Centre at BAE Systems' Warton facility.

One of the drawings, also used in the P.10 brochure, carries a series of scrap views that show prospective bomb configurations for the bomber version of the English Electric P.10. The first shows a semi-recessed 54in (137cm) diameter cylindrical store, not unlike a Blockbuster, with a length of 12ft (3.7m) and fairings fore and aft carrying fuel. The bomb doors were designed to clasp the store with a portion of the store itself exposed. To smooth the intersection of the doors and the fuselage, a fairing runs along each side of the fuselage. These fairings allowed the use of a simpler two-piece bomb door to close around the 54in weapon and produced a clean weapon bay area after the store and its fore and aft fairings were dropped.

Two further scrap views show 36in (91cm) and 45in (114cm) cylindrical stores inside the

Convair's B-58 Hustler is the closest operational type to the OR.330 aircraft. The Americans overcame the weapons release problem by using the two-stage ventral pod. The large outer pod enveloped a smaller weapons pod. When the fuel in the outer pod was consumed it was dropped to reveal the small weapon pod. *USAF*

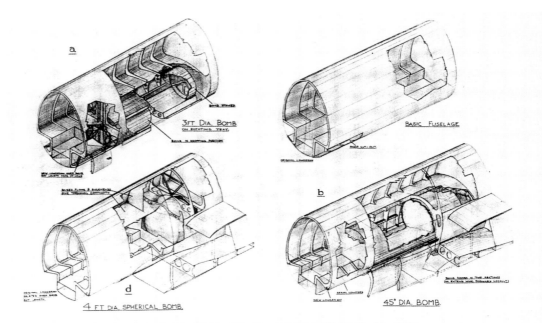

Weapons installations on the EECo P.10. The 3ft Dia. Bomb was mounted on a rotating bomb door, the 45" Dia. Bomb required large clamshell doors. Of most interest is the 4ft Dia. Spherical Bomb. Was this the Air Staff's Tumbling Bomb? *BAE Systems/ North West Heritage Group*

To accommodate the larger British weapons such as the 54in Dia. bomb, this P.10 bomber variant required semi-recessed carriage. With fore-and-aft fairings, the bomb doors clasped the weapon, closing flush once the bomb and fairings were released.

P.10's weapons bay. The fact that the weapons are represented as cylinders does not mean that they were that shape, but merely reflect the dimensions that the weapon designers were allowed to disclose and the aircraft developers made provision for these. There is a distinct possibility that these drawings were prepared for a later, tactical bomber study by English Electric, but similar studies would have been carried out in an attempt to meet RB.156.

The 36in (91cm) store is shown mounted on a rotating bomb door, a feature patented in 1950 by the Glenn L. Martin Company and developed for the Martin XB-51. The rotating bomb door was also fitted to the Blackburn Buccaneer, designed to meet Admiralty requirement NA.39 for a strike aircraft to carry Green Cheese and Red Beard. Rotary bomb doors allow stores to be delivered at higher speeds than conventional clamshell bomb doors by effectively converting internal carriage of stores to external carriage in a very short time. The rotating bomb door in its open and closed positions sealed the bay and thus prevented turbulent flow in and around an open bomb bay. It also removed the drag caused by doors opening into the airstream. Another feature of such doors is that weapons ejection mechanisms can be fitted to push the store away from the aircraft thus providing greater control of the bomb's movement on release. Despite plans to fit the Canberra with a rotating bomb door (the US-built Martin B-57 was thus fitted) English Electric never received the funding to add this to the Canberra.

The fourth scrap view shows something very interesting – a 48in (122cm) spherical bomb, carried wholly within the aircraft's bomb bay. While 48 inches is slightly larger than the 44 inches defined by AWRE for the Green Bamboo warhead, the later Orange Herald may have fitted within such a sphere. Perhaps English Electric, who had already pre-empted the Ministry's requirement for shorter radar antennae on the OR.330 type, also foresaw a major reduction in nuclear warhead size.

The above is conjecture on the author's part; but what better shape than a sphere when an object has to be ejected into a Mach 2.5 environment?

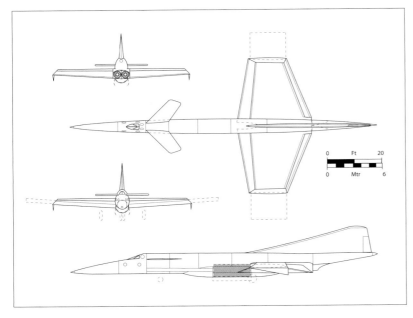

Remote Red Drover – Reconnaissance Drones

'Russian industry is so dispersed that it is unlikely to be a profitable air target' – conclusion to the plan for Operation Unthinkable, 1945.

Winston Churchill in May 1945 asked General Alan Brooke, Chief of the Imperial Defence Staff, to draw up plans to carry on the war against Russia to liberate Poland from Soviet occupation. Called *Operation Unthinkable*, this was Churchill's attempt to honour the original reason for Britain and France going to war against Nazi Germany in the first place – Polish independence. The Air Staff planners concluded that western air power could be used effectively against Soviet communications but 'Russian industry is so dispersed that it is unlikely to be a profitable air target' and that dispersion was to create targeting problems for years to come.

The lack of targeting information for strikes against the Soviet Union in the early 1950s was partially alleviated by the use of modified English Electric Canberra PR.3s on flights over Soviet territory to acquire photographic and electronic reconnaissance information. These missions began in August 1953 and were carried out to gather data that the USAF and RAF could use in identifying and selecting targets. The RAF Canberra aircraft were fitted with American camera systems and had by April 1954 evolved into Project Robin. While these missions could provide photographic intelligence and prove the steady evolution of Soviet air defences, they could not provide the radar imagery that the OR.330 types could.

It was hoped that the OR.330 aircraft would be immune to Soviet fighters and heavy anti-aircraft guns such as the KS-30 130mm anti-aircraft gun that could trace its roots back to the German 128mm (5in) Flak 40 of World War Two (or to a Soviet naval gun, depending on what side of the Iron Curtain the source resided). The KS-30 was combined with the SON-30 radar (NATO reporting name *Fire Wheel*) and PUAZO-30 fire director, producing a weapon capable of defending a target to an effective altitude of 45,000ft (13,716m) at a rate of around 20 rounds per minute.

The availability by 1955 of a Q-band sideways looking airborne radar (SLAR) with a smaller antenna introduced a startling possibility. Rather than a massive supersonic aircraft with a three-man crew on the scale of the Avro 730, a smaller machine could be developed by one simple change: dispense with the crew. Another incentive to develop an unmanned reconnaissance type was the certain knowledge that the Soviet Union was developing surface-to-air guided weapons on a par with the British Bloodhound and Thunderbird missiles or US Nike MIM-3 Ajax. A smaller, high-speed reconnaissance platform would pose a problem for the defenders as it streaked through their airspace.

A crewless bomber had been examined in the late 1940s by way of the Blue Moon projects, with the guidance of such aircraft being a perennial problem. The difference between a bomber and a reconnaissance type was the bomber's mission was to attack a pinpoint target whereas a reconnaissance aircraft could fly on a pre-programmed course across the Soviet Union. It was not only the removal of the crew and their seats that made an unmanned aircraft much lighter and smaller; an aircraft with the performance of the Avro 730 required a large amount of ancillary equipment for the three or four man crew. This included life-support systems, air-conditioning plant to keep the crew cool and survival gear. All this added to a considerable weight and volume of kit that had to be accommodated in a larger airframe which in turn required more engine power and more fuel for the same range. Remove the crew and the aircraft can be considerably smaller for an equivalent range and performance. This also made for a much cheaper production and operating costs, all of which were a factor in English Electric's philosophy with the two-man P.10, a type that was designed for the smaller Red Drover radar from the start.

Avro saw an opportunity to apply many of the aerodynamic and materials lessons learned in development of the Type 730 and Blue Steel to this new challenge. Avro's aircraft division had also suggested a supersonic decoy to support their 730 reconnaissance bomber. The 50ft (15.2m) long Type 734 shared the 730's canard configuration with the compound-sweep delta

Not all of Avro's drones were for reconnaissance. The Type 734 was a 'free-running decoy' intended to support the supersonic bomber operations. Carried to the edge of hostile airspace by a Vulcan, the 734 would then be launched and accompany the Avro 730 into the target zone. *BAE Systems/ Avro Heritage*

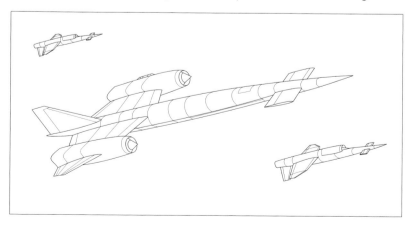

Avro's WRD design studies for radar reconnaissance drones included the TRM-1, a Vulcan-launched expendable; the TRM-2 recoverable and the two-stage TRM-3.

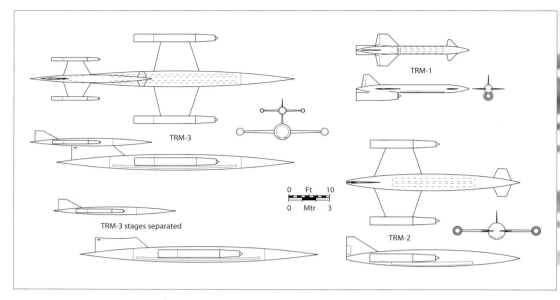

wing, spanning 19ft (5.8m) minus the mid–span engine pods, but with a forward-swept trailing edge. The single Armstrong Siddeley P176 turbojet, rated at 19,400 lbf (86.3kN), was in a dorsal installation with the half-cone intake above the forward fuselage. When operated as a decoy, the Type 734 was carried by Vulcans in the bomber support role with each Vulcan carrying one 734 under each wing. The operational plan for using such decoys was for the Vulcans and their Type 734s to take off and approach Soviet airspace ahead of the Avro 730s. As the supersonic bombers overtook the subsonic Vulcans, the 734s were released and accelerated to fly in loose formation with the 730s to draw the fire of radar-directed air defences.

The first Avro Weapons Research Division (WRD) design study for a reconnaissance drone was the P39Z (also described as the TRM-1) which was a small air-launched single-engined unmanned aircraft carrying Q-band sideways-looking radar. Dating from February 1955 P39Z was of canard configuration with the straight tapered wings towards the rear of the fuselage

and the foreplanes almost at the nose. As with the OR.330 submissions, the canard allowed the 10ft (3.05m) long antennae to be placed along the length of the fuselage between the aerodynamic surfaces and have an unrestricted view of the ground below.

Propulsion was to be provided by a Rolls-Royce RB.121 turbojet, an engine that had been proposed for the OR.330 proposals from Vickers and Handley Page, installed under the rear fuselage. Fed by an axisymetric intake with a conical centrebody, the RB.121 with reheat was capable of powering the 4,000 lb (1,814kg) P39Z to a cruising speed of Mach 2 at 20,000ft (6,096m) for 200nm (370km). The Q-band radar was to cover a swathe of ground 20nm (37km) each side of the drone over a linear distance of 100nm. To make best use of this valuable data some means of returning it to the intelligence and targeting officers was a top priority.

In the 1980s Lockheed U-2R reconnaissance aircraft were observed with large aerodynamic fairings mounted on a dorsal pylon. This system, called Senior Span, was a satellite communications system that allowed the U-2 to transmit its imagery, signals and communications intelligence back to base via satellite. Back in 1955 the communications satellite was but an idea proposed by Arthur C. Clarke; therefore another means of returning the intelligence take was required.

Avro's first attempt also involved transmission of data. After launch from an Avro Vulcan or HP Victor, the P39Z embarked on its radar reconnaissance mission over hostile territory with the radar imagery transmitted by data link back to the launch aircraft. The 'mother ship' was to remain outside the target area in line of

A Lockheed U-2R/S fitted with the Senior Span satellite datalink antenna in the dorsal pod. This allowed transmission of reconnaissance data back to base. Avro's TRM-1 predated this by transmitting its data to a Vulcan mother ship.
Via Kev Darling

sight of the drone. How this data link worked was not described in Avro's documentation, but a scheme along the lines of the AN/ART-28 Bellhop data link that was used to transmit the radar picture from the Fairey Gannet AEW.3 to surface ships may have formed the basis of such a system. At the end of the run and having transmitted its radar data, the P39Z dived to destruction on the ground, no doubt helped by demolition charges on any equipment deemed to be security sensitive.

A range of 200nm still meant that, unless the carrier aircraft penetrated Soviet airspace, the areas of interest deep within the Russian interior remained very much a mystery. To this end, in June 1955, Avro proposed a larger, twin-engined, air-launched reconnaissance drone, the P38Z. Also known as the TRM-2, this was twice the size and four times the weight of the P39Z. Like its predecessor, the P.38Z was launched from a Vulcan, the Victor being capable of carrying such a large payload only after much modification.

With a launch weight of 16,500 lb (7,843kg), the P38Z shared the canard configuration of the original Avro Type 730 and with a turbojet on each wingtip, the P.38Z very much resembled a scaled-down version of that aircraft. The 42ft (12.8m) long circular-section fuselage carried the two 20ft (6.1m) Red Drover antennae on either side of the lower fuselage to sweep a strip of land 20 nautical miles (37km) either side of the aircraft over a distance of 200nm (370km). P38Z was to have a range of 2,400nm (4,445km) when launched from a Vulcan and would have carried out its mission by cruising at Mach 2 at 50,000ft (15,240m) under inertial guidance. The main difference from the TRM-1 was that the TRM-2 had to perform a return mission to bring back the radar information it had recorded rather than transmit it to a control aircraft. At the end of its radar reconnaissance run the TRM-2 was intended to return to friendly territory under inertial control until a point where it could be brought under radio control and guided in for a conventional landing. As such this type could be re-used and its recorded radar data was no doubt of much higher quality than the data transmitted over a data link of relatively narrow bandwidth.

The parallels with the American Lockheed D-21 ramjet-powered drone that was developed for the USAF in the 1960s are obvious, with this type performing its missions at Mach 3+. The D-21 was launched from an M-21 carrier aircraft based on a modified Lockheed A-12 reconnaissance aircraft. After problems were encountered with separation from M-21 at high speed, the D-21 was launched from a pylon under the wing of a Boeing B-52H. This low-speed launch required a large solid rocket booster to accelerate the D-21 to the Mach 3 speed required to light its Marquardt ramjet. The D-21 was used on four operational flights over the People's Republic of China with disappointing results.

Yet again the vastness of Soviet territory posed a problem that could only be solved by increased range, which inevitably forced a larger airframe on the designers. As outlined above a manned aircraft requires enough fuel to return to base with its crew. A reconnaissance aircraft has a need to provide its reconnaissance haul to the intelligence officers, so some means of returning the newly-gathered material was required. Data transmission technology was in its infancy and historically a manned reconnaissance aircraft recovered to friendly territory, as its material was of great importance to future operations.

Avro's answer was drawn up in September 1955. The P.33Z/TRM-3 was a longer-ranged type with a twist: essentially a two-stage, composite, unmanned aircraft capable of cruising at Mach 2.5. The 60ft 6in (18.4m) long first stage was powered by two large supersonic turbojets

The mission profiles of the Avro strategic reconnaissance drones. Such systems would be replicated in the 1970s by the American Lockheed D-21 and U-2 Senior Span and in the 1990s with the Global Hawk.

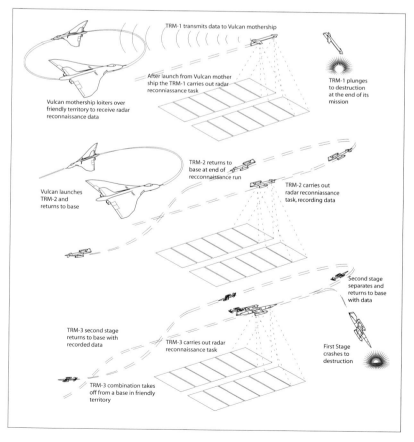

TRM-1 transmits data to Vulcan mothership

After launch from Vulcan mother ship the TRM-1 carries out radar reconnaissance task

Vulcan mothership loiters over friendly territory to receive radar reconnaissance data

TRM-1 plunges to destruction at the end of its mission

TRM-2 returns to base at end of recconnaissance run

TRM-2 carries out radar reconnaissance task, recording data

Vulcan launches TRM-2 and returns to base

Second stage separates and returns to base with data

TRM-3 second stage returns to base with recorded data

TRM-3 carries out radar reconnaissance task

First Stage crashes to destruction

TRM-3 combination takes off from a base in friendly territory

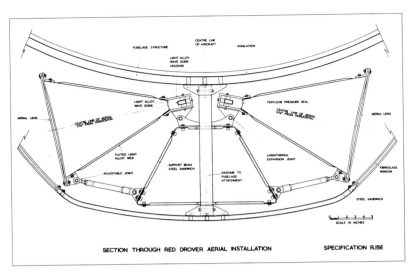

FUSELAGE STRUCTURE
CENTRE LINE OF AIRCRAFT
INSULATION
LIGHT ALLOY WAVE GUIDE HOUSING
LIGHT ALLOY WAVE GUIDE
TERYLENE PRESSURE SEAL
AERIAL LENS
CENTRE LINE OF AERIAL 11½° FROM HORIZONTAL
CENTRE LINE OF AERIAL 11½° FROM HORIZONTAL
AERIAL LENS
FLUTED LIGHT ALLOY WEB
FLUTED LIGHT ALLOY WEB
SUPPORT BEAM STEEL SANDWICH
LONGITUDINAL EXPANSION JOINT
FIBREGLASS WINDOW
ADJUSTABLE JOINT
RADOME TO FUSELAGE ATTACHMENT
STEEL SANDWICH
SCALE IN INCHES

SECTION THROUGH RED DROVER AERIAL INSTALLATION
SPECIFICATION R.156

A detailed cross-section through the EMI Type 800 Red Drover. These early sideways-looking radars paved the way for the future leading to SLAR and synthetic aperture radars on a new generation of drones (now called UAVs) in widespread use today.
BAE Systems/ Avro Heritage

mounted on each wingtip. Described as DH Gyrons, these engines may have been the DH Gyron PS.48 rated at 18,510 lbf (82.3kN) intended for the OR.330 types or the PS.52 rated at 25,000 lbf (111.2kN) designed for the OR.329 interceptors. The fuselage carried the 30ft (9.1m) Red Drover antennae and most of the fuel for the sortie. The second stage was more or less a 75% scaled TRM-2 mounted atop a pylon that doubled as the tail fin of the first stage, thus the second stage formed the horizontal stabiliser for the first stage.

The complete aircraft was to be capable of performing radar reconnaissance of a strip of terrain 20nm (37km) wide and 200nm (370km) long at a distance of 2,000nm (3,700km) from base. The maximum range of the P33Z/TRM-3 was stated as being 4500 nautical miles (8,334km). This performance data appears to overlook the fact that the Gyron turbojet was notoriously thirsty and for a radius of action of 2,000nm (3,700km) the P33Z/TRM-3's airframe could not possibly carry enough fuel for a return mission.

The P33Z/TRM-3's trick was the two-stage configuration with the first stage carrying and powering the radar to collect the data which was then transferred to a recording device in the second stage mounted atop the fin. The end of the reconnaissance run saw the engines on the smaller aircraft started up and the two airframes separated. The first stage fell away to destruction on the ground while the second stage with its recorded radar information returned under autopilot with inertial guidance until it could be brought under radio control to land at a friendly airfield.

That Avro's efforts in the field of strategic reconnaissance drones came to nought will come as no surprise given the era and defence policies followed in the late 1950s. In April

1957 the UK government published its Defence White Paper that changed the deterrent policy from an airborne deterrent to ballistic missiles. This event was followed on 4th October 1957 when the Soviet Union launched Sputnik, the world's first artificial satellite which paved the way for the development of surveillance satellites such as the American KH4 Corona, first launched in June 1959. Further impetus to end overflights of the Soviet Union came on May Day 1960 when a CIA U-2, piloted by Gary Powers was shot down by a salvo of S75 guided weapons (NATO reporting name *Guideline*) over Sverdlovsk. Although the Guidelines did not reach the U-2's altitude, the shock-waves from their explosions affected Powers' aircraft, causing it to break up.

Sixty years on from the TRM-3 a ground-launched, recoverable drone conducts its missions over the mountains of Afghanistan and transmits the output from its sideways-looking radar over a datalink back to base. The Northrop Grumman RQ-4A Global Hawk has swapped speed for stealth and multiple stages for satellite transmission, but it may be an indirect descendant of Avro's TRM series of studies from 1955.

Tactical Drones

Avro WRD, by 1960 renamed Hawker Siddeley Dynamics, returned to the development of reconnaissance drones. The British Army in 1962 issued GSOR.1095 for a tactical reconnaissance drone that would be used to support the Royal Artillery and replace the Radioplane SD-1 that had entered service in 1960.

The first attempt was the Z.112 that was drawn up in April 1962 and described as a long-range recoverable reconnaissance drone. Compared with earlier attempts the Z.112 was hardly long-ranged, with a radius of action around 100 nautical miles (185km), but as a tactical drone for the Royal Artillery, this was long-range. Borrowing much from the low-level stand-off weapons developed by the WRD, Z.112 was a sleek tailed delta with a solid rocket motor installed in the rear fuselage and a Turboméca Marboré turbojet rated at 880 lbf (3.9kN) mounted on a dorsal pylon that doubled as a fin and carried the rudder. The Marboré had been used previously in the Nord CT20 target drone and R20 reconnaissance drone used by the French Army. Avro WRD had a close relationship with Nord Aviation having co-operated on the CT.41 supersonic target. This was displayed alongside a Blue Steel on the Avro stand at the 1958 Farnborough Air Show.

The Z.112 was probably too long-ranged and complex in operation for the tactical needs of the Army, who wanted a system that could be deployed quickly, used in quantity and produce rapid results. The Army requirement was for a basic machine that could answer the Duke of Wellington's famous question about what was on the other side of the hill.

The drone was to be rocket-powered for simplicity and possess a range of about 30nm (56km) and since it was to carry a photographic reconnaissance pack, had to be recovered. The design team at the WRD came up with the Z.113, a recoverable, rocket-powered reconnaissance vehicle that when fitted with its tandem boost was 15ft 6in (4.7m) long. The drone itself was 9ft 6in (2.9m) long with the rear 3ft (0.9m) taken up by a pair of parachutes installed around the rocket blast tube for the recovery. The sustainer was to be a packaged liquid-fuelled rocket engine of similar thrust rating as the Spartan that had been proposed by de Havilland for the Red Top Mk.2 air-to-air missile.

Z.113 proved unsatisfactory due to its large size, a consequence of the need to carry recovery kit and enough propellant to return to base for recovery of the film. The size limited the number of drones that could be carried by a unit's support truck and the use of wet film introduced a time delay on the intelligence that was untenable in the fluid environment of a battlefield.

The first problem addressed by Hawker Siddeley was the need to return the drone to base. As described above, the technology to transmit data was maturing so the main question was what sensor should replace wet film? A television system was considered and, given the era, might have held sway for a realtime reconnaissance tool. Television guidance was in vogue for guided weapons such as the AJ.168 Martel, but as a short-range reconnaissance tool TV was thought to be susceptible to interference, was difficult to transmit over a narrow bandwidth datalink and required recording and playback equipment. The preferred solution was a linescan system whereby a sensor swept rapidly from side-to-side as the aircraft flew over an area of interest. Linescan systems can use visible or infrared spectra to produce a picture built up as a series of lines across the image normal to the direction of flight. Since the drone was to fly at a constant height, bearing and speed, linescan was ideal, with the data being transmitted to base and printed out on a continuous strip of paper.

With the linescan system selected for the drone a major reduction in size was possible so the designers drew up a study called W.150 that was described as 'a small drone, fitted with a reliable propulsion system and scanning system, flying low over the target area'. To study this vehicle Hawker Siddeley were awarded contract KV/K/2/CB.44b to conduct a feasibility study in late 1961 and by September 1962 had produced a report on their study.

The aim was a 'squaddie-proof' system that could be set up and launched rapidly and sustain operations for extended periods. The next vehicle was the Z.114 that comprised a 9ft 6in (2.9m) long cigar-shaped fuselage with three all-moving fins at the rear. The centre of the fuselage was formed by the dual-chamber solid rocket motor that would power the drone to Mach 1.2 with the control system and fin actuators disposed around the blast tube of the rocket. Facing rearwards on a raised portion of the rear fuselage was the antenna for the data link that transmitted the signal back to a tracking aerial on a control truck in the launch area.

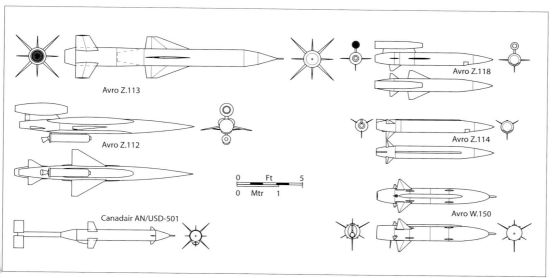

Avro Z.113

Avro Z.112

Canadair AN/USD-501

Avro Z.118

Avro Z.114

Avro W.150

As well as helping the RAF see into Russia, Avro's WRD aimed at helping the British Army see over the hill. Work on drone vehicles for the Army included rocket, turbojet and ramjet types. Ultimately the MoD acquired the Canadian AN/USD-501 as the Midge.

The nose housed the linescan equipment that allowed a field of view of 120° of the ground below the vehicle through optically flat glass panels on the underside.

Rather than increase the size of the rocket motors to increase range and maintain the return to base capability, HSD fitted the Z.114 with a dorsal ramjet to create the Z.118. The ramjet had been viewed as a means of increasing the range of unmanned rocket-powered vehicles since the first guided weapons appeared. The internal sustainer rocket motor was converted to a boost motor by changing the propellant compound and internal profile to increase the thrust and reduce the burn time. This produced a booster that could accelerate the Z.118 to sufficient speed to light the ramjet. The Z.118 was fitted with small delta wings at the mid-fuselage position while the 120° indexed fins of the Z.114 were replaced by a pair of horizontal tailplanes and a vertical fin under the rear fuselage.

By August 1963 Hawker Siddeley produced a much modified W.150. Shorter and more rounded, the new W.150 introduced a two-chamber rocket motor with separate high-thrust boost motor and lower thrust sustainer that formed the mid-body section of the fuselage. This motor propelled the W.150 to an altitude of 2,500ft (762m) and cruised at Mach 0.9 over a distance of 15nm (28km) in a flight that lasted one minute and fifteen seconds. By increasing the thrust of the boost motor by 18% the range could be increased to 30nm (56km) and that improvement could be achieved by extending the fuselage by 12in (30cm) to house a larger boost motor. These changes would increase the launch weight to 87lb (39kg). The control system was modified to use a trio of fixed fins to produce symmetrical aerodynamic properties. Control in pitch, yaw and roll was provided by three interdigitated all-moving fins slightly to the rear of the fixed fins. As before the datalink transmitter was fitted in the flattened rear of the drone, above the sustainer rocket blast pipe. Ultimately the British Army acquired the AN/USD-501 Midge, a variant of the Canadair CL-89 as its tactical reconnaissance drone.

The Duke of Wellington's most memorable quote is 'The whole art of war consists in getting at what is on the other side of the hill.' In the 1950s this could have been paraphrased by substituting 'Iron Curtain' for 'hill'. Seeing what was inside the Soviet Union would prove as problematic as getting to it and many an imaginative project to this end would be studied with little or no progress. In the end it would take space-based reconnaissance to find the targets and ballistic missiles to destroy them, but in the 1950s this was but a pipedream.

Sons of Vulcan – leading particulars

Type	Length	Span	Weight	Propulsion	Speed	Range
Avro 730 (initial)	163ft 6in	59ft 9in	222,000lb	4 x ASM P.176 turbojets	Mach 2.5	4,500nm
Avro 730 (final)	159ft	65ft 7in	292,000lb	8 x ASM P.159 turbojets	Mach 2.5	3,500nm
Vickers SP4	133ft	63ft 3in	209,000lb	16 x RB.121 turbojets	Mach 2.5	4,400nm
EECo P10	108ft 9in	50ft	123,000lb	Split-wing ramjet 2 x RB.123 turbojet	Mach 3	4,500nm
Convair B-58 Hustler	96ft 10in	56ft 9in	67,871lb	4 x J79 turbojets	Mach 2.0	4,000nm
EECo P10/16	124ft	61ft 6in	n/a	16 x RB.121 turbojet		n/a
EECo P10B	100ft	50ft	n/a	Split-wing ramjet	Mach 3	n/a
EECo P10C	104ft	58ft	n/a	2 x Bristol ramjets	Mach 3	n/a
EECo P10E	80ft	44ft	58,000lb	8 x ramjets 8 x RB.121	Mach 3	n/a
Convair F-106	70ft 8in	38ft 3in	34,510lb	J75 turbojet	Mach 2.3	1,600nm
Avro TRM-1	26ft 8in	8ft	4,000lb	RB.121 turbojet	Mach 2	200nm
Avro TRM-2	42ft	19ft	16,500lb	2 x turbojets	Mach 2	2,400nm
Avro TRM-3	56ft	20ft	28,200lb	4 x turbojets	Mach 2.5	4,500nm
Lockheed D-21	42ft 2in	19ft	11,000lb	Marquardt ramjet	Mach 3.3	3,000nm
Avro 734	50ft	19ft	17,000lb	ASM P.176 turbojet	Mach 2.5	1,564nm

3 Gravity Bombs

'We've got to have it and it's got to have a bloody Union Jack on it.' – Ernest Bevin, Foreign Secretary, 1947

United Kingdom deterrence began with the atomic bomb, a large weapon dropped from a large aircraft flying over a target. Denied US help, the UK developed a number of nuclear bombs, some more successful than others. The quest for a weapon that could be released before the aircraft entered a defended area led to glide bombs to reduce the force's exposure to enemy anti-aircraft systems. The massive investment in the V-Force made the Air Staff very aware of its vulnerability to attack on the ground. Dispersal was the answer but still relied on long runways and airfield facilities. The answers to these problems lay in the development of a stand-off weapon and vertical take-off aircraft that did not need runways, effectively a VTOL V-Force.

Bomber Command intended using the atomic bomb to Soviet attack cities, a skill it had honed in the war through massed attacks with high-explosive and incendiary bombs. The only differences between an attack on Germany and one on the Soviet Union were the distances and number of aircraft involved. Nuclear weapons allowed devastation on the scale of Hamburg or Dresden to be visited on Leningrad or Kiev by a single aircraft with a single bomb and as in the last war that would have been a free-fall bomb.

The rather surprising fact about the V-Force was that free-fall nuclear weapons figured in its armoury throughout its life and continued in service on Tornados long after the last Vulcan bomber had been retired in 1982. The free-fall bomb is the stock-in-trade of any 'bomber' aircraft and being uncontrollable after release relies on the aircraft aiming systems for accuracy.

The term free-fall suggests that an aircraft merely flew over a target, opened its bomb

A pair of Avro 727s with P35Z glide bombs return to base after an operational exercise.
Adrian Mann

Vickers Valiant B(PR).1 WP223 drops an inert Blue Danube during ballistic trials at the A&AEE. The size of Blue Danube was due to the size of the Hurricane-derived physics package within. *Via Terry Panopalis*

Bomb delivery methods evolved from the original high-altitude drop to a variety of methods to including toss/loft, dive toss and over the shoulder toss. In this diagram delivery of WE.177 by TSR.2 is shown.

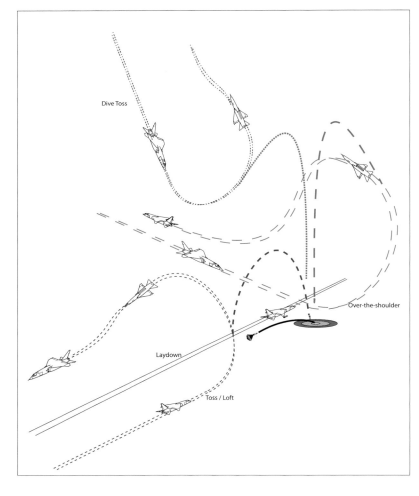

doors and released a bomb. As ever the situation was not that simple. Initially, that was how the British atomic weapons were to be delivered. A V-bomber flew towards the target at an altitude of around 50,000ft (15,240m) and, using its H2S Mk.9 and NBS to aim the weapon, released it. The aircraft then performed a high-rate turn away from the target area to escape the blast. This was employed by V-bombers delivering Blue Danube, Red Beard and Yellow Sun while Canberra bombers used Red Beard in this manner.

As the Fifties became the Sixties, Soviet air defences had improved to such an extent that the V-Force was required to change tactics to a low-level environment. This would have reduced the amount of time for the bomber to escape the blast, so a different delivery method was required.

The first, used mainly by the V-bombers to deliver Yellow Sun and also widely used by Canberras to deliver Red Beard, was the pop-up delivery. This involved the aircraft approaching the target at low level, followed by a rapid climb to 12,500ft (3,810m) where the weapon was released.

The third method, low-altitude bombing system (LABS), came in two variants used by strike aircraft to deliver Red Beard and WE.177. The 'long toss' involved the aircraft approaching the target at low level and when indicated by the LABS bomb aiming computer, entering a 45° climb. The aiming system would release the weapon at a point in the climb, followed by the aircraft performing a half loop to depart the area on a reciprocal bearing at 7,000ft (2,134m). The bomb continued upward until, under the force of gravity, it tipped over and fell onto the target. The 'over the shoulder' delivery was similar to the toss method apart from the aircraft overflying the target at 200ft (61m) before entering the loop manoeuvre. The weapon was released near the top of the loop and the aircraft continued through the loop until pulling out at low altitude to egress the target area. Again, the bomb continued upwards before falling to land on the target.

The last method was laydown, the technique employed with the WE.177 bomb. The aircraft approached the target at low level and released the weapon when almost on top of the target. The aircraft continued on at low level while the bomb, retarded by parachutes, made a 'fairly soft' landing on the target. After a time delay to allow the aircraft to escape, the weapon detonated.

British Free Fall Nuclear Weapons

Blue Danube

Introduced to RAF service in 1953, Blue Danube (known variously as Littleboy and Mk.1 Atom Bomb during early development) was Britain's first nuclear weapon and was the 'Special Weapon' that the Valiant, Victor and Vulcan were designed around. 'Designed around' is probably a misleading description as the dimensions and weight of the weapon had been laid out in OR.1001, issued in August 1946. The dimensions of the V-bomber weapons bays were drawn up to fit these guidelines set out in the various bomber requirements including specification B.35/46 issued in January 1947.

Rather than a weapon in its own right, Blue Danube should be considered as a bomb casing, even a test vehicle, for various physics packages. The confusing litany of the Ministry of Supply's rainbow code system certainly fulfilled its goal of covering the precise nature of the equipment involved. Blue Danube was an aerodynamic fairing that enclosed the device and stabilised it during air dropping. Physics package was an apt description of the weapon rather than one of the many euphemisms associated with British nuclear weapons. Blue Danube's first physics package, an implosion device developed by the Atomic Weapons Research Establishment (AWRE), differed only in detail from the device tested in Operation Hurricane in 1952 and possessed a yield of at least 10Kt.

The RAF was very wary of its new atomic weapons but unlike American devices, it did not use in-flight core insertion to prevent accidental detonation during take-off. Once armed, Blue Danube had four separate trigger mechanisms; a primary radar detonation system with back up from barostatic and timer and, if all those failed, inertia switches to detonate on impact. The barostatic and timer systems were to be used to circumvent jamming of the radar system. This wariness was compounded after an inert Blue Danube hung up in the bomb-bay of a Valiant. On landing to investigate the incident, the ground crew opened the bomb bay doors and out popped the Blue Danube! Had it been armed, the inertia switches would have triggered the bomb. This incident prompted a change in procedures and subsequently any air-

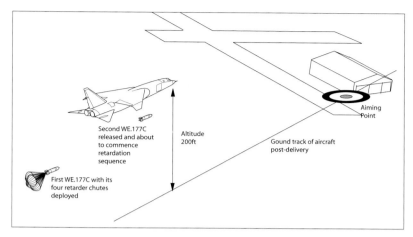

Second WE.177C released and about to commence retardation sequence

First WE.177C with its four retarder chutes deployed

Altitude 200ft

Aiming Point

Gound track of aircraft post-delivery

craft suffering a hung-up weapon was to be ditched.

Having described Blue Danube as a test vehicle might sound odd, but it served that role very well. Contrary to popular belief, its shape was not derived from the largest bomb that the RAF had deployed, the Grand Slam of World War Two, nor was Barnes Wallis involved in its design. Blue Danube, a shapely device, certainly shared that weapon's aerodynamic cleanliness but test drops revealed that it had a somewhat alarming characteristic. On release from the Valiant's weapons bay the bomb resolutely refused to drop and it tracked the aircraft as it moved slowly away, much to the consternation of the crew.

Fitting of parachutes to retard the weapon and allow the aircraft to escape the blast on detonation was considered but not adopted. Another problem, caused by transonic and supersonic airflow over the Blue Danube casing at its Mach 2.2 terminal velocity, was the generation of shockwaves that affected the barometric fuzes.

Blue Danube was declared operational at RAF Wittering in November 1953 as 'Bomb, Aircraft, HE 10,000 lb MC'. Unfortunately there were no aircraft capable of carrying it until April

The WE.177C Laydown Bomb was intended for low-level delivery from types such as the BAC TSR.2. WE.177 eventually came in three types with a variety of delivery methods.

Blue Danube also known as Small Boy and Special Weapon was Britain's first operational nuclear weapon. Blue Danube referred to the casing that could contain a variety of warheads including Green Grass. Its shape was developed from data acquired in the Emulsion trials that used borrowed USAF B-29s.
Via Terry Panopalis

There was a time when the airbrush would have been applied to the large store at the front of this impressive display of Buccaneer weapons. Buccaneers with Red Beard took over the tactical nuclear strike role from Scimitars in 1965.
Via Terry Panopalis

Cutaway showing the major components of the Red Beard/Target Marker Bomb.
Via Brian Burnell

1954 when 1321 Flight was established to integrate Blue Danube with the Valiant. This unit came under the auspices of No.138 Squadron on its reformation as the first Valiant squadron in 1955. Blue Danube continued in service until 1962, by which time it had been replaced by Red Beard.

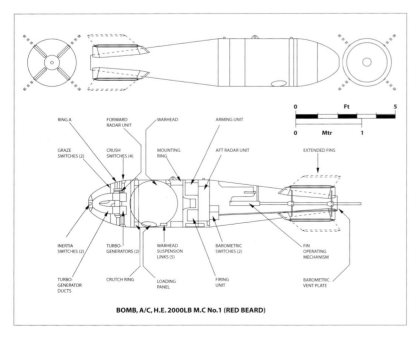

RING A
FORWARD RADAR UNIT
WARHEAD
ARMING UNIT
GRAZE SWITCHES (2)
CRUSH SWITCHES (4)
MOUNTING RING
AFT RADAR UNIT
EXTENDED FINS
INERTIA SWITCHES (2)
TURBO-GENERATORS (2)
WARHEAD SUSPENSION LINKS (5)
BAROMETRIC SWITCHES (2)
FIN OPERATING MECHANISM
TURBO-GENERATOR DUCTS
CRUTCH RING
LOADING PANEL
FIRING UNIT
BAROMETRIC VENT PLATE

0   Ft   5
0   Mtr   1

BOMB, A/C, H.E. 2000LB M.C No.1 (RED BEARD)

Red Beard/TMB

All countries and companies involved in weapon research apply code or cover names to their wares. Some exalt the supposed capabilities of their weaponry while others opt for a more mundane approach. Britain had two cracks of the cover name whip: a codename was applied to a weapon during its development and then a service name applied once operational. The service name was generally in the exultant style but in some cases a euphemism was applied, particularly to new technology. Possibly the finest of these was applied to Britain's second atomic weapon and first tactical bomb. Known as Red Beard during its development, the bomb to meet OR.1127, a 2,000 lb (907kg) tactical weapon, entered service in 1962 under the name Target Marker Bomb (TMB). This euphemism allowed the weapon to be listed on inventories and used in loading paperwork without revealing its true identity as a 15Kt nuclear weapon.

Red Beard was originally known as the Javelin Bomb, being intended for the bomber version of the Gloster Thin-wing Javelin, drawn up to meet OR.328 as one of numerous attempts at Canberra replacement. It utilised a physics package of similar design to Blue

Danube but much smaller and came in four variants: Mk.1 had a yield of 15Kt while the Mk.2 had improved weather-proofing for naval use and a yield of 25Kt. Further sub-divisions were the No.1 intended for high-altitude delivery by Vulcan, Victor or Canberra and No.2 for LABS (low-altitude bombing system) delivery by Supermarine Scimitar or Blackburn Buccaneer strike aircraft.

Despite its service designation of 'Bomb, HE, 2,000 lb, MC', the weapon weighed in at 1,750 lb (793.7kg) and MC, which normally stood for 'Medium Capacity' on a conventional bomb, identified Red Beard as possessing a yield in the Kiloton range. Red Beard spawned a couple of derivatives either based on the entire weapon or its physics package. The earliest was Nuclear Highball that dated from the mid Fifties and involved fitting the Red Beard physics package into a 3ft (0.9m) diameter spherical bouncing bomb. The only extant image of what may be this weapon shows it in the weapons bay of an English Electric P.10 Mach 3 bomber. The reasoning behind this application is unknown; however the drawings have been recently identified with a tactical application of the P.10 that superseded the RB.156 requirement. Alternatively the spherical weapon may be a response to the tumbling effect of dropping a weapon at Mach 3.

A later development from 1958 was the Winged Target Marker (WTM). This took the basic Red Beard and added a ventral fin and a small swept wing attached by a pair of hoops fastened around the girth of the casing. Winged Target Marker used a similar principle to Wallis' Momentum Bomb and was intended to arm low-level strike aircraft such as the Eng-

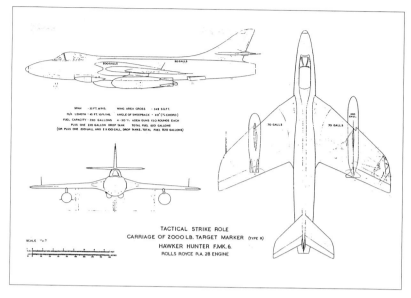

lish Electric P.17 and its successor, TSR.2. After launch the WTM climbed upwards to around 10,000ft (3,048m) before looping over and descending onto the target. This loop manoeuvre allowed the aircraft to escape at low altitude and avoided the climb that an aircraft performed in a LABS run.

Red Beard entered service in 1962 and was in use by the Fleet Air Arm and the RAF until replacement by WE.177 in 1969. At one stage Red Beard was suggested as an anti-aircraft weapon, to be tossed from Gloster Javelins and English Electric Lightnings at incoming Soviet bombers to airburst within the formations. Improvements to guided weapons and the defeat of such weapons by bombers flying further apart made the use of such nuclear weapons against bomber formations obsolete.

Although the Hawker Hunter is not normally associated with nuclear strike, this Hawker study shows the large size of British nuclear weapons. The Red Beard bomb under the port wing was the smallest of the British free-fall weapons during the 1950s.
BAE Systems/ Brooklands Museum

Red Beard/Target Marker Bomb installed on the port inboard pylon of a Fleet Air Arm Supermarine Scimitar. Red Beard replaced the Green Cheese missile in the anti-ship role.
Via Terry Panopalis

Buccaneer XV162 of Fleet Air Arm NAS 801 releases a Red Beard. The recess for its semi-recessed carriage on the rotating bomb bay door can be seen clearly. *Via Terry Panopalis*

Equipped with freefall bombs such as Yellow Sun these Handley Page Victor B.1As of 55 Squadron are spotted on an Operational Readiness Platform at RAF Honington. The quick-start trolley in the foreground allowed all four engines to be started at once. *Author's Collection*

Violet Club

Having embarked on development of the Blue Danube fission bomb, the goalposts moved in the nuclear deterrent game on 1st November 1952. On that date the Americans exploded the first thermonuclear weapon: the hydrogen bomb. Denied American help under the McMahon Act and still striving for a place at the nuclear top table, Britain embarked on creating its own fusion weapon in July 1954.

Deception in warfare is as old as war itself and aims to persuade an enemy that any attack would be too costly to contemplate. When combined with deterrence there is a need to convince the enemy that offensive action would result in their complete and utter destruction. The advent of thermonuclear weapons brought these two aspects together and nowhere more so than in the United Kingdom.

Violet Club is an example of how deception can be applied against enemy and ally alike while causing great annoyance to the user of the weapon. Pending development of thermonuclear warheads, AWRE came up with what they described as the Interim Megaton Weapon. This was a high yield, but not thermonuclear, physics package called Green Grass that when fitted in a Blue Danube casing became Violet Club.

AWRE declared that the Green Grass/Violet Club weapon was 'in the megaton range' but the Air Staff were decidedly unconvinced by 'Bomb, Aircraft, HE 9,000 lb HC'. Their reasoning was that the weapon had a yield of 500Kt, which AWRE insisted was 'half a megaton' hence the 'HC' in its designation. That exercise in semantics was not the Air Staff's primary concern about Violet Club.

Its unboosted fission design used a hollow sphere of highly enriched uranium (HEU) surrounded by a high-explosive implosion system comprising 72 explosive lenses. That sphere of HEU had an uncompressed mass in excess of the required critical mass once compressed in the explosion of detonation. This gave the Air Staff cause for concern as the weapon could be crushed or damaged in transit or in a crash, causing partial compression and potentially initiate fission. AWRE's solution to this was to fill the void within the sphere with steel ball-bearings, 20,000 to be precise, which increased the bomb's loaded weight to 11,250 lb (5,102kg). This weight exceeded the bomb release mechanism of the Vulcan and precluded flight with the safety devices in place.

To arm the device the weapon was loaded into the aircraft and once ready to embark on its mission, a plastic bung was removed and that allowed the bearings to flow out of the bomb before take-off. This could take up to half an hour at best. It was soon discovered that the rubber liner inside the sphere perished and the ball bearings stuck to it. This required the replacement of the liner on a regular basis. The RAF were most annoyed by this as the bearings increased the weight of the bomb to such an extent that it could not be transported in unarmed condition, nor could it be used for extended alerts as cold weather caused the bearings to freeze together thus rendering the bomb useless as a weapon. Airborne alert was not possible because, once armed, the weapon could not be made safe for landing, with take-off being the first hazard for any aircraft carrying Violet Club. Even ground running of engines was frowned upon before Violet Club was armed for fear that the bung would fall out, followed closely by 20,000 steel balls. Only five Violet Club bombs were built. From the RAF's point of view, that was probably five too many.

Ultimately what most annoyed the Air Staff was AWRE's reference to Violet Club being in the megaton range when in fact it was closer to 400Kt. By describing Violet Club as a weapon in the megaton class and having demonstrated a fairly convincing megaton range bomb test in the 1957 Grapple series at Christmas Island, Her Majesty's Government managed to influence the Americans to resume nuclear co-operation in 1958. Not so easily persuaded were the Bomber Command officers who were of the opinion that, with the Interim Megaton Weapon, they 'had been sold a lemon'. However, Violet Club wasn't alone in this ambiguity.

Yellow Sun Mk.1 and Mk.2

Codenames, as noted above, are intended to conceal the nature of the subject, so why would the name Yellow Sun be applied to a nuclear bomb? The simple answer would be deception: if ever a name suggested a fusion weapon, it's Yellow Sun. Again this name applies more to the casing than the entire weapon; it came in two variants defined as ever by their physics packages. Fitted with that AWRE-designed Green Grass, 'Bomb, Aircraft, HE 7,000 lb HC Mk.1' incorporated lessons learned from Violet Club including the use of 133,000 smaller ball-bearings. Like the physics package in Violet Club, Yellow Sun Mk.1 was not a fusion device but had a yield of 500Kt (or in AWRE parlance, 0.5Mt) and was touted as a megaton weapon, hence the 'HC' in the official name. This economy with the actualité served to convince the

Americans and Soviets that Britain possessed a viable thermonuclear capability.

Yellow Sun Mk.2

Britain's success in developing that apparent thermonuclear weapon contributed to the repeal of the McMahon Act in 1958. This opened the door to collaboration between AWRE and American nuclear weapons developers and Green Grass was the last wholly British nuclear device. Under the 1958 US-UK Mutual Defence Agreement, the Americans gave AWRE access to their fusion weapon designs, which the British would manufacture using their own materials. This renewal of co-operation with the Americans opened up new possibilities at AWRE who could 'Anglicise' the more compact American bomb designs. As ever there were differences in detail between US and UK devices. Apart from using British fissile material, the main difference was the explosives used for the fission devices, with the American PBX-9404 deemed too sensitive to shocks for use in British weapons.

This new-found spirit of co-operation led to a modified American W-28 warhead being used in Yellow Sun Mk.2. The Mk.28 warhead was familiar as it had already been used by the RAF under the Project E protocols. Re-engineered to meet RAF requirements, the Mk.28 warhead became known as Red Snow and was

Yellow Sun with a Victor B.1. The bluff nose was to ensure it dropped cleanly from the aircraft and prevent the weapon accelerating to transonic speeds. The shockwaves generated at transonic speeds had affected the barometric fuze on Blue Danube.
Via Terry Panopalis

Yellow Sun Mark.1 with the Green Grass warhead taking up the entire centre section of the bomb. When the Red Snow warhead was fitted, ballast had to be added to preserve its ballistic properties.
Via Terry Panopalis

Top left: Yellow Sun Mark 2 showing the Red Snow capsule derived from the American W28 physics package. The size difference between warhead and casing is apparent, requiring ballast to maintain aerodynamic and ballistic properties. *Via Terry Panopalis*

Top right: The Red Snow capsule as fitted to Yellow Sun Mk.2 and Blue Steel. Derived from the US Mk.28 warhead engineered to British standards, the small compact size of Red Snow is not apparent in this photograph. *Via Terry Panopalis*

fitted in the Yellow Sun casing to become 'Bomb, Aircraft, 7,000 lb, HC Mk.2'. In this instance the 'HC' did signify a megaton weapon as the stated yield for Red Snow was 1Mt. Although Red Snow was a fraction of the size and weight of Green Grass, the Yellow Sun casing was used as the handling gear and procedures for Yellow Sun Mk.1 were still useable. To maintain the Mk.1's delivery characteristics, ballast was added in the casing to keep the Mk.2 weapon's weight similar to the Mk.1. At last the RAF had a true fusion weapon and with the aid of US experience AWRE could reduce the size of the casings.

WE.177

The low-level role became standard practice for strike aircraft from the late 1950s and it soon became clear that Red Beard was not an ideal weapon for external carriage. In August 1959 a requirement, OR.1177, was issued to cover a replacement for Red Beard with a variety of yields up to 300Kt and weighing no more than 1,000 lb (454kg). This weapon soon became known as the Improved Kiloton Weapon. The Admiralty also issued a requirement, GDA.10, to replace Red Beard.

As this weapon was to be delivered at low altitude by strike aircraft such as the TSR.2, it soon became known as the Laydown Bomb. The tail section of the bomb held a drogue and four main parachutes. These served to retard the weapon and after a fairly soft landing, bring it to a halt on the ground before a delayed detonation which allowed the strike aircraft to escape the blast. To survive the rigours of a laydown delivery on land, only the warhead section of the bomb was robust, the equipment in the tail and nose sections needed no such protection as it was redundant as soon as the bomb impacted.

UK Nuclear Gravity Bombs

Above: A WE.177C fitted to a bomb carrier for the Vulcan awaits loading. The width of the bomb carrier structure shows the size of the Vulcan weapons bay and how far British bombs had progressed from the Blue Danube. *Via Terry Panopalis*

Type	Length	Yield	Diameter	Weight	Carrier
Blue Danube	24ft 1in	20Kt	5ft 2in	10,250 lb	Valiant, Vulcan, Victor
Red Beard	12ft	Mk.1: 5Kt Mk.2: 25Kt	2ft 4in	1,650 lb	Valiant, Victor Vulcan, Buccaneer, Canberra
Violet Club	24ft 1in	400Kt (originally 0.5Mt)	5ft 2in	9,000 lb	Vulcan
Yellow Sun Mk.1	20ft	400Kt	4ft	7,250 lb	Vulcan
Yellow Sun Mk.2	20ft	1.1Mt	4ft	7,250 lb	Victor, Vulcan
WE.177A	9ft 4in	0.5-10Kt	1ft 5in	620 lb	Buccaneer, Wessex, Wasp, Nimrod
WE.177B	11ft 1in	450Kt	1ft 5in	1,008 lb	Vulcan
WE.177C	11ft 1in	190Kt	1ft 5in	1,008 lb	Buccaneer, Jaguar, Tornado

However it was intended to be delivered by the gamut of techniques and as it was also required for the Royal Navy as a nuclear depth bomb, it acquired the Ministry of Aviation reference WE.177. The initial version was WE.177A, known to the Services as 'Bomb, Aircraft, HE 600 lb MC' with a variable yield (0.5-10Kt) boosted fission warhead and matched most closely the Admiralty's GDA.10 Red Beard replacement requirement. The WE.177A was only issued to the RAF's maritime strike squadrons after the retirement of HMS *Ark Royal*. The reason for the low yield of 0.5Kt was to allow the weapon to be used against submarines in shallow water without endangering nearby shipping.

In 1962, in the fallout from Skybolt cancellation, emphasis changed to producing a higher yield WE.177 for strategic use by the V-Force. This became WE.177B, also known as Weapon X, which entered service on RAF Vulcans in September 1966. Designated as 'Bomb, Aircraft, HE 950 lb MC' and with fixed yield of 450kt it used the RE.179 fusion warhead intended for Skybolt. To accommodate the thermonuclear warhead a 2ft 2in (0.7m) section was added to the WE.177 bringing the total length to 11ft 1in (3.4m). On retirement of the Vulcan bomber force in 1982, the WE.177B was carried by the Tornado GR.1 until all British free-fall nuclear weapons were withdrawn in 1998.

The RAF also required a tactical nuclear weapon in the 200Kt range for use on the European battlefield. The 10Kt yield of the WE.177A was too small to destroy a large target such as an airfield while the 450Kt yield of WE.177B was too large for such use. NATO doctrine held that a warhead with a yield of 200Kt was the maximum for use on the battlefield. The result was WE.177C, a 190Kt yield weapon believed to use warhead components from the British Polaris warhead, ET.317. These warheads became available when the Polaris improvement project known as Chevaline got under way. The Chevaline version of Polaris carried two ET.317 warheads rather than three, with the space for the third warhead being taken up by penetration aids.

WE.177C shared the same stretched casing as the B model and entered service in the mid-1970s as the RAF's Buccaneer and Jaguar strike aircraft were replacing Canberra and Phantom respectively. Recent speculation has centred on the tactics for delivering WE.177C, particularly onto a wide area target. Dropping pairs of weapons to maximise damage may have been considered. Another matter raised at a confer-

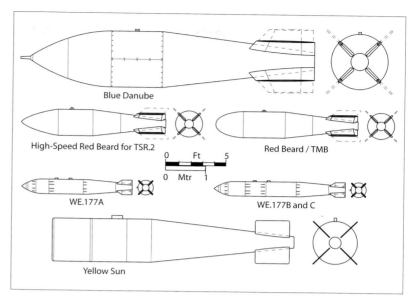

Blue Danube

High-Speed Red Beard for TSR.2   Red Beard / TMB

WE.177A   WE.177B and C

Yellow Sun

ence in 2009 involved the possibility of the weapon being vulnerable in the delay period prior to detonation. Given the preponderance of light anti-aircraft weapons around a Warsaw Pact airfield, could these have been used to disrupt the weapon before detonation? Possibly the reason the RAF considered dropping pairs.

By 1998 the free-fall nuclear weapon had been withdrawn from British service, leaving the Trident SLBM as Britain's deterrent. All WE.177 bombs had been withdrawn, de-activated and a few examples were donated to museums around the country, where they sit on trolleys looking completely innocuous. Their small size actually gives them a rather benign appearance. Only by reading the label can the uninformed public learn that such small weapons could destroy the surrounding area over a radius of three miles.

Before the Steel Age – Glide Bombs

On 21st July 1943 a flight of Dornier 217K-2 medium bombers from *Gruppe* III of *Kampfgeschwader* 100 approached the Italian port of Augusta, north of the city of Syracuse on Sicily. On dropping their bombs, rather than accelerating away from the anti-aircraft fire, these Dorniers slowed down by entering a steep climb before levelling out. Six weeks later the Italian battleship *Roma* lay at the bottom of the Straits of Bonifacio, between Sardinia and Corsica, sunk by bombs from the same Dornier 217s that exhibited similar behaviour. Then on 16th September another battleship, HMS *Warspite*, was struck and severely damaged off

The relative sizes of British free-fall bombs can be seen in this diagram. By 1957 the Red Beard/Target Marker Bomb was the smallest nuclear weapon available to the British. In comparison the Americans were deploying the W33 8in (203mm) artillery shell with a yield of up to 40kt. Note the changes involved in conversion of Red Beard for TSR.2 and high-speed delivery.

53

Salerno. A second weapon struck the sea close by and, had it hit the ship, would probably have sunk *Warspite*.

Attacks with bombs on ships under way had until that point been the preserve of the dive bomber with its ability to adjust its aim as the target weaved and turned. These attacks were different. No dive bombers, just conventional medium bombers with the ability to put bomb after bomb on their targets, with particular preference for capital ships.

It soon became apparent that the Dorniers were using a guided bomb called Fritz-X or to give it is official name: Ruhrstahl SD 1400 X. During the Spanish Civil War the Luftwaffe had discovered that ships at sea made for very difficult targets and embarked on a research programme to produce specialised weapons for this task under the direction of Dipl. Ing. Max Kramer at the *Deutsche Versuchsanstalt für Luftfahrt*. Fritz-X was a radio-controlled glide bomb with a stand-off range of around 5km (2.7nm) and was fitted with tracking flares to allow the operator to see the bomb in flight. The sudden deceleration of the Dorniers was to allow the bomb to overtake the aircraft and enter the operator's field of vision. The operator then used a joystick and radio link to guide the bomb to its target. The 320kg (700lb) armour-piercing warhead was designed specifically to attack capital ships.

To address the same problem the British had been developing large anti-ship rockets such as Uncle Tom for use by anti-ship Mosquitoes or in the immediate postwar period, Red Angel by the Westland Wyvern and fired at low level and short range into the sea 30ft (9.1m) abeam of the ship. On entering the water the rockets arced upward to strike the hull below the ship's armour. This of course required the launch aircraft to run the gauntlet of the ships anti-aircraft guns and, whether on land or at sea, the Germans were masters of the use of light flak guns. To attack ships at anchor the RAF used its Tallboy earthquake bombs with great effect against vessels such as the battleship *Tirpitz*. Unfortunately it took thirty Avro Lancasters from No.617 and No.9 squadrons to sink the *Tirpitz* with three bomb hits out of thirty, so some means of improving accuracy was required.

The Germans decided that dropping a controllable bomb from outside the ship's defences was the best approach and Fritz-X, this earliest guided stand-off bomb, was developed. Intrigued by this guided bomb and its success, and comparing German efforts with that of the RAF, the Admiralty began examining a guided bomb along similar lines to Fritz-X. What the Admiralty really wanted was bomb that could be stowed and carried like standard bombs, but it was quickly realised that the existing guidance systems, such as television, could only be fitted to large weapons in the 10,000lb (4,534kg) class without affecting the explosive/weight ratio of the bomb.

The Germans had accomplished the successful use of the Fritz-X by being first; the shock of the new allowed Fritz-X its initial devastating success but the British expertise in radio countermeasures soon saw Fritz-X more or less neutralised. Fritz-X had two effects on the Admiralty who decided that action was required; firstly to create an effective countermeasure and secondly to produce a similar weapon. The first took the form of the requirements for the LOP/GAP anti-aircraft projectile and the postwar Popsy and Mopsy SAMs. These weapons were to intercept the bombs themselves, mainly because the carrier aircraft were out of range of the ships' anti-aircraft guns, which had also proven ineffective at destroying the warhead.

The steps to produce a similar British weapon were well under way by the time Fritz-X appeared and these could be traced back to the Toraplane, an anti-ship glide bomb developed by Dennis Burney in 1918 and re-assessed in the late 1930s. By 1943 Major-General Millis Rowland Jefferis began to examine the problems of attacking ships from aircraft. Jefferis had been successful in developing a number of innovative weapons during the Second World War particularly those that used the High Explosive Squash Head (HESH) anti-armour warhead. Jefferis and Lord Cherwell, Winston Churchill's scientific advisor, in 1944 drew up plans to use the HESH warhead on a homing bomb for use against Japanese warships in the Pacific. The Ministry of Aircraft Production and the Air Staff were very interested in this and gave it their support. This became known as the Cherwell-Jefferis Bomb and as development progressed the weapon acquired the name Journey's End. Fitted with a TV camera and a very basic one-shot 'bonker' control to correct its trajectory, Journey's End failed to meet the required performance and was scrapped in 1947.

Meanwhile, as attention was turning to attacks on the Soviet Union, the requirement was changed from hitting capital ships to precision attacks on fixed targets such as bridges, factories and airfields. The new generation of bombers such as the B.35/46 that led to the Valiant, were designed to carry the large

Special Weapon that became Blue Danube and would therefore be capable of carrying a large, guided, glide bomb.

At Vickers, Barnes Wallis, the father of the earthquake bomb, began to look at improving the accuracy of his Tallboy. Wallis designed a Tallboy with enlarged tail fins and a pair of vertical fins at the nose that were fitted with spoilers. Rather than spinning to provide stability, the Line-Controlled Tallboy used radio commands to control the bomb's line of flight by operating the spoilers and thus altering the bomb's azimuth in a much more controllable manner than a single-shot bonker.

During the war the British discovered that guidance and control systems for guided projectiles were not a simple matter of radio-commanded servo systems applied to the actuation of control surfaces. In 1941 while developing anti-aircraft projectiles, the RAE, for want of a rocket with more power, had been forced to rely on the 3in (7.6cm) solid rocket motor for propulsion. This forced the RAE to simplify and miniaturise the components of guided weapons, leading to such systems as the bonker on Journey's End. The axial rolling of projectiles was a major problem for early developers, so much so that Flt Lt Benson of the RAE used the roll to advantage and created a radial-scanning seeker on the Artemis AAM. The German guided weapon developers on the other hand had no need to miniaturise, as the liquid-fuelled rocket engines produced enough power to allow larger, heavier weapons that could use more or less conventional systems. By 1945 the Germans had learned what the British guided weapons developers had discovered in 1942.

A great deal of work was required on stabilisation and basic rethinking of how such vehicles worked so a series of test vehicles were developed and flown by the RAE. One such vehicle, the Rocket Test Vehicle RTV.1, was used to iron out basic problems such as the aforementioned roll-control and development of servo systems. Well under way in 1947, this work was beginning to show promise and the foundations for a guided weapons development programme were laid. Journey's End was cancelled and a new operational requirement for 'Control of Bombs' was issued as OR.1059 in April 1946. The new weapon that grew from OR.1059 was assigned the MoS codename 'Blue Boar' in 1949.

Vickers commenced development of a weapon to meet OR.1059 under the designation 'Project G' and embarked on the construction of a series of test vehicles, called the Bomb Test Vehicles (BTV), with the basic vehicle being a cylinder with a rounded nose and a tapered tail. Along the main body of the bomb were four retractable strakes that formed the wings, with the aft end of each strake a control surface. To accommodate these bombs in the forthcoming V-bombers, particularly the larger

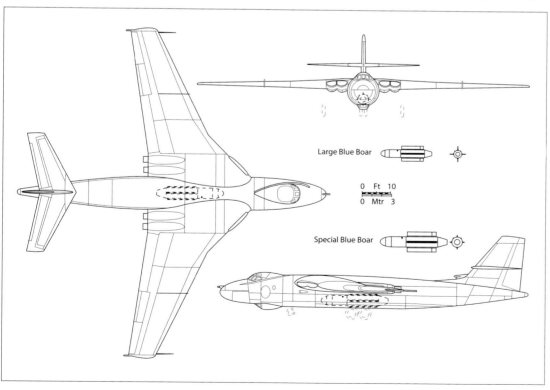

Large Blue Boar

Special Blue Boar

0 Ft 10
0 Mtr 3

Blue Boar was intended to arm the Vickers Valiant. It would have provided a stand-off range of 25nm (46km) from a high-altitude delivery. Night delivery of the TV-guided bomb required a second illuminator bomb releasing flares.

55

bombs that Vickers were planning, the Air Staff specified that these strakes should be retractable. The strakes would supply roll-stabilisation and lift to provide a 40° glide angle, which provided a stand-off range of 25nm (46.3km) if Blue Boar was dropped from 50,000ft (15,240m).

A range of Blue Boars was drawn up, with the 1,000 lb (454kg) model being deemed too small to carry a useful amount of explosive although it would be useful for training. The main versions were the Standard with a diameter of 32in (81.3cm) and weighing in at 5,000 lb (2,267kg) and the Large, with a diameter of 40in (101cm), weighing 10,000 lb (4,540kg). These models were the main types for the RAF, with the service weapon based on the Large Blue Boar to be called the BTB.12. The Extra Large Blue Boar had a diameter of 53in (134.6cm) and weighed 13,700 lb (6,213kg) while a variant of this, 'Special' Blue Boar, was to be armed, as the name suggests, with a nuclear warhead, probably based on the Blue Danube physics package, but the later Red Beard was also considered. The larger Blue Boars were also being considered for guidance via the H2S radars of the V-bombers under blind-bombing conditions. In the case of Special Blue Boar, the hope was that this would replace the Blue Danube weapon and afford the V-Force with a degree of stand-off.

A Vickers Valiant could carry two Standard Blue Boars in its bomb bay, or a single Large, Extra Large or Special with the wings retracted. Perhaps the most interesting Blue Boar was the Extra Large configured as a Master Bomb. This version was fitted out with the standard guidance system but could pass its commands to Standard Blue Boars and allow a single bomb-aimer to fly a stick of bombs onto a large target such as an airfield. The effect of a formation of Blue Boars hitting such a target would have been akin to a small nuclear weapon.

Guidance was to be via an EMI Engineering Division (EMIED) television camera in the nose, with the images transmitted back to the launch aircraft by microwave radio link. The bomb-aimer kept the target in the centre of the image by controlling the bomb's trajectory via a joystick and transmitting the control commands back to the Blue Boar autopilot on a radio link. These radio links could suffer interference from ground reflections so a helical polarised signal from 16in (40.6cm) 'paraboloidal' antennae on bomb and aircraft allowed narrow beams of 14° to be used between the Blue Boar and carrier. For bombing through cloud, the target was first identified on H2S and the bomb, with a transponder that could be seen on the 'green porridge' H2S display, guided towards it until breaking through the cloud base. It was thought that the operator would have at least six seconds to acquire the target on the TV screen and correct the bomb's trajectory if cloud base was 10,000ft (3,281m). Darkness presented a different problem and since these early TV cameras had very limited low-light capability some means of illuminating the target was required. Previously a target marker aircraft was used for such work, dropping parachute flares over the target, but this was not possible with a stand-off weapon such as Blue Boar. The solution was to use a second Blue Boar as an illuminator for the armed weapon. A 5,000 lb (2,268kg) Blue Boar was fitted with 250 high-intensity flares arranged in six banks along the fuselage. The Flare Bomb was to be launched three seconds after the armed bomb and fly a parallel trajectory above it, ejecting its flares as it fell, to provide illumination for the TV camera in the lower bomb.

The TV system to meet OR.1089 underwent initial trials in a Vickers Valetta transport aircraft but later, more realistic, high-speed trials were undertaken in the nose of Gloster Meteor NF.11 (WM262) before the whole system was tested in a full-sized Blue Boar test vehicle. The initial tests involved dropping small-scale models of Blue Boar from an Avro Lincoln, its aerodynamics having been proven by ground-launched models. Full-scale tests of the 5,000 lb (2,268kg) BTV10 were carried out using a Lincoln and later a Boeing B-29 Washington. An English Electric Canberra was used for high-speed drops of the 1,000 lb (454kg) BTV.1 to

A litter of Blue Boars. Despite an attempt to use the V-bombers' H2S radar for guidance, like Hitler and Napoleon, Blue Boar was thwarted by the Russian climate. Test vehicles went on to aid development of Green Cheese.

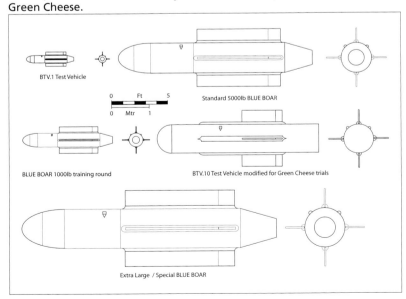

BTV.1 Test Vehicle

Standard 5000lb BLUE BOAR

0 Ft 5
0 Mtr 1

BLUE BOAR 1000lb training round

BTV.10 Test Vehicle modified for Green Cheese trials

Extra Large / Special BLUE BOAR

simulate delivery from V-bombers. Initial drop trials were held at Salisbury Plain and Aberporth; but a clip of film also exists that shows a BTV being dropped over the Orford Ness range in Suffolk.

Reading the description of how Blue Boar worked, it seemed a lot of trouble to go to for the delivery of what was actually a small amount of explosive on a high-value target. Why develop such a complex weapon to deliver such a small warhead? The obvious conclusion is that it only becomes a useful weapon when used with a nuclear warhead. Blue Boar was cancelled in 1954 by which time it was clear that the British atomic bomb was viable and the early studies of rocket-powered bombs were under way. Perhaps Blue Boar was actually intended as a back-up to the British atomic bomb? Blue Boar's TV guidance was its Achilles Heel as the radio datalink could be lost or jammed, but more importantly, its optical guidance could be defeated by the Russian weather. Although radar guidance was possible using H2S/NBC, meeting the accuracy requirement forced the use of the TV system. The trials had shown that, if a cloud base of 10,000ft (3,048m) was assumed, only six seconds were available to acquire the target and guide the Blue Boar on to it. In reality the cloud base over the Soviet Union, particularly in winter, would be much lower and the time available for TV guidance much reduced. Another factor was the prospect of inertial and astro navigators that could allow autonomous guidance of missiles and when combined with rocket propulsion provide a much better weapon. The last attempt to make Blue Boar a viable weapon involved the bomb homing in on a Blue Sugar beacon planted by agents or Pathfinder forces.

An adjunct to the Blue Boar story is Green Cheese, an anti-ship missile that was to meet OR.1123 as a weapon for the carrier-borne strike aircraft to meet Specification M.148, which ultimately became the Buccaneer. Green Cheese used some of the control systems from Blue Boar and some of the Blue Boar test vehicles were used for Green Cheese development. While not a true stand-off weapon, Green Cheese began as glide-bomb but soon evolved into a radar-guided, rocket-propelled missile for use against ships. The Vickers Valiant would have been able to carry four rounds on its wing pylons, this external carriage driven by the need for the active seeker in the missile nose to see its target before launch. Internal carriage would have required lowering from the bomb bay to allow target acquisition. The Green Cheese for

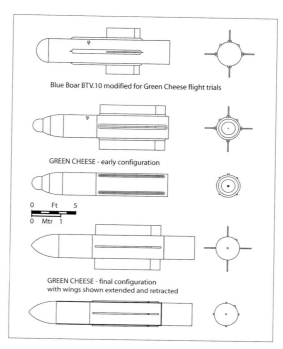

Blue Boar BTV.10 modified for Green Cheese flight trials

GREEN CHEESE - early configuration

0   Ft   5
0   Mtr   1

GREEN CHEESE - final configuration
with wings shown extended and retracted

Green Cheese was to be carried on the Valiant's wing pylons to allow the X-band seeker to acquire its target before the weapon was released.

the Valiant would have been optimised for 'dry' hits above the waterline of warships and had an armour-piercing warhead. A nuclear warhead based on Red Beard was proposed for Green Cheese with the missile renamed Green Flash. Given the MoS' preference for meaningless, even silly, codenames such as Green Flash, its allusion to the bright flash of a nuclear explosion may have been far too obvious, and was possibly a clue to the amount of effort put into Green Flash. Like Yellow Sun, its true nature may have been far from that suggested by its name.

After Blue Danube, Blue Boar and Green Cheese were amongst the earliest of weapons for the V-Bombers. They were under development at a time of great advances in the miniaturisation of components and warheads. This rapid development in the technology of weapons far outpaced that of the weapons developers, leaving a project that had been specified in 1949 obsolete before it had entered final development in 1954, never mind service. In the rush to give the RAF a weapon that emulated the success of the Fritz-X, did the Air Staff go up a blind alley with Blue Boar? Perhaps, but had Blue Boar not been subject to development delays it could have provided the V-Bombers with a basic stand-off weapon. With a nuclear warhead fitted, Blue Boar could have been a viable alternative to Blue Danube.

By the end of May 1952 the Vickers progress reports were beginning with the words 'Generally speaking progress has been disappointing, and the programme has fallen considerably behind schedule.' Eddie Smyth of Vickers Special Projects Section identified a lack of workers with the necessary skills for the manufacture of development rounds.

Overall, Vickers Guided Weapons admitted that they had underestimated the resources needed to develop Blue Boar, particularly man-power and facilities: 'Considerable embarrassment has occurred due to inadequate working space.' To address this Vickers GW were given access to a hangar that the Ministry of Food had been using, into which Vickers Aircraft promptly installed a mock-up of the V.1000 transport aircraft. Further delays with service-ability of aircraft such as a trials Canberra that suffered reliability problems in Australia and the delayed arrival of test vehicles at Woomera, compounded the disappointment. Blue Boar and Green Cheese were the earliest examples of this situation, where a delay in one of the myriad of components that made a guided weapon could hold up the entire project. Blue Boar and Green Cheese were cancelled in good time; however the finest exemplar of this (and one that wasn't cancelled) was Blue Steel.

Supersonic glide bomb

Aircraft technology had leapt forward in the decade that followed the end of World War Two. Blue Boar had been designed in the era of the piston engine and showed it: large, blunt and utilitarian. By 1953 there had been a revolution in aviation, aided by the rapid development of the gas turbine and the glide bomb reflected this.

Avro's P.35Z dated from May 1955 was a very sleek weapon; 40ft (12.2m) long and with a launch weight of 6,610lb (2,998kg) of which 4,000lb (1,814kg) was the warhead. The weapon's diameter of 52in (132cm) was large enough to accommodate a nuclear warhead such as the forthcoming Green Bamboo, although the warhead weight was optimistic. The P.35Z was a canard design with trapezoidal wings spanning 12ft (3.7m) with a similar shaped ventral fin.

Also called the SBM-2, the P35Z glide bomb was to be released at a speed of Mach 2 and an altitude of 60,000ft (18,288m) from the 'Avro 730 supersonic bomber' to provide a stand-off range of 23nm (43km). The reference to the Avro 730 is odd as that type was intended to release its weapon at Mach 2.5 and only became a bomber on the issue of RB.156 in October 1955 The answer to this may lie in an earlier proposal for a glide bomb that dates from mid-1953 and is shown in a semi-recessed mounting on a rather spectacular aircraft.

As noted above, the gas turbine revolutionised aircraft design and opened up a plethora of possibilities including supersonic flight and vertical take-off and landing (VTOL). Supersonic flight had been the obvious application for the jet engine, but the compact, high-power turbojet allowed the use of direct lift to propel an aircraft straight up without the use of a runway. The Air Staff were mindful of an attack on their airfields as a result of Operation Bodenplatte on 1st January 1945 when the Luftwaffe struck a number of Allied airfields in Holland and were not intending be caught out again. They had already discussed dispersal of the V-Force around the UK, but VTOL would multiply the number of potential operating bases many-fold.

A further development was the delta wing, derived from the advances made in the aerodynamic field in Germany and carried on at the Royal Aircraft Establishment at Farnborough. All these features were combined in a single type, a supersonic, VTOL delta aircraft armed with what appears to be an early version of the

Avro's Type 727, later renamed as a Type 730 study, was a supersonic VTOL aircraft with a battery of lift engines within the fuselage. Such designs usually originated in the engine companies.

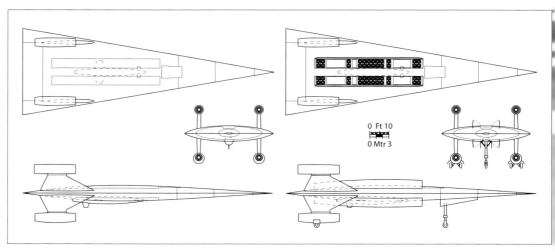

P.35Z glide bomb that Avro drew up in November 1953. All that exists in the Avro Heritage archive is a drawing labelled 'Type 727' although the number has been crossed out and '730' appended above, almost as though Avro had dug it out when specification RB.156 was issued. The Type 727 was described variously as a fighter bomber and a strike fighter but the aircraft as drawn is over 100ft (30.5m) long, somewhat large for a fighter bomber in the 1950s. Perhaps this study represents the earliest example of Avro's thinking on the supersonic bomber, as being dated November 1953, it predates the issue of OR.330/R.156. It is also radical in its design and operation.

The aircraft is a blended delta, a flying wing in fact, with no distinct fuselage, a 75° sweep to the leading edge and a straight trailing edge. Much of the trailing edge forms a pair of elevons, with rudders on the four vertical fins completing the control surfaces. Four engines, possibly Bristol Olympus, are shown with each in a pod at the tip of four trapezoidal fins/engine pylons, two above and two below the wing. On the original general arrangement drawing the engine intakes are simple pitot types, but a later amendment has a new fin shape of greater area and the addition of a centre-body in each intake.

The aircraft has a flattened oval cross-section that apart from the fins/engine pylons is completely devoid of any excrescences. The upper and lower surfaces are each dominated by a pair of long doors that cover two bays either side of the centreline. These bays are approximately 60ft (18.3m) long and appear to hold 24 lift engines apiece, arranged in five blocks, something that may explain the size of the aircraft. The main block of twelve engines is located at the aircraft's centre of gravity while a block of four is fitted at either end of the bay. This suggests that the Avro 730, (née 727) is a VTOL type. The cross-sectional drawing shows that the blocks of four are mounted on pivots that allowed the engine to swivel fore and aft to provide a measure of directional thrust for manoeuvring.

Further pointers to the Type 727 being a VTOL aircraft include the undercarriage, which does not look robust enough to allow an aircraft with a take-off weight that must be around 100,000 lb (45,359kg) to operate from conventional runways. The single nosewheel is fitted on a rather long leg while two main wheels are mounted on short legs fitted in each of the lower engine pods. That undercarriage could not have absorbed the shock loads associated with the high landing speed and use of aerodynamic braking on landing. Like all high-performance aircraft the greatest loads on an undercarriage and its braking systems are on take-off, particularly an aborted take-off at full loading. In the early Fifties, before the development of high-performance tyres, carbon or ceramic disk brakes and anti-lock braking systems, stopping a large high-performance aircraft was fraught with problems.

Vertical take-off and landing presented one solution to this but until undercarriage technologies caught up with aircraft performance in the 1960s, the answer was concrete. The long runways, in excess of 10,000ft (3,048m), such as Bruntingthorpe, Elvington and Machrihanish were built to support the operations of the V-Force and Strategic Air Command, with the supersonic bomber in mind. As time and engine development progressed, even concrete was superseded by the use of thrust reversers and drag chutes, but the ultimate answer was high-capacity braking systems.

There was another driver for the VTOL aircraft in the United Kingdom: Dr A A Griffith. In the early days of gas turbine development, Griffith had the ear of the Air Ministry and was employed by Rolls-Royce where he was working on a contraflow gas turbine to drive a propeller, rather than the jet propulsion system under development by Frank Whittle. After the war and with Whittle's designs adopted as the norm, Griffith was keen to apply the jet engine as much as possible to allow VTOL. From interceptors to long-range passenger transports, Griffith drew up design studies that shared two features: a multitude of lift engines and a highly-swept, blended delta wing and fuselage. As an employee of an engine manufacturer, Griffith had an interest in peddling gas turbines, so perhaps he had a hand in the design of the Avro 727 with its 48 lift engines.

The Vulcan Jump Jet

While not armed with a glide bomb, Avro proposed in June 1959 another VTOL deterrent in the shape of the Type 769 that was essentially a VTOL Vulcan. Intended for dispersal at remote, pre-surveyed locations, the Type 769 was to be armed with a single WS-138 Charlie-1 (an early version of Skybolt) under the starboard wing and a large fuel tank under the port. The Vulcan's capacious bomb bay was filled with ten lift jets, Bristol Engines BE.59 turbofan rated at 14,000 lbf (62.3kN) that as the BS.59 went on to be proposed for various transport aircraft in the early Sixties. This amount of

Avro's Type 769 weapons system was a VTOL version of the Vulcan equipped with a Charlie 1 version of WS-138, an early Skybolt. Ten BS.59 lift engines and switched-in thrust deflectors for the Olympus turbojets provided the necessary thrust.

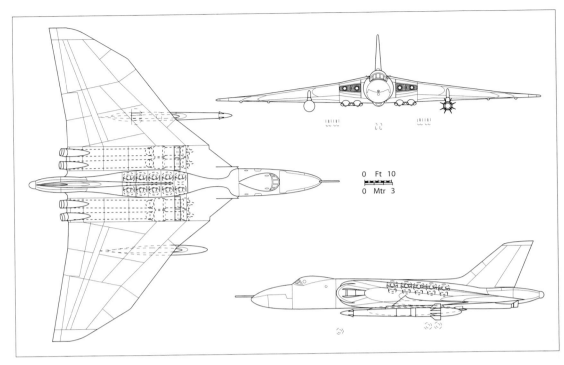

The Rolls-Royce RB.153 could be fitted with a deflector section that could direct the thrust downwards for VTOL. Such a device would have been required for the VTOL Vulcan's Olympus engines.
Author's Collection

thrust was not enough to lift a Vulcan with an AUW of 188,400 lb (85,457kg), so a deflection system was to be fitted in the jet pipes of the Bristol Olympus engines to deflect their thrust downwards vertically to produce a lift thrust of 212,000 lbf (943kN).

These deflection systems may have benefited from experience gained from a Westland Aircraft project that took a Gloster Meteor Mk.4 and re-engined it with Rolls-Royce Nene turbojets. These engines were fitted with deflection equipment developed by the National Gas Turbine Establishment (NGTE) to investigate the use of deflected thrust as a means of reducing landing speeds of high-performance aircraft. Rolls-Royce continued with this work, culminating in the 'twisting' jetpipe intended for the Hawker P.1154 but ultimately used in the Yakovlev Yak-141 *Freestyle* and the

Lockheed Martin F-35B. Bristol Engines eschewed the jet pipe deflection system and adopted a completely different 'four poster' system with swivelling nozzles that came to characterise the Hawker Harrier family.

A fuel load of 67,100 lb (30,431kg) was factored in, with 6,600 lb (2,993kg) of fuel considered to be sufficient for five minutes of hovering. The remaining fuel allowed a range of 3,000nm (4,828km) at economic cruise speed, which combined with the 1,000nm (1,852km) range of the Charlie-1 ALBM, would have been able to reach many of the targets on the Air Staff's list.

An Updated Blue Boar

Avro Aircraft attempted to get into the stand-off bomb business by way of the glide bomb. They had an airframe already available that had a fuselage sized to accommodate the large warheads that AWRE were advising the missile makers to make allowances for. Warheads such as Green Bamboo and Green Grass would have been at least as big as the Blue Danube weapon, with a diameter of around 45in (114cm) and weighing around 4,500 lb (2,041kg). Avro's alternative to Blue Steel was to be a glide bomb based on the Type 707, a 1/3 scale analogue of the Vulcan intended to aid development of the larger aircraft. The single-seat 707A and 707B were intended as research aircraft, while the two-seat 707C was to be a trainer for Vulcan pilots.

Avro took the wings and tail of the Type 707A and added a new fuselage that lacked the Rolls-Royce Derwent engine, cockpit and landing gear. A 5ft (1.5m) diameter cigar-shaped fuselage was fitted with a large warhead in a bay situated at the centre of gravity. The delta wings lacked intakes and were similar in planform to the Avro 707A with the only other major changes being deletion of main undercarriage, air brakes and dive recovery flaps. A swept ventral fin was added under the rear fuselage. The 707A was selected as it was a high-speed version of the two types of 707 that Avro built whereas the B model had a dorsal intake ahead of the tail fin. The original aircraft had a wing span of 33ft (10m), whereas the glide bomb, thanks to its larger diameter fuselage, had a span of 35ft (10.7m).

The Glide Bomb could have been carried by the Vulcan, but was probably too large for the Victor. Released from 40,000ft (12,192m) and Mach 0.8, the glide Bomb would fly towards its target. If the weapon possessed a similar lift/drag ratio as the Vulcan, its glide angle would be more than enough to provide a decent stand-off range, better than Blue Boar's 25nm (46.3km). The Avro Glide bomb could be considered as a shapelier Blue Boar with a delta wing, with more range, possibly close to Blue Steel. Unfortunately it would have been highly vulnerable to interception by fighters and SAMs due to its low speed.

Wallis' Weapons

By 1960 the deterrent weapon would take off vertically, but was to be a ballistic launched from a silo or a submarine. Meanwhile at Weybridge, Barnes Wallis had different ideas and proposed an unusual aircraft called Cascade as a deterrent carrier and a weapon called the Momentum Bomb to arm the RAF. Wallis was a brilliant engineer with a string of engineering innovations stretching back to the Thirties, from the structure of the R100 airship and the Vickers Wellington, while the Forties saw his most famous device, the Upkeep mine, better known as the Bouncing Bomb.

On 28th January 1960, Barnes Wallis had a meeting over lunch at the Athenaeum Club in Pall Mall with Sir Solly Zuckerman, Chief Scientific Adviser to the MoD. Wallis outlined his ideas on the British deterrent and its carrier. Research on the carrier aircraft was under way at Vickers at Weybridge under the codename 'Cascade'. He considered the 'static deterrent' such as Blue Streak in its silos to be defunct by

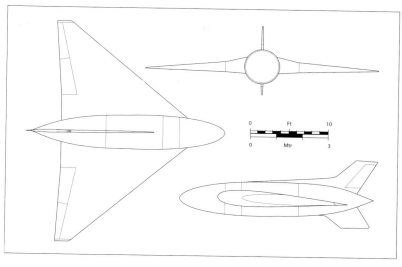

way of a Soviet first strike on known locations. Wallis was interested in what was known as the 'fluid deterrent' whereby the deterrent was moved around or carried by aircraft or submarine.

The Cascade aircraft was intended to cruise at Mach 4.5 at an altitude of 93,000ft (28,346m) and thus be immune from interception. Wallis' concept involved a supersonic short take-off and landing (STOL) aircraft with an AUW of 50,000lb (22,680kg) including a payload of a 3,000lb (1,360kg) 'deterrent weapon', all in the air after a take-off run of 185 yards (169m). Such aircraft could operate from '…a great number of aerodromes dispersed throughout the Commonwealth' that would pose as much a problem to the Soviets as targets such as the location of 'closed cities' posed to the Western air forces. In fact Wallis was of the opinion that Cascade would cause offensive action by the Soviet Union or China to 'become impracticable'.

Sir Solly questioned Wallis about Cascade and how it compared with Swallow that had been proposed for RB.156/OR.336 in the mid Fifties. Wallis advised that Cascade was 'so simple' in concept and construction and hoped to have a single-seat prototype flying within three years, with the full-scale bomber available three years later. Sir Solly informed Wallis that he would discuss the matter with the Minister, Harold Watkinson and the Chief of the Defence Staff, Lord Mountbatten.

At first glance Cascade was a two-seat delta aircraft powered by a combination engine in the portion of the rear fuselage that extended aft of the wing. The combination engine comprising two Rolls-Royce RB.153 turbojets rated at 6,850lbf (30.5kN) mounted above a ramjet, all fed from a common pitot intake in the nose

The Avro Type 707 was an analogue of the Vulcan intended for training and research into the aerodynamics of delta wings. By substituting the cockpit and engine for a warhead, a glide bomb for the V-Force was possible. *Via David Fildes, Avro Heritage*

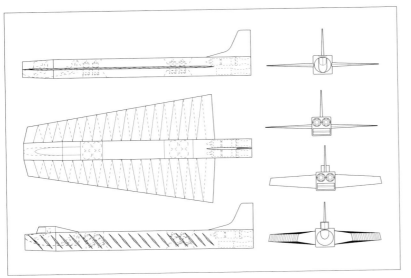

Barnes Wallis tempted the Air Staff with his Cascade deterrent carrier. Intended for dispersed deployment, Wallis' 'fluid deterrent' would have taken off in 185 yards and had a maximum speed of Mach 4.5. The Air Staff were not particularly interested.

with the diffuser housing the cockpit. Cascade was 58ft (17.7m) long with a wingspan of 29ft 6in (9m), with a leading edge sweep of 80°, apart from the forward portion of the wing that was cut off at a sweep angle of 7°. So far, so conventional and as a supersonic aircraft, it looked the part.

As might be expected from a Wallis project, Cascade had a couple of tricks up its sleeve. Cascade's STOL performance came courtesy of two banks of four Rolls-Royce RB.162 lift engines rated at 6,000 lbf (26.7kN) that could swivel aft through 30° to direct their thrust rearwards. To get airborne after a take-off roll of 185yds (169m) with a wing optimised for Mach 4.5 required more than eight swivelling RB.162 lift jets and the power of two RB.153 turbojets.

Lift can be augmented by increasing the angle of incidence on the wing. On a delta wing such as that on Cascade, the wing's chord, 47ft 9in (14.5m) was too great and the incidence increase would have been too much to allow safe, controlled flight. Wallis' approach was to transform the large area of the Cascade's wing into a series of 19 smaller trapezoidal wing sections. The sections overlapped fore and aft to present a single wing surface top and bottom; however when an increase in incidence was required, each wing section rotated span-wise through 45° on a swivel at the root.

This, according to Wallis, produced a wing so thin that wave drag was negligible while the sections rotated to increase lift as required. This, when coupled with the eight lift engines, would provide Cascade with very short take-off distances and an unstick speed of 80kts (148km/h) rather than 1,000yds (914m) and 122kts (226km/h). After take-off and as the aircraft accelerated under the power of the RB.153s

and the deflected RB.162s, lift increased and the angle of the wing sections could be reduced and the lift jets shut down. Once the Cascade had reached a speed where the ramjets could operate efficiently, the ramjet took over for the cruise, turbojets being unable to operate at speeds in excess of Mach 2.5. Landing involved using the variable incidence sections to provide lift at slow speeds until the lift jets could take over for a vertical landing.

Zuckerman's views on Cascade are not recorded, but Morien Morgan, the Scientific Advisor, Air Ministry, in a memo to the Deputy Chief of the Air Staff was not particularly impressed with Wallis' 'Venetian Blind aeroplane'. Despite finding the idea 'fascinating', Morgan though that if any lift engines were put in an aircraft why not '…go the whole hog and put in still more lightweight engines.' This, he considered 'would obviate the need for the multi-slatted wing.' The advisor also considered that development would need a strong design team from a manufacturer 'Wallis' own team just isn't strong enough to undertake such a study.' Morgan pointed out that a similar situation had arisen with the Swallow project. How qualified was Morgan to comment on this? He had been at the Royal Aircraft Establishment (RAE) Aerodynamics Department since 1935 before being appointed as Scientific Advisor in 1959. He would later be appointed Director of the RAE and became known as the 'Father of Concorde'.

Apple Turnover and the Winged TMB

Wallis' other proposal in the early 1960s was as innovative as it was simple. The writing was on the wall for high-altitude bombers, whatever their speed, as advances in long-range air surveillance radars and high-performance SAMs saw off the North American B-70 and the British Avro 730. Bombers abandoned the stratosphere and headed for the tree-tops, creating a new generation of under-the-radar strike aircraft that was on the drawing boards. The outcome of this work was the BAC TSR.2 to meet GOR.339 for the RAF and the General Dynamics F-111 for the Air Force portion of the USAF/USN TFX requirement. Both the TSR.2 and F-111 were intended for high-speed penetration missions into hostile territory for a tactical nuclear strike role.

The question of arming these types soon arose. The RAF had armed their English Electric

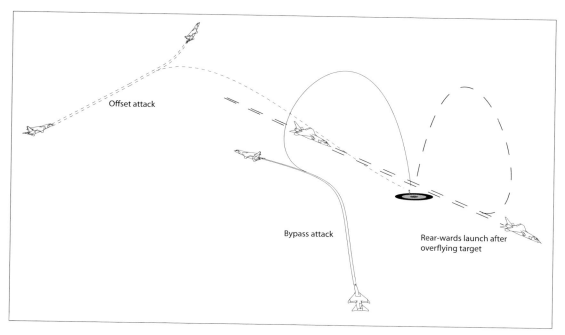

Offset attack

Bypass attack

Rear-wards launch after
overflying target

Wallis' Momentum
Bomb was of
interest to the Air
Staff. Delivery
methods for the
Momentum Bomb
included Offset,
Rearwards and
Bypass attacks.
Such tactics kept
the strike aircraft
out of the range of
low altitude
defences.

Canberra tactical strike squadrons with the Red Beard, a weapon to meet OR.1127 while the same weapon to meet Admiralty requirement AW.330 was in service with the Fleet Air Arm on its Blackburn Buccaneer and Supermarine Scimitars. The tactic involved in delivering was LABS, low altitude bombing system, using a sighting system developed under OR.1148. On a LABS delivery the aircraft flew towards the target and at a point determined by the sighting system, pulled up into a climb at an angle determined by the aiming equipment until the release altitude was reached. Having released the weapon, the aircraft performed a half-loop and dived back to low altitude to egress the target area.

LABS delivery required the aircraft to climb out of the comparative safety of low altitude and expose itself to the local air defences, the short-range SAMs and light anti-aircraft artillery (AAA) into which the Soviets had invested heavily. The stand-off bomb was the answer and unfortunately these were large, expensive and at this point in time, reserved for strategic use. By 1960 the nuclear warheads had been miniaturised whereas guidance and propulsion systems had not benefited from such size reduction. The answer was to remove these and produce a glide bomb whose guidance system was in the aircraft.

Barnes Wallis at Vickers proposed a weapon he called the Apple Turnover, later known by the more technical term 'Momentum Bomb', and was a winged weapon that when released at low altitude was trimmed to use lift gained from the forward speed, its momentum, to maintain a constant or increasing altitude to allow an element of stand-off. The wings were of a symmetrical section, utilising the weapon's incidence to generate lift. The control surfaces were basic elevators on the tailplanes. This delivery method allowed the aircraft to remain low and turn away from the defences as soon as the bomb was released. As Wallis developed his idea he produced a design for the Momentum Bomb that provided a much more flexible delivery and longer range. On release, the bomb pulled up and entered a loop before levelling out on a reciprocal bearing to that on which it was released and flying to the target. While that might sound odd it allowed attacks to be made on targets behind the aircraft. This had the benefit of avoiding the need to fly over the target and its defences as an offset course could be flown with a turn made to position the target behind the aircraft, before releasing the Momentum Bomb.

Meanwhile at English Electric's Warton plant the P.17, predecessor of the BAC TSR.2, had been under development since 1956 as a low-altitude strike aircraft; the P.17 was to be armed with a variety of weapons for the strike role, including the Red Beard tactical nuclear weapon. As noted elsewhere, this was also known as the Target Marker Bomb and was intended for LABS delivery for which the P.17 was to be fitted with a rotary bomb bay door. To avoid exposure to the defences English Electric took the standard Red Beard casing and added wings and a new tail with a ventral fin and tailplanes.

This Winged Target Marker was also described as the Manoeuvring Bomb and was carried semi-

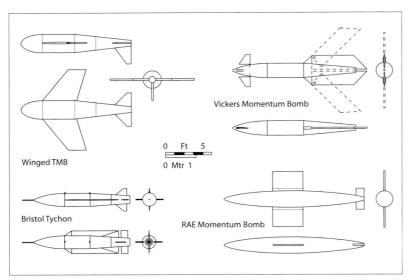

Winged TMB

Vickers Momentum Bomb

Bristol Tychon

RAE Momentum Bomb

0 Ft 5

0 Mtr 1

Four versions of the Momentum Bomb were proposed; although the English Electric Winged TMB differed slightly in operation, the principle was the same for all.

recessed on the rotary bomb door of the P.17. After launch at an altitude of 500ft (152m), the Manoeuvring Bomb climbed steeply before entering a backwards loop up to an altitude of 7,000ft (2,134m). At the top of the loop the bomb's controls operated to direct the bomb into a terminal vertical dive for an air or ground burst.

Tychon – Accurate Bristolian

In 1962 joint requirement NASR.1168 was issued covering development of a weapon to replace the Martin AGM-12 Bullpup that the Fleet Air Arm had been using since 1960. Bristol Aircraft tendered a design called Tychon that used a similar principle to the Momentum Bomb although Tychon retained the facility for high-altitude and high-speed release. From 40,000ft (12,192m) and launched at a speed of Mach 2.0, Tychon would have had a stand-off

range of 50nm (93km) for a ground burst.

Launched at 200ft (61m) and Mach 0.95 from a TSR.2 type, Tychon could have struck a target 15nm (28km) way. The weapon could be aimed visually or by radar using the target itself or a known offset point and had a CEP of 150yds (137m) at 15nm and 1nm (1.8km) at maximum range. Having released the weapon, the aircraft had complete freedom of action to make good its escape.

Tychon was intended to be a modular weapon with HE or nuclear warheads and could be fitted with terminal guidance systems such as TV or radar homing heads. A further proposal saw the warhead replaced by a reconnaissance package to provide stand-off reconnaissance, pre- or post-strike. Tychon would weigh 1,000lb (454kg) and was to be 11ft 8in (3.6m) long with a body diameter of 1ft 6in (0.46m) and a 3ft (0.9m) span to its long chord wings that ran along the body. Canberras could accommodate a single Tychon and the V-bombers a pair in their bomb bays while the TSR.2 could have carried four on its pylons. Bristol Aircraft advised that the weapon was '…suitable for high or low delivery from future generations of military aircraft including Swallow and sub-orbital bombers.'

Tychon came to nought as the RAF opted for the Anglo-French MARTel missile that became the AJ.168 and AS.37 missiles. Neither of these weapons had a particularly good Cold War. The Momentum Bomb and its ilk were developed to avoid strike aircraft being exposed to AAA and SAM defences and with their predictable delivery flight path, the glide bombs themselves were now vulnerable to interception and the focus sharpened on powered bombs.

Glide Bombs

Type	Length	Span	Diameter	Weight	Range
Fritz X	11ft	5ft	2ft 8in	3,000lb	3nm
Blue Boar	17ft 6in	5ft 2in	2ft 6in	5,000lb	25nm
Large Blue Boar	22ft	6ft 6in	3ft 4in	10,000lb	25nm
Special / Extra Large Blue Boar	22ft 6in	9ft 2in	4ft 5in	13,700lb	25nm
Green Cheese	15ft	5ft 2in	2ft 6in	3,800lb	
Winged TMB	12ft	8ft	2ft 4in	2,000lb	n/a
Bristol Tychon	11ft 8in	3ft	1ft 6in	1,000lb	15nm
Vickers Momentum Bomb	12ft	9ft	1ft 6in	10,000lb	n/a
Avro P.35Z	40ft	12ft	4ft 4in	6,610lb	23nm
Avro Glide bomb	38ft	35ft	5ft	10,000lb	n/a

4 The Steam Engine

'The major disadvantage of the bi-fuel rocket is the highly active chemical propellants but the technique of using these fuels is now well established.'
Avro WRD report on OR.1132, August 1955

By 1954 the writing was on the wall for the high-altitude free-fall bomber and with the failure of Blue Boar, a new approach was required. Blue Steel has long been criticised by users and historians alike. Few have outlined its history in any detail or attempted to explain its shortcomings. Attempting the development of one of the most complex vehicles ever built in the UK was a considerable challenge that Avro met in time. Unfortunately the time taken to meet these challenges saw the high-technology of 1955 become the old-hat of 1963.

Seventies Britain probably had some of the best science and technology TV presenters in the world. Specialists like Reginald Turnhill and Geoffrey Pardoe covered aerospace technology for mainstream TV news while programmes such as *Tomorrow's World* boasted the likes of James Burke, a consummate professional when it came to explaining technological matters to the masses. Way back then, with three TV channels, a good proportion of the viewing public would be receiving, possibly subliminally, some level of scientific knowledge.

Undoubtedly at the pinnacle of scientific broadcasting were the Royal Institution Christmas Lectures. These were transmitted between Christmas and New Year and always guaranteed to be delivered by a scientific Titan, a scientist or engineer who had made significant

A Vulcan with its Blue Steel undergoes checks on a rain-soaked dispersal somewhere in England. This view shows the anhedral outer wing of Blue Steel, necessary to ensure clearance of the Vulcan's engine nacelles. *Via Kev Darling*

contributions to their field. Two lecturers stick in this author's memory: Professors R V Jones and Eric Laithwaite. Aside from my interest in his recent book 'Most Secret War', I had seen Jones walking across the campus at Aberdeen University and always wondered what his lectures were like. Entertaining is the only description that could be applied.

Laithwaite on the other hand I had only seen on TV in the mid Seventies, a medium for which he was a natural, demonstrating his linear induction motor (of which, more later) on the BBC's technology programme, *Tomorrow's World*. Laithwaite's 1974 Royal Society lecture concentrated on another field of interest, gyroscopes. The lecture proved controversial; Laithwaite's paper was rejected by the Royal Institution, but that furore washed over this author, unlike his demonstration of an application for gyroscopes. What impressed this 12-year-old was a large metal box on castors that was wheeled in by a brown-coated lab technician. Having fiddled with the control panel on the top, Laithwaite instructed the assistant to push the box across the room and read out the figures on its display. This operation was repeated twice more until the box was back where it started. On its return to where Laithwaite stood, he read out the figures himself and summed up the demonstration by describing how the box had travelled fifteen metres but had a displacement of zero metres, that is, it was back where it had started.

In what was probably the first public display of such technology, Laithwaite had demonstrated an inertial navigator, a Ferranti FINAS from a Hawker Siddeley Harrier to be precise. He then proceeded to describe how an inertial navigator worked, using gyroscopes and accelerometers to measure the displacement of the vehicle in each dimension, integrating this raw data to produce positioning information and ultimately, a means of navigation. Having spent much of the war at the Royal Aircraft Establishment working on autopilots, such devices must have appealed to Laithwaite's curiosity. Twenty years later this author would watch the same technology, merely called the Ferranti Gyro Tool, being lowered into oil wells to determine the exact path of the hole, critical information on a production platform with 36 wells radiating from it.

So what does a brown-coated man pushing a metal box across lecture theatre floor under the direction of a man in a suit before an audience of children or a tool for finding where a hole has been drilled have to do with the

weaponry of the V-Force? An awful lot actually. The forerunners of the equipment in the metal trolley provided the information that guided the V-Force aircraft and the Blue Steel missile to their targets. The inertial navigator, with its pros and cons, governed the shape and form of the deterrent.

In its simplest form an inertial navigation system uses gyroscopes to measure angular velocity and accelerometers to measure linear acceleration. These measurements are passed to a calculator that integrates the data for use in kinematic calculations. To work accurately the equipment requires to be initialised, which means it is set to a known start position that is then used to calculate its displacement and subsequently its current position as the vehicle moves. This information can be used to guide the carrying vehicle to a specified point and the entire device is called an inertial navigation system, INS. If the system is given the location of its destination the system can calculate the change in direction required to reach that target and pass the course changes to the control system. Note that a guidance system directs the control system to change the course of the vehicle.

INS benefited from being unjammable, required no external signals transmitted nor received, was not dependent on clear skies and worked in the air, the sea, underground and in space. As such INS provided a perfect solution for use in the guidance systems of the deterrent, particularly over the expanse of the Soviet Union. Its development for the American Minuteman ICBM and Apollo space programme hastened the miniaturising of electronics in the 1960s.

They did have one major flaw: integration drift caused by the system using the output from the gyros in its calculations. This was a time-dependent inaccuracy where subsequent iterations of the integration process produced a drift in the output values. The computer used this data, which compounded the errors, so the system therefore lost accuracy over time. This could lead to a navigation error of around 0.6 nautical miles (1.1km) after an hour of operation. Being time-dependent, there was a simple solution to the so-called gyro drift problem: fly faster or reduce the range. For this reason INS was the favoured guidance for ballistic missiles and rocket-powered bombs such as Skybolt and Blue Steel respectively.

The high loss-rate suffered by the bomber formations in the Second World War prompted a change of thinking on the postwar conduct of bomber operations. The Luftwaffe was first to adopt what would become known as a stand-off weapon in the shape of Fritz X and the air-launched V-1. Carriage of the V-1 on Heinkel He 111s was forced upon the Luftwaffe for two reasons: firstly the short range of the V-1 pre-cluded surface-launched attacks against targets in the industrial regions of the English Midlands and secondly, the late 1944 loss of the areas in Northern France used for launching the V-1. On the Allied side, the Americans followed suit with a variety of trials using Boeing B-17s to launch the Republic Aviation JB-2, a reverse-engineered V-1 that could have been in service by the end of 1945.

The postwar development of stand-off weapons was driven by the improvement in air defences, particularly surface-to-air guided weapons, with the intention of allowing the bomber force to attack a target from outside the range of its defences. The advent of the nuclear weapon allowed a significant reduction in the number of aircraft required to wreak havoc on a city, echoing Clement Attlee's thoughts on deterrence. This in turn led to there being fewer targets for the defences, so more likelihood of the bomber being intercepted before it dropped its destructive cargo. A stand-off missile would be smaller, probably faster, and present a more difficult target for fighters and anti-aircraft missiles.

Project Mastiff was a USAAF study from early 1946 to investigate an air-to-surface guided weapon that could carry an atomic warhead. Bell were awarded a contract in April 1946 and commenced development of a subsonic, rocket-powered missile with a range of 300 miles (483km). By October 1947 Bell had concluded that the rocket engine could not meet the stated range, so this was reduced to 100 miles (160km). Unfortunately range was not the Mastiff's only difficulty; guidance over such distances proved problematic. Mastiff led to MX-776 that split to become the MX-776A, the X-9 aerodynamic test vehicle, and the MX-776B development vehicle for the B-63 RASCAL, an air-to-surface missile with a range of 86nm (160km). In 1955 the designation was changed to GAM-63 when the USAF stopped assigning aircraft designations to missiles. The first launch of a B-63 RASCAL powered by a Bell XLR-67 rocket engine occurred in September 1952

The name RASCAL was derived from *RA*dar *SCA*nning *L*ink which described the guidance system. The GAM-63 RASCAL was pro-grammed to follow a route to the target from a predefined release point. The missile was equipped with a ground-mapping radar (similar to H2S) and a video link. The radar picture was transmitted back to the launch aircraft where the bombardier guided the missile onto the target via a command link, providing a CEP of 3,000ft (914m). Unfortunately the command links could be jammed so a modified version, the GAM-63A, was fitted with an inertial navi-gator and this improved the CEP to 1,500m (457m) and removed the susceptibility to jam-ming. Despite these efforts the RASCAL never became fully operational with the USAF and it

The Bell RASCAL provided the USAF B-36 and B-47 with a stand-off range of 100nm (185km). Initially using radar guidance as proposed for the H2S-controlled Blue Boar, it became apparent that inertial guidance was superior.
Author's Collection

and its director/carrier bombers were withdrawn in 1959 in favour of the GAM-77 Hound Dog on the Boeing B-52.

RASCAL showed that a rocket-powered missile with inertial guidance was feasible, but much work was required to produce a worthwhile weapon. RASCAL, by its rapid obsolescence, also highlighted the rapid pace of development. Meanwhile, across the Atlantic, the RAF and RAE watched with interest. The United Kingdom faced a similar problem, but believed that its faster and higher flying V-bombers with advanced ECM would be immune from interception. As the Fifties dawned the Air Staff and RAE came to the conclusion that, despite attempts at providing some stand-off with Blue Boar, a powered bomb was required. The Air Ministry convened a series of discussions in February 1954 under the title 'The Future Pattern of the Offensive' that drew on the experience of Bomber Command and the military intelligence services. The Vulcan was yet to enter service but the Air Ministry voiced concerns about improvements to Soviet air defences.

Their prime concern was the guided weapon rather than fighters as they were confident that the high-flying Vulcan and Victor were immune from the current and next generations of Soviet fighters. Neither was anti-aircraft artillery seen as a threat to the V-bombers. If required, an additional 6,000ft (1,830m) in height of target could be gained by re-engining the Victor and the Vulcan, preferably with improved versions of the current Conway and Olympus. If this was not feasible, a new centre wing for the Victor capable of taking larger engines was considered, but this impacted fuel capacity and therefore range. The Vulcan on the other hand could be fitted with a podded engine under each wing or replacement of each pair of Olympus turbojets with a trio of smaller engines. Both these schemes allowed extra fuel to be carried and thus had no effect on range. It soon became apparent that more height would not future-proof the V-Force beyond 1960.

The Air Ministry was party to information on UK surface-to-air guided weapons projects and was of the opinion that by 1960 a SAGW with a range of 22nm (40km) would be in Soviet service, as was the case in the UK with the Bloodhound Mk.1 missile. A free-fall bomb dropped from 60,000ft (18,288m) would travel 15 miles (24km) before impacting, so any SAGW with a range in the same class as Bloodhound was a threat to a free-fall bomber.

The Ministry's next suggestion was a development of the supersonic reconnaissance aircraft: a supersonic unmanned bomber with Mach 3 performance and range of around 2,000nm (3,704km). Materials problems associated with Mach 3 flight were mentioned and the difficulty of guidance arose yet again. Inertial guidance was the only option and, as noted above, was prone to errors, particularly in the early forms of the equipment available in 1954. Although such a missile would be cheaper than a supersonic bomber, its guidance, particularly in the terminal phase would result in a great deal of delay. This concern over terminal guidance harkened back to the problems with the TV-guided Blue Boar bomb that was rendered ineffective by cloudy weather. The lack of tactical flexibility made this weapon less attractive than a manned bomber and the Chief of the Air Staff pointed out that the Americans had been developing such a weapon for a long time at great expense. Funding for such cutting-edge but non-critical projects was something that was not easily available in 1954.

Low-level bombers such as those proposed for OR.324 were considered but despite presenting the Soviets with a difficult target, it would be of limited use due to problems with low-altitude navigation and adverse weather conditions. It would also prompt the Soviets into expending effort in countering the threat. The type would also require a stand-off bomb to prevent self-destruction on delivering an atomic weapon.

Assistant Chief of the Air Staff, ACM Tuttle summarised the meetings in a letter to ACM Sir John Baker, Controller of Aircraft. Tuttle advised that the long-term solution was the ballistic missile 'similar to the V-2' and the Ministry was well aware that the technology was in its infancy so considered 1968 as the earliest possible in-service date. In the short term, by 1960 the Air Ministry decided that there was no point upgrading the V-bombers but equipping them with a 'powered inertia bomb' was feasible. Such a weapon should have a range of at least 70nm (130km) as at such ranges the Soviet missile defences would need a mid-course guidance system. Based on British experience with the Bristol Blue Envoy long-range SAGW, development of such guidance systems was difficult and the Soviets would no doubt be in similar circumstances. In fact information received from debriefs of German scientists returned from the USSR had revealed that the Russians considered SAGW defence of their vast country uneconomic and that fighters would be the best defence. Having identified the powered bomb as the best option the question of the selection of targets arose. Reconnaissance versions of the Victor and Vulcan were proposed, but the Air Ministry were set on acquiring a supersonic reconnaissance-bomber to provide the targeting information for the V-Force.

The propulsion system

Of the four principal components of the missile, the system that was expected to be the most difficult to develop was the propulsion system. In the postwar era British high-speed propulsion development was dominated by the ramjet. There were a couple of reasons for this emphasis, the first being the much greater range available from ramjets in a high-speed vehicle and second the preference for solid rocket motors in British missiles driven by the Navy's unpleasant experience with the Sea Slug SAM and its liquid fuels. Tales of a rum ration being issued whenever a Sea Slug succeeded in flying its course may not be exaggerated.

When the Air Staff began examining a long-range high-speed missile they considered four propulsion systems: variable-thrust liquid-fuelled rocket engines, solid-rocket booster and small liquid-fuelled sustainer, gas turbines and finally ramjet with solid boost motor. Though capable of meeting the range requirement, ramjets and gas turbines required intakes that increased the missile's frontal area and therefore its drag. The supersonic turbojets of the early 1950s were in need of much development plus their performance at Mach 2.5 and beyond was unknown. The lack of intakes and much smaller frontal area made rockets more attractive both aerodynamically and from the aspect of easier installation in a carrying aircraft. Rockets brought their own problems with control of thrust levels, hence the solid boost and liquid sustainer, but the liquid engines use of highly-active chemical propellants was also problematic. Despite this, the liquid-fuelled engine's ability to readily attain the speed required made them attractive.

Controlling the thrust to maximise economy of propellant and therefore range was a priority for the missile so a powerplant that could operate over a range of thrust levels was needed. The bi-fuel rocket was most applicable, with two combinations under consideration: liquid oxygen and kerosene or High Test Peroxide (HTP) and kerosene. The liquid oxygen/kerosene engine was dismissed at an early stage as the HTP/kerosene offered advantages

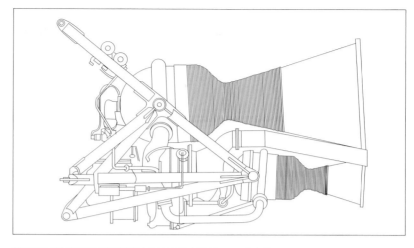

particularly that the high density of HTP, typically 1.46g/cc, allowed more fuel to be carried while liquid oxygen suffered from excessive evaporation. These were deemed to outweigh the logistical disadvantages of using HTP as the oxidiser.

Famously used as an oxidiser in the Walter rocket engines of the Messerschmitt Me 163 interceptor during the last year of the Second World War, High Test Peroxide is an 85-95% solution of hydrogen peroxide (H_2O_2) in water. HTP could be used as a fuel in its own right, a monopropellant, if it is passed through a catalyst such as silver-plated wire gauze, in an exothermic decomposition reaction to produce steam at 500° (932°F) and free oxygen. Used in the bipropellant application, kerosene is sprayed into the hot steam and ignites spontaneously in the presence of the free oxygen. When this reaction is carried out in a rocket combustion chamber combined with a rocket nozzle, the result is thrust.

The main drawback to using HTP, one of the aforementioned logistical disadvantages, was its propensity to catalyse with many common materials such as iron and copper. Contact with human skin produced extensive burns if not washed off within seconds, with blindness resulting from HTP entering the eyes. As a

The Armstrong Siddeley Stentor two-chamber rocket engine. The combustion chambers are wrapped in pipework through which propellants were pumped to cool the chamber.

Compact and powerful the two chambers allowed a high-thrust boost and low-thrust sustainer phase. Fuelled by High Test Peroxide and kerosene, the large chamber operated in the initial boost phase with the small chamber running at Mach 2.5 at the end of the climb. Low-level launch used both chambers at once. This engine is on display at Newark Air Museum. *Author's Collection*

result it required careful handling with specialised protective clothing and equipment. Invariably an HTP handling station had emergency showers and a bathtub full of water to allow operators to jump into in the event of being splashed. This, of course, was never used for horseplay.

For the initial development of the missile that would become Blue Steel, Avro WRD engineers decided that the de Havilland Spectre engine, rated at 8,000 lbf (35.6kN) thrust, would be ideal. This engine was already under development for the mixed-powerplant interceptor to meet OR.337 for the RAF and NA.37 for the Fleet Air Arm and as the RDS.15, a rocket-assisted take-off unit for the V-Force. The Spectre was fitted to the Saunders-Roe SR.53 technology demonstrator for the programme that was to lead to the Saro SR.177 and Avro Type 720. As a rocket for use in a manned aircraft, this also ensured that the engine was safe for carriage in a bomber. In developing the 720 with its Armstrong Siddeley Screamer rated at 8,000 lb (35.6kN) thrust, Avro had gained experience of the liquid-fuelled rockets and liquid oxygen/kerosene propellants. This experience may have had a hand in the WRD adopting HTP/kerosene and the Spectre for Blue Steel.

The Powered Bomb – Essentially a Two-Stage Aircraft

'We simply cannot accept these slippages; should we send for Roy Dobson again or wait?' – Harold Watkinson, Minister of Defence, January 1961

Having found the Blue Boar wanting due to guidance difficulties caused by the weather over Russia, the aircraft companies turned their attention to arming the low-level bomber that was to meet OR.324. The Low Altitude Bomber came into existence in June 1951 as a complement to the V-bombers and to address the Air Staff's realisation that the V-bombers would soon be vulnerable to Soviet fighters and surface-to-air missiles. By January 1952 the Air Staff were concerned that the forthcoming V-bombers would be limited to operations at heights of more than 40,000ft (12,192m) that would give the Soviets timely warning of their approach and allow their defences to be concentrated on the V-bombers. The solution was to attack at altitudes that would deny the Soviets that warning.

Red Cat

The original requirement, OR.314 and the accompanying Specification B.126 was issued in May 1952 and laid out the Air Staff's need for a Low Altitude Bomber capable of delivering a 10,000 lb (4,536kg) powered winged bomb, to a target 2,500nm (4,633km) from base. The weapon dimensions stated in B.126 were a diameter of 62in (1.6m) and a length of 24ft 2in (7.4m) so it was presumably based on Blue Danube physics package.

By the end of October 1953 the requirement had become OR.324 covering an aircraft that would be capable of carrying one of three types of 'Special Bomb' and the nature of that special bomb had been clarified. The requirement also stated that the still air range at 1,500ft (457m) was to be 5,000nm (9,260km), which in hindsight was a tall order.

The special bomb was to be a winged, powered, inertial-guided stand-off weapon to meet OR.1125 that was issued on 17th November 1953 and would receive the Ministry of Supply rainbow code 'Red Cat'. The RAE's Bomb Group listed three options for OR.1125 in Tech Memo 1460: a Large Subsonic Bomb weighing 14,000 lb (6,350kg), a diameter of 62in (1.6m) and a length of 45ft (13.7m); the Small Supersonic Bomb weighing 13,000 lb (6,897kg), a diameter of 33in (84cm) and a length of 35ft (10.7m) and finally the Small Subsonic Bomb weighing 7,500 lb (3,402kg), a diameter of 33in (84cm) and again 35ft (10.7m) long. Aiming was to be either visual or by radar, but how any target information for the stand-off bomb was to be acquired at an altitude of less than 1,000ft (304m) was not detailed. However, a new Navigation and Bombing System (NBS) to meet OR.3567, issued in January 1954, would allow the Low Altitude Bomber to find its target and attack it blind with the OR.1125 weapon. The targeting system would use visual sights, forward looking and sideways-looking radar to provide navigation and sighting information. Interestingly the use of the forward-looking radar for terrain clearance was only considered in July 1953 rather than from the start of the project.

The Air Staff were concerned about release of the weapon and went to great pains to point out that external carriage would be admissible if that eased delivery. The requirement also noted that the long, low-altitude flight would be fatiguing so '…the greatest attention is to be paid to crew comfort.' To this end an integrated control system was drawn up to meet OR.941

issued in early February 1954, with one item of particular interest being the ability to restrict aircraft manoeuvres to keep within airframe limits. As time and discussions by the Low Altitude Bomber working party progressed there was a move towards making the aircraft and weapon a single requirement, in what is possibly the earliest example of a British project being treated as a complete weapon system. In response to this, Bristol and Handley Page tendered weapons with which to arm their respective aircraft to meet OR.324/OR.1125.

Bristol's Type 186 was an odd-looking aircraft whose cigar-shaped fuselage carried a clean, swept, mid-mounted wing and fitted with a butterfly tail to ensure that the dorsal mounted weapon had a clean release. The two Olympus 101 turbojets were mounted on pylons at the two o'clock and ten o'clock positions on the rear fuselage. The Red Cat weapon was to be carried in a recess above the wing box and the missile elevated on jacks before launch. The missile itself was 31ft 9in (9.7m) long with a diameter of 62in (155cm) and shared the Type 186's fuselage shape but carried small, square wings with a span of 11ft 4in (3.4m) that folded upward for stowage. As the hydraulic jacks lifted the weapon clear of the fuselage for launch, the wing and tail surfaces fell into place. Unfortunately Bristol's efforts came to nought as on 13th October 1953 the MoS decided that as Bristol were too busy with other projects such as the Britannia and the 'Mach 2 Aircraft' (what became the Bristol 188 research aircraft) they should be denied the chance to tender for OR.324/OR.1125.

Handley Page on the other hand tendered the HP.99, another odd-looking type, with a compound swept wing and somewhat vestigial tailplanes. Two Rolls-Royce Avon RA.14 turbojets were mounted in double nacelles on underwing pylons. The main undercarriage was to be installed within the same nacelles and the pylons were sufficiently deep to allow short oleos, but still maintain adequate ground clearance (the requirement stated a minimum of 68in/173cm) to install the Red Cat in the ventral weapons bay.

The HP missile to OR.1125 followed the Bristol theme in being cigar-shaped and 62in (155cm) in diameter, although that is where the similarity ended. The fuselage was much longer at 39ft 6in (12m) while the short, swept wings that spanned 17ft (5.2m) did not need to fold as they were mounted low on the fuselage to allow semi-recessed carriage on the HP.99. The missile was to be mounted on a removable pallet in the weapons bay that could be replaced with racks for conventional bombs, thus satisfying the August 1952 instruction from Charles Lea, the Director of Armament Research and Development, that the aircraft must not be tied to a single weapon.

By September 1954 the Deputy Chief of the Air Staff, AM Sir Thomas Pike, advised that the American adoption of low-level unmanned weapons would force the Soviets to focus on low-altitude defence and thus also make OR.324 vulnerable. The requirement fell by the wayside when it was realised that the necessary performance would only be attainable in aircraft that were restricted to the low-level regime and produce an inflexible weapon unsuitable to address evolving threats. The Chief of the Air Staff, ACM Sir William Dickson, added to these comments and was of the opinion that OR.324 should be cut '…because we have left it so late we could not expect to have appreciable numbers of this aircraft in Bomber Command until after 1965 when we could expect to have a ballistic rocket with nuclear warhead that would have the same degree of penetration…'. On 7th October 1954, the Air Staff cancelled OR.1125 and OR.324. The low-level bomber had been an interesting exercise that flagged a number of potential problems for the role such as navigation and targeting. This knowledge was to provide the basis for a later low-level bomber, TSR.2.

While the Air Staff examined a low-level threat, the Royal Aircraft Establishment (RAE) were considering a weapon for the forthcoming V-bombers. The RAE's Armament Department had had an interest in a powered bomb from early 1953, with the aim of prolonging the

Handley Page addressed the OR.324 requirement with the HP.99. The weapon under the fuselage is probably Red Cat to OR.1125. Low-level flight to Moscow would prove much more difficult than originally thought. *Handley Page Association*

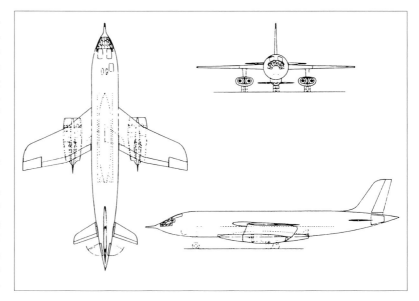

capability of the V-Force beyond the turn of the decade. Amongst the RAE's objectives were the ability to carry the forthcoming thermonuclear warhead in a delivery vehicle that would be immune from interception and using a guidance system that could not be jammed or otherwise interfered with. Red Cat had shown that guidance of such a vehicle was fraught with problems without a new navigation and guidance system. As a consequence of a trip to the USA by RAE and Radar Research Establishment (RRE) personnel to examine American work, inertial navigation was selected.

The weapon that became Blue Steel evolved from the Air Staff's requirement OR.1132 for a weapon that the V-bombers could launch against targets defended by SAGWs with ranges in the region of 25nm (46km). When used against large, heavily-defended cities such as Moscow or Leningrad, a stand-off range of more than 60nm (111km) was required, with 75nm (139km) deemed more than adequate. A range of 100nm (160km) would allow greater tactical freedom to put the open space of Russia to good use and this is the range that the Air Staff finally decided to aim for. The 100nm (185km) range would also allow an inertial navigator to be used to guide the weapon to a target and achieve accuracy of 1nm (1.9km) radius, whereas a 250nm (463km) missile would require Doppler navigation to achieve a comparable accuracy. Intended for use against fixed, industrial targets whose locations were fairly well-known the powered bomb would be able to navigate its route without external assistance.

Gyro drift has long been blamed for the inaccuracy of inertial navigation systems in the 1950s, but the main source of inaccuracy was the errors in the definition of the vertical position (the altitude) and azimuth (direction) at launch. The influence of vertical position increased with the square of the flight time and this outweighed any gyro wander by a significant factor until flight times were in excess of 800 seconds (13.3 minutes). Since the powered bomb would be flying at Mach 2.5 for 100nm (185km) giving a flight time of 4.5 minutes, gyro wander was less of a problem. Once inertial navigation had been selected, Elliott Brothers Ltd were tasked with developing the navigation system with the RAE Instrument and Photographic (IAP) Department as design authority.

The Air Staff were also intending to specify the use of radar-absorbing materials and other techniques to reduce the missile's radar echoing area of the missile. The RAE advised that this request was incompatible with the thermal regime associated with the Mach 2.5 speeds of the missile.

The main constraints were the size of the nuclear warhead and the means of fitting to the V-bombers. The first of these constraints was a complete unknown as the fusion weapon had yet to be tested experimentally, never mind converted to an operational weapon, so the diameter of the missile would depend on the diameter of the warhead. The Atomic Weapons Research Establishment (AWRE) at Aldermaston was somewhat vague on the size of such warheads and would not guarantee any of the warhead diameters that were suggested by the RAE. The RAE ultimately advised that the maximum diameters for powered bombs be based on the size of the V-bombers' bomb bays. Despite this advice AWRE refused to be pinned down, so the RAE conducted a series of paper studies that examined weapons based on a variety of missile fuselage diameters and concluded that despite a preference for internal carriage a semi-recessed mounting would allow the vagaries of the AWRE warhead diameter to be accommodated.

This uncertainty around warhead size and the possibility of a large missile even prompted the RAE to consider a method adopted by the Germans (and examined by the British) during the Second World War. One way to carry additional fuel was to carry it in a fuel tank fitted with aerodynamic surfaces towed behind the aircraft. This 'rigid tow' called *Deichselschlepp* (literally shaft tow) by the Germans, allowed aircraft to tow long-range fuel tanks and trials were carried out in Britain by Miles Aircraft using

A variety of configurations were examined by the RAE but with information on warhead size being hazy at best, these could be somewhat large. This Vulcan is shown carrying the RAE 4ft Dia. and 5ft Dia. powered bombs.

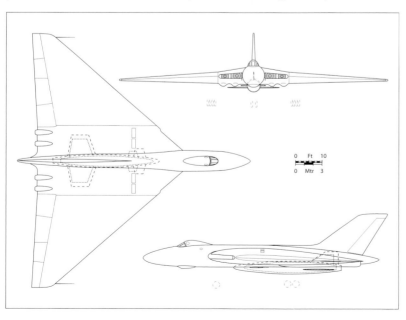

a Magister trainer with towed fuel tank. A towed missile could be as large as required, but the RAE were concerned about inaccuracy caused by azimuth corrections relative to the towing aircraft and dropped the idea.

The RAE were fairly secure in designing a weapon around the known dimensions of existing warheads and by early 1955 had produced a series of studies based on diameters of 3ft, 4ft and 5ft 6in (0.9m, 1.2m and 1.7m) each with rocket, ramjet or turbojet propulsion. These were simply described by their diameter and propulsion type, such as '4ft Dia. Turbojet'. To maintain fineness ratio and reduce drag, their lengths varied with diameter, with the '5.5ft Dia. Rocket Missile' being 45ft (13.7m) long. Handley Page was also conducting studies at this time with particular interest in the aerodynamics of a powered bomb for use on the Victor.

As knowledge of warhead types (Green Bamboo and Orange Herald were the current preferences) and their dimensions became more realistic, the RAE's studies looked at further configurations and powerplant options in what was called the 'W' series. These were of no relation to the similarly-named W-type from Avro's WRD. The RAE's studies were intended to carry a thermonuclear warhead for a distance of 50-100nm (93-185km), a distance more or less dictated by the volume of propellant that could be accommodated within the missile once the volume occupied by the warhead (the important component) and navigator had been used up.

The RAE's W.1 missile came in four configurations, A to D, with the basic format being a canard. W.1A and W.1B shared the same basic layout with cropped-delta wings towards the rear with ventral and dorsal fins. The foreplanes were set just aft of the nose, allowing a continuous fuselage bay for a 2,000lb (907kg) warhead and propellant. The rearmost bay housed the liquid-fuelled rocket engine. The W.1A was 28ft (8.5m) long with a diameter of 2ft 11in (0.9m) while the W.1B was 25% larger with a length of 35ft (10.7m) and a diameter of 3ft 1in (0.9m). Their respective launch weights were 7,550lb and 9,100lb (3,425kg and 4,128kg) with 3,000lb and 4,300lb (1,361kg and 1,951kg) of propellant. The W.1B could have been carried internally by all three V-bombers if rotated 45° from wings level or with the lower fins projecting out into the open through slots in the weapons bay doors. Interestingly the Valiant, by dint of its high wing, could have carried a W.1B under each wing, doubling its warload compared with its younger brethren. This

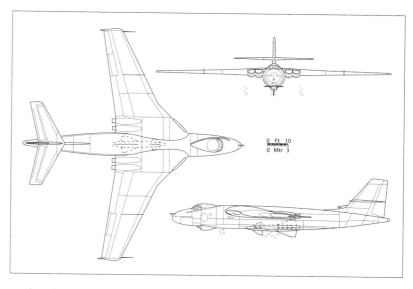

underwing carriage is not shown for the Vulcan despite that aircraft having adequate clearance. This may be due to the Valiant carrying the missiles on the hard point used for large drop tanks. The larger W.1B could be mounted on a ventral pylon on the Vulcan, but not be carried by the Valiant or Victor.

W.1C harked back to the earlier RAE '5.5ft Dia. Rocket Missile' in that it was 5ft 6in (1.6m) in diameter and shared the earlier missile's straight equi-taper wings and foreplane. This larger weapon was designed to carry a warhead weighing 7,500lb (3,402kg) and was 41ft (12.5m) long, so had to be carried in a semi-recessed mounting in any of the V-bomber's weapons bays.

The uncertainty about the size of a thermonuclear warhead is exemplified by Missile W.1D. Despite maintaining the required maximum fuselage width of 5ft 2in (1.6m) to allow stowage within V-bomber weapons bays, W.1D was 8ft 6in (2.6m) deep. The overall length of the missile was 46ft (14m) which was more or less the maximum length to allow carriage on a Vulcan, the only V-bomber with sufficient ground clearance to accommodate this monster. The main reason for the depth of the W.1D's fuselage was to provide sufficient fuel capacity to meet the range requirement as much of the fuselage was taken up by the warhead. This was massive, weighing 15,000lb (6,804kg), was 20ft (6.1m) long and a stated diameter of 5ft (1.5m). Overall the W.1D missile had a launch weight of 32,000lb (14,515kg) that included 10,000lb (4,536kg) of propellant. This size reflects the contemporary thinking behind the size of nuclear weapons and the belief that a thermonuclear device would be much larger than a fission weapon. These mis-

The RAE produced a variety of studies for a powered bomb. This example for the Valiant was the W1A (no relation to the later Avro W-Series). The RAE dictated that the same weapon was to be carried by all the V-bombers.

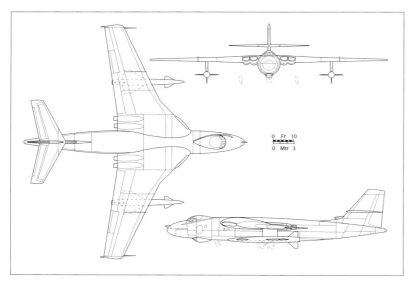

Underwing carriage was considered for the powered bomb, but problems with azimuth setting on the inertial guidance system made ventral carriage, on the centreline, the preferred method. This Valiant carries a pair of W1B powered bombs on its wing pylons.

they should have sole control over the powered bomb project. The Ministry of Supply (MoS) on the other hand had other ideas. The MoS had initially intended that a company with no interest in V-bomber manufacture should be involved in Blue Steel, thus dismissing Vickers, Avro and Handley Page. Their prime concern was that an aircraft builder would tailor the weapon to their own aircraft. The Royal Aircraft Establishment on the other hand had other ideas and, despite that initial desire to control the entire project, latterly had no qualms about the V-bomber firms working on Blue Steel. Vickers had a good track record in the guided weapons field and had been developing the Blue Boar guided bomb for the V-Force. In fact Vickers had disclosed that they could develop the weapon to meet OR.1132 in two years if the RAE became directly involved.

siles were designed a year after the USA detonated its first 'weaponised' thermonuclear device, at a test called Castle Bravo. The physics package, called 'Shrimp' weighed 23,500 lb (10,659kg), was 53in (135cm) in diameter and 15ft (4.6m) long. The physicists at AWRE may have had some idea about Shrimp's size and so advised the RAE, who drew up W.1D in response and included a bit of room for growth. In some ways the W.1D could be seen as insurance against a British fusion weapon project that produced a viable hydrogen bomb, but at the expense of size and weight.

Having carried out the W studies, the RAE Controlled Weapons Department decided that

In November 1954 Avro's WRD already had a stand-off weapon on the drawing board that predated the issue of OR.1132 in the shape of the P43Z. This was also described as the 38/27 and was tailor-made for the Vulcan. Weighing 10,000 lb (4,535kg) and powered by a de Havilland Spectre engine, the P.43Z was 26ft (7.9m) long and its broad-chord, low aspect-ratio wings had a span of 9ft (2.7m) and so could fit in the Vulcan's bomb bay with ease. One interesting aspect of the P.43Z was its parabolic nose, that for the same length, allowed greater stowage volume than a conventional radius curved taper.

This diagram demonstrates how vague the Atomic Weapons Research Establishment was on the subject of warhead size. These Vulcan prototypes are shown carrying powered bombs, with the slim RAE W1B on the left and massive W1D on the right. Note how the vertical fins on the W1B rotate for stowage.

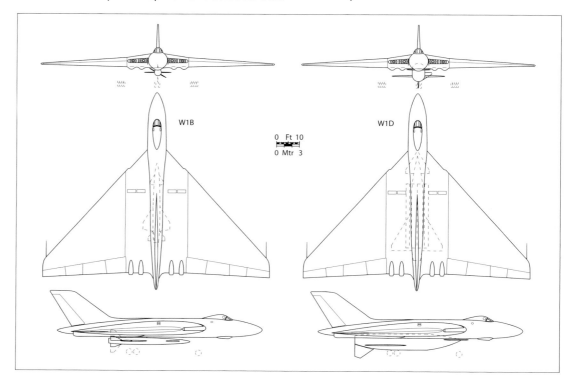

Vickers' thoughts on the powered bomb were similar to the RAE's 4ft diameter missile in two versions. Their rocket-powered missile was shorter than the RAE's while their turbojet variant used the rear-mounted tail configuration. A smaller version based on a 3ft (0.9m) diameter fuselage was deemed capable of underwing carriage, while the larger version caused interference with the undercarriage and therefore had to be carried ventrally. The RAE was against underwing carriage of the weapons because, as with the towed weapon, they considered the azimuth corrections too complex. The MoS voiced concern about launching the rear-tailed missile, something Vickers proposed be addressed by lowering the missile on a trapeze system.

Handley Page's thoughts on the powered bomb were quite probably more advanced than any other company's proposals. In drawing up a rocket-boosted, ramjet-powered missile, HP foresaw the need for longer range and higher speed. At an altitude of 80,000ft (24,384m) and a speed of Mach 3, HP's missile was capable of a range of 500nm (926km) but the main stumbling block would be guidance, as the inertial systems of the time could not provide sufficient accuracy at such range. The MoS considered HP's proposal to be somewhat optimistic and stuck with the 100nm (185km) requirement.

Deputations from the MoS had in November 1954 visited the three V-bomber builders, on an informal and unofficial basis, to assess their suitability as developers of a missile to meet OR.1132. Handley Page was described as 'most enthusiastic and offered to do a considerable amount of work. In particular they are willing to study in detail the possible methods of installing the various sizes of bombs on the existing Victor.' Vickers was described as 'equally co-operative, although of course the Valiant cannot carry as large a bomb as the Victor. They also are keen to help in the same way as HPs.'

The MoS delegations's third visit was less successful. Avro at Woodford were: '...not co-operative. Their general attitude was that the bomb size should be decided, or rather guessed, and that they would then arrange to carry it without any penalty.' There was some light at the end of the tunnel, as G A Whitfield of the MoS noted 'I think, however, that they will help, particularly because their aerodynamicist is interested and sensible.' It turned out that Avro may have been ahead of the other companies all along and had been '...in fact, doing some work under the counter and want more information

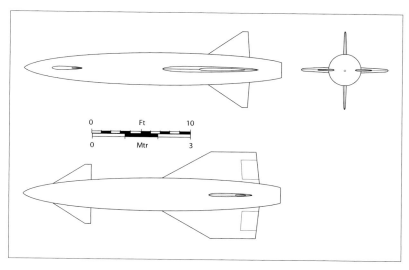

about possible sizes and shapes of bombs.' The P.43Z may indicate how far Avro's work had gone and may even have been the under-the-counter job. This situation was supported by Handley Page being worried that Avro's had been supplied with additional information by R H Francis (who had recently departed the RAE) and this gave Avro's an advantage. Whitfield's memo ends with the news that the Director of Military Aircraft Research and Development had cleared the way for all three firms to carry on with their work.

Why had Avro, a company with absolutely no track record in guided weapons, become so involved in the development of the powered bomb that they could take such a high-handed attitude to the MoS? Secure in the knowledge that that the RAE would be in control of the powered bomb, Avro's engineers, of whom six (including Chief Engineer R H Francis) were former RAE employees, felt they were well-placed to gain the contract.

The original Avro proposal for OR.1132. The P.43Z was to be carried in the Vulcan bomb bay and was shaped to maximise its internal volume.

The RAE's W1A powered bomb on a Handley Page Victor. The RAE dictat that all V-bombers should carry the OR.1132 weapon was quietly dropped.

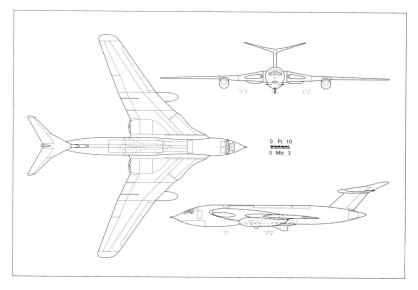

In August 1955 Avro's Weapons Research Division (WRD) submitted to the Ministries and Air Staff a brochure, WRB.1, entitled 'A Weapon to OR.1132' that laid out Avro's proposals for a stand-off weapon. WRB.1 also outlined a sextet of proposals based on their configuration study 48/35 (based on the diameter in inches and length in feet) to meet OR.1132 and beyond. Identified as Stages 1 through 4, WRD laid out not only a missile to meet OR.1132 but a programme for future development that could keep pace with both the perceived improvement in Soviet air defences and the RAF's future plans for offensive aircraft. Each was to carry a 4,500lb (2,041kg)/45in (114cm) diameter Green Bamboo thermonuclear warhead with the prospect of a lighter 2,000lb (907kg) Orange Herald warhead in the future. The lighter warhead was thought to allow extra propellant for a range increase of 70nm (129km)

Stage 1a was the baseline model for OR.1132 that was to be launched from a V-Bomber, capable of Mach 2.5 cruise at 75,000ft (22,860m) and deliver its warhead to a range of 100nm (185km). The Stage 1a would be in RAF service in 1960, while a longer-ranged, 180nm (333km), Stage 1b that weighed in at 15,000lb (6,803kg) was to enter service a year later. Further development would improve performance to such an extent that Stage 2 would reach Mach 4.5 at 85,000ft (25,908m) and weigh 16,000lb (7,257kg) while its range would have been 240nm (444km). The wings of Stage 1 would be unsuitable for the

higher speeds of Stage 2, so a new thinner wing with sharper leading edge was required. By 1963 WRD hoped to have improved the Stage 2 to such an extent that as Stage 3, with a saddleback propellant tank and two additional boost engines, it would have almost double the range of Stage 2 at 450nm (833km) for a launch weight of 25,000lb (11,334kg). The saddle tank and boost engines would be jettisoned prior to commencing the cruise phase. A larger wing would also have been required to cope with the additional weight.

Stage 4 was a Stage 2 lengthened to 40ft (12.2m) intended for supersonic launch from a development of the Avro Type 730 aircraft to meet the recently specified RB.156. Estimated to achieve service by 1964, Stage 4a had a projected range of 600nm (1,111km) and weighed 18,000lb (8,165kg) with a cruising speed of Mach 5. An even longer version, Stage 4b, was to be 50ft (15.2m) long with an estimated launch weight of 26,000lb (11,793kg) and a projected range of 900nm (1,667km). The last two proposals were really pushing the flight envelope into the hypersonic regime that in the mid-1950s was seen as the future of flight.

All used inertial navigation apart from Stage 4 which used a combination of automatic-astro and inertial navigators to maintain accuracy over the longer ranges. The propulsion system was to be the Armstrong Siddeley RB.9/2, a two-chamber HTP/Kerosene rocket engine whose chambers differed in size to allow for different thrust requirements in boost, 30,000lbf (133.4kN) and cruise, 4,000lbf (17.8kN) phases. Stage 3 dif-

Early configurations for Blue Steel included the 1/8th-scale 6/5 ground-launched test vehicle and 2/5-scale 19/15 air-launched vehicle. The 48/35 full-scale vehicle led to a number of studies including W.100 and the long-range Stage 3 with saddle tank.

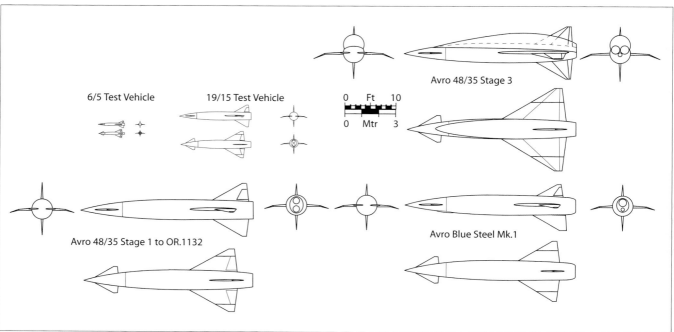

6/5 Test Vehicle

19/15 Test Vehicle

Avro 48/35 Stage 3

Avro 48/35 Stage 1 to OR.1132

Avro Blue Steel Mk.1

fered in using two large chambers producing 26,000 lbf (115.6kN) apiece as boosters and the small chamber for the cruise. The RB.9/2 would ultimately become the Stentor, the engine used in the production Blue Steel.

The canard delta configuration was preferred for a number of reasons including stability at all speeds due to the centre of pressure (CoP) moving fore and aft in a predictable manner as speed increased. At transonic speeds the CoP moved aft until true supersonic speed was achieved, at which point it moved forward. Another reason was the ease with which a warhead (whose dimensions were still vague) could be fitted between wing and foreplane structures. A cropped-delta wing with 60° sweep was chosen because it had good transonic characteristics and generated sufficient lift at the critical point in the boost phase when the missile achieved Mach 1.3 and began its climb.

A thickness/chord ratio of 4.5% was chosen, a compromise between the aerodynamic and structural requirements, and this was maintained across the span. The section was a variation on the RAE 101, with the rearmost 46% simplified to be a straight taper, rather than curved, to ease construction. Oddly enough, this simplification of construction was taken to extreme in August 1955 with the P.36Z that was an attempt to design a Blue Steel using straight lines and flat surfaces. Also known as the Utility Bomber Missile, the P36Z used simple shapes such as cones and cylinders to produce a much simplified version of the 48/35 configuration. This included squared aerodynamic surfaces with simple bi-conic sections. Its basic aerodynamic parameters were checked against the standard 48/35 configuration, but no detailed analysis was made to assess the effect on stability and range.

Contract is signed

On 4th May 1956 the MoS awarded contract G/Proj/6220/GW35A to A.V. Roe as co-ordinating contractor for the development of a stand-off weapon to meet OR.1132, the weapon that became known as Blue Steel. As outlined in the original requirement, Blue Steel was to be carried by all three V-Bombers, have a range of at least 100nm (185km) and carry a warhead weighing 4,500 lb (2,041kg).

Avro, who had been conducting private venture work on a stand-off weapon, had a further advantage in the form of their experience in the field of high-speed structures. OR.1132 called for a missile capable of flying at speeds ranging

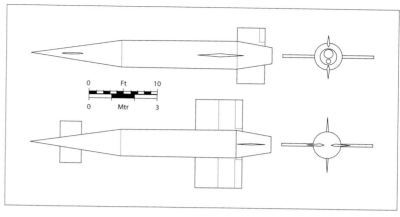

from Mach 0.8 to Mach 2.5, with later development to speeds in excess of Mach 3 and beyond. Such speeds required a structure that could withstand the temperature range and stresses caused by flight in excess of Mach 2.0. Avro, who by 1955 had been granted the contract to develop the OR.330 reconnaissance aircraft as the Type 730, were well placed to use the experience of fabricating the airframes for high-speed flight. Unfortunately this was a bet that Avro lost when the Avro 730 was cancelled and so they had to learn a great deal about stainless steel fabrication and forming from scratch.

On being presented with the contract for OR.1132, Avro commenced recruitment of suitable engineers and other relevant personnel. As co-ordinating contractor Avro was also required to oversee the work of Elliott Brothers on the inertial navigator and Armstrong Siddeley with the rocket engine. Having built a team, development of the missile began in earnest, with 1/20 and 1/48 scale wind tunnel and free-flight models being prepared and put to work. The first free-flight models were the P41Z, known as the 6/5; this was a 1/8th scale vehicle with limited telemetry and ground-launched on a Mayfly rocket booster at Aberporth to check the aerodynamics and stability in flight. The first flight of a 6/5 was made on 1st April 1954 and continued throughout that year. The 6/5 came in two variants for different flight regimes, with the Mayfly-boosted version good for Mach 2.7 while a second version, for flight up to Mach 1.5, used a Demon solid boost.

To enable trials of full-scale systems for the final missile, particularly guidance systems, Avro proposed using one of their forthcoming small delta fighters, such as the Type 720. This proposal came to nought as the Type 720 was cancelled with OR.301 in 1957. In fact the ultimate solution of using light-alloy versions of the missile itself no doubt gave better value in the long run both financially and in more relevant results.

The fabrication problems encountered by WRD on Blue Steel should have been solved during the Type 730 project. WRD had to work out how to form three-dimensional shapes in stainless steel. The P36Z was a utility version without the complex shapes.

19/15 – The Trail Blazer

Test vehicles were, and to a certain extent remain today, a fundamental element of guided weapons development and their use to prove aerodynamics and systems function normally help to speed development. Avro's first test vehicles had been ground-launched, rocket-boosted models such as the 1/8th scale 6/5 vehicle. The first air-launched free-flight vehicle was the 2/5th-scale 19/15. This was used to prove the aerodynamics and control systems, all monitored by a 24-channel telemetry system. Almost the entire top surface of the 19/15 was removable to allow access to the internal equipment, with the vehicle powered by a Jackdaw solid rocket motor. Developed by the Propellant and Explosives Research and Manufacturing Establishment (PERME) at Westcott and built by Bristol Aerojet, the Jackdaw was novel in using a single combustion chamber with two superimposed blast tubes. This mimicked the proposed propulsion system configuration of the operational missile.

The 19/15's aerodynamic control systems were essentially the same as the full-size Blue Steel missile, with the vehicle's trajectory pre-programmed in the autopilot. Carried aloft in the weapons bay of a Valiant, thus avoiding exposure to the elements on the climb to launch height, the test vehicle was dropped in the same manner as a free-fall bomb. Once clear of the aircraft the Jackdaw motor fired and the vehicle commenced its test manoeuvres over a period of several minutes before a destruct system fired, ending the trial.

The 19/15 series were the first test vehicles to use the stainless steel structure of the full-scale vehicle, essentially to gain fabrication experience and it was during their construction that the early indications of manufacturing problems arose with stretch-forming DDT.166 stainless steel sheet. The challenge of forming the complex curves of 19/15 and the larger Blue Steel were what led to Avro considering a radical redesign in the aforementioned P.36Z simplified W.100.

These early setbacks prompted a change in material to the FV.520 stainless steel used in the later vehicles. FV.520 was a precipitation-hardened stainless steel that included 16% chromium and 6% nickel. Delays caused by fabrication problems were further compounded by problems that Avro were encountering in obtaining the services of a Valiant to use in trials. This lack of suitable aircraft for trials work was a continual problem for Avro throughout the programme's duration and had also plagued the earlier Blue Boar trials.

These trials were used to determine the accuracy of the flight dynamics calculations and to check the flight control equations in practice, particularly in the transonic regime. They also provided training for personnel, but most importantly provided valuable information that could be transferred directly to the full-scale

The 19/15 test vehicle production line. This 2/5th-scale vehicle taught WRD a great deal about almost every aspect of the Blue Steel manufacturing process and was also proposed as the basis for a weapon.
BAE Systems/ Avro Heritage

Blue Steel and therefore fulfilled the requirement of any test vehicle to facilitate development of the final weapon. By late 1958 the 19/15 trials had been completed successfully and apart from a handful of training flights in 1959, the programme was concluded and the effort transferred to the later full-scale vehicles derived from the 48/35 configuration.

As a missile in its own right, the 19/15 was a challenge. Until 1956 the majority of British missiles were small, short-range and possessed short flight times. The Blue Steel test vehicles were highly complex, pilotless aircraft whose manufacture, systems, flight envelope and trajectory were such a departure from previous experience in guided weapons development, that no-one could really be surprised that delays occurred. Fortunately for Avro, had these problems been encountered in the full-scale missile, the delays would have been much more serious.

48/35 – The Basis of the Weapon

While the 19/15 test vehicle was used confirm the control and dynamics of the missile, full-scale test vehicles were required for aerodynamic, carriage, component and systems trials. Avro had more or less finalised the configuration of the Blue Steel weapons in a configuration called 48/35 that formed the basis of a range of full-scale vehicles, W.100 to W.105. The W.100 would allow the full spectrum of trials to be made while the others in the range were designed for specific tasks.

Avro were well aware that stainless steel construction would be problematic with potential delays in the fabrication process holding up development. For carriage and low-speed flight tests, the heat-resistant properties of stainless steel were not required. These trials included investigation of the effects of prolonged high-altitude carriage on components, the release sequence, aircraft missile interface trials and hydraulic and electrical power systems. Therefore Avro opted to construct an inert version of Blue Steel using aluminium alloy. Called the W.102, this was an unpowered vehicle with fixed controls, no hydraulic or power systems and constructed by Air Service Training (AST). This came in two variants: the W.102 fitted with limited telemetry and used for drop trials, while the W.102A vehicles lacked telemetry and were used solely for carriage trials in the V-bombers. A total of three W.102 and six W.102A were built and used throughout the trials period.

For flight trials in the launch and boost to supersonic speeds, Gloster Aircraft at Huccle-

cote were contracted to construct the W.103 and W.103A. Again, construction was of aluminium alloy with the eleven W.103 having full controls driven by a non-circulating hydraulic system while electric power was supplied by batteries. Propulsion came from a de Havilland Double Spectre rocket engine and the W.103 was used for speeds up to Mach 2.

For trials more representative of the final missile and to test hydraulic and electrical power systems, six W.103A were built by Glosters. These incorporated a 7ft 6in (2.3m) bay sized to accommodate the Green Bamboo warhead and were powered by either a Double Spectre or Armstrong Siddeley PR.9 engine. Hydraulic and electrical power was supplied by iso-propyl nitrate (IPN) turbines. Glosters were also put in charge of developing a third alloy test vehicle, the W.104. This was to be a recoverable, re-usable test vehicle equipped with a retractable skid undercarriage. Ultimately the W.104 was not built, as it was not required and Avro's WRD thought that work on it would hold up development of the final weapon.

The only major configuration change made as a result of the various trials was a change in size of the dorsal and ventral fins. The original 48/35 configuration sported fins of equal size; however carriage trials soon revealed that a reduced area dorsal fin with a correspondingly larger ventral fin not only helped with carriage and launch but improved stability as the ventral fin was not blanked in certain phases of the flight regime when the missile was operating at high angles of incidence such as the boost climb.

The test vehicles were also used to develop the environmental control systems that were important to Blue Steel's success. The missile would experience temperatures ranging from -45°C (-49°F) in the high-altitude flight under the bomber to 300°C (572°F) in the supersonic

Gloster Aircraft built the light alloy trials specimens for the Blue Steel programme. This poor quality photo shows the wings and rear fuselage of a W.103 under construction.
BAE Systems/ Avro Heritage

cruise. Such temperatures would wreak havoc with internal systems such as the warhead that required a steady, fairly benign environment and required heating or the inertial navigator and flight rules computer that generated a lot of heat and therefore needed cooling. The environmental control of adjacent bays with divergent temperature limits posed a serious problem to the designers who had to design equipment such a Freon refrigeration packs from scratch. Blue Steel was paving the way to a high-speed flight aircraft. If such a vehicle was to be manned, thermal management would be a priority

Flight trials by No.4 Joint Services Trials Unit (JSTU) were carried out at two ranges: initial UK trials at Aberporth in Wales covered short-range and captive flights while long-range, full-capability testing was conducted at the Woomera range in Australia. The British base for trials was Avro's Woodford airfield where a Valiant (WZ370), two Vulcans (XA903 and XL317) and a pair of Victors (XH675 and XL161) were dedicated to Blue Steel flight trials over the range at Aberporth using the ground track-

ing systems already developed for British guided weapons testing.

The use of Woomera for long-range testing required extension of the range facilities, in particular the installation of additional tracking and telemetry systems including radars and optical tracking equipment such as kinetheodolites. The new facilities were required to cover the longer distances, in comparison to earlier missiles such as Blue Boar, of the Blue Steel flight trajectories. The Blue Steel test vehicles utilised the existing RAE 465MHz 24-channel telemetry systems as the staff on both test ranges were familiar with its operation. Early trials used up to four telemetry sets per vehicle, but as experience was gained, the number was reduced to two per missile.

Most test vehicles and operational trials missiles were transported to Woomera by sea with urgent or small items by air freight. In 1960 the need to speed up the trials prompted the despatch of eighteen preproduction Blue Steels to Woomera under the codename Blue Ranger. Blue Steel trials rounds were carried by Vulcan and Victor aircraft from Woodford via transit points such as Gan in the Indian Ocean. This operation was officially described as a series of long-range carriage trials, but in reality was a means of transporting missiles to No.4 JSTU at Edinburgh Field, near Elizabeth in South Australia by the fastest possible method.

Full-Scale Trials

The description of the long series of Blue Steel trials is beyond the scope of this book and has been covered in the detail it deserves elsewhere, specifically in Peter Morton's excellent *Fire Across the Desert*. From 1957 until 1965 No.4 JSTU carried out more than fifty trials involving carry tests, drop checks and fully-guided launches over the Weapons Research Establishment range at Woomera. These trials were the subject of great scrutiny by the authorities back in the UK, particularly the Right Honourable Harold Watkinson, who awaited the results each test flight with anticipation. As will become clear, Watkinson had more than a successful flight on his mind.

The Minister's Tale

In October 1959 Harold Watkinson MP was appointed as Her Majesty's Secretary of State for Defence in Harold Macmillan's Government. Watkinson took over from Duncan Sandys and inherited Sandys' policies. These included development of a weapon to meet OR.1159, the Blue Streak MRBM, TSR.2 and the ongoing saga that was Blue Steel. Some of Watkinson's decisions saw the cancellation of OR.1159 and Blue Streak, to be replaced by the Douglas Skybolt, a fairly sensible decision under the circumstances. So by April 1960 Watkinson had rationalised the UK's deterrence plans but there was one project that Watkinson appeared to have difficulty dealing with: Blue Steel. Having opted for Skybolt and with Blue Steel experiencing delay after delay, Watkinson considered what to do with a project that had cost almost £55M by 1960.

Avro got wind of Watkinson's doubts about Blue Steel and organised a meeting between the Chairman, Sir Roy Dobson, and Watkinson's Scientific Advisor, Sir Solly Zuckerman. Over lunch at the Royal Aero Club, Dobson was adamant that 'We must get Blue Steel Mk.I into service in order to get a lot of experience with it.', especially after the trials phase. Nor was he amused by Zuckerman's implication that Blue Steel be seen as a learning process and stated that 'It is demoralising to regard Mk.I as a test vehicle not only to the R+D teams but to the RAF.'

In May 1960 Watkinson admitted to being attracted to a 'mixed bag of clubs' in the guise of a deterrent that comprised the ballistic Skybolt on the Vulcan and the cruise-type Blue Steel on the Victor to provide two separate threats. However when it came to Blue Steel, Watkinson was '…gravely concerned at the delay in providing the services with this weapon.' and compared this with the American Hound Dog which was started after and was more advanced than Blue Steel that had been 'bogged down by minor technical problems'.

On 25th May 1960 at a meeting at the Ministry of Aviation to discuss Blue Steel's status, the Minister of Defence stated that only an operational weapon was of any use to him and wanted a date for Initial Operational Capability

The elegant lines of Handley Page's Victor B.2 were somewhat spoiled by the addition of Blue Steel. This photograph shows the nose-down carriage of the weapon and its large size relative to the aircraft. *Author's Collection*

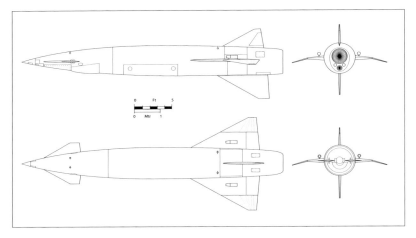

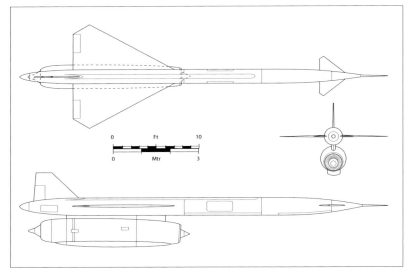

General arrangement drawing of Blue Steel W.105 (as Avro referred to it). At 35 feet long Blue Steel was a monster, its size dictated by the diameter of its Green Grass warhead.

Hound Dog. Much to the chagrin of the Air Staff and Air Ministry, this American missile started development after Blue Steel, entered service before Blue Steel and had superior capability.

(IOC). Sir Roy Dobson pointed out that much of the delay was down to the programme being interrupted by a new warhead (Red Snow) in January 1959 and that the Air Staff were well aware of this. James Kay, Avro's Managing Director of the Blue Steel project described how the greatest problem was a lack of craftsmen and that the threat of cancellation had hindered recruitment, something that the Minister of Aviation, Duncan Sandys, considered to be a valid point. Solly Zuckerman pointed out that the UK had never installed a nuclear warhead in a missile before and that '...the proving of this might take more than two years.'

On the subject of delays with the trials, range time was seen as 'crucial', with 57 flights planned in the next 18 months. Despite these admittedly valid reasons for the delays, Watkinson and Sandys were of the opinion that Avro's WRD should initiate a crash programme to progress Blue Steel to a stage that an IOC could be declared. By the third week of June Watkinson appears to have been distracted by Avro's next proposal for a modified Blue Steel. This

was the Blue Steel Mk.II (of which more later) that Watkinson was assured would be available at a 'reasonable cost' as an insurance against the failure of Skybolt. Watkinson was keen on this project, unlike the Defence Committee who were exceedingly sceptical of the comments on cost as the source was '...an off the cuff remark from an Avro technical director.'

Avro's next proposal from early July, the Blue Steel Mk.1*, failed to elicit a response other than add to the growing impatience in Whitehall. Watkinson's advisors discovered that while Avro quoted a cruise speed of Mach 4, the range increase to 320nm (593km) was gained by the missile gliding towards the target, with its speed decreasing to Mach 1.4 on the approach to the target, thus it would be vulnerable to Soviet SAMs. The Mk.1* represented a fundamental redesign of the basic missile and even Avro must have thought they'd tried the Government's patience. So they proposed the less radical modification of fitting solid boost motors to Blue Steel Mk.I to save fuel for the cruise and provide the same range as the Mk.1*.

By mid July it had come to Watkinson's attention that Blue Steel was being held up by '...the difficulty of clearing the nuclear warhead from a safety and operational point of view.' The origin of this is not detailed in Watkinson's typically terse memo to Solly Zuckerman, who was asked to investigate. Less than a week later, the Chief Scientist replied and informed the Minister that 'Aldermaston knows nothing of the warhead that is holding up Blue Steel.' and was in fact awaiting a Blue Steel missile to carry out their own tests.

The Chief Scientist also pointed out that it would be useful if the identity of Watkinson's informant was known. Watkinson scribbled a few lines on Zuckerman's memo that reveal the informant to be a 'MoA representative' and asked when a Blue Steel would be supplied to Aldermaston. 'Seems surprising to me that they have not got one already.' were Watkinson's final thoughts on the matter.

In August came a surprise for Watkinson. Avro had been approached by the French Government with the intention of fitting a version of Blue Steel to the Dassault Mirage IV. Duncan Sandys had discussed it with Monsieur Pierre Messmer, the French defence minister and Sandys had passed this on to Watkinson who was quite happy for this to happen as long as it didn't interfere with the British Blue Steel programme. A sceptical Richard Chilver, MoD

This Vulcan B.2 carries a Blue Steel drill round. Operational weapons were painted white, drill rounds pale blue and trials rounds were black. Surveillance warheads were fitted to drill and operational rounds.
Via Terry Panopalis

Deputy Secretary, was of the opinion that it would come to nought and since Blue Steel was 'seriously behindhand' already, if the French became involved they could share the costs. Chilver also thought that French co-operation would 'help to restore some of our industry's lost prestige to be taking part in the design of a strategic missile for the up-and-coming French.'

Yet again Watkinson appeared to be distracted from putting 'some ginger into Avro' and became bogged down in looking at the pros and cons of the deterrent. Options listed in a minute dated 23rd September 1960 included developing TSR.2 as a strategic nuclear strike aircraft, an air-launched version of the Blue Water tactical ballistic missile or carry on with Blue Steel. By this date, thanks in part to Gary Powers languishing in a Soviet prison cell, it had become obvious that a cruise-type missile was becoming vulnerable to enemy air defences.

At the beginning of October 1960 Watkinson visited the Weapons Research Division at Avro's Woodford plant and was supplied by Air Commodore Hughes at the Ministry of Aviation with a few awkward questions (and as is the way with civil servants, the probable answers) to put to Avro's R H Francis. One question involved the flight of the first navigated Blue Steel (Round 6), a major milestone in the programme that had slipped by seven months over a period of almost a year. Round 6 and its status was a recurring subject in the memo traffic between the Ministries. The answer could have come from Lewis Carroll: Round 6 was now Round 11 as Round 6's goals had been superseded by those of Round 11.

One of Hughes' more pertinent questions was about the ten flights that had been aborted (out of 22 trials) due to a failure in the EPCU, the power supply control unit. The MoD were convinced that this was 'a rather higher failure rate than would be expected.' and was no doubt due to the system being overloaded.

On the subject of vulnerability, R H Francis told Watkinson that Blue Steel '…could be made to jink without loss of navigational accuracy.' A member of Watkinson's staff, Mr A G Tough asserted that this idea was nonsense as without additional equipment to react to attack, the jinking would be pre-programmed and therefore make no difference to vulnerability. Tough also pointed out that the missile was most vulnerable in the final attack phase, where jinking was not possible.

Watkinson returned to London to a note from the Treasury that said that the Chancellor of the Exchequer would like 'a chat'. The Chancellor, Selwyn Lloyd had been appointed in late July 1960 and was concerned that the cost of the deterrent was escalating and had shown no sign of levelling off. This, according to Watkinson, was because the deterrent was changing from Blue Steel to Skybolt to Polaris. This state-

Blue Steel trajectory showing the initial dive to 32,000ft to accelerate through the sound barrier before pitching up to climb to high altitude for the cruise.

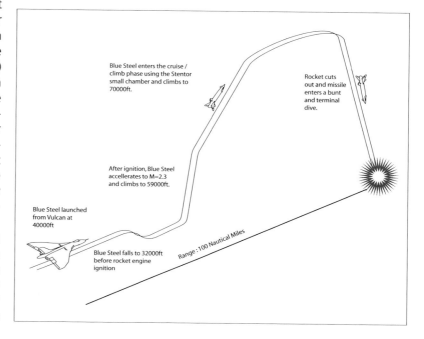

Blue Steel enters the cruise / climb phase using the Stentor small chamber and climbs to 70000ft.

Rocket cuts out and missile enters a bunt and terminal dive.

After ignition, Blue Steel accelerates to M=2.3 and climbs to 59000ft.

Blue Steel launched from Vulcan at 40000ft

Blue Steel falls to 32000ft before rocket engine ignition

Range : 100 Nautical Miles

ment shows that there was an intention to buy Polaris in 1960; however this proposal to buy Polaris was for a joint NATO deterrence plan, not the independent deterrent that was to be Skybolt and the scope of this plan would affect the size of the order for Blue Steel. Watkinson had more or less told the Americans that the UK would buy Skybolt *and* Polaris, to be used as part of the NATO force and in doing so may have exceeded his remit.

Not much happened on the subject of Blue Steel until the turn of the year, almost as if the MoD had decided to give Avro time sort out the problems. Then on the 13th of January 1961, Watkinson was informed by the MoA that '…the prospects about Blue Steel have continued to deteriorate' and that technical release would be delayed by six months. 'This is very alarming.' was Watkinson's response and penned a memo to the Secretary of State for the Air, Julian Amery, (who was Macmillan's son-in-law) in which he stated 'I know that you realise the importance of my being able to declare an IOC for Blue Steel at the earliest possible date.'

Watkinson observed that Blue Steel had cost £60M with little to show for it, particularly as a weapon. He continued 'It certainly would be helpful if we could have even one squadron with an Initial Operational Blue Steel Capability in January 1962.' The work to produce the Mk.2 Victor and Vulcan was well under way and in the light of a lack of Blue Steel would have to revert to the free-fall role using Yellow Sun Mk.2 and that this would involve 300 man-hours per aircraft. This was crucial as it also became apparent that the Red Snow warhead would not be available before March 1962 at the earliest.

By the end of January Watkinson was becoming increasingly impatient with the lack of progress 'We simply cannot accept these slippages; should we send for Roy Dobson again or wait?' and in the first week of February was urging for more pressure to be placed on Avro. Peter Thorneycroft, the Minister of Aviation, asserted that the maximum pressure was being applied. The Secretary of State for Air, Julian Amery, suggested that an IOC by January 1962 was possible. Amery also said 'The only real question is whether we will know that Blue Steel will work by that date. The answer appears to be no'; possibly an indication of the MoA's scepticism on the matter. It also transpired that the IOC would only be possible '…by interim use of Yellow Sun warheads' and that this would allow the Minister of Defence to claim an emergency operational capability for Blue Steel with the Yellow Sun warhead. This was more or less what Watkinson wanted to hear. He could declare an IOC for Blue Steel, albeit an emergency, and appeared to be happy that he had what he required. As ever the Deputy Secretary of the MoD was not convinced.

At the end of March 1961 with an IOC date in the bag, Richard Chilver wrote a rather damning précis of the Blue Steel programme and was particularly critical of the Ministry of Aviation's project managers who did not 'appreciate the crisis caused by the delays' with Blue Steel. Bomber Command was criticised for not providing sufficient support for the aircraft involved in trials specifically the 'reliance on old and inadequately-equipped aircraft' and '…could have done more to get the aircraft serviceable.'

Range facilities in the UK were insufficient, there being a shortage of capacity and a definite shortage of good weather, forcing a reliance on the Woomera range in Australia with the attendant long logistics chain. The Americans had far fewer problems – 'What stands out above all is that compared with the Americans we try to do this kind of thing on a shoestring. They may be lavish but we have overdone carefulness.' Chilver also observed 'that we ought not to spread ourselves over such a wide range of projects' and that the story of Blue Steel illustrates very well the trouble that those in charge of a development project have to tackle.' Perhaps Chilver's most prescient words were 'It is frightening that in future these troubles should be tackled by management that are responsible to several different countries at once.'

When it came to the relationship between Whitehall and an aviation company, few contracts prompted such bitterness as the one for Blue Steel. The Ministry of Aviation considered Avro's programming of the entire Blue Steel project to be 'weak and in need of overhauling'. By late 1961 the word 'crisis' was being bandied about in relation to Blue Steel as the Ministries realised the immensity of the task in hand. In January 1962 the first firings of the W.100A preproduction round were carried out but these only served to make the Ministries assess the situation. Having seen Hound Dog overhaul Blue Steel in the conception-to-service stakes, the MoD and Ministry of Aviation were aghast to realise that Skybolt might even be in service before Blue Steel Mk.I had finished trials.

This unidentified 617 Squadron Vulcan B.2 just after IOC was attained has but a single Red Shrimp ECM antenna on the starboard engine nacelle. Later B.2 models had Red Shrimp under each nacelle.
Via Terry Panopalis

The view from the ground

Once Blue Steel achieved Watkinson's desired IOC in September 1962, nine months later than the Minister had demanded, it was down to the servicemen of the RAF to make it work. The first unit to operate Blue Steel was 617 Squadron, The Dam Busters; though their Vulcans were able to carry Blue Steel, launching it was strictly forbidden! This was not Watkinson's IOC, it was an emergency operating capability and to compound matters the Deputy Chief of the Air Staff was of the opinion that IOC could only be attained if at least six missiles were in service.

After 617 Squadron, 27 and 83 Squadrons eventually became equipped with Blue Steel at Scampton (already the home of 18 Joint Service Trials Unit) on the Vulcan B.2, while two

The two Red Shrimp ECM antennae can be seen on this B.2 as can the wider jetpipes of the uprated Olympus 301 engines.
Via Terry Panopalis

squadrons of Victor B.2, 139 and 100 were so equipped at Wittering. A third Victor B.2 squadron was converted to strategic reconnaissance as the SR.2 rather than completed as a Blue Steel carrier due to delays in the manufacture of the Victor B.2.

Ground crew called Blue Steel 'the Steam Engine', a reference to the decomposition of HTP to steam that drove the turbopumps and the reaction in the combustion chamber prior to the addition of kerosene. To prepare a Blue Steel-armed Vulcan for QRA involved a process that took four hours and once prepared, the fully-fuelled missile could remain at readiness on the aircraft for a week. A fuelled Blue Steel at readiness needed what could only be described as a vigil: constant monitoring of the missile temperature was required to prevent the HTP from undergoing decomposition in the tank. On a flight mission with a fuelled Blue Steel an additional task for the navigator was to monitor and plot the HTP temperature on a graph. If the temperature went outside certain limits, the aircraft was required to land and offload the HTP within forty minutes. The home bases of Blue Steel-equipped squadrons, such as Scampton for the Vulcan and Wittering for the Victor, were equipped with purpose-dug pits for fuel off-load. If this was required the airfield fire trucks and water bowser were required to fill the pit to ensure the HTP was diluted. In the event that the home base was too far away, each aircraft carried a nine-man dinghy to be filled with water from the station fire trucks. This was to be used as an emergency water-bath if a crew member or, more likely, ground-crew had any HTP spilled upon them.

After a week on standby the missile had to be de-fuelled and the HTP tank cleaned and dried thoroughly. Where HTP was concerned, cleanliness was next to Godliness as it reacted with ferrous metals and any dirt in the tanks. Although the shed where the Blue Steels were kept was called the Piggery, the term referred to the fat, white shapes of the missiles in serried ranks rather the state of the place.

Blue Steel's service readiness left a lot to be desired with the greatest cause of poor service-ability being the inertial navigator and the cooling system. On one sortie it took were twelve attempts to clear the fuelled-up round for a flight mission. The inertial platform took forty minutes to 'get going' which was not ideal for a QRA mission when the requirement was for fifteen minutes readiness. The answer was to take off and fly on a fixed heading for forty minutes to allow the inertial platform to stabilise.

Anecdotal evidence suggests that no Blue Steel ever flew with a live warhead although 'Surveillance Warheads'; inert Red Snow warheads that used natural uranium 238 were flown. A surveillance warhead was fitted and the missile fuelled up with a mixture of 20% HTP with a trace of nitric acid as corrosion inhibitor to ensure that the missile had the correct weight and centre of gravity. The Blue Steels with surveillance warheads and their inert fuel were used for crew familiarisation and to monitor how Red Snow reacted under operational conditions. On describing in January 1962, the surveillance round, the Assistant Under Secretary for Air, D A J West reassured the Deputy Chief of the Air Staff that 'The natural uranium used in a surveillance warhead is less toxic than lead.'

Once in the air, there was only a 40% chance that a Blue Steel was viable at the point of launch. If launched successfully, the missile had a 75% chance of reaching the target, so in hard numbers: of thirty six missiles despatched fourteen could be launched of which eleven would reach its target. Missiles that could not launch would be dropped as free-fall bombs. Trials showed that the ideal stand-off distance to launch Blue Steel was 50nm (93km), which was quite apt as Blue Steel had been described as 'the short-ranged weapon' since 1960 when Skybolt had been ordered.

Blue Steel served as the RAF's 'big stick' until QRA ended on 30th June 1969, although 617 Squadron continued to carry Blue Steel into 1970

Expanding the Herd

Of all the criticisms thrown at Avro, and the WRD in particular, by the Air Staff and Ministries was that they spent too much time fiddling with Blue Steel rather getting the basics right. A glance at the list of WRD projects in Appendix A shows how prolific they were; however any company involved in cutting edge military technology must push the boundaries of knowledge to avoid being left behind. The Ministries criticism was especially duplicitous as they would be the first to ask 'Where's our equivalent?' when the Soviets unveiled their latest weapons in Red Square. Another factor was that as weapons became more complex, their development times became longer and this extended period gave the customer plenty of time to change their requirement.

The MK.I* mentioned above was only one of a series of attempts WRD made to interest the Air Staff in improved Blue Steel. A further six models were proposed on a serious basis, with many others drawn up as design exercises. The latter included the Z.63 from January 1960 that featured a reshaped rear fuselage to hold a quartet of rocket boosters and a Stentor small chamber. Despite an increase in launch weight of 420 lb (191kg) from the boosters, the range of the Z.63 was expected to be 168nm (31km). No equivalent information is available for the Z.64 that used a trio of rocket engines. The additional weight of 2,920 lb (1,325kg) over the standard W.100 must have had some impact on range.

Of the more in-depth Blue Steel studies using rocket propulsion (as opposed to the air-breathers of OR.1149 and OR.1159 described in Chapter Five) the aim was to increase range, speed and cruise altitude. Many of these used new engines and exotic fuels, which are examined in Chapter Eight. The first of the serious studies was the Z.74, that became the Mk.I* of July 1960 that replaced the Stentor with a Bristol Siddeley PR.41/1 four-chamber rocket engine rated at 2800–5,400 lbf (12.5-24kN). Further external modifications included a fairing under each wing, a larger wing with 66° sweep and modified rear fuselage. The MK.I* performance was to be improved to cruise at Mach 4 for 500nm (926km) at 90,000ft (27,432m) which was indeed an improvement. This was at the expense of missile weight: 20,400 lb (9,253kg) at launch, due to the greater density of the fuel amongst other things. This came at the price of using a new propellant mix of 95% HTP and unsymmetrical di-methyl hydrazine (UDMH). These were pretty nasty chemicals, even compared with 'normal' HTP at 85% concentration. The Ministries were not happy about using such fluids, as fuels such as UDMH were not widely available in the UK. Nor were they happy that the missiles with the larger wings and modified tanks would need to be built from scratch rather than use the existing airframes.

The next variants from August 1960 were the Z.81, Z.84, Z.85, Z.86, Z.87 and Z88. The

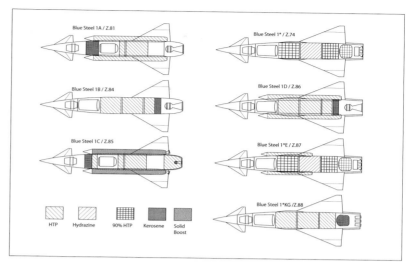

Z.81 was known as the Blue Steel Mk.IA and was even heavier at 21,300 lb (9,662kg) due to the addition of two jettisonable fuel tanks along the fuselage to hold more HTP. This modification could be made to existing Blue Steel Mk.I types and increased range to 245nm (454km). The Z.84 or Blue Steel Mk.IB dispensed with the external tanks and was fitted with a smaller lighter warhead that could be located further forward, allowing the internal tanks to be rearranged and volume increased. This greater fuel volume produced a range of 175nm (324km).

The Z.85 or Mk.IC saw the removal of the Stentor's large boost chamber and replacing the volume saved with new tanks for HTP and Kerosene. Boost power was to be provided by a pair of strap-on solid rockets in the same position as the external tanks on the Mk.IA. By replacing the large chamber with solid boosts the remaining small chamber had the entire propellant volume available and the estimated range was 275nm (509km). From the very start of the project the requirement had stated that external boosts increased the drag on the carrying aircraft and thus reduced its range. Avro

Throughout development of Blue Steel Mk.1, Avro WRD pursued the goal of extending its range with minimal change. These generally involved different boost configurations, new engines and new fuels. The Air Staff became increasingly annoyed by what they saw as distractions.

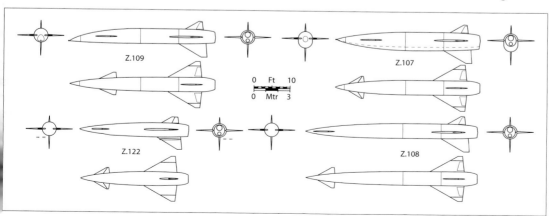

Four proposals for post-Skybolt Blue Steels included stretched versions with longer range such as the Z.108 and Z.109, while the shortened Z.122 was to arm the TSR.2. The Z.107 acquired a ventral pannier for extra fuel.

did not elaborate on how much the aircraft range would be affected by this. Further rearrangement of the internal tanks and the addition of two shorter external tanks produced the Z.86 or Mk.ID. This also sported the enlarged wing and retained the Stentor two-chamber engine to give a range of 395nm (732km) and increased cruise speed to Mach 4.

August 1960 certainly produced a good crop of Blue Steels. The Z.87 or Mk.I*E took the Mk.1* that had been dismissed by the powers that be and swapped the four-chamber PR.41 for a three chamber PR.41 of increased specific impulse and added two external tanks containing HTP. Despite all these changes the range actually *reduced* to 450nm (833km). Oddly enough it appeared that Avro listened to the Ministers et al and drew up the Z.88, Blue Steel Mk.I*KG. This took the Mk.I* and replaced the 90% HTP and UDMH propellants with traditional kerosene/HTP and substituted a three-chamber version of Bristol Siddeley Gamma for the Stentor engine. By October 1960 Avro had merely opted to fit Blue Steel with external tanks, the smaller warhead and internal modifications to the tankage. This they called the Blue Steel Mk.IS.

For the next year or so, no new Blue Steel variants appeared as Avro concentrated on getting the Mk.I to work properly. Yet more Stentor-powered models were drawn up in January 1962. The Z.107 featured a 3ft (0.9m) extension of the fuselage, which was deepened along its entire length to produce a double-bubble cross-section. An RE.179 warhead from Skybolt was fitted in the lower fuselage and with extra tankage, range was 320nm (593km). However it was soon discovered that since the Z.107 cruised at Mach 4, the hoped-for range extension from the new ventral fairing was only 10%, much less than had been expected.

Stretching Blue Steel produced problems of stowage on the Victor and Vulcan as longer missiles fouled the nose undercarriage on the Vulcan and, due to the tilted mounting on Victor would have reduced ground clearance. Z.108 featured a 10ft (3m) fuselage extension and was intended for the Vulcan Phase 6 (see Chapter Six) and while the Z.108 could not be carried by Vulcan, a less radical 3ft (0.9m) stretch could be accommodated but the Z.109 took on a somewhat comical look as it featured a drooped nose to allow stowage in existing Vulcan and Victor mountings. The Z.109 also carried the Skybolt warhead and increased fuel volume to give a range of 500nm (926km) at Mach 4.

The final Blue Steel, W.200 of 1963, saw the weapon's development come full circle: a weapon launched at low-level from a bomber that had penetrated at low-level to avoid Soviet defences. After ten years the systems outlined in OR.324 had arrived. Unfortunately a lot of time, money and angst had been expended.

As the only game in town Blue Steel had to be brought into service. It could have been cancelled at an early stage, but when the Sandys White Paper appeared, its delays were not critical. Watkinson could have taken the radical step of scrapping it but with Skybolt on the stocks and the OR.1149 and OR.1159 cancelled for a number of reasons, the 'jam tomorrow' view of Blue Steel kept it in development. The only conclusion that can be drawn is that Richard Chilver was correct. The British were too cautious. Having mentioned putative replacements for Blue Steel these must also be examined to determine whether any lessons had been learned.

The Steam Engines

Type	Length	Span	Diameter	Weight	Propulsion	Speed	Range
W.1A	28ft	9ft	2.9ft	7,550 lb	Rocket	Mach 2.5	100nm
W.1B	35ft	11ft 7in	3.1ft	9,100 lb	Rocket	Mach 2.5	100nm
W.1C	41ft	20ft	5.2ft	26,400 lb	Rocket	Mach 2.5	100nm
W.1D	46ft	22ft	5.2 x 8ft	32,000 lb	Rocket	Mach 2.5	100nm
4ft Dia. R	36ft	17ft	4ft	14,700 lb	Rocket	Mach 2.5	100nm
4ft Dia. TJ	42ft	21.4ft	4ft	13,900 lb	Turbojet	Mach 2.5	100nm
P.43Z	26ft	9ft	3ft	10,000 lb	Rocket	Mach 2.5	100nm
RASCAL	32ft	16ft 8in	4ft	18,200 lb	Rocket	Mach 1.6	86nm
19/15	14ft 10in	5ft 2in	1ft 7in	1,380 lb	Rocket	Mach 1.8	50nm
48/35	35ft	13ft	4ft	13,000 lb	Rocket	Mach 2.5	110nm
W.100	35ft	13ft	4ft	16,000 lb	Rocket	Mach 2.5	100nm

5 The Long-Range Job

Less than two years after drawing up OR.1132 the Air Staff realised their mistake in the 100nm (185km) range requirement. In response they demanded 1,000nm (1,850km) for OR.1149 but after a further two years they realised that was also unfeasible and issued OR.1159, which was duly cancelled a year later. Throughout all this Avro attempted to bring Blue Steel into service in the face of numerous technical problems and changes. These changes to the operational requirements led to a variety of proposals for a long-range deterrent, only to be snuffed out by a star-struck Air Staff.

By 1955 all the powers involved in the Cold War were aware of the threat posed by a powered bomb with a typical range of 100nm (160km) and had embarked on the development of long-range surface-to-air missiles (SAM) to counter them. The Americans already had such

a weapon in the shape of the IM-99 Bomarc with its 200nm (320km) range to defend their northern airspace. Meanwhile the British continued their Stage Plan with the 150nm (278km) range Blue Envoy to meet Stage 1¾ and the much longer-ranged Green Sparkler Stage 2 SAMs. One concern of the Air Staff was that they were investing in an air defence system for Northern France and Belgium; such was the range of Stage 2. The Soviets, although details were sparse at the time, had a vigorous SAM development programme that led to the S-75 (SA-2 *Guideline*) and the S-200 (SA-5 *Gammon*) with a range of 160nm (296km). All of these weapons were intended to intercept the launch aircraft before the powered bombs could be released.

Long-range SAMs were still very much an unknown quantity in 1955 and their successful development was not a foregone conclusion so a second, more traditional, defence was under development. In the UK fast reaction interceptors such as the Saro SR.177 mixed powerplant fighter and the English Electric P.1B were also intended to counter inbound Soviet missile car-

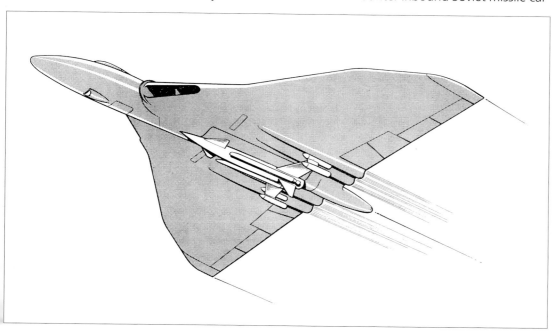

Avro's W.112 Long Range Guided Bomb to OR.1149 carried by a Vulcan B.2. The number of studies that the WRD made under OR.1149 defies belief, all in vain as the range requirement was beyond the state of the art.
BAE Systems/ RAF Museum

riers before they could launch their stores. While the Soviets developed the Sukhoi Su-11 *Fishpot* and Su-15 *Flagon* interceptor, they also opted for long-endurance interceptors such as the Tu-128 *Fiddler* that fulfilled a similar role and filled the gaps in the SAM belts.

The Soviet Union was investing heavily in upgrading its air defences, with a branch of the Soviet armed forces, the *ProvitoVozdushnaya Oborona Strany, (PVO Strany)* dedicated to the defence of the Motherland. NATO intelligence estimates saw no real threat from Soviet SAMs until 1962 so planned accordingly. The events of May Day 1960, that catapulted the U-2 and Gary Powers into the limelight, were to show how the Soviet defences had progressed greatly since RAF Canberras had conducted the Project Robin overflights virtually unmolested in the early 1950s. The V-bombers would have flown into the face of the *PVO Strany's* defences to launch their Blue Steel missiles and would be vulnerable en route to the launch points. The extended range available to the SAM defences also affected the tactical routing that had driven the requirement for Blue Steel's 100nm (160km) range rather than the 75nm (139km) that was considered originally.

The obvious counter to the long-range SAM and interceptors was to go for low-level penetration or increase the range of the stand-off weapons. The former was a non-starter; the experience of OR.324 had shown how difficult this was from scratch, never mind modifying existing types such as the Victor and Vulcan. The trajectory of the Blue Steel also made low-level launch difficult without exposing the carrier aircraft as it climbed to a suitable launch altitude. Great faith was placed in new ECM systems for the Mk.2 V-bombers; however it was observed that on-going electronic intelligence gathering was required and this would be difficult until the RB.156 aircraft was available.

Avro WRD and Handley Page had outlined long-range stand-off weapons for their submissions to OR.1132 but their thoughts on a missile with a range of 500nm (926km) were small beer compared with what the Air Staff and Air Ministry had in mind. The discussions led to what became the Long Range Guided Bomb (LRGB) and this was to be carried by the V-bombers and the RB.156 aircraft. The issue in May 1956 of OR.1149 as a requirement for a 'long-range air-to-surface missile to be carried on the developed V-bomber aircraft and in service in 1962' could be construed as an admission that the original OR.1132 was obsolete. There was also the impending deployment

of the Blue Streak MRBM, scheduled for 1962, with 1965 looking more likely. Unfortunately the RAF's need for a stand-off weapon, indeed a credible deterrent of any description, was such that even one that would be in service for only two years would be a boost. The Directorate of Air Armament went on to outline the basics of the requirement which was very similar to OR.1132 in that a 4,500lb (2,041kg) warhead would be carried at an altitude of 80,000ft (24,384m) and a speed of Mach 3. There were two major differences between the two requirements: the range and trajectory. A USAF study had shown that the cost (in aircraft and crews rather than direct monetary value) of inflicting a measurable amount of damage to a target decreased as the range of the powered bomb increased. This was down to the aircraft spending less time in enemy airspace. The Air Staff found these findings reassuring so opted for a range of 1,000nm (1,852km) with the possibility of the last 100nm (186km) being flown at low altitude. A missile with a range of 1,000nm (1,852km) would allow 90% of the RAF's designated targets to be attacked without the aircraft entering enemy airspace. That range, an order of magnitude greater than Blue Steel, would be a challenge, firstly in achieving the range and secondly, accurate navigation. Added to this wish-list was the need to be immune from interception by fighters up to Mach 2 and 75,000ft (22,860m) or SAMs at Mach 2.5 and 80,000ft (24,384m).

On the subject of accuracy, the Staff pointed out that this was not a great problem as the objectives were '…large targets and the lethal radius large so that errors of a few miles can be tolerated.' The navigation system could take a known azimuth and position before entering enemy territory thus allowing the LRGB to navigate to the target with 'tolerable accuracy'.

Assessing the options, the Air Ministry made comparisons with the unmanned bomber and noted that the LRGB had none of the launch and endurance limitations of the expendable bomber but did preserve the flexibility of the manned bomber. To maximise aerodynamic efficiency of the combination the Ministry considered a purpose-built LRGB carrier but given the timescale involved, the best solution was an LRGB designed to use the existing V-bombers. This made the LRGB/V-bomber option 'doubly attractive' by extending the V-bombers' useful lives.

As for the missile itself, to meet the range and speed requirements a long, thin missile would be most suitable, with a length in the region of 50ft (15.4m). R H Francis at Avro WRD was of the opinion that such a weapon would be possible, but it would be more useful to develop a more advanced stand-off missile with the requisite range and with Mach 5 performance at an altitude of 120,000ft (36,576m). Francis said that this weapon would '…provide a threat of much greater flexibility and more accuracy than the MRBM while providing almost as difficult a problem to the defences' while maintaining a conventional bomber force for alternative tasks.

A missile for the RB.156 supersonic bomber was examined and the ideal shape for carriage at Mach 2.5 was a length/diameter ratio of 15/1 although release of such a weapon would have been problematic. Dorsal carriage with the ability to impart incidence on the missile at launch was recommended to guarantee clean separation by ensuring that lift was in excess of the missile weight. A further interesting observation was that the combination would be somewhat inefficient; underpowered on the outbound leg and overpowered on the return and more so when carrying a LRGB. This could be overcome by using the missile's propulsion system to contribute to the total thrust, although integration of missile and carrier from the start would be the best option. The Directorate of Airborne Armament (DAA) Working Party on OR.1149 began to look at possible configurations for the missile at the end of 1955 and reported its findings on 12th December 1956.

The DAA considered studies from the RAE Armament Department and the Avro WRD.

Three configurations were examined: conventional with wings, tail and fin; canard and narrow delta with wingtip controls and tail fin. Powerplant development was seen as the lynchpin to the range so studies were carried out on two types: the DH Gyron turbojet and the Armstrong Siddeley PR 9/2 rocket. Guidance was to be based around three techniques: inertial, Doppler/inertial with fixed azimuth monitoring and Doppler with astro fix.

The RAE configurations included the S1 with a single, integrated Bristol Olympus turbojet with a half-cone two-shock intake in a conventional wing/tail/fin layout, with the fin fitted ventrally. The S2 followed a similar layout apart from a DH Gyron Junior on each wingtip. The S1 and S2 were 36ft 6in (11.1m) and 36ft (10.9m) in length respectively with wingspans of 25ft (7.6m). The RAE's third configuration, Missile C was a handsome canard delta with a span of 18ft (5.5m) powered by a pair of reheated DH Gyron Juniors installed in the fuselage. Missile C was 50ft 6in (15.4m) in length while the similar Missile B was 46ft (14m), the difference being due to the C model carrying more fuel to allow the Gyron Juniors to run in reheat for the entire flight. These designations were later changed to Missile A through D.

The impression gained from studying the Air Ministry files in the UK National Archives is that only the RAE and Avro were involved in these studies. Interestingly, during a research trip to the North West Heritage Group at Warton the author was shown a series of English Electric

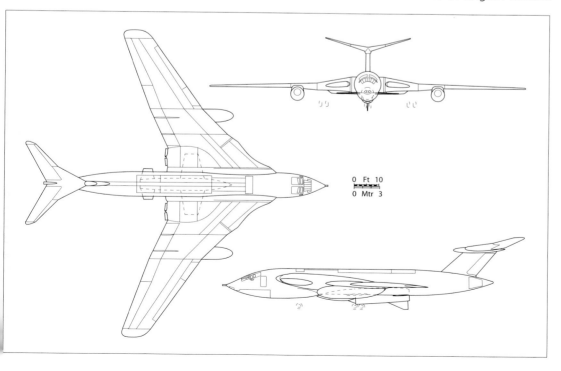

As ever the RAE were involved in the studies towards an OR.1149 missile. This S1 on a Victor also looks suspiciously like one of EECo's proposals.

0 Ft 10
0 Mtr 3

Aviation (EEA) proposals for OR.1149. On making the observation that EEA had used the RAE's configurations for the studies, it was pointed out, in no uncertain terms, that these were original EEA configurations and that the RAE had 'borrowed' them and that they did it all the time! The suggestion that the RAE favoured its former colleagues at Woodford was not made, but could be implied.

Avro's submissions were radically different from the RAE (or were they EEA's?) configurations and featured 'swallow-tail' deltas with the long trailing wingtips forming elevons, the so-called Eggers configuration. The first two proposals were dimensionally identical; 54ft 8in (16.7m) long with a wingspan of 24ft (7.3m), differing only in their powerplant. The W.107 was to be powered by a single reheated DH Gyron Junior turbojet fed by a ventral half-cone, three-shock intake that spoiled the lines of the missile. Avro's W.108 was a much cleaner design powered by an ASM PR.9/2 HTP/Kerosene rocket engine giving the fuselage a half-cone shape surmounted by the delta wing. Use of rocket propulsion allowed a smaller airframe to be used and this was reflected in the W.109, with a length of 43ft (13.1m) and a span of 18ft 8in (5.7m). The trick up the W.109's sleeve was to use a dorsal drop tank to carry additional propellant for its PR.9/2 rocket, producing a winged cone. The propellant in the dorsal tank was used for the launch and acceleration phase, being shed once the fuel had been consumed prior to entering the cruise phase.

The Air Ministry and RAE analysis of these proposals was dismissive of the W.107, concerned that Avro's estimated performance figures were based on a simple half-cone fuselage, ignoring the effect of the engine installation, particularly the intake. They also thought that Avro had not considered the size of the warhead when sizing the fuselage. The planform, while innovative, was seen as being potentially unstable, difficult to control and would require a lot of wind tunnel and free-flight model trials work. To address these concerns Avro WRD drew up a free-flight model called the P.5Z that was boosted in two phases with four Gosling BRMs to boost it off the ground with a fifth Gosling to accelerate the model W.107 to Mach 4.8.

Use of the single Gyron Junior was considered unwise as the single engine had insufficient thrust for the initial phase of the trajectory producing slow acceleration to the Mach 3 cruise speed and that this would impact on the range of the missile. Avro countered by suggesting that two Gamma rockets be fitted, thus reducing the acceleration time to Mach 3. The Gyron Junior was an unknown quantity at the high altitudes and Mach Numbers that the LRGB would operate at so the Ministry suggested a test vehicle based on Blue Steel. On the operational missile the turbojet would operate in reheat until the cruise was established and then only operate as required to maintain the required cruise Mach Number.

The RAE reserved its greatest criticism for the intake on the W.107 and was of the opinion that the fixed three-shock intake would be less stable than the two-shock intake on the RAE's S1. Intake instability was a severe problem with such fixed-geometry intakes as the intake could choke, causing the engine to flameout. This was a particular problem under yawed flight when the airflow was off the axis of the

Missile D – whatever its provenance, it was a handsome vehicle that shared is configuration with the North American Navaho. BAE Systems/ North West Heritage Group

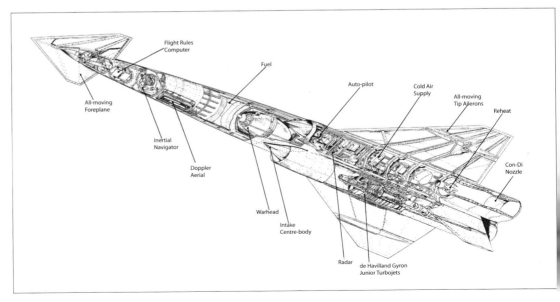

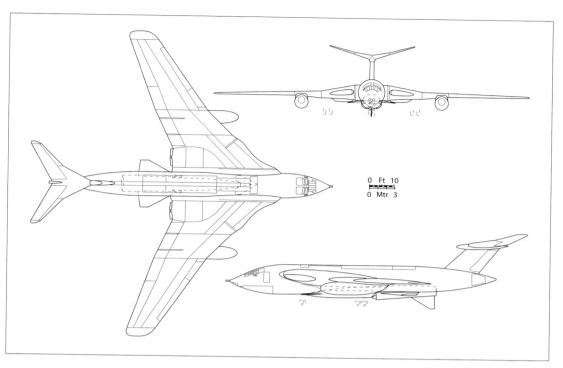

Missile D was undoubtedly too large to be carried by the Victor. The shorter Missile C may have been a possibility.

intake. The Ministry's scepticism was well founded as a turbojet that was required to operate from Mach 0.8 to 3+ would need a variable geometry intake.

W.108 and W.109 were to be powered by the same Armstrong Siddeley PR.9/2 rocket as the W.100 Blue Steel; however the Air Ministry were of the opinion that the range would be a problem for the rocket despite its shortened flight time at Mach 5. This was a particular problem with the 4,500 lb (2,045 kg) Green Bamboo warhead, although meeting the range requirement was just possible when carrying the 2,500 lb (1,134 kg) Orange Herald warhead. To carry the heavy warhead for the 1,000 nm

(1,852 km) specified in OR.1149 required a turbojet. The Air Ministry were also critical of Avro's W.107/8/9 series as they appeared to have designed their missiles around the smaller, lighter warhead rather than the more likely result of thermonuclear research, Green Bamboo.

Despite all this the Ministry and Air Staff were keen on Avro's missile: '...a missile with performance better than the OR.330 aircraft, in service before it, and capable of higher speed development is worth having.' A change of powerplant was considered, with the Armstrong Siddeley P.170 turborocket, under development to meet specification TE 10/56, suggested as a replacement for the Gyron Jun-

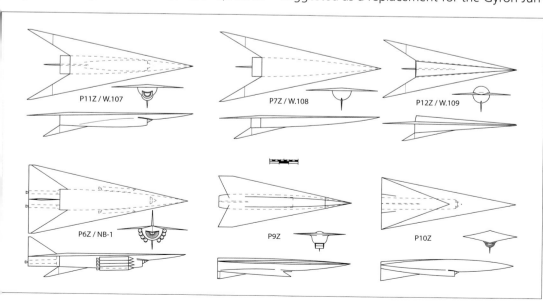

Avro's WRD proposed a variety of delta-winged missiles to meet OR.1149, including the surface-launched NB -1 with internal and external solid boosts. The entire upper fuselage of the W.109 formed a drop tank. The P10Z with its compound curves would have taken too long to build.

Navaho on its liquid-fuelled booster awaits launch. Ramjet powered, the Navaho and its X-10 demonstrator were rendered obsolete by the ballistic missile. *USAF*

Missiles C and D differed in their operation, with the D model intended to operate with the engines in reheat for the entire flight. How accurate the rugby-ball shape of the warhead was in this hypothetical cutaway is not known. *BAE Systems*

iors. Turborockets use small rocket engines to drive turbines in a basic turbojet which on attaining adequate forward speed, converts to a ramjet. This allows the engine to operate, unlike a ramjet, from a standstill to high Mach Numbers, unlike a turbojet. With this engine change the Ministry were of the opinion that even with high-calorific value (zip) fuels, the maximum range would be in the region of 700nm (1,296km).

Astute readers may have recognised the layout of the RAE, or EEA, Missile B and C as not dissimilar to the North American SM-64 Navaho

that had its origins as an American 'winged V-2' in 1946. By 1956 the subscale X-10 canard delta test vehicle had been flying, powered by a pair of Westinghouse J-40 reheated turbojets, and had proved the configuration. Unfortunately the full-scale, rocket-boosted, ramjet-propelled XM-64 never flew, having been superseded by ICBMs and cancelled in 1958.

Borrowing the configuration allowed the RAE (or EEA) to save time and money by using a proven design, albeit much larger than the intended LRGB. The Air Ministry commented that 'A good deal is already known about this form of layout' whereas the Avro deltas were an unknown quantity. On the other hand the Ministry liked the idea of the W.109 with its drop tank, but were concerned that only dorsal carriage would be possible.

...and the Old Guard?

English Electric Aviation has been mentioned previously in this search for the LRGB. EEA were very much newcomers to the aircraft design and construction business, some thirty years behind the Old Guard of British Aviation. Of course when it came to the new field of guided weapons, it was a level playing field, with a possible advantage lying with those firms with experience of electronics, such as Vickers Supermarine and English Electric or advanced aerodynamics such as Handley Page. As noted in the story of the W.100 Blue Steel, there was some puzzlement as to why Avro landed such a prestigious guided weapon contract with absolutely no experience in the field. When it came to OR.1149, Handley Page and English Electric were back in the fray and each was determined to succeed.

Vickers had been stung by the criticism levelled at them over the Blue Boar affair and, to use a colloquialism, threw bodies at their LRGB project. They were able to do this after manpower, including the design team, was freed up by the cancellation of the Red Rapier flying bomb. Vickers proposed a missile called the Type 569 powered by a pair of turborockets mounted at the tips of a very low aspect-ratio trapezoidal wing. Parametric studies soon showed that the turborocket suffered high specific fuel consumption for little or no improvement in performance over turbojets particularly in the acceleration and climb phase. Strapping on solid rocket motors improved the performance of the overall vehicle, particularly in the boost phase, but the fuel consumption eroded the range figures.

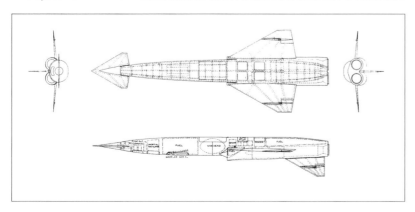

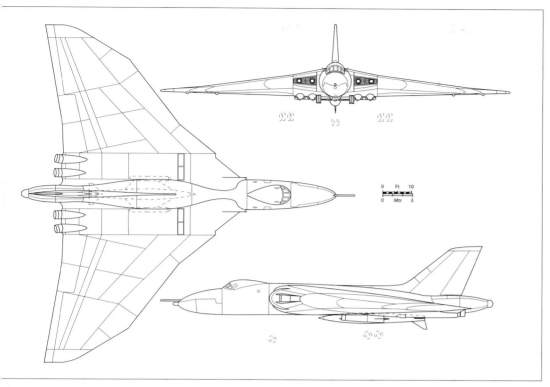

0 Ft 10
0 Mtr 3

Vickers' type 569 was dismissed from the OR.1149 tendering process at an early stage due to its effect on the carrying aircraft's centre of gravity. Vickers proposed fuelling the missile from the aircraft's tanks after take-off. The Air Staff were unimpressed.

Bristol Engines, the leading exponents of ramjets in Europe, were contracted by Vickers to examine ramjet propulsion for the Type 569 and called their study RP.4. Again the calculations showed that the 30in (76cm) BRJ.1000 ramjet offered little advantage over the turbo-rockets so faced with these results, Vickers fitted four Rolls-Royce RB.93 Soar turbojets.

The Type 569's woes were not at an end with the engine selection. The configuration of the Type 569 should have made installation in the V-bombers a simple enough practice. Unfortunately the missile with its heavy turbojets affected the centre of gravity of the carrier when it was loaded in the fully fuelled-up condition. Vickers suggestion that the 569 be loaded empty and filled with fuel in flight from the aircraft fuel tanks was dismissed by the Air Staff and Ministry. Both thought the idea of using the aircraft fuel load to fill up the missile after take-off, thus reducing the aircraft range, was laughable. Another factor against the Type 569 was its cruise speed of Mach 2.7, a limit imposed by the missiles light-alloy construction.

For OR.1132 Handley Page had proposed a missile with ramjet propulsion and its initial boost phase powered by solid rocket motors, providing a range of 500nm (926km). This had been dismissed by the Air Staff and Air Ministry as too far for the inertial navigator to operate accurately, so when the Staff issued OR.1149, HP could be forgiven a touch of smugness.

Bristol Engines became involved in stand-off weapons through Handley Page with a study called RP.6 (Ramjet Project 6) that was examining the possibility of fitting a 40in (101.6cm) ramjet in a missile that was described by T V Somerville of the RAE as having a '…most unusual shape for a supersonic aircraft.' – The HP.106M. This was indeed an understatement that described a missile that was stubby and fat, possibly as close to a winged brick as missiles come, but designed to carry as much fuel as possible.

For OR.1149 HP dispensed with the ramjets and opted for the reheated Gyron Junior in the

Handley Page's HP.106M was the only submission to OR.1149 that came close to meeting the 1,000nm range requirement. It achieved this through use of diesel fuel with a higher density than kerosene. Later long-range weapons would use high-density fuels such as Shelldyne to increase range. *Handley Page Association*

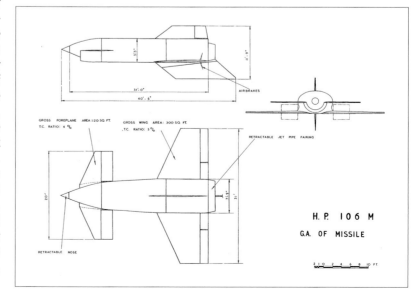

GROSS FOREPLANE AREA:120 SQ. FT.
T.C. RATIO: 4 %

GROSS WING AREA: 300 SQ. FT.
T.C. RATIO: 5 %

AIRBRAKES

RETRACTABLE JET PIPE FAIRING

RETRACTABLE NOSE

H. P. 106 M

G.A. OF MISSILE

HP.106M. With an overall length of 40ft 6in (12.3m), a wingspan of 31ft (9.4m) and a canard with a 20ft (6.1m) span. The wing and foreplane shared a similar shape with a swept leading and straight trailing edge with the foreplane having an area 40% that of the wing. The wing trailing edge featured ailerons in the outboard two-thirds and the inboard third a split trailing edge that opened to form airbrakes for the bunt into the terminal dive. The foreplanes were fixed and carried elevators across their span, the canard being adopted for the usual reason of maintaining an uncluttered warhead bay.

The overall length of the HP.106M was 40ft 6in (12.3m) which precluded storage in the weapons bay of the Victor or the Vulcan; the HP.106M did have a retractable nosecone and jet pipe fairing that allowed it fit into the bomb bay. HP ignored the RAE's thinking on the shape of the missile and produced a fuselage with a length:diameter ratio of 4.5:1. This had an oval cross section with the wing mounted flush with the undersurface, a stubby trapezoidal dorsal fin also carried the rudder while a very large folding highly-swept ventral fin completed the aerodynamic surfaces.

The fuselage held two reheated Gyron Juniors fed by an intake that wrapped around the lower nose, giving the impression of a smile. Prior to launch the intake was closed off by a series of flaps that prevented drag caused by the windmilling of turbomachinery. The unsatisfactory performance of the Gyron Junior in general prompted a major change in the HP.106M propulsion system. The Rolls-Royce RB.93 was an odd selection for a high-performance missile: rated at 1,375 lbf (6.1kN) without reheat to replace the Gyron Junior rated at 8,000 lbf (35.6kN). How could a puny disposable turbojet designed for use on sub-sonic flying bombs like Red Rapier cut the mustard at Mach 3? Each Gyron Junior was replaced by no fewer than four Soars, set in two-by-two block upstream of a very large reheat section in the rear fuselage. Such installations had been all the rage for the OR.330 supersonic bomber studies, mainly because 'big' supersonic turbojets such as the Gyron were proving difficult to develop.

One innovation employed by Handley Page was the use of diesel fuel to meet the 1,000nm (1,852km) range requirement. Gas turbines generally run on kerosene, such as Jet A which has a density of 0.775g/cc and a heating value of 42.8MegaJoules per kilogram. Diesel on the other hand has a density of 0.832g/cc and a heating value 43.1Megajoules per kilogram. This means, in very rough terms, that for a given volume, diesel can supply 7% more energy than kerosene which in turn could provide up to 7% extra endurance. Another factor in choosing diesel was its higher boiling point meaning that there was less loss from evaporation at the high temperatures encountered in the cruise. For a missile that is required to fly for 1,000nm (1,852km) that 70nm (130km) made the differ

The short, stubby HP.106M was ideal for the Victor and when the nosecone and jet pipes were retracted, fitted nicely in the Victor's bomb bay. It made maximum use of available volume and despite its configuration, had a good turn of speed. A similar Avro WRD study was drawn up, possibly out of mere curiosity. *Handley Page Association*

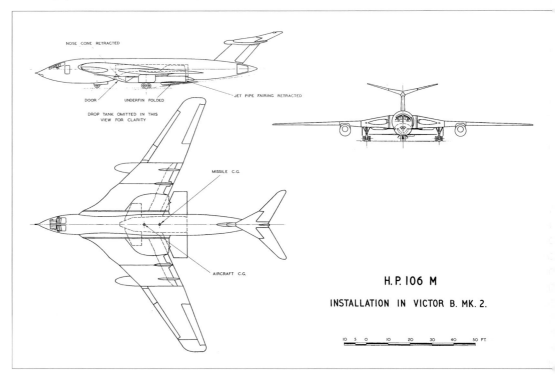

H.P. 106 M

INSTALLATION IN VICTOR B. MK. 2.

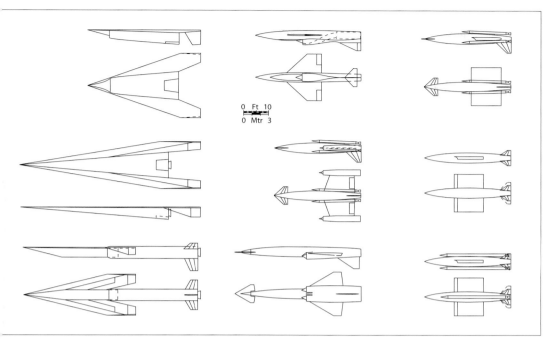

0 Ft 10
0 Mtr 3

Although Avro produced many design studies for OR.1149, EECo's efforts were almost as varied. Note the inclusion of a missile very similar to the RAE's Missile D. Unfortunately no detail on these studies has been found. *Redrawn from BAE Systems/ North West Heritage Group document*

ence between success and failure in meeting the requirement. The HP.106M could be carried with no great penalty by the Victor and Vulcan, with aerodynamic fairings fore and aft. Unsurprisingly it was a better fit in the more capacious bomb bay of the Victor producing an installation with less drag than that of the Vulcan.

Meanwhile in Warton, English Electric Aviation's project office was examining the Long Range Guided Bomb and although little information on the work is available, it appears that EEA produced nine configurations to meet OR.1149. The most striking was the twin-Gyron Junior canard delta that the RAE called Missile B and C (or C and D, depending on whether you read Air Staff or Air Ministry documentation). EEA also looked at using a turborocket, fitted in the tail of a missile with a tailed-delta configuration and fed by a ventral half-cone intake. A couple of Eggers configuration rocket-propelled deltas were proposed, one of which was boosted by a very large tandem boost motor.

Another design mentioned, but not illustrated, was to be powered by an integrated ramjet and it was described as having a tail with 'emciform' controls. This integrated ramjet project did show up another advantage of the canard configuration as it was found that the noise from the ramjets caused excessive vibration in tail surfaces. The other interesting feature of this design was that just before entering its terminal dive, the wings were jettisoned and the body behaved like a ballistic bomb, thus reducing 'the vulnerability of the missile during the most valuable phase of its flight.'

This integrated project was scrapped as the disposable wings were deemed too complicated so a new Eggers configuration with an integrated ramjet based on recent NACA work was drawn up. This missile was to weigh in at 24,000 lb (10,884kg) and the EEA document states that 'This missile would fly at Mach 4 at an altitude of 600,000ft and has an aerodynamic efficiency 4% greater than that of the missile project submitted in this brochure.' It is worth quoting this sentence in full as the stated altitude of 600,000ft (182,880m) must be taken with a pinch of salt and the project mentioned is presumably the P.10D, which is described below.

The unnamed vehicle was particularly interesting as it follows a similar configuration as the Avro WRD W.107/8/9 series, with wing atop the fuselage that carried the integrated ramjet, with a multi-shock half-cone intake forming the apex of the delta wing/fuselage. Interestingly rather than carrying a single folding fin under the fuselage, EEA fitted twin vertical stabilisers under the wingtips of these missiles. This did not help with carriage on the V-bombers: 'Its shape is not compatible with this requirement and a design of this type would only be installed pick-a-pack (sic) style.' and like the similar designs from Avro would need dorsal carriage.

Only one of the EEA missile studies used ramjets, fitted in pods at the end of each stubby wing, but it was the use of the Napier/EEA split-wing ramjet that set EEA's proposals for OR.1149 apart. This had been developed for the P.10 Mach 3 aircraft to

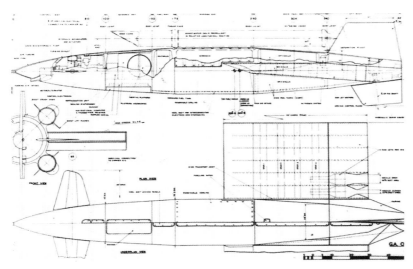

This drawing of EECo's P.10D shows the split-wing ramjet wing with six combustors. P.10D was not a Blue Steel with a split wing, although Avro did explore the option. *BAE Systems/ North West Heritage Group*

The utilitarian lines of RAE's Controlled Weapons Section proposal for OR.1149. It avoided the complex three-dimensional curves that posed such a problem during Blue Steel manufacture. *BAE Systems/ North West Heritage Group*

meet OR.330/R.156. Despite losing out to the Avro 730, EEA had continued development of the P.10 as a possible bomber, 'covert reconnaissance aircraft' and fighter, with the RAE interested enough to consider it as a research aircraft. The split-wing ramjet is described Chapter Two, and being optimised for efficient flight at Mach 3, was an obvious choice for the LRGB. EEA took a cigar-shaped fuselage, sized to accommodate the Green Bamboo warhead, and fitted it with a split-wing ramjet comprising five combustors. Two of the studies used rear-mounted cruciform control surfaces that folded flat for stowage, while a third was fitted with the usual canard foreplane plus a ventral fin and rudder. The canard design was boosted by three solid boosters, indexed around the fuselage, while the cruciform tail types could be boosted by a pair of external boosts or a single internal rocket boost, possibly an HTP/Kerosene engine. The canard was indeed a superior design not only for the usual reasons but also the elimination of noise-induced fatigue in the tail.

These split wing studies led to an EEA design for LRGB called P.10D that EEA tendered for OR.1149. On submission of the tender, Gerrie Willox, Senior Engineer of EEA's Project Office had a meeting with the RAE Controlled Weapons Section at Farnborough. This meeting proved more insightful to EEA than it did to the RAE, mainly because Mr J S Elliott, the RAE engineer with overall responsibility for OR.1149 designs, was not present due to illness.

On presenting the P.10D design the RAE engineers admitted that they were impressed with the P.10D and '...thought we had something with the integrated ramjet wing.' Despite this the RAE delegation voiced concern about flow separation due to the angles of the divergent nozzle and Willox agreed that this would be looked into. Discussions then turned to the RAE's Missile D whose design, as noted above, EEA may have had a hand in. Willox was of the opinion that the RAE had '...neglected pre-entry drag' in the design; however it was indicated that the thrust levels used for calculating the missile's performance had not been net thrust (thrust available after engine/intake drag taken into account) but stub thrust (calculated thrust from engine). Willox was also concerned that the RAE's choice of intake was '...quite impracticable and that if they were worried about flow breakaway in the exhaust nozzles of P.10D then they ought to be more worried about flow breakaway in the subsonic diffusers of Missile D.'

The discussions then turned to the RAE Controlled Weapons Section's work on an integrated ramjet missile. The design that the RAE were considering has the appearance of a finned box with a wedge at the front; its angular lines could have come direct from the fabrication department of a Chris Wren cartoon and made Avro WRD's P.36Z, the utility Blue Steel, look sleek.

As the meeting progressed it became clear that the RAE were dabbling in many studies for OR.1149, including a rocket-boosted glide missile with a range of 700nm (1,296km). Willox queried the figures, particularly the weight ratio, but '...got a very evasive reply which did not answer his question.' and the impression gained was that the RAE were a bit wide of the mark. Perhaps Willox's impression would have been better had Mr Elliott been at work that day. On his return to Warton, Gerrie Willox reported to Ollie Heath and Ray Creasey that 'The Controlled Weapons Section agreed that our P.10D was a very good design and they definitely thought that we had something with the integrated ramjet wing.'

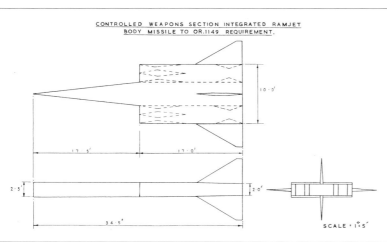

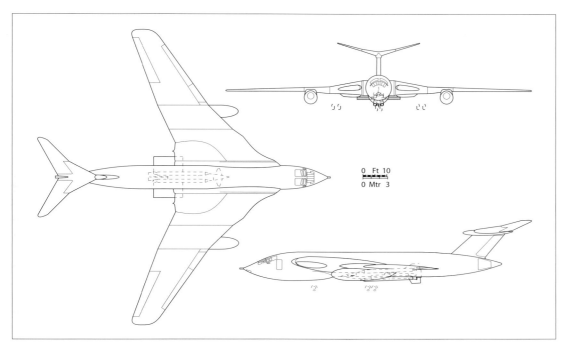

The EECo P.10D fitted easily into the capacious bomb bay of the Victor. The drag induced by the boosters and the split wing ramjet may have been considered excessive despite the P.10D possessing adequate range.

At first glance the P.10D looked pretty much a Blue Steel with the English Electric split wing ramjet but it was a completely different design. Although Avro had considered fitting Blue Steel with the EEA propulsion system, that was about as far as it went as Avro preferred the proven podded ramjets from Bristol Siddeley.

The P.10D was derived from the trio of studies described above and employed six, rather than the original five, combustors within the low-aspect ratio rectangular wing in a canard configuration. The foreplanes were fairly small in comparison with Blue Steel, with straight taper and cut-back Mach tips. A fixed dorsal fin provided directional stability while directional control was provided by an all-moving ventral fin and the foreplanes. To boost the P.10D from its Mach 0.8 launch speed to the Mach 1.2 light-up speed of the ramjet required a quartet of boost rocket motors indexed around the fuselage. Acceleration continued on ramjet and boosters until Mach 1.5 at which point full ramjet thrust was available to propel the P.10D to the 1,000nm demanded by the requirement at an altitude in excess of 80,000ft (24,384m) and a speed of Mach 4. How the low altitude portion of the trajectory was to be achieved was not outlined.

EEA also proposed a much longer range version of the P.10D that could have achieved 2,000nm (3,704km) by scaling up the missile. At 43ft (13.1m) and with a diameter of 52in (132cm) the missile possessed an improved fineness ratio that increased its aerodynamic efficiency by 23%. The ramjets had longer com-

bustion chambers, 5ft (1.5m) versus 3ft (0.9m) that improved their performance by allowing light-up at Mach 0.84 and full thrust at Mach 1.25 which permitted lighter boost motors to be used.

So, why was the P.10D so favoured for OR.1149 by the RAE? It essentially met the requirement and could be installed in the Victor and Vulcan with minimal modifications to the aircraft. What more could be desired? The Air Ministry was by 1957 taking a jaundiced view of any guided weapon development timetables submitted by the companies and were particularly sceptical of the timescales that Warton were quoting for in-service dates. The integrated ramjet wing was untested and could be fraught with delays, so given the urgent need to update the Blue Steel, the ministry returned to its maker for the replacement.

P10D was to be mounted semi-recessed on telescopic pylons within the V-bomber's bomb bay. For launch, the pylons would have extended to lower the missile clear of the aircraft before release. *BAE Systems/North West Heritage Group*

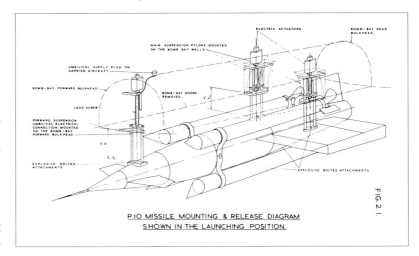

P.10 MISSILE MOUNTING & RELEASE DIAGRAM
SHOWN IN THE LAUNCHING POSITION.

FIG 2.1

Woodford's WRD Studies

Given the size of their investment made in the WRD, Avro's studies for OR.1149 certainly reflect that outlay in their number and variety. These ranged from a Blue Steel fitted with a ventral turbojet to blended wing/fuselage all-delta designs. In addition to the W.107/8/9 Eggers deltas, WRD investigated other delta planform missiles that addressed the Air Staff and Air Ministry criticism about the size of the fuselage and the integrated propulsion systems.

The ultimate aim was, of course, to meet the OR.1149 requirement and that 1,000nm (1,852km) range was the main problem. Rockets, be they solid- or liquid-fuelled, could not compete with the turbojet when it came to range, but as already noted, the rocket provided superior acceleration to cruise speed. To achieve the best of both worlds, a mix of gas turbine and rocket engine was seen as the best option.

Described as a 'turbine-powered version of Blue Steel' the P.22Z was powered by a pair of Rolls-Royce RB.121 turbojets and a DH Spectre rocket engine, all installed in a new rear fuselage. The RB.121's intakes were semi-circular with boundary layer splitters and half-cone centre-bodies and were placed halfway along the fuselage, low on the flanks to maximise efficiency at high incidence in the boost phase. All the P.22Z's aerodynamic surfaces were from the Blue Steel, which would have simplified conversion of existing missiles if required.

Another turbojet-powered Blue Steel was the even simpler P.21Z with the entire Blue Steel forward of the engine bay tacked onto new propulsion and propellant bay in a new, wider rear fuselage. This carried four Rolls-Royce Soar turbojets and two DH Spectre rocket engines, with the Soars fed by an intake that wrapped around each side of the fuselage, making the P.21Z a very handsome machine. Aimed at reducing the amount of modifications to the basic Blue Steel, the P.19Z took Blue Steel and added a single reheated DH Gyron Junior in a nacelle faired-in under the rear fuselage. The bay that previously held the Stentor engine was fitted out with three Gamma rocket engines.

Before submitting the W.107/8/9 Eggers deltas, Avro drew up in April 1956 five conventional, straight trailing edge, delta-planform missiles; P.17Z to P.13Z. Two of these, P.17Z and P.15Z were powered by integrated turbojets fed by ventral two-dimensional wedge intakes. The Bristol BE.38, rated at 5,590lbf (24.9kN), and DH Gyron Junior powered the P.17Z and P.13Z respectively. Additional boost was provided by three Armstrong Siddeley Gamma rocket engines in the P.17Z while the boost for the P.15Z was provided by a DH Spectre rocket engine. The BE.38 is an interesting turbojet as it was an all-steel derivative of the Bristol Orpheus that was designed for supersonic performance and intended to power high-speed aircraft such as the Vickers Swallow variable geometry research aircraft.

The P.16Z, P.14Z and P.13Z all shared the same basic configuration: a mid-mounted delta with cruise powerplant fitted in wingtip nacelles. The P.16Z was powered by a pair of Bristol BE.38 turbojet and three Gamma rockets in the rear fuselage. The P.14Z saw the BE.38s replaced by Rolls-Royce Soar turbojets while the P.13Z opted for ramjets.

WRD looked at a different form of delta in July 1956 and drew up a design called P.10Z

Yet more Avro WRD OR.1149 studies. Avro recognised that the delta was an ideal planform for a long-range missile, combining stability at supersonic speed with robust structure. The P18Z was intended for carriage and launch from the Avro supersonic bomber.

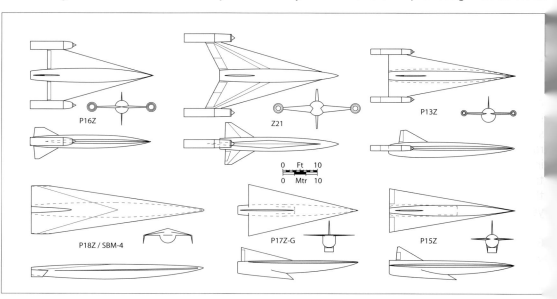

using what was called a Newby delta, a pure 75° delta wing, blended into the fuselage that held the usual Blue Steel equipment. Again the rear fuselage held a DH Gyron Junior and two Gamma rocket engines, the turbojet being fed by a ventral semi-circular intake with half-cone centre-body. Viewed from front or rear, the blended Newby delta looked like a flat diamond with concave edges. Avro's comment on this study was that the configuration was 'Discontinued because of a lack of high-speed experimental data.' Another more practical reason for it being discontinued was without doubt its complex shape and attendant manufacturing costs. Avro had learned something from Blue Steel.

Avro's WRD was not only interested in innovative wing shapes and engine installations. Into this mix WRD added reaction control systems as alternatives to the ailerons and spoilers of aerodynamic controls. The P.9Z was drawn up in May 1956 and was powered by the usual OR.1149 mix of DH Gyron Junior and two Gamma rockets. The arrowhead delta wing was blended into the top of the fuselage with the two-dimensional scoop intake underneath. What sets the P.9Z apart was its lack of conventional flight controls other than a ventral fin and rudder. Rather than using a canard configuration for pitch control, vertical movement of the hinged nose and the forward portions of the delta wing was to replace the usual foreplanes. Roll control was by directing air from the engine compressor through ducts to nozzles on the wingtips. When a manoeuvre was commanded by the autopilot, the high-pressure air was ducted to the relevant nozzle on the wingtip to roll the aircraft. Such a control system is now used for low-speed manoeuvring by BAe Harrier STOVL fighter and, of course, for the reaction controls on spacecraft.

Back to the business in hand

These diversions into unconventional planforms and controls probably added to the Air Ministry's suspicions that Avro and its WRD were spending too much time on project studies rather than working on the business of producing a viable deterrent. By November 1956 a new train of thought was running through WRD and the task of meeting OR.1149 was resumed with yet another LRGB study.

Looking like a cross between the W.100 Blue Steel and the W.107, P.8Z utilised the forward section and wings of Blue Steel married to a deeper rear fuselage that housed the usual powerplants with a ventral half-cone intake à la

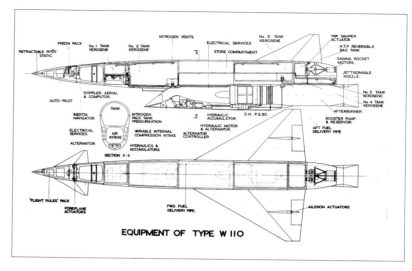

EQUIPMENT OF TYPE W 110

W.107. The P8Z was much larger than the standard Blue Steel, 45ft (13.7m) long and weighing in at 20,000 lb (9,070kg) with the larger fuselage carrying enough fuel for a range of 1,500nm (2,778km) at a speed of Mach 3 and altitude of 80,000ft (24,384m). One odd aspect of the P.8Z, given the need to install it in a V-bomber bomb bay was a tall dorsal fin and the lack of a ventral fin, which was surprising given the earlier statements regarding its importance at high incidence.

By June 1957 having spent 1956 looking in all sorts of directions and quite possibly annoying the Air Ministry at a time when the Blue Steel was making little progress, Avro's WRD had firmed up their OR.1149 submissions. Three designs were taken further, aiming to meet the LRGB requirement.

The first of this trio was the P.8Z modified to produce the Z.1, also known as the W.110. This application of a W designation shows how serious Avro were about the W.110, not a flight of fancy with reaction controls or blended airframe but a serviceable weapon.

By tacking a new rear fuselage and larger wing onto a Blue Steel forebody, WRD sought to produce a missile that could meet OR.1149. For a change Avro outlined how they would do so: two Gamma rocket engines for the boost and climb to a cruise altitude of 70,000ft, where the Gyron Junior took over, running in reheat for the duration. At a point 100nm (185km) from the target the W.110 jettisoned its reheat convergent/divergent nozzle and descended to low-altitude, as little as 500ft (152.4m), for the final 50nm (93km) low-level run in to the target under dry power, controlled by a radar altimeter. At the end of the low-altitude run it was to climb to a suitable altitude for the Green Bamboo warhead to air burst.

Avro's W.110 was a promising study for OR.1149 that used the DH Gyron supersonic turbojet with reheat for the cruise. On descending to low level for the final stage of the trajectory, the divergent section of the con/di nozzle was jettisoned. *BAE Systems/ RAF Museum*

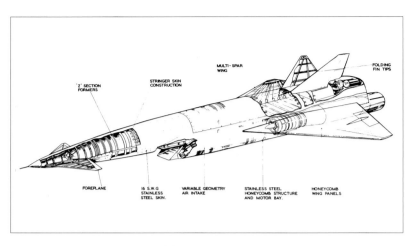

Cutaway drawing of the W.110 to OR.1149. When the promising W.110 study was under way, the Air Staff instructed WRD to produce a minimum-change Blue Steel powered by turbojets. *BAE Systems/ RAF Museum*

If fitted with a Short Granite warhead the W.110 could reach a range of 810nm (1,500km); however if the Green Bamboo warhead was installed it reduced range by 90nm (167km) due to the larger size of the warhead bay taking up fuel space.

To accommodate the disparate performance envelopes of high-speed/high-altitude and low-altitude/high-speed the W.110 was fitted with a variable three-shock intake that could alter its capture area to match the speed/height conditions. To test the turbojet propulsion system including the intake and disposable reheat system, WRD proposed building the Z.15, a reusable test vehicle with wheeled undercarriage that could be air-launched from a Vulcan.

With a length of 45ft (13.7m) the W.110 sported a larger 60° delta wing with a 19ft (6.8m) span with anhedral from root to tip. Another change from the P.8Z was the replacement of the single tall dorsal fin by a pair of

canted fins whose top third folded inwards for stowage in the bomb bay. Stowage was the main problem with the W.110; the length and the depth of its fuselage made installation on the Victor a problem. A further difficulty was that the thirsty Gyron Junior reduced the range of the missile to around 700nm (1,296km), something Avro addressed by adding underwing fuel tanks. The Air Staff were unimpressed; the OR.1149 weapon had to be carried by both Victor and Vulcan, while the use of external tanks and their attendant drag affected the performance of both carrier and missile adversely.

The next proposal was the W.111, based on the Z.12 study which was itself derived from the P.13Z, which took a more or less unaltered 48/35 fuselage complete with the large dorsal fin and ASM Stentor engine to boost the missile to Mach 2. The Blue Steel foreplanes and wings were replaced by a 7% thickness arrowhead delta wing that held the fuel for the wingtip-mounted Bristol BRJ.1000 32in (81.3cm) ramjets that lit up at Mach 2 and continued the acceleration to the cruise speed of Mach 3.5. The propulsion system for the Z.12 was developed by Bristol Engines as RP.2 to ensure that engine and airframe were matched. With ramjet power the W.111 exceeded the range requirement at 1,100nm (2,037km) and by using the 48/35 fuselage and with a span between the ramjet axes of 21ft 8in (6.6m) could be carried without problem in the Victor and Vulcan. An alternative study that used a pair of Rolls-Royce turbojets was the Z.19, but no details of this have been found.

The number of design studies carried out by Avro had variations on the turbojet-powered theme. This wide range of projects is particularly surprising when the selected design turned out to be a re-engined Blue Steel with a new wing, the W.112.

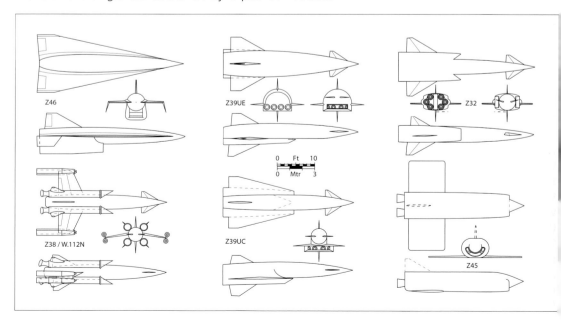

An extended-range version of the W.111 was the Z.21, scaled up by 33% to produce a range of 1,500nm (2,778km). Unfortunately the 45ft (13.7m) long fuselage and 27ft 10in (8.4m) span between the ramjet axes would have made the Z.21 difficult to install on the V-bombers without much modification of the aircraft. The ramjet in this study may have been the engine being examined by Bristol as the RP.6, a 40in (101.6cm) diameter ramjet that was also suggested for the HP.106M.

Neither the W.110 nor W.111 would be available before 1962 (probably 1964 in reality) and combined with the need to develop the missile and modify the V-bombers to carry them, prompted Avro to look at extending the range of the standard Blue Steel with as few changes as possible. Out of this grew the W.112.

Blue Steel Phase Two

W.110 and W.111 were radical but ambitious designs that would require far too much effort to develop and put into service in the required time frame. To address these factors, Avro WRD proposed the W.112, a minimum-change Blue Steel W.100 that used turbojet or ramjet power, external solid rocket boosters and a revised Doppler/inertial guidance system. Being a minimal-change Blue Steel, this weapon would fit in the existing V-bombers and the only snag was that its range would be around 700nm (1,296km), better than Blue Steel, but 30% less than the OR.1149 requirement demanded.

The evolution of the W.112 can be traced back to May 1957 and the Z.4 study for a long-range ramjet missile, a Blue Steel fuselage with twin canted fins powered by four 23in (58.4cm) Bristol BRJ.1300 ramjets on the wingtips and boosted to ramjet light-up speed by a pair of DH Spectre rocket engines in jettisonable pods. This was a very complex propulsion system and was soon discarded.

This led to the Z.16, the first study to which the W.112 designation was applied and the first named as Blue Steel Phase 2. Again the W.100 fuselage was used, minus the Stentor engine, with its space taken up by a Doppler navigation system and extra fuel. The twin canted fins from the Z.4 were retained but a new straight wing with a span between engine axes of 18ft 4in (5.6m) and root-to-tip anhedral was fitted to the existing Blue Steel wing root attachment points. These new wings carried an engine nacelle on each tip that held a pair of stacked Rolls-Royce RB.93/4 Soar turbojets. A pair of Gosling 10in (25.4cm) diameter boost rocket

motors (as used on the Bloodhound SAM) were fitted under the fuselage and were jettisoned when a speed of Mach 1.3 was attained, with the four Soars continuing the acceleration to Mach 3 to give a range of 635nm (1,176km).

By replacing the Soar turbojets with a quartet of Bristol BRJ.851 19in (48.2cm) ramjets on the Z.20 the range of the W.112 was increased to 730nm (1,352km). The extra inch of diameter over the BRJ.824 was to improve the cooling of the ramjet and increase its performance, something that was also helped by the use of higher power Raven 17in (43.2cm) boosts that were retained until Mach 2 was achieved. The other reason for the bigger boosts was that ramjets were tailored to a speed range of Mach 2 to 3 and would not produce maximum thrust before Mach 2 was reached. This lack of thrust below Mach 2 forced a somewhat radical trajectory on the Z.20: a dive from the launch altitude powered by the Ravens until Mach 1.7 was reached at around 21,000ft (6,401m) followed by a pull up and acceleration to Mach 3 in a climb to 69,000ft (21,031m) with the Raven boosts dropped at Mach 2.2 once the BRJ.851s were at full thrust. Once at cruise altitude the Z.20 cruise/climbed to 74,000ft (22,555m) and once the target was reached, entered a bunt followed by the terminal dive. W.112, being based on the standard Blue Steel could be accommodated in the Victor and Vulcan without a problem, the W.112's anhedral wings providing more than sufficient clearance between the Vulcan's jet pipes and the missile ramjets.

One study that was rejected quickly was the Z.18 from July 1957 that acquired the designation W.113 for a short time. This was a minimal-change Blue Steel with the twin canted fins and a large ventral propellant tank. This only increased range to 340nm (630km), a drop in the OR.1149 ocean, so the proposal was scrapped and the W.113 designator applied to the later Z.36.

The Air Ministry and the Air Staff had been observing the activities of the various companies as they strove to meet OR.1149. The main problem they all had was achieving the range, followed by the low-level approach. Missiles that could meet all this were generally too large for the V-bombers. As ever the source of this was the size of the Green Bamboo warhead that required a 9ft (2.7m) bay to house it while the weight of 4,500lb (2,041kg) affected range and speed performance. At one point Avro WRD heard a rumour that the warhead would weigh nearer to 5,000lb (2,268kg) prompting a flurry of activity. Eventually the Staff and the

Avro artwork
showing a W.114
in its terminal dive
onto the target.
*BAE Systems/
RAF Museum*

Ministry realised that the game was up for OR.1149 so it was cancelled in early 1958. The range was beyond the state of the art in engineering and aerodynamics.

Phase Two not Mark Two

'This misunderstanding which you mention about Mk.II undoubtedly arose because officially there has never been a "Mk.II". Nevertheless the development of Blue Steel to produce the answer to OR.1159 was sometimes called "Blue Steel Mk.II".'
Sir William Farren, Director, Hawker Siddeley Aviation in a letter to Sir Solly Zuckerman, Government Scientific Advisor. 26th April 1960.

The quote above is taken from correspondence between Hawker Siddeley's board and the Ministry of Defence in the spring of 1960 as they tried to assure the British Government that Blue Steel would enter service. The Government, in the shape of Sir Solly Zuckerman, Chief Scientific advisor and not a fan of Blue Steel, was particularly unimpressed when Sir William Farren proposed Blue Steel Mk.II.

Astute readers will have noticed that, until now, there has been no mention of Blue Steel Mk.II, not even in the previous discussion of OR.1149, where the missile studies were described as Blue Steel Phase Two. For five years the Air Staff and Air Ministry had discussed back and forth the development of Blue Steel Mk.II absolutely unaware that Avro were discussing something completely different. While this may be the ultimate example of compartmented security, this was not the intention, as Hawker Siddeley appeared to be blissfully ignorant of this when they proposed, much to the

annoyance of the Ministry, an extended-range re-engined Blue Steel with hydrazine propellant as Blue Steel Mk.II.

The OR.1149 and its OR.1159 successor have been called Blue Steel Mk.II in a myriad of books and papers over the years (including previous work by the author) and this revelation was very much a surprise to the author on reading the correspondence on the subject in the UK National Archives file DEFE 19/6. So who is correct? As far as Avro were concerned, Blue Steel Mk.II did not exist until April 1960 and the missile the Government called Blue Steel Mk.II was known to Avro as the Long Range Guided Bomb, or when based on the W.114, Blue Steel Phase Two. In this work, to preserve the nomenclature used throughout, the descriptions of A.V. Roe have been used.

The opening exchange of this section took place in 1960; two years after OR.1149 had been withdrawn. What had happened in the intervening 24 months? OR.1159 was what happened and this operational requirement was issued in May 1958 along with Specification UB.200 and a new OR for a nuclear warhead, OR.1160, issued in June 1958. This new warhead was known initially as the 'One Ton Warhead' and was originally one of the Granite series until a new warhead appeared which was allocated the MoS rainbow code Red Snow. This was the result of the revoking of the McMahon Act in the USA and the US/UK Mutual Defence Agreement which opened up American advances in nuclear weapons to the British who took the US W-28 warhead in September 1958 and Anglicised it as Red Snow. This replaced the Green Bamboo and Orange Herald warheads intended for Blue Steel and the Yellow Sun free-fall bomb and in comparison with these warheads, Red Snow was tiny. This prompted changes to the internal layout of Blue Steel, like Yellow Sun Mk.2 to maintain centre of gravity and balance.

Given the ongoing delays in the development of Blue Steel, the RAF was still without a credible deterrent. That is if a stand-off weapon with a range of 100nm (185km) could be described as credible five years after it was first drawn up in an era when the pace of weapons development was extremely rapid. Avro were estimating an in-service date for Blue Steel of 1961 which had been the original in-service date for the OR.1149 missile. This did not placate the Air Staff and Air Ministry, nor did it fill them with confidence for the recently issued OR.1159. Therefore speed was of the essence so Avro got the job with a target service date of late 1963 under contract KF/G/01/CB.23(b). Even Avro admitted that the issue of OR.1159 '…resulted in a period of intense project studies.' Avro also noted that 'The over-riding consideration has been given to the need to get the missile into services as soon as possible.' and to this end as few changes as possible were to be made to the Blue Steel missile.

The difference between OR.1149 and OR.1159 was the range, cut from 1,000nm (1,852km) to 600nm (1,111km) with the low-level portion of the trajectory quietly dropped after its delaying effect on the programme was assessed. Guidance was not seen as a problem, with the inertial system backed up by a Doppler navigation package called Blue Jacket based on the navigation system from the Blackburn Buccaneer.

The initial Avro study was Z.44, a ramjet-powered canard missile that offered a range of 750nm (1,389km) at high altitude while the Soar-powered Z.39 addressed the high/low trajectory with 500nm (926km) at high altitude and Mach 3 and the last 100nm (185km) flown at Mach 0.8 at low altitude. A solely high-level trajectory would give a range at 750nm (1,389km). Both of these designs were essentially a Blue Steel with wingtip engines. These studies firmed up into the W.114 missile that featured a pair of solid boosts fitted dorsally as it was found that the four boosts used earlier destabilised the missile in pitch and yaw when they were jettisoned. The lower boosts also caused drag while the missile was being carried on the aircraft. The two boosts were also connected so that they would separate cleanly from the missile

The dorsal boosts forced the removal of the dorsal fin and changing the shape of the ventral fin. One benefit of the wingtip-mounted ramjets was that they acted as endplates that increased lift and it was this that allowed the trailing edge of the wing to be moved forward out of the ramjet efflux. Although the preferred selection was a turbojet, the choice of ramjet power, with the Bristol 18in (45.7cm) BRJ.822 from the Blue Envoy SAM being favoured, was down to the ramjets being available 18 months before a suitable turbojet would be on hand. If the low-level trajectory was required, the Rolls-Royce RB.145, rated at 2,750/3,650 lbf reheated (12.2/16.2kN reheated) would be the engine of choice. A version powered by Soar turbojets was available, but even this would be 18 months behind the ramjet version, so by August 1958 the Controller, Aircraft had confirmed to the Deputy Chief of the Air Staff that the ramjet version, in the high-level trajectory version, was to go ahead as it would have the earliest in-service date.

As already described, the improved cooling possible by increasing the ramjet's diameter from 18in (46cm) to 19in (48cm) improved combustor efficiency and helped provide better power and range for the same fuel load. Another way to increase range was described by R H Francis in a September 1958 meeting of the OR.1159 working party. If Bristol's work on variable-geometry ramjets could be applied to the BRJ.822, the ramjets' performance could be fine-tuned to the operating conditions in the cruise phase. A range increase in the order of 100nm (185km) could have been gained by fitting the BRJ.822 with a variable jetpipe, achieved by installing a translating centre-body in the exhaust. Such a ramjet, the R.2, was under development at Bristol Engines for cruise applications.

Although the idea was to have a minimum of changes to the standard Blue Steel, some quite radical modifications were indeed made. The smaller warhead allowed the internals to be re-arranged to fit more fuel into the fuselage with a total of 746 UK gallons (3,391 litres) usable fuel on board at launch. The Stentor bay was now empty, with the engine replaced by an Elliott Brothers inertial navigation system with the Blue Jacket Doppler system and antenna fitted underneath.

The most obvious differences were to the wings. Although the leading-edge sweep angle was the same as Blue Steel, the wingspan was greater at 14ft 6in (4.4m) rather than 13ft (3.9m) and the entire wing had 7.5° anhedral. Two BRJ.822 ramjets were fitted at the wingtips, set down 5° on the wing chord. This planform replaced the straight wings of the W.112 for OR.1149 as it had been found that

Blue Steel Phase II to OR.1159. Once the Air Staff realised that the aviation companies were not exaggerating the difficulties of OR.1149, they issued OR.1159. To make up for lost time Avro produced a minimum change version of Blue Steel with ramjets and Doppler navigation.

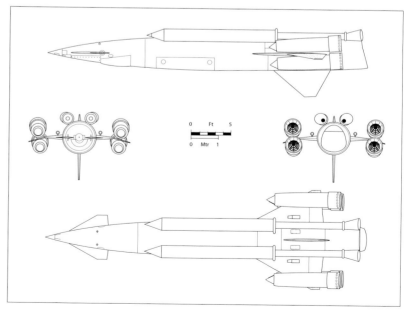

the greater span of the W.112 fouled RATO units when fitted to the Victor.

All this added up to a launch weight of 18,800 lb (8,527kg) with the 'One Ton Warhead' and capable of flying at Mach 3 for 750nm (1,389km) at an altitude of 76,000ft (23,165m). The flight trajectory saw the missile drop away from the aircraft for two seconds and enter a dive before the boosts lit and accelerated the missile to Mach 2.1 in a dive to 34,000ft (10,363m) where the boosts separated. The ramjets were to start at Mach 1.2 and by 25,000ft (7,620m) the missile would have reached Mach 2.2 where it was to pull up into a 14° climb to 69,000ft (21,031m) and enter the cruise-climb until it reached 76,000ft (23,165m). On approaching the target the ramjets were to be cut and jettisoned before the missile bunted into a 40° terminal dive.

Extra range could have been achieved by inserting a 1ft (0.3m) plug in the fuselage to increase the size of the main fuel tank and this additional fuel could have increased range by 100nm (185km). The W.114 would have been a tight squeeze into the bomb bays of the Victor and Vulcan, so much so that Avro planned to fit castors on the rear of the missiles with channels for these to run in installed on the rear bulkheads of the bays.

The choice of the W.114 for OR.1159 appears to have been a straightforward decision based on the rational need to get a viable weapon into service as fast as possible. As might be construed from the development of the Long Range Guided Bomb, there was more to OR.1159 than the Air Staff's quick decision suggests.

There were quite a few Avro WRD studies to choose from. The first such study, which dates from June 1958, was the Z.36 that also re-used the W.113 designation. This comprised the Blue Steel fuselage and foreplane married to new wings carrying a Bristol BRJ.1300 23in (58.4cm) ramjet on the wingtip, with an incidence of 5°

to the missile horizontal. A third BRJ.1300 ramjet was mounted on a dorsal pylon that raised the ramjet 3ft (0.9m) above the missile to ensure smooth airflow into the intake when the missile attained its 5° nose-up incidence in the cruise. Unlike the other two, this ramjet was not inclined to match the missile's incidence in the cruise. Ramjets are notoriously sensitive to off-axis airflow so perhaps the third ramjet was only used to accelerate and jettisoned once the cruise had been established and less thrust required. Two Smokey Joe boost rocket motors were attached under the wings and jettisoned at Mach 2 once the ramjets were running. With a launch weight of 19,800 lb (8,981kg) the Z.36/W.113 was to have a range of 970nm (1,796km) with a payload of the 'One Ton Warhead' that weighed 2,240 lb (1,016kg) and a cruise speed of Mach 3. The Z.36 found no favour with the Air Staff or Ministry mainly due to its BRJ.1300 ramjets being in early development unlike the BRJ.822 that was undergoing trials before the Blue Envoy SAM was cancelled in April 1957.

Turbojet power allowed flexibility in trajectory and as noted above was the preferred propulsion system for OR.1159. WRD studied a number of designs that used the Rolls-Royce Soar. Z.39/S was a configuration study that involved a completely new airframe apart from the nose and foreplane. The Z.39S was powered by a quartet of Soars fitted in a cluster in the rear fuselage with their rectangular intakes on the fuselage flanks with their trunking faired into the rear fuselage. The clean 60° delta wing was fitted under the fuselage, which also carried a conformal ventral fuel tank. Z.39T/3 was derived from the W.112 for OR.1149 and capable of high- and low-level flight. The Z.39T/3 carried its four Soars in wingtip nacelles with reduced span wings to allow carriage on a Victor fitted with RATO pods. In the high-level mode it cruised at Mach 3 at 74,000ft (33,566m) or Mach 0.8 at 500ft (227m) with a stated range of 850nm (1,574km) while carrying the 'One Ton Warhead'.

Z.39UC was another configuration study that used very little of the existing Blue Steel airframe. Four Soars were installed in a row within a ventral intake/engine fairing that merged into the new rear fuselage. A very narrow 75° delta wing was fitted at the upper edge of the engine nacelle, giving a tip-to-tip span of 14ft (4.3m) but 8ft (2.4m) of the span was taken up by engine nacelle. The need to fair-in the engine nacelle and fuselage led to the Z.39UE that saw an enlarged fuselage with the same width as

The cutaway shows the definitive W.114 Blue Steel Phase 2. The boost configuration was aimed at drag reduction while being carried by the Vulcan and Victor. This size of the Green Grass warhead can be seen, as can the inertial navigator in the rear fuselage. *BAE Systems/ RAF Museum*

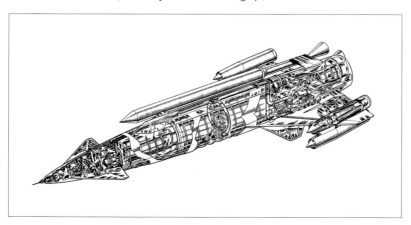

the engine nacelle curved over to form a rounded, squat missile with a 60° cropped delta wing, more like an upturned rowing boat than a missile. These designs were far too radical, would have required a long development period and the description 'Configuration Study' shows that they were never looked into with any serious intent.

The final fling for low-level flight requirement was the Z.41 that used the Blue Steel fuselage, twin canted fins and the revised wing with four tip-mounted BRJ.861 19in (48.3cm) ramjets. As already noted the extra inch on these ramjets denoted that they were modified to improve the cooling of the combustor, allowing higher combustion temperatures and therefore more power. The Z.41 was also fitted with a Bristol Orpheus rated at 4,950lbf (22kN) in the rear fuselage bay that had previously held the Stentor rocket engine on Blue Steel. This bay was converted into a fuel tank and would be filled with kerosene for the ramjets, immersing the Orpheus, and once this fuel had been used, the bottom of the bay opened as an air intake and the turbojet could be used for the low-level phase of the trajectory. Unsurprisingly this idea was dismissed due to potential technical problems.

By September 1958 the low-level portion of the trajectory had been forgotten in the name of expediency, so Avro took the Z.41, removed the Orpheus and produced the Z.42 while the Z.40 used four BRJ.822 ramjets from the Z.20 and took its wings from the Z.39. These were optimised for high-altitude missions with no low-level role at all.

In January 1959 a new variation of the W.114 was submitted, the Z.53. Rolls-Royce's RB.145 was still not available, so each pair of ramjets was replaced by a single Gyron Junior. Unfortunately the W.114 with ramjets was well into its development programme and changing horses midstream to the Gyron Junior would have caused a major delay in a project that hinged upon rapid progress.

One Avro design that had proven to be of interest during the OR.1149 programme was the W.110, but it had been criticised for its size and problems with stowage on the Victor. WRD addressed this by scaling the W.110 down to give length of 35ft (10.7m) with a wingspan of 14ft (4.3m) and produced the Z.43. The intake for the reheated Gyron Junior is much farther forwards on the fuselage than the W.110 and, being optimised for high altitude; the disposable reheat section was not required. All-in-all the Z.43 is a much better looking type than the W.110. Unfortunately, the Victor still could not accommodate it.

The Flying Brick Boomerangs Back

Despite Air Staff and Ministry comments, Handley Page must have been onto something with the HP.106M, if imitation is the sincerest form of flattery. Avro's WRD must have been curious about HP's submission for OR.1149, particularly how it had managed to meet the range requirement in a design that looked so unmissile-like.

Essentially a winged flattened cylinder with a nose cone and chin intake, the Z.45 was 34ft (10.4m) long and towards the rear of the fuselage was a low, rectangular wing with a span of 25ft. This wing made no concessions to high speed, having straight, parallel leading and trailing edges. Lacking canard foreplanes and with a retractable dorsal fin, the Z.45 looked very odd indeed. The bluff rear fuselage of the Z.45 carried the jetpipes of the two Gyron Juniors that powered this most unlikely-looking Mach 3 vehicle. Parametric studies had shown that Avro's Z.45 had a calculated range of 760nm (1,408km), which was less than the HP.106M. Perhaps Handley Page were onto something with the cheap and short-lived Soars and a fuselage that maximised the available space for diesel fuel.

Was the Z.45 a result of parallel evolution or merely WRD attempting to satisfy their curiosity? The HP.106M configuration was so radically different from Avro's ideas for meeting the same requirement that it would have made sense to have examined the layout just in case they had missed something.

The End of OR.1159 weapon

By mid-1959 two separate activities were bringing their influence to bear on OR.1159: the first came from 20 yards (18m) along the corridor at Woodford, while the other originated 4,605nm (8,530km) away in Long Beach, California.

The much-delayed Blue Steel had yet to begin its full-scale trials in Australia and the top brass at the RAF were becoming somewhat irate as the in-service date slipped away. The OR.1149 missile to replace Blue Steel was to have been in service by late 1962. Given the rate of progress on Blue Steel, that date would be the service entry rather than replacement date for Blue Steel. Meanwhile the Air Ministry had been asking awkward questions about the delays to Blue Steel and continued to do so throughout 1959.

Having overcome the fabrication problems, particularly the forming of two-dimensional curves in stainless steel, further delays caused by the lack of trials aircraft in Australia and problems with missile power supplies dogged the project. The Ministry and Air Staff, under pressure from Parliament and becoming exasperated by continual hold-ups finally lost patience.

After the General Election on 8th October 1959 the Conservatives were returned to office with an increased majority. Some people certainly never had it so good, but the ministers at the Ministry of Defence (MoD) and newly created Ministry of Aviation (under the control of one D Sandys) were aiming to make life less tolerable for Avro and Blue Steel. Harold Watkinson at the MoD took a dim view of what he perceived as Avro's reluctance to sort out Blue Steel, rather than spread their effort over a number of projects. One project that he had in mind was OR.1159, Blue Steel Phase Two. On 1st January 1960 the requirement was cancelled, ostensibly to avoid WRD being distracted from bringing Blue Steel up to scratch. The Douglas Skybolt programme for the USAF had been under way for some time and by mid 1959 was being considered for use by the Vulcan and Victor.

OR.1159 was not alone in being scrapped by Watkinson; Sandys' Blue Streak MRBM was felled by Watkinson's axe on 24th February 1960 as it was deemed vulnerable to a pre-emptive strike. On 13th April 1960 the Douglas Skybolt air-launched ballistic missile (ALBM) was adopted as Britain's credible deterrent. It was at this point in the proceedings that Hawker Siddeley director Sir William Farren arrived at the Ministry with his proposal for Blue Steel Mk.II in late April 1960. The Minister of Defence, Harold Watkinson and the Chief Scientific Advisor Sir Solly Zuckerman could be forgiven for their confusion on the matter of Blue Steel. Both had been under the impression that the weapon that had been under development by Avro to meet OR.1149 and later OR.1159 was Blue Steel Mk.II. The Air Staff thought the same and were somewhat dismayed by Farren's new missile.

Farren's Blue Steel Mk.II was sold as a Blue Steel Mk.I with a lighter warhead (the British One Ton Warhead) and range in the region of 500nm (926km). This amazing increase in the missile's range was made possible in part by a lighter and smaller warhead that allowed part of the warhead bay to be used for propellant. The fuel was changed from kerosene to hydrazine, with HTP retained as the oxidiser. The mention of hydrazine did not fill the Air Staff or MoD with enthusiasm nor was the news that the HTP would be more concentrated at 95%. HTP was hazardous and required protective suits, emergency showers, water bowsers and plunge baths to dilute and wash away any spills; highly-toxic hydrazine on the other hand was a different matter. In the Twenty-First Century hydrazine is an important industrial catalyst and precursor material plus a key component in the airbag systems in cars. Not so in the 1950s when hydrazine was a deadly poison whose main application was as a rocket fuel, originally as C-stoff in the Walter rocket engine for the Messerschmitt Me163.

A further irritation to the Air Staff was that hydrazine was not manufactured in Britain and had to be imported from the USA. Hawker Siddeley WRD countered all these criticisms by pointing out that the RAF would be used to handling HTP and that the hydrazine would be supplied in sealed capsules that could be inserted into the missile at little additional risk over operations involving the Blue Steel Mk.I missile.

Farren's bad timing can be forgiven as Avro did not appear to be aware of the strength of feeling that pervaded the Air Staff and Ministries whenever Blue Steel matters were discussed. Perhaps Farren should have introduced Blue Steel Mk.II over lunch at his club. Meanwhile in the USA a new type of weapon was in the early stages of development and attracting attention amongst the Air Staff. The future was Skybolt.

The Long-Range Job

Type	Length	Span	Diameter	Weight	Propulsion	Speed	Range
HP.106M	40ft 6in	31ft	n/a	26,500lb	8 x Soar turbojets	Mach 3	1,000nm
EECo P.10D	35ft	18ft 6in	4ft 6in	19,000lb	Split-wing ramjet	Mach 4	1,000nm
Vickers 569	44ft	14ft 6in	4ft 6in	23,900lb	4 x Soar turbojets	Mach 2.7	1,000nm
Avro W.107	54ft 7in	26ft	n/a	19,260lb	2 x DH Gyron Jr.	Mach 3	1500
Avro W.109	46ft	20ft	n/a	25,580lb	PR.9 Rocket	Mach 5	850nm
Avro W.110	45ft	19ft	n/a	23,740lb	2 x ASM Gamma 2 x DH Gyron Jr.	Mach 3	810nm
Avro W.112	37.4ft	18ft 4in	4ft 6in	21,100lb	4 x BRJ.851 ramjets	Mach 3	730nm
Missile D	50ft 6in	18ft	n/a	22,000lb	2 x DH Gyron Jr.	Mach 3	975nm
Avro W.114	35ft	11ft 2in	4ft 6in	16,700lb	4 x BRJ.822	Mach 3	520nm

6 Pofflers
The V-Force and Skybolt

'From the moment that the idea of Skybolt was conceived, the American Air Staff sought the support of the RAF which from early 1959 had started to send officers and Ministry of Aviation officials to the States to keep in touch with what was afoot.' – Solly Zuckerman. *Monkeys, Men and Missiles*, 1988

After five years of to-and-fro with Blue Steel, Skybolt was a breath of fresh air. In 1960 it promised a new lease of life for the V-Force and released its officers from a future under concrete. In reality it was but a minor part of the huge American R+D effort that had gained momentum amongst the British Government and Air Staff, who bet the lent on it. Skybolt had a major effect on the British deterrent and spawned a number of projects, one of which could yet be resurrected in the unlikely cause of fuel efficiency.

Having in 1960 taken the decision to acquire the Skybolt system in lieu of Blue Streak, there was the question of its deployment. The options were considered by the Air Staff and British Nuclear Deterrent Study Group (BNDSG) and the pros and cons of each were weighed up. BNDSG comprised senior officers, civil servants and scientists who were charged with developing the most efficient use of Britain's nuclear weapons to create the credible deterrent the government needed.

BNDSG had played a major role in the cancellation of Blue Streak, a system that they had advised as being obsolete due to its liquid-fuelled engines and not being available for service until after 1965 but it was Blue Streak's basing that posed a problem. The MRBM was intended to be based and launched from 64 underground silos whose construction would be an expensive project and would have consumed a large proportion of the UK's concrete

The Douglas GAM-87 Skybolt on its transport trolley before loading on a Boeing B-52. The relative size of the large, fixed stabiliser fins and smaller control fins is readily apparent.
Via Terry Panopalis

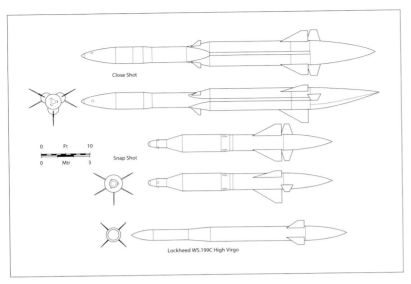

Close Shot

0   Ft   10
0   Mtr   3

Snap Shot

Lockheed WS.199C High Virgo

Before the WS-138 requirement was issued, a number of technology demonstrators were built and tested. These proved the feasibility of an air-launched ballistic missile.

GA of the Convair B-58B. Its main armament was to be the WS-138 ALBM that became Skybolt. The B-58B and WS-138 were originally intended as insurance against failure of the B-70 bomber.

production. There was also the small matter of the sedimentary rocks of eastern England being largely unsuitable for silo construction due to the high water-table and if the Soviets used large enough warheads, the silos would be shifted out of alignment or even popped out by seismic liquefaction.

BNDSG next turned its attention to Skybolt. The RAF was keen on Skybolt, an air-launched missile much more in the RAF's line of work than a concrete-lined hole in the ground. Skybolt was an American ballistic missile that had grown out of the USAF's GAM-77 Hound Dog project. GAM-77 was a turbojet powered stand-off weapon that had utilised some of the technologies developed for Navaho. In the tendering process for WS-131 that led to Hound Dog, several of the companies proposed air-launched ballistic missiles. While this was of interest to the USAF, they opted for the quicker development

of an air-breathing cruise missile. Despite this Lockheed/Convair, Martin, McDonnell and Douglas were awarded study contracts to investigate the air-launched ballistic missile (ALBM) under the designation WS-199A. The projects arising from WS-199A used existing hardware to produce working test vehicles. Martin's WS-199B Bold Orion was also tested as an anti-satellite weapon and proved the air-launched ballistic missile concept to be sound. The joint Lockheed/Convair project WS-199C High Virgo, was tested as a satellite interception vehicle, and intended as the main weapon for the Convair B-58B while McDonnell's WS-199D Alpha Draco was involved in boost/glide vehicle research.

These studies proved the feasibility of launching large missiles from supersonic and subsonic aircraft and in January 1959 General Operational Requirement No.177 was issued for a rocket-powered, strategic air-to-surface missile system, to be designated as the WS-138A and to be used by the USAF and RAF. This was to have a range of 1,000nm (1,852km) and be compatible '…with the B-58, B-52, Victor Mk.2 and Vulcan Mk.2 and, if possible, with the B-70 and KC-135.' thus allowing its use by both air forces. The reference to the B-70 was quickly dropped and very little work was ever carried out to integrate the WS-138 with the Valkyrie.

Three months later the USAF embarked on a design competition to develop an ALBM. Fifteen companies tendered designs, mainly two-stage, solid-rocket, ballistic schemes, but Temco and Raytheon proposed boost/glide vehicles with Temco and RCA opting for liquid fuel rocket engines. Douglas was awarded the contract for the missile portion of WS-138A, designated GAM-87A, in May 1959 and subcontracted the guidance system to Northrop while General Electric handled the re-entry vehicle.

Meanwhile in Britain, two missile projects were being considered for the deterrent. The first was the Blue Streak MRBM and the second the OR.1159 stand-off weapon, referred to by the Air Staff as Blue Steel Mk.II. Blue Streak was subject to changes in technology and basing options while OR.1159 had by 1959 been through a complete rewrite from its initial iteration (as OR.1149) to make the stand-off missile viable, specifically a reduction in the range from 1,000nm (1,852km) to 600nm (1,111km). Both were delayed and the Air Staff and Air Ministry were becoming impatient; in fact by August 1959 a Mr Treble at the Air Ministry wrote '…OR.1159 offers too little, too late and I doubt that it is worth spending £1M to preserve it to the end of the year.'

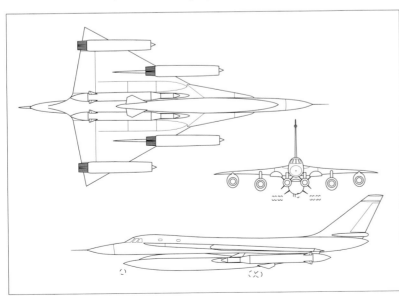

The classic shot of a Vulcan and its Skybolt missiles. The Skybolts shown in this photograph are the early cone/cylinder/flare/cylinder Delta 2 configuration. *Via Terry Panopalis*

When the first reports of what would become WS-138A reached the Air Staff, they couldn't believe their luck. Here was the answer to their prayers: Skybolt combined the command and control flexibility of a bomber (the Go/No Go option of recall on a false alarm), the invulnerability of a ballistic missile and life extension for the V-bombers. It would keep the RAF in the deterrent game and would be available by 1964. Excellent, and rather than the troglodytic life in a missile silo, WS-138A would provide RAF officers with plenty of stick time. The USAF took a similar view, with head of Strategic Air Command, General Curtis Le May, being especially enthusiastic about Skybolt. There was also the small matter of being able to keep the V-bombers viable for longer. Indeed the Secretary of State for Air, George Ward declared '…we must have it or something like it to ensure that the V-bomber force, in which we have invested so many millions of pounds, remains a worthwhile and effective contribution to the deterrent in the years after 1965.'

Not everyone was as keen on Skybolt as the Air Staff. Just after Blue Streak was cancelled, the Minister of Aviation, Duncan Sandys, wrote on 25th February 1960 to the Prime Minister questioning the viability of Skybolt on the V-bombers: 'However, this depends upon the ability of our bomber force to get off the ground within a short warning period available, or to maintain a substantial standing patrol in periods of tension which may be prolonged.' This somewhat belies Sandys' reputation as a lover of missiles of any description and shows that he was very much a realist when it came to deterrence. Sandys was ultimately correct about the V-bombers and Skybolt in that they could not have maintained the intensity of operation required by the airborne patrol role.

Despite Sandys' misgivings, President Eisenhower and Prime Minister Macmillan struck a deal for 144 Skybolts (minus warheads) in March 1960 and the agreement between the US and UK governments was signed on 6th June 1960. Skybolt was coming to Britain.

Skybolt and the V-bombers

Douglas' initial configuration for what the USAF called the XGAM-87, Able 1 designed for the B-58B, was more or less incompatible with the Victor and Vulcan, but crucially the B-52 as well. The problem was that the bulbous first stage not only had a large diameter, but carried eight identical fins that stabilised the missile during the initial launch phase. These fins gave the Able 1 an overall diameter of 8ft (2.4m) which precluded mounting under the wings of Vulcan and Victor. There was also the matter of the quartet of canard fins on the second stage. The XGAM-87 was fitted with an inertial navigation system updated by a star-tracker mounted on the aircraft, passing data to the missile. This was due to the B-58B carrying its missiles under the wing roots with no view of the sky. On a wing pylon, each missile would have an unrestricted field of view and thus could have a star-tracker built in.

In June 1959 a team comprising representatives of the MoS, Avro and Handley Page visited the Douglas Aircraft Company in Los Angeles to

Handley Page was quick to adopt the air-launched ballistic missile for the Victor. This model was exhibited at the Farnborough air show and shows a Victor B.2 with four generic ALBMs. *Handley Page Association*

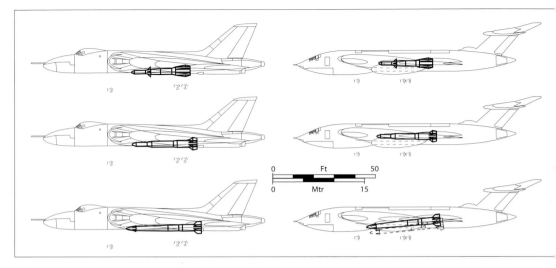

Early Skybolts were to be carried on the V-bomber centreline. The Victor's inclusion in these studies shows that it was intended to carry Skybolt from the start. Victor only fell from favour when wing carriage allowed two missiles per aircraft, thus reducing the number of aircraft required and since the Vulcan required fewer changes, they alone would be used.

The evolution of Skybolt. Able 1 was too fat, Charlie 1 was too long but Delta 2 was just right. Avro's Z.72 ALBM proposal, sized for internal carriage on the Vulcan, is also shown.

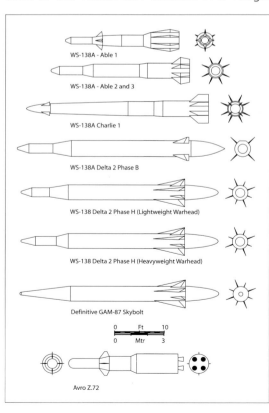

WS-138A - Able 1

WS-138A - Able 2 and 3

WS-138A Charlie 1

WS-138A Delta 2 Phase B

WS-138 Delta 2 Phase H (Lightweight Warhead)

WS-138 Delta 2 Phase H (Heavyweight Warhead)

Definitive GAM-87 Skybolt

Avro Z.72

assess the application of the WS-138A to the Mk.2 V-bombers. The size of the Able 1's first stage and its fins posed a problem with ground and airframe clearances on the Vulcan and particularly on the Victor. One option examined by the Air Staff, was the installation of the missile in the bomb bay of the Vulcan and Victor, the simplest solution. Able 1 could be housed within the Vulcan and Victor's large bomb bays, albeit with some tweaks.

Interestingly for an American weapon, its length had been tailored to fit the Vulcan's bomb-bay. The most radical of the modifications to the Vulcan saw deletion of a 150gal (682 litres) dorsal fuel tank and re-routing the fuel piping. This allowed the installation of a Douglas-designed 'light link data transfer system' that allowed the missile's inertial platform to be updated by a dorsal star-tracker. While internal carriage did allow both types to carry the XGAM-87, only one round could be loaded. Oddly enough, in the light of future events, the Able 1 was best suited to the Victor thanks to its particularly capacious bomb bay, whereas Able 1 could only be carried semi-submerged on the Vulcan, despite its bespoke length.

In February 1960 Avro's WRD, despite the ongoing Blue Steel delays and setbacks, also proposed an ALBM, the Z.72. Like Able 1 this was intended for internal carriage on the Vulcan and Victor. The Z.72 was a three-stage device with a launch weight of 16,000 lb (7,257kg). The third stage was the re-entry vehicle with a total weight at final separation of 1,350 lb (612kg), 1,000 lb (454kg) of that being the warhead itself. Avro stated that the Z.72 had a range of up to 1,000nm (1,850km) but received little response from the Air Staff and Defence Ministries who no doubt looked upon Avro's ALBM as yet another distraction from getting Blue Steel into service.

Meantime in the USA, changes were afoot for the XGAM-87 programme due to problems integrating it with its intended carrier, the B-58B. The short, fat Able 1 was having the same clearance problems with the B-58B, and since the missile was to be that type's main armament, something had to be done. So, it was back to the drawing board for Douglas, who had by 5th August 1959 produced a further three versions with lengthened airframe and reduced maximum diameter, giving it better aerodynamics and larger fins for better stability in the boost phase. A further modification was o move the star-tracker to the missile itself, which was made possible by the cancellation of the Convair B-58B in late 1959. The first of the new versions was Able 2, which was much slimmer, 32in (81cm) longer and carried the larger tail fins. Able 3 used the same basic airframe but with the star-tracker moved forward. This was prompted by the discovery that when mounted as a pair on a single pylon on the B-52, the inboard missile's star-tracker suffered from a restricted view of the sky.

Both models could be carried on the British types either on underwing pylons or semi-submerged in the bomb-bay à la Blue Steel. On the Victor, the fins would need to be removed and replaced after loading. The Air Staff did point out that the ground and airframe clearances were critical when mounted under the wings of a Victor and this would require further investigation. Internal/semi-submerged carriage was preferred to avoid such clearance and aerodynamic problems. Semi-submerged carriage of Able 3 on the Victor would require that aircraft's direction finding aerial be moved to install the light link tube. Under these circumstances, wing mounting made sense. The pylon design itself was based on that for the Firestreak on the Gloster Javelin.

Loading on external wing pylons would have involved major modifications to the wiring of both aircraft and the Victor's electrical systems to be beefed up to cope with the additional loads needed to heat two nuclear weapons. For the Vulcan B.2, further changes included new centimetric ECM antennae as the missile/pylon configuration was incompatible with the Red Shrimp aerials on the engine nacelles. On the mission front, external carriage of such large, drag-inducing stores would incur a sizeable range penalty.

The Charlie 1 was a radical change, 6ft (1.8m) longer and bizarrely, could be carried semi-recessed on the Vulcan, but would not fit in the Victor's bomb bay unless installed at an angle. This would be unsatisfactory as it would require additional fairings and the missile's incidence would create problems on launch. Four large tail fins were fitted as well as four canards around the nose. The length of the Charlie 1 posed problems for wing attachments on both aircraft, which would need structural reinforcement, while the Victor would suffer ground fouling in the event of a hard landing, defined as one with sink rate greater than 7ft/sec (2.1m/sec) or one that compressed the oleos fully and burst all the tyres. Therefore the Air Staff considered the Charlie 1 unsuitable for the Victor and possibly the Vulcan as well.

The name Skybolt was applied to WS-138 in mid-1959, making official the nickname 'Sky Bolt' that the USAF Chief-of-Staff General White had used for some time. By this time the USAF was intending Skybolt to be carried by the B-52 alone; even the option of mounting it on the Boeing C-135 was looking unlikely.

Skybolt Evolves

By March 1960 the Charlie configuration had been much improved, cleaned up, with four smaller fins at the tail to produce the Delta 2 Phase B. Further changes to the Phase B included installing a second-stage motor with a single nozzle rather than four as fitted previously. This became the Delta 2 Phase H/J with the overall length reduced by 16in (40cm) by deletion of a terminal guidance system aft of the warhead. Phase H/J also introduced a new fin arrangement comprising four long, fixed fins and four smaller control fins indexed around the fuselage. These eight fins gave a greater overall diameter of 6ft 6in (2m). Compared with the Phase B, this made underwing installation on the Vulcan difficult and 'impossible' on the Victor due to reduced ground clearance. In fact there was no ground clearance at rotation or touchdown. This runs contrary to the received wisdom that the eight fin arrangement was adopted to allow carriage by the Victor.

The engineers at Handley Page admitted that the earlier work they had done on clearances had been somewhat arbitrary, so went back to their drawing boards and slide rules. It now transpired that GAM-87's fins contacted the ground at a bank angle of 8° during take-off. The engineers gleefully informed the Air Staff that a fully-deflected aileron would impact at a bank of 7.5°. Handley Page, in the guise of Sir Frederick himself, lobbied hard for the Victor to be fitted for GAM-87 and eventually HP told the Air Staff that Skybolt on Victor was possible by extending the undercarriage by 6in (12.7cm). An unimpressed Air Staff considered

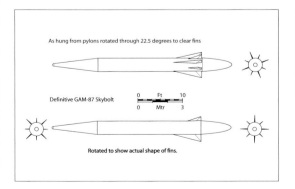

The definitive GAM-87 Skybolt missile as built in late 1962. The lower drawing shows the actual shape of the fins.

Aerodynamic work by Handley Page included this wind-tunnel half-model of a Victor B.1 with two Skybolt ALBMs. Note how far forward the missiles are mounted on the wing, which improved the ground clearance. *Handley Page Association*

Handley Page prepared this diagram to show that even the Able 1 could be carried by Victor despite what one of their employees had told the Air Staff. In fact the airframe impacted the ground before the missile.

this too costly, so HP replied that all this was unnecessary as all that needed done was to move the missile forward by 18in (0.46m), restrict bank on take-off to less than 6.5° and the problem would be solved. On inquiring amongst Victor pilots, 6.5° of bank on take-off was considered to be excessive as 2° of bank was the equivalent of having one main oleo compressed and the other fully extended and that such a situation could only improve as the aircraft lifted off.

In practice, the Victor was never a real contender as a Skybolt carrier. Only 140 rounds were to be bought and these would arm the 72 Vulcan Mk.2 aircraft (to be called the Vulcan B.2S) that were to enter service. This would save the money that would have been spent on modifying Victors. In fact the Air Ministry had eliminated Victor fairly early in the process when it appeared that modifications to the Victor and/or Skybolt were required. Anything that reduced the commonality between USAF and RAF Skybolts was frowned upon. The Ministry was also of the opinion that HP was stretched and the effort involved in fitting the Victor for

Skybolt could tip the company into crisis. There was also the small matter of Handley Page's reluctance to participate in the rationalisation of the UK aerospace industry under Duncan Sandys' master plan.

The Delta Phase H/J became the definitive WS-138 configuration in 1960 and integration with the B-52, Victor and Vulcan commenced in earnest, alongside development and trials of the missile itself. As a weapon system in USAF service launched from B-52, WS-138 was to be armed with either the 'light' Mk.47 or 'heavy' Mk.28 warhead. In British service, Air Staff Requirement ASR.1187 was issued in April 1961 calling for an air-launched ballistic missile for the V-Force. Attendant requirements and specifications included B.222 for an ALBM carrier and OR.1179 for a nuclear warhead for the WS-138. The aim was for commonality but the American missile could not carry a UK warhead. British warhead design differed greatly from that of the Americans, particularly in the amount of fissile material they used. On this matter, Mr Treble at the Ministry of Aviation opined in March 1959 that 'The American warhead uses relatively much larger amounts of scarce material.'

The RAF's warhead was to be an indigenous design labelled RE.179 under the MoA's new digraph/trinome system that replaced the Ministry of Supply's rainbow code system. The RE.179 thermonuclear warhead used a primary called CLEO and this would live on in a variety of British nuclear weapons such as the WE.177A lay-down bomb.

The RE.179 warhead for WS-138 in RAF service was an Anglicised version of the American W59 warhead with a yield of 400Kt. Another warhead proposed for the UK WS-138 was STEVEN, the AWRE cover name for a British version of the Mk.47 warhead used on the American WS-138 and Polaris A1 SLBM. Other UK warheads mooted for the UK WS-138 included the Type A, a 500Kt yield warhead design to meet OR.1179 with an estimated weight of 850 lb (385kg) and Type B, a development of the Type A warhead to give, for the same size and weight, a maximum yield of 850Kt.

Once the political discussions between the US and the UK governments had been concluded in May 1960 work began on integrating Skybolt with the Vulcan. Given the less than cordial relations between HM government and Avro Weapons Research Division over Blue Steel, it may come as a surprise to learn that Avro was selected as prime contractor for Skybolt integration. Soon after, in mid 1960, a

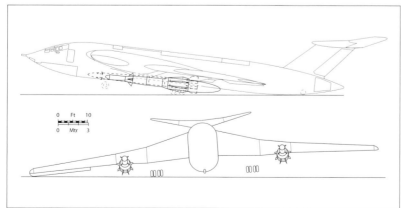

Vulcan was seen flying from Avro's Woodford airfield with a long, white store under each wing. The first drop trials of dummy Skybolts were performed in December 1961 over the West Freugh range near Stranraer in Wigtownshire. Testing and integration on both sides of the Atlantic was now well under way.

Two Skybolt variants underwent carriage and drop testing on Vulcan XH538. These were the initial service version, with a cylindrical forward fuselage (cone/cylinder/flare/cylinder in the parlance of missile description) and the definitive Skybolt with a conical nose (cone/cylinder) configuration. The conical re-entry vehicle offered increased range of up to 30nm (56km) and reduced the effect on stability produced by differential erosion of the RV skin.

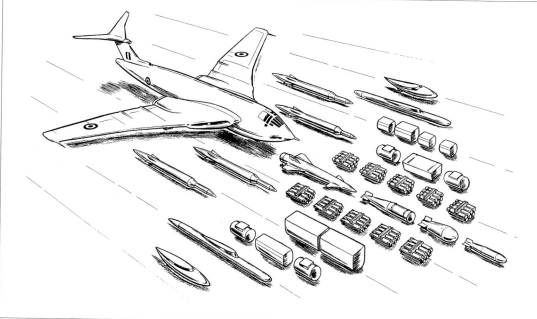

This wind-tunnel model appears to be a Victor B.2 fitted with wingtip fuel tanks and four ALBMs. This later led to the HP.114 Patrol Missile Carrier. *Handley Page Association*

Handley Page were keen to show how the Victor could fulfil a variety of roles including Skybolt carrier. This illustration shows the Victor with an array of weapons including an American Mk.5 bomb (second row, middle) supplied under Project E. The cigar-shaped stores inboard of the slipper tanks are Red Neck radar pods. Ultimately Victor was to carry Blue Steel to complement the Skybolt-equipped Vulcans. *Handley Page Association*

This image shows two different Skybolts, the Delta 2 and the definitive GAM-87. The later conical nose could take a range of warheads. *Via Terry Panopalis*

115

Skybolt as a weapon

Skybolt operations, whether on the scramble basis or airborne alert, followed a fairly rigid set of rules. For maximum range, the missile had to be launched as high as possible with the aircraft on a track directed at the target. This latter requirement was not set in stone, but off-track launches incurred a range penalty. The preferred launch altitude was around 40,000ft (12,192m) but the Vulcan could exceed this. For maximum range, launch from the aircraft in a steep climb would be best, but for best accuracy, being dropped during straight and level flight gave the most accurate targeting. To hit a target with any level of accuracy a ballistic weapon needs to know its launch point. The launch sequence involved the inertial platform being updated from the astro-navigation star-tracker to provide the point of origin at launch.

Although the inertial platform would have been initialised at the base before take-off, such systems were subject to inaccuracy that increased over time. Therefore the longer the time period since initialisation, the less accurate the targeting and in the 1960s one hour was considered the maximum. The star-tracker served to initialise the inertial navigator in flight just prior to launch.

Having initialised the navigation system, the missile was launched. Released from the pylon the weapon was in free-fall for two seconds to provide at least 50ft (15m) separation from the aircraft. Four explosive bolts blew off the aerodynamic fairing on the tail and the first-stage motor fired. The four control fins commanded the missile into a pre-programmed climb for 40 seconds until the motor cut and the first stage separated. The second stage with the warhead coasted for a few seconds before the motor

ignited to propel the missile upwards guided by the INS and controlled by the gimballed nozzle. Once the missile had reached a velocity for the required range, four burst disks on the front of the motor blew to provide 'reverse thrust' to control the velocity. Once set on its course, the warhead in its General Electric-designed re-entry vehicle separated and continued in a ballistic trajectory to re-enter the atmosphere and plunge onto its target.

The RAF would have operated its 104 Vulcan B.2S on a scramble basis (later known as Quick Reaction Alert when applied to Blue Steel operations) from dispersed airfields around the UK. Oddly enough some of the same arguments against Blue Streak were levelled at Skybolt, that the bases and aircraft could be destroyed by a Soviet first strike. Skybolt would be the British deterrent, unlike the US who would field a triad of deterrence that wasn't dependent on a single weapon like the UK would be with Skybolt. The USAF had a different attitude to Skybolt, which they saw as a means to blast a path through the Soviet defences to allow B-52s to attack valuable or hardened targets by precision attacks with free-fall nuclear weapons.

Patrol Missile Carrier

The USAF also faced the prospect of being destroyed on the ground by a pre-emptive strike and had addressed this keeping fully-armed B-52s on constant airborne alert under codenames such as Chrome Dome and Head Start. The Air Staff and the Ministry of Aviation looked at these operations in 1960 and considered airborne alert, for which they coined the term 'poffler', to be a viable option for the survival of a deterrent force. A poffle is a Scots

A Vulcan B.2 fitted with pylons for Skybolt drop trials over the West Freugh range in south-west Scotland. The pylons were based on the design used on the Gloster Javelin for Blue Jay/Firestreak. *Via Terry Panopalis*

term for a small area of farmland, so a poffler would be a small farmer. No doubt the same civil servant who came up with the name Dominie (Scots for a schoolmaster) for the HS.125 trainer had a hand in this.

Unfortunately the Vulcan B.1 and Victor B.1 armed with Yellow Sun free-fall bombs and the forthcoming Mk.2 V-bombers lacked the endurance to maintain such poffling patrols without serious impact on their serviceability, so much so that they could only mount such patrols for a period of four to six weeks before being forced to stand down for heavy servicing.

The Air Staff's thinking on continuous airborne alert missions with Skybolt involved the V–bombers taking off from bases in eastern England and entering a cruise-climb to a patrol area over Norway or, if based on Cyprus, the Adriatic or Turkey. The existing B.2 variants of the Victor and Vulcan could not mount such missions without a major effort on the part of the squadrons. With a seven hour sortie period the time on patrol would be less than five hours, requiring many more aircraft than in the scramble role.

Faced with this, the Air Staff approached Avro and Handley Page with requests in mid 1960 for studies to produce a poffler armed with Skybolt that would become what was called a Patrol Missile Carrier. The aim of these studies was to produce a poffler that could perform a mission of at least twelve hours, carrying an adequate weapons load and keep the British nuclear forces safe from a pre-emptive strike. The extended endurance would reduce the workload of the support staff on RAF stations and hasten in a true round-the-clock deterrent.

Avro's approach to the poffler, submitted in May 1960, was the Vulcan Phase 6 which, had it progressed, would have been the Vulcan B.3. This had an enlarged wing spanning 121ft

(36.9m) with increased fuel capacity that was further increased by the addition of a dorsal spine enclosing even more fuel tanks, doubling the fuel capacity. Bristol Siddeley Olympus 301 rated at 20,000 lbf (88.9kN) dry thrust, possibly 30,000 lbf (133.4kN) with reheat, produced the extra thrust to power the large aircraft carrying four Skybolts on a patrol lasting up to eleven hours. This compared favourably with the seven hours with two Skybolts of the Vulcan B.2S. An enlarged fin and new four-wheel main undercarriage to carry the B.3's AUW of 339,000 lb (153,742kg) completed the modifications.

Such missions placed a great workload on the crew and the original Phase 6 five-man crew in standard Vulcan B.2 accommodation was not ideal for long missions. The next Phase 6 Vulcan study, dated from October 1960, introduced a 10ft 9in (3.3m) plug inserted into the fuselage ahead of the wing to give an overall length of 110ft (33.5m). Within this section was a new cabin with forward-facing crew stations and, in a first for the Vulcan, all crew seated on ejection seats. The increase in crew from five to six allowed an extra relief pilot to be carried for

Skybolt was originally developed for the B-58, B-52 and Vulcan. The B-52 could carry four Skybolts, in this case the GAM-87 definitive variant and maintain airborne alert missions around the clock.
Via Terry Panopalis

What would have become a familiar sight around the UK from the mid-1960s: a Vulcan with a pair of Skybolts. Had Skybolt entered service, V-Force Vulcans would have maintained a QRA role. The Vulcan establishment could not have maintained a continuous air alert role for any length of time.
Via Terry Panopalis

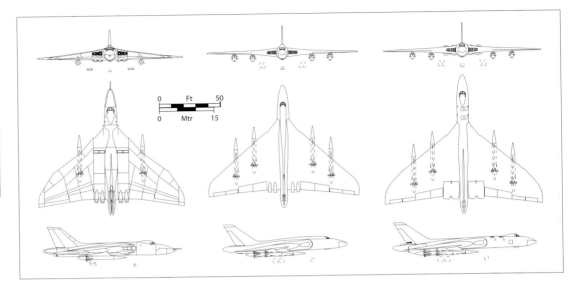

Comparison of the patrol missile carrier 'Poffler' versions of the Vulcan. Left to right: Vulcan B.2S, Vulcan Phase 6, Vulcan Phase 6 stretched. The Phase 6 could carry up to six Skybolts while the stretched version included a crew rest area.

Handley Page's HP.114 was based on the Victor B.2 with changes that included ventral fuel tanks, wing pylons for the Skybolts (including a dummy Skybolt full of fuel if required) and new outer wings with tip tanks.
Adrian Mann

long missions, but increased AUW to 349,000 lb (158,276kg). Another modification to the later Phase 6 was the application of aft-fan technology to the Olympus 301 engines. Aft fans added a free-running rear stage behind the turbine that drove a large diameter fan in ducts above and below the wing which provided more thrust and greater efficiency. This technique was overtaken by the shaft-driven front fan of the high bypass ratio engines so familiar today.

Meanwhile at Radlett, Handley Page's development department were making similar changes to the Victor and by March 1960 had produced a brochure entitled 'Victor B.Mk.2 Patrol Missile Carrier'. HP described a two-phase process, with Phase One being a fairly straightforward conversion carried out at the RAF stations. This involved fitting new outer wings with 1,200gal (5,455 litres) tip tanks and a pair of fuel tanks in the bomb bay carrying a further 11,000gal (50,007 litres) to produce a Victor that could carry two Skybolts on a 14-hour mission. The bomb bay fuel tanks extended below the fuselage line, faired-in to lie flush with the radar bulge below the cockpit. This was to be called the HP.114.

Phase Two HP.114 could carry four missiles for the same duration and involved more radical modifications at the Handley Page works. A new six-wheel bogie main undercarriage was required to cater for the take-off weight of 310,000 lb (140,589kg) and to increase ground

clearance for the outboard missiles. To improve take-off performance two of the Conway 17 turbofans could be fitted with reheat or a pair of de Havilland Spectre RATO units attached under the wing roots. The rear fuselage was to be strengthened and the same Phase One outer wings with tip tanks were to be fitted. To further extend endurance, the Phase Two HP.114 could carry three Skybolts with a dummy Skybolt on the No.4 station that was configured as a drop tank.

Ploughshare to Sword – Following the Vulcan

The V-bombers were designed for war and intended for discrete missions, such as a seven-hour conventional raid, perhaps twice a week, or a one-off nuclear strike if the Cold War turned hot. They were not designed for the repeated take-off and landings (what airlines call cycles) of the poffler role and as such had a fatigue life of around 10,000 hours. Poffling would eat into that life, gobbling up the V-Force's equipment in less than five years, even at a fairly conservative sortie rate. Sandys' prescient observation on standing patrols was correct and all the Russians had to do was create a period of tension long enough for the RAF's Vulcan/Skybolt force to be grounded through over-use.

Airliners on the other hand were designed for constant use as an aircraft on the ground isn't making money. Britain had learned much from the de Havilland Comet saga and by 1958 Vickers had commenced development of an airliner that would become the VC10. A large aircraft, the VC10 was ordered by BOAC as an airliner and by the RAF as a troop and cargo transport. Although airliner life is generally measured in cycles, the VC10 was intended to

have a fatigue life in the region of 30,000 hours, making the type much more suitable for the poffler mission. Vickers, like all aircraft manufacturers, was ever mindful of expanding the roles for its products and began to look at further military developments of the VC10. Hand-in-hand with the patrol missile carrier went tanker support and in 1960 that role was filled by the Vickers Valiant but sustaining the pofflers would also use up the Valiant's fatigue life.

When the RAF began looking at the patrol missile carrier, Vickers saw an opportunity to utilise the size, power and endurance of the VC10 and proposed a variant that could carry up to eight Skybolts on underwing pylons. The VC10 was particularly suited to the poffler role: it had the speed to transit to the launch areas, the performance to reach the ideal launch altitude and a capacious fuselage into which up to six fuel tanks could be fitted. In total 24,550gal (111,607 litres) of fuel could be carried allowing a VC10 to carry eight Skybolts on a sortie lasting up to 13 hours.

Of course all this fuel and eight Skybolts increased the AUW of the VC10 to 380,000lb (172,336kg) and Vickers proposed a couple of techniques to get it into the air. The first was to fit reheat to the Rolls-Royce Conway R.Co.43 turbofans while the second involved

The Sud Aviation VII Caravelle with General Electric CJ-805-23 engines fitted with aft fans. Larger aft fans were proposed for the Phase 6 Vulcan. The aft fan was eclipsed by the high bypass ratio turbofan that has been a standard fit on airliners since the early 1970s. *Author's Collection*

Vickers artwork showing the Patrol Missile Carrier/ poffler version of the VC10. Shown with six ALBMs, the VC10 could carry up to eight Skybolts and operate at very high take-off weights. Plans to fit engines with reheat and/or RATO units were also aimed at increasing the endurance. *BAE Systems/ Brooklands Museum*

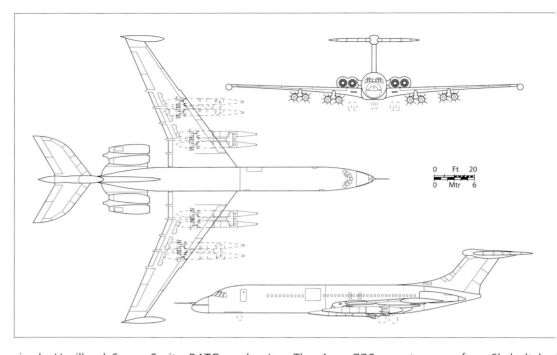

General arrangement the VC10 poffler with four Skybolts and a optional further four on the outboard pylons. Other changes included a crew rest area behind the flightdeck and six fuel tanks in the cabin. The VC10 could revert to a tanker/transport role in less tense times.

six de Havilland Super Sprite RATO packs. In hot/high conditions both techniques may have been required and a VC10 embarking on a pof-fling mission would have been a spectacle of flame, smoke and steam from the HTP-fuelled Super Sprites. The increased AUW would have normally required strengthening of the aircraft's structure but Vickers advised that if the type was limited to 2.15G while at these high weights, a beefed-up structure was not neces-sary. Should the Cold War become less tense, the VC10 could also double as a transport or tanker aircraft by removing the fuel tanks, Sky-bolt control systems and missile pylons.

Hawker Siddeley were also interested in the poffler role and submitted a variant of the Avro 776 maritime reconnaissance aircraft that was in turn derived from the HS.121 Trident airliner.

The Avro 776 was to carry four Skybolt but could not compete with the sheer power and endurance of the VC10, not to mention its abil-ity to lift up to eight Skybolts.

Turboprops have always been more efficient than even a bypass turbofan and have been used for many roles that required long range or endurance. The only large turboprop aircraft under development in Britain during the early 1960s was the Shorts SC.5 Belfast. This started out as the Britannic, that mated a capacious fuselage with the wings and Rolls-Royce Tyne engines of the Bristol Britannia. Shorts devel-oped the Belfast as a strategic transport for the RAF but in 1961 they proposed the SC.5/35 variant for use in the patrol missile carrier role with one proposal having the missiles launched out the rear cargo door of the Belfast.

The Belfast looked great on paper, capable of long sorties of up to twenty hours and able to accommodate the additional crew required for this length of mission. Unfortunately the Belfast poffler had an Achilles Heel in the form of the weather. As noted above, Skybolt relied on a pre-launch update of its inertial platform from the star-tracker. The need for a clear view of the sky above the aircraft has also been men-tioned in relation to the airframe obscuration on the B-52 and B-58B. However, what if that obscuration was due to the weather? This was the main problem with the Belfast. As a turbo-prop its cruising ceiling was much lower than the jet-powered V-bombers and VC10. Its launch altitude of 30,000ft (9,144m) already affected the maximum range of the Skybolt,

What made the Shorts Belfast attractive as a Poffler was its long endurance. Unfortunately the Belfast operated at a lower altitude than the VC10, which limited the range of the Skybolt.

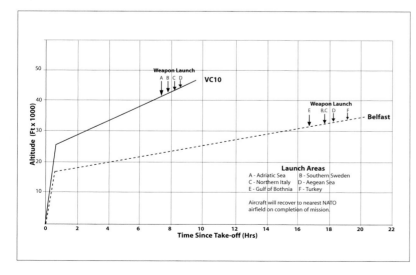

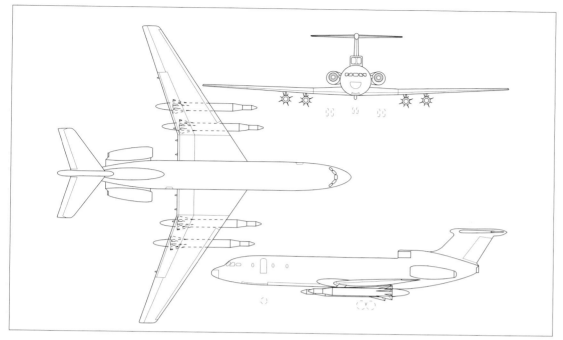

Avro also suggested a Poffler variant of the HS.121 Trident airliner. This was designated the Avro 776 and could carry up to four Skybolts.

Designed to meet OR.371, the Shorts Belfast was suggested as a long-endurance patrol missile carrier. Four Skybolts were to be carried internally and launched via the rear cargo door. *Author's Collection*

In addition to its effect on the Skybolt range, the Belfast's patrol altitude reduced the missile's accuracy due to cloud cover obscuring the sky from the missile's star-tracker for the pre-launch astro-fix.

estimated as 850 nautical miles (1,574km) and there were also concerns about the accuracy of the Skybolt if the star-tracker was compromised by cloud. Even thin cirrus cloud could prevent the star tracker locating its reference stars.

The Air Staff asked for analysis of this problem and produced a series of graphs that compared the cloud cover at various altitudes and latitudes. At the Equator cloud cover averaged 25% at 45,000ft (13,716m) but averaged 38% at 30,000ft (9,144m). Fortunately the situation was much improved in the higher latitudes where the pofflers would be flying. At the VC10's launch height of 45,000ft (13,716m) there was no cloud at 55°N and 80°N. Also much improved was the Belfast's launch altitude of 30,000ft (9,144m) with 15% cover at 55°N and no cloud at 80°N.

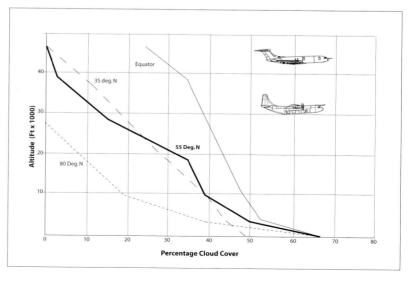

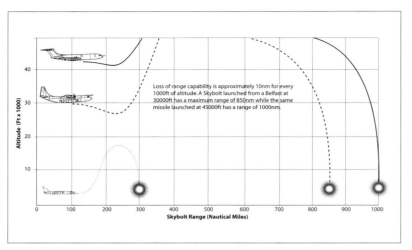

Loss of range capability is approximately 10nm for every 1000ft of altitude. A Skybolt launched from a Belfast at 30000ft has a maximum range of 850nm while the same missile launched at 45000ft has a range of 1000nm.

The effect of launch altitude on Skybolt range. The TSR.2 would not have carried Skybolt for a variety of reasons, but the main reason was that there was little point due to the very limited range.

The reduction in range caused by the lower launch altitude had another effect on a poffler mission. The launch aircraft would need to fly closer to Soviet territory to attack the same targets. In effect the greater endurance would have been used to place the Belfast further away from its bases and it would take much longer to reach the launch area. When compared with the VC10, the Belfast was slower, lower and its ability affected by clouds. Meanwhile at Radlett, Handley Page had another iron in the poffling fire, the HP.117 and its story merits a separate discussion.

Low-level Skybolt

One of the oddest suggestions for a Skybolt carrier was the BAC TSR.2 strike aircraft. As described above, the Ministry of Aviation had in 1960 examined the possibilities for arming various types with stand-off weapons, focussing on converted transport aircraft. When it came to the TSR.2 the Ministry had previously dismissed it as a Blue Steel carrier due to that missile's weight, but at 11,000 lb (4,989kg) Skybolt was not too heavy nor too large at 3ft (0.9m) in diameter as opposed to 5ft (1.4m) so it was hoped that TSR.2 with a payload in excess of 20,000 lb (9,070kg) could carry a pair.

UK National Archives file AVIA 65/911 includes an analysis of this scheme written in September 1960. Initial proposals involved the simple expedient of mounting a Skybolt on the fuselage centreline but this was soon revealed as a non-starter for two reasons. The first was the blanking of the TSR.2's Doppler antenna which would affect the aircraft's navigation system and the second was the airframe covering the missile's star-tracker window. Next proposal was to fit a Skybolt under each wing, which cured both of the above problems, but created

more. The underwing mounting would cause aerodynamic interference with the tailplane, which would be a short distance aft of the missile and the wing structure might need additional strengthening.

The third option was overwing carriage which would solve the aerodynamic interference of the tailplane, but would transfer these problems to the tailfin. Structural strengthening of the wing would no doubt be required again. One further feature of the overwing pylons would be the need to invert the aircraft to get an astro fix and to launch the Skybolts. Due to the requirement that UK and US Skybolts should be identical apart from the warhead, the attachment lugs and interfaces were on the upper side of the missile so it would be need to be mounted upside down with the star tracker pointing to the ground. Launch would involve the aircraft rolling inverted and maintaining this attitude until the missile had achieved a fix, then released. This was not a manoeuvre to be carried out at low-level.

So from a carriage point of view, Skybolt on TSR.2 was a non-starter although there were other, more fundamental, reasons not to mount Skybolt on this type. The Air Staff had always viewed stand-off weapons as the sole preserve of the bomber force while the tactical force should utilise fast, low-level strike aircraft such as the Canberra and its replacement. TSR.2 was to be a penetrator, carrying the Lay-Down Bomb: WE.177C or, if used in the strategic role the WE.177B. Stand-off weapons were a threat to this penetration mission and would in fact negate the need for TSR.2 altogether. Fit Skybolt and there was no need for TSR.2 in the first place, so even within the Air Staff there was a conflict between the strategic and tactical factions.

In the case of a TSR.2 carrying two Skybolts the aircraft's radius of action was much less than 1,000nm (1,852km) and the range of Skybolt would be 300nm (556km) if launched at low level. If a pop-up manoeuvre to 25,000ft (7,620m) was performed this increased Skybolt range to 800nm (1,482km). As noted above, altitude and latitude could have considerable effect on the star-tracker's ability to gain a fix. This would degrade accuracy and produce a circular error probable of 4nm (7km) rather than the 1.5nm (2.8km) of a high-altitude launch. In short there was nothing to be gained by fitting Skybolt to the TSR.2 as it could be better used for more suitable tactical missions.

That knowledge did not prevent BAC from proposing TSR.2 for the poffler role in January 1963, armed with WE.177 or air-launched Blue

Water. In a brochure entitled 'TSR2 Strategic Weapons System – Air Alert' BAC outlined a TSR.2 with beefed up undercarriage, to handle 21,000 lb (9,525 lb) of extra fuel that brought the type's AUW to 118,000 lb (53,524kg). With two refuellings from Victor K.1 tankers, the TSR.2 poffler could remain on patrol for up to eight hours. BAC suggested that to maintain a continuous patrol of ten TSR.2 aircraft, a force of 60 aircraft would be required.

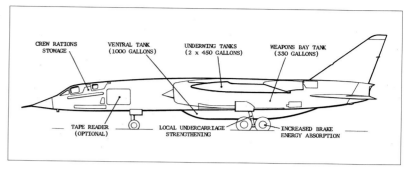

Skybolt Fallout

The odd thing about Skybolt was that the RAF was so keen on it, as were the Ministries, before its technology had even been demonstrated as a practicality never mind as a weapon system.

The entire WS-138 programme had been a research project, a fact that the Minister of defence, Harold Watkinson, admitted at the time in a memo that went on to describe how its supply to the RAF was dependent on its successful development. Solly Zuckerman had pointed out in January 1961 that the Americans were only continuing its development because the British requirement. The Admiralty were just as enthusiastic about the competing weapon, the Polaris submarine-launched ballistic missile that was considered to be a much more challenging system than Skybolt. Polaris plodded along through its trials with comparatively few problems, possibly because the potential for development setbacks had been flagged-up extensively.

By March 1961, two months after Kennedy's inauguration, the MoD and MoA had got wind of a change in US policy towards Skybolt. Peter Thorneycroft at the Ministry of Aviation evidently began to make plans for alternatives in the event of the Americans cancelling the programme. Thorneycroft was keen to broaden the scope of the long-range cruise missile feasibility studies as insurance (see Chapter Seven) and stated that if Skybolt was cancelled 'Our present view in the Ministry of Aviation is that if the Americans give up Skybolt the cheapest and most effective course for us to take would be to carry on where they leave off.'

One such setback for Skybolt involved its guidance system being incompatible with that on the Vulcan. Watkinson wrote to Thorneycroft on the subject of the astro-navigation system of Skybolt requiring an accurate position fix from the Vulcan. 'I am told that the present day navigation equipment in British V-bombers is so markedly more inaccurate than the American counterpart that in certain circumstances Sky-

bolt would be virtually unusable as a weapon.' Solving this would require modifications to the Vulcan systems and would have incurred costs.

In fact this potential problem of fixing the missile's position prior to launch, whether by US or UK equipment, had been raised as far back as July 1959 by the Fletcher Committee of the US Congress who recommended that 'the program should not be approved.' Nor was the Fletcher committee alone in its scepticism on Skybolt as the President's Science Advisory Committee and the Pentagon's Weapons Systems Evaluation Group had recommended its cancellation on an annual basis since Skybolt's inception.

By September 1962 McNamara and Peter Thorneycroft, now British Defence Minister, held talks on Skybolt. Harold Watkinson had been dismissed by Macmillan on 13th July 1962 in 'The Night of the Long Knives' reshuffle. Thorneycroft learned that five Skybolt tests had been carried out and all had failed to meet their goals. McNamara also intimated that Skybolt's costs were increasing and that the complexity of the weapon was such that successful testing might take some time. In short McNamara was telling the Minister that Skybolt was about to be cancelled.

Poffler did not refer solely to aircraft armed with Skybolt. It could also apply to aircraft with freefall weapons or other stand-off missiles. The TSR.2 was proposed as a poffler, equipped with extra fuel tanks and up-rated brakes.
BAE Systems/ RAF Museum

Avro's Z.89 was suggested as an alternative to Skybolt and would comprise an air-launched version of Z.82. Both Z.82 and Z.89 were tandem-boosted W.130 with the Z.89 using a liquid-fuelled sustainer. Here it is mounted on the Skybolt pylons on a Vulcan B.2

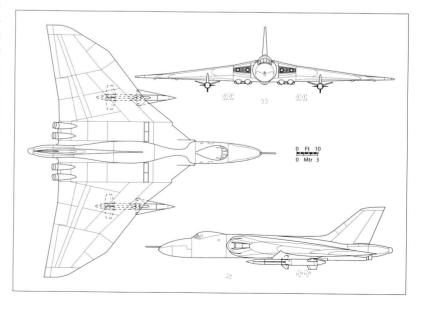

The Ministry of Aviation were not entirely convinced by McNamara's warnings on the technical difficulties with Skybolt and had acquired some data on the other ballistic missiles' tests. The initial trials of the Polaris AX involved 13 flights, of which only four were successful and the first five were complete failures. The Minuteman ICBM fared better with three of the first six flights logged as failures. Skybolt's initial failure rate appeared to be par for the course.

At a meeting in Whitehall on 11th December 1962 the US Secretary of Defense and the UK Minister of Defence discussed an aide-memoire that Mr McNamara had prepared on the American position on Skybolt and that their position was unfavourable to continued Skybolt development. At the end of the meeting Peter Thorneycroft thanked Robert McNamara and then Thorneycroft '…went on to stress that Mr McNamara's statement raised political and military implications of the gravest character.'

In an analysis of that aide-memoire on Skybolt, the analyst informed the Minister of Defence that 'Mr McNamara argued that the United States could score more 'megadeaths per megabuck' from Polaris and Minuteman than from Skybolt.' and that despite what the aide-memoire stated, the American technicians involved had '…not changed their minds about their ability to complete development successfully.'

By December 1962, McNamara was telling the UK Government that the delays in Skybolt trials made the possibility remote of it being a reliable and worthwhile weapon within a reasonable timescale. In fact McNamara admitted he had never had much faith in Skybolt as a weapon from the start. Thorneycroft outlined how Skybolt was the key to British defence policy to which McNamara proposed alternatives to Skybolt. Firstly was that the British took over the development of Skybolt, secondly the Americans provided the GAM-77 Hound Dog and thirdly the British joined a multinational submarine-based deterrent scheme.

Only the first option was viable as Hound Dog could not be fitted to the V-bombers and the multinational deterrent force lacked the independence the British sought. The upshot of this was that a series of top-level talks were scheduled for mid-December at Nassau in the Bahamas. These discussions between Macmillan and Kennedy concentrated on the British deterrent and the effect that the cancellation of Skybolt would have.

Kennedy explained that Skybolt would exceed the time and cost estimates by a considerable amount and, since he appreciated Skybolt's importance to the British, offered to continue it to fill the British requirement. Macmillan, possibly mindful of the delays on Blue Steel, took the President's dire warnings of cost and delays seriously and agreed to Skybolt's cancellation. The Hound Dog option was dismissed due to technical reasons as it could not be mounted on the V-bombers and would take five years to enter service, so that left Polaris. Macmillan came back from Nassau with a new deterrent, Polaris, that would probably not be in service until the end of the decade and Blue Steel would not be credible past 1965.

The British appear to have been blind to the fact that the Americans viewed Skybolt as merely another weapon study within their massive defence research programme. Skybolt seemed too good to be true and that's how the saga panned out. It was time to examine the insurance policy.

Initial drop tests were carried out using the Delta 2 variant of Skybolt. The dark fairings under the wingtips and the fuselage centreline held cameras to record the drop.
Via Terry Panopalis

Laminar Launcher

'The first aircraft was a motorised glider. This conception of the aeroplane has persisted for over 50 years and is still being followed by the majority of aircraft designers.' Dr Gustav Lachmann, 1957

The second generation of pofflers were based on existing types, such as the Vickers VC10, Shorts Belfast and variants of the Avro 776 (which later became the Trident airliner). Of these designs only the VC10 provided the mission endurance, useful deterrent payload and launch envelope the role required.

There was one other design that could have fulfilled all these criteria and, had it been developed, it would have heralded a new era, if not a revolution, in aviation. That revolution was intended to be in the field of air travel, with the intent of bringing it to the masses by massive reductions on the seat/mile cost of passenger transport. As a poffler, the aircraft possessed the endurance and payload required while being available for strategic airlift tasks in less tense times. That type was the Handley Page HP.117 laminar flow transport aircraft and as an example of the high-technology related to the UK deterrent, it deserves discussion in any work on that subject.

Dr Gustav Lachmann (1896-1966) had been chief designer at Albatros Flugzeugwerke in Berlin until 1925 and four years later came to Britain to take up an appointment with Hand-

ley Page Aviation. While at Handley Page, Lachmann developed an interest in improving the efficiency of aircraft and took the view that to allow airlines to make money, aircraft needed to be larger and carry more passengers. Lachmann saw that the future of air travel was in the mass market, rather than with the privileged few on diplomatic and military journeys in the service of the British Empire.

The key to reducing the seat/mile cost was, and still is, to reduce fuel burn and that is what Lachmann set out to do, aiming for a trans-Atlantic air fare of £11. In 1955 that was the equivalent of £192 in 2010 whilst one-way economy class fares from London to New York cost around £600 in 2010. Lachmann was looking for a 60% reduction in operating costs for the airlines.

An HP.117 Poffler launches its payload of Skybolts over Norway.
Adrian Mann

Artist's impression of the Handley Page HP.117. Intended as a high-capacity transport aircraft for cargo and passengers. Handley Page promoted the HP.117 as a multipurpose aircraft with a patrol missile carrier/poffler being one proposal.
Author's Collection

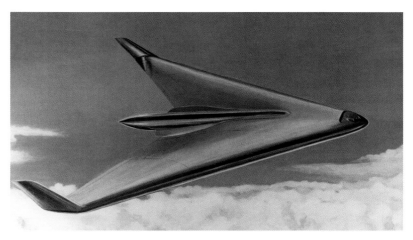

HP's Laminar Flow Projects

'If the rate of engine development had been maintained, airliners would have landed with more fuel than when they took off.' This oft repeated joke will be familiar to any reader of aviation titles in the late 1970s and 1980s. Nonsense of course, but gives an idea of the magnitude of the advances made in engine technology since the jet airliner was introduced in 1949. Much of this improvement was driven by the massive hike in oil prices in 1973 and ostensibly the need to reduce emissions that contributed to greenhouse gasses. Since the Seventies, fuel cost has been the driving force behind improving engine efficiencies and as a result, by the 1990s turbofan technology had reached a development plateau. Attention turned to efficient airframes in the 1990s with lighter composite materials in airframes culminating in the Airbus A350 and Boeing 787 Dreamliner. A more advanced approach was the Blended Wing Body being developed to test advanced aerodynamics and airframe shaping in the pursuit of lower fuel consumption. There being nothing new under the Sun, these merely applied modern technology to ideas that Handley Page had espoused much earlier.

Forty years previously, at the dawn of the jet age, the gas turbine was a thirsty beast. Luckily fuel was cheap and at the mid-point of the Petroleum Age fuel efficiency was a fairly low priority for airlines. Even if they desired more fuel efficiency the engine technology wasn't available nor would it be until development was driven by the upwards spiral of crude oil prices and subsequent economic crises of the Seventies. What airlines did want was an expanding market and this needed cheaper tickets to open up a mass market for air travel. This would require larger aircraft, which would burn more fuel due to higher weight and drag. With fuel efficiency being a fairly fixed parameter in the running costs of airliners, the way to cut the costs of operating turbojet-powered airliners was to increase the overall efficiency of the aircraft itself. After weight, the aircraft designer's biggest headache is drag, which comes in many forms, each with its particular characteristics. If fuel efficiency was constant, seat/mile cost could be reduced by lowering drag. This work is most definitely not a book on aerodynamics, so what follows is much simplified as better, more technical explanations are available elsewhere. The two main types of drag that affect an aircraft are induced and parasitic. Induced is created when air is diverted around an object to generate lift, for example around a wing. Induced drag becomes lower as airspeed increases. Parasitic drag is the sum of many distinct drag components with the principal types being: form, interference and skin friction. More simply parasitic drag is caused by the non-lift-generating parts of the airframe. A low-drag airframe required less thrust to propel it which in turn allowed the installation of smaller engines with lower fuel consumption.

Trans-Atlantic passengers were to be carried by these designs. The earlier version on the right had different engines for take-off and cruise. These types and the intercontinental transports only had LFC on the wings; the fuselage still generated drag. The LFC system only operated once the aircraft was in the cruise.

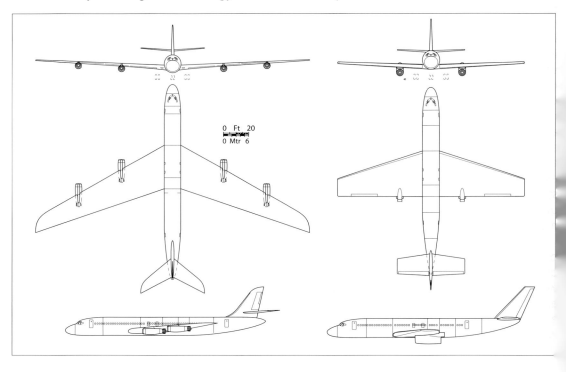

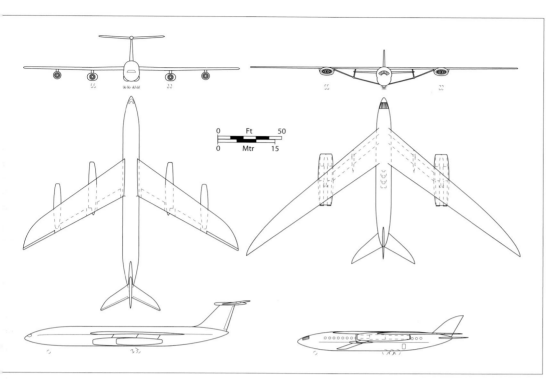

0 Ft 50
0 Mtr 15

Lachman and Lees examined a variety of fairly conventional LFC long-range airliners before opting for the flying wing. These intercontinental transports were to carry up to 250 passengers in double-bubble fuselages.

This had been a well-known aerodynamic fact since the dawn of the aviation era and the solution was the all-wing aircraft or flying wing whereby the entire structure served as a lift surface. This was a simple solution to parasite drag, but not without complications and lift-induced drag was another matter.

Any fluid passing over a surface will become stratified into layers of different velocity parallel to that surface with fluid velocity lowest in the layers closest to the surface due to friction. This causes the layers to break up and produce what is termed turbulent flow as speed increases. This is called the boundary layer and can be made to work for and against efficient aerodynamics depending on how the boundary layer is treated. Untouched, the boundary layer contributes to drag but if energised by blowing high-pressure air through slots or ports in the leading edge of a surface, the boundary layer is controlled and can contribute to lift at low speeds. The finest example of this is the Blackburn Buccaneer naval strike aircraft with what is called a 'blown wing' utilising boundary layer control (BLC) for maximum lift efficiency at low speed.

Alternatively the boundary layer with its turbulent flow and drag can be removed, to produce what is called laminar flow, a regime where the layers of fluid remain stacked neatly and pass over the surface smoothly. This can be achieved by shaping and so-called laminar flow wing profiles were a feature of wartime aircraft such as the North American Aviation P-51 Mus-

tang and Supermarine Spiteful, but these were passive measures. Active measures, called laminarisation, were aimed at increasing the efficiency of the overall aircraft. When combined with the postwar interest in flying wings, laminarisation had the potential to provide great advances in efficiency thus reducing the costs of air travel and opening up a mass market the airlines would only see two decades later with the advent of the Boeing 747 in 1970.

Two aircraft companies carried the torch for laminarisation in Britain: Armstrong Whitworth Aircraft (AWA) at Baginton in Warwickshire and Handley Page Aviation (HPA) at Radlett. AWA and HPA had shown great interest in flying wings and tailless aircraft having flown the AW.52 and HP.75 Manx in the 1940s but it would be the early 1950s before attempts at truly laminarised flying wings would be investigated. HP were not particularly interested in

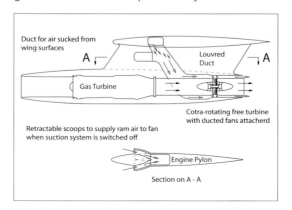

This cross-section through the engine installation on the intercontinental transports; suction was to be provided by a free turbine in the jet pipe that operated in a similar manner to the aft fans discussed earlier.

The Handley Page HP.113 was a very clean aircraft with its engines buried in the rear fuselage. As with the long-range airliners, only the wing was fitted with LFC. The right-hand plan view shows the amount of 'plumbing' required for LFC of the wings.

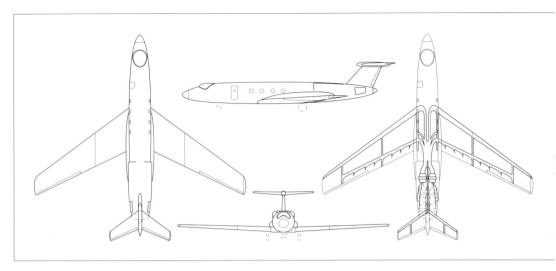

that Great British obsession of the late Fifties, the development of a supersonic transport, seeing this as a means of moving the elite rather than the masses. Even in the 1950s, ideas for large passenger aircraft were old-hat, dating back to the 1920s with types such as the Dornier Do.X and in the immediate postwar period when Bristol designed and built the Brabazon. Despite their size, these were only capable of carrying around a hundred passengers in relative luxury whereas HP intended carrying hun-

dreds. To do this they saw the volume available within a flying wing as the key and by laminarising that wing, could produce the seat/mile cos that would have the airlines beating a path to their door. Oddly enough the protagonists o the supersonic transport held similar views.

Handley Page briefed the Ministry and Ai Staff on its views at the 1956 Farnborough dis play by describing how, especially in long-range aircraft, laminarisation could produce cost sav ings. HP's first attempt at a laminarised airline

The Lockheed JetStar entered service with the USAF as the C-140 for VIP transport. Handley Page proposed the HP.113 for this requirement.
Author's Collection

The HS.125 Dominie was to form the basis of the HP.130 laminar flow control test bed. Due to the Ministry of Aviation policy of amalgamation and Handley Page's opposition, the HP.130 would have been sub-contracted to HP by Hawker Siddeley.
Via Terry Panopalis

was a conventional low-wing design with low aspect-ratio wings that carried its engines in an underwing nacelle at mid-span towards the trailing edge. The wings and tail surfaces had a fairly high thickness/chord ratio and were laminarised, but not the fuselage. Each engine nacelle carried two engines: one with high thrust for take-off and climb and the second, a lower power turbofan for high-altitude cruise. The latter drew much of its mass flow from the laminar suction system.

This initial attempt at an airliner was too small and its configuration less than ideal. The high thickness/chord ratio may have been driven by the need to install the ducting and equipment associated with the laminarisation system. Another drawback was the different types of engine, a feature that airlines did not like due to the costs of doubling up on engine maintenance and spares stock.

Working with Godfrey Lee, fresh from the Victor project, Lachmann's next design was the larger Project A, the Global Range Airliner that had a layout similar to the Boeing 707, with the four Conway engines mounted on the leading edge of the low, 30° swept wings that spanned 198ft (60.4m) but possessed much higher aspect and lower thickness/chord ratio than the earlier study. As before, the laminarisation system was designed into the wing, which with a series of slots in its skin, allowed the boundary layer to be drawn away through a series of ducts within the wing. Another Global Range Airliner, Project B was a more ambitious design with high, strut-braced wings swept at 42° with a span of 220ft (67m). Again the four Conways were mounted as pairs in the wing at mid-span. Both of these aircraft were designed for long range, London to Sydney with one stop at Fremantle. Lachmann and Lee's next study traded range for payload and was described as the Economic Transatlantic Transport Aircraft. Designed to carry heavy payloads over medium ranges, this type could have carried 240 economy-class passengers across the Atlantic within its double-bubble fuselage. This mid-winged type with a span of 167ft (50.9m) also sported all-moving tailplanes reminiscent of the Victor atop its fin. The four engines were to be mounted on pylons on the 35° swept wings, the inboard nacelle holding outriggers for the main undercarriage, Victor main bogies, in the fuselage. In comparison, the Boeing 747-100 of 1969 had a span of 195ft (59.4m).

None of these studies were assigned project numbers nor did they progress beyond initial drafts. The first laminar flow design to make

significant progress and carry a Handley Page project number was the HP.113, a 12-seat rear-engined airliner. Handley Page showed this design at the 1958 SBAC display at Farnborough and advised that the HP.113 would be capable of non-stop Atlantic crossings in just over six hours. This type progressed far enough for it to be proposed to fill the UC/X requirement for the USAF, ultimately filled by the Lockheed JetStar. This equipment took up internal volume that could be used for fuel and since only the wings and tail surfaces were laminarised, the drag from the fuselage was still a factor to be considered. The answer, of course, was the flying wing. In 1959 Lachmann proposed the HP.117, a fully-laminarised flying wing with a wingspan of 125ft (38.1m) and an all-up-weight of 330,000lb (149,659kg) to be powered by up to four RB.163 low-bypass turbofans. The full-sized HP.117 would have introduced an awful lot of new technology into a very large aircraft so the decision was taken to produce a scaled analogue called the HP.119. Unfortunately the expenditure on the HP.119 was estimated at between five and eight million pounds and so the project was rejected by the

Lachmann's initial foray into flying wings with LFC were the HP.117 and smaller HP.119. The HP.117's vestigial fuselage was not laminarised, so an annular intake collected the boundary layer and transferred it to the Spey turbofans.

Lachmann and Lee's final HP.117 was a flying wing with fins at the wingtips. The entire surface was subject to LFC with the minimum of doors and hatches left 'unsucked'. The passenger cabin and cargo holds were accessed via the undercarriage wells and their non-laminarised doors.

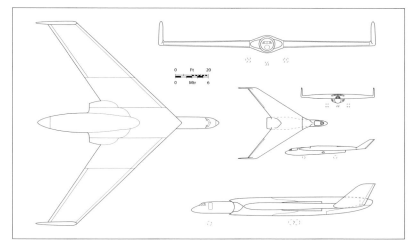

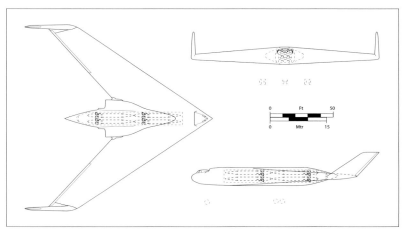

Handley Page drew up a range of laminarised transports under the HP.130 studies. The Type A based on the Herald was too slow to show any benefit, so the HS.125 was the basis of the remaining proposals.

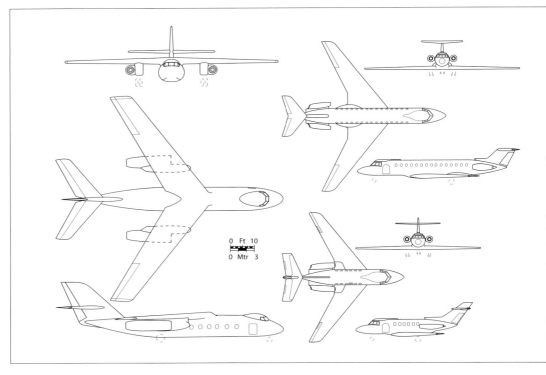

The HP.130 proved that LFC could provide efficiency benefits even if the wings alone were fitted for LFC. This drawing shows the two Gnome gas turbines used to suck the boundary layer from the wing surfaces. The LFC system took up space that could have been used for fuel.

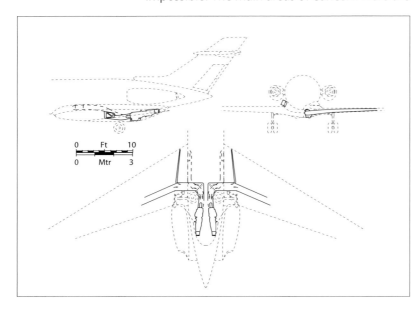

Ministry of Supply's Research and Development (R+D) Board in July 1961.

At the beginning of 1963 the R+D Board encouraged HP to investigate a less costly technology demonstration project with the aim of proving that laminarisation worked and that it could be applied to existing aircraft. This was to be based on either HP's Herald or the Hawker Siddeley HS.125 and the green light was given for this project in March 1963, leading to the HP.130.

As the design studies for the HP.117 progressed, it became increasingly obvious that complete laminarisation of the airframe was impossible. The main areas of concern were the entry doors and escape hatches for passenger access to the freight bays plus the undercarriage doors. The cockpit area with its glazing also proved problematic and not to be defeated Lee and Lachmann had a fairly simple solution. By adding a vestigial fuselage with cockpit, passenger access and nose undercarriage door ahead of the main wing and having its boundary layer swallowed by an annular intake at the wing/fuselage join; any turbulent airflow was prevented from affecting the wing.

A recurring problem was that the vestigial fuselage still contributed drag, so Lee and Lachmann examined the problem of the doors by doubling up on their function. Access to the passenger cabins would be via doors incorporated into the undercarriage bays. The cockpit glazing still posed a problem by being raised above the line of the wing upper surface. This was resolved by installing the intake for the six Rolls-Royce Spey turbofans immediately behind the cockpit. While this intake may have appeared too small to feed six turbofans, the laminar flow suction system drew the air from the boundary layer through a series of ducts that fed into the engine intakes.

In parallel with the HP.117 studies the HP.130 was an interesting design study for a research aircraft on a much smaller scale than the HP.117 or 119, with potential for retrofit onto existing designs. Initial studies concentrated on fitting the HPR.7 Herald with a laminarised wing and turbofans but this was soon dismissed as th

The Northrop X-21A was a radically redesigned Douglas B-66 fitted with a laminar flow control wing. The HP.130 would have fulfilled a similar development role. One problem revealed by the X-21A was debris and insects being sucked onto the wing surface. The solution was to keep the suction system switched off until a safe altitude had been reached. *USAF*

Herald was a fairly slow turboprop feeder-liner that would not benefit greatly from laminarisation. A high-subsonic type on the other hand would show significant gain from the technique. HP drew up a small rear-engined executive jet (looking not unlike a modern Embraer 145) with a laminarised swept wing. The last HP laminar flow project was the HP.135, a large transport aircraft with a maximum take-off weight of 475,000lb (215,456kg) to meet OR.371, later met by the Shorts Belfast.

The Laminar Flow Launcher

As an 'air alert deterrent' platform the HP.117 would have had an AUW of 354,000lb (160,544kg) when operating with eight Skybolts on a patrol lasting 12 hours. The HP.117 poffler was different from the VC10 or V-bombers in that it carried its eight Skybolts internally in the cargo bay. The missiles were mounted in two quartets, one behind the other on rails and launched out of the rear of the fuselage. By ejecting them rearwards through specially-designed doors set in the rear fuselage, the missiles are moving at relatively low velocity relative to the aircraft. This meant that they did not suffer a reduction in speed and maintained an air speed within the missile's flight envelope. The missiles were to be launched singly,

with each 'rail' of missiles having its own door.

Had the HP.117 been developed, it could have given the VC10 a run for its money in the poffler role. Had the situation been different and HP been given funding for its laminar flow research, who knows where it might have taken

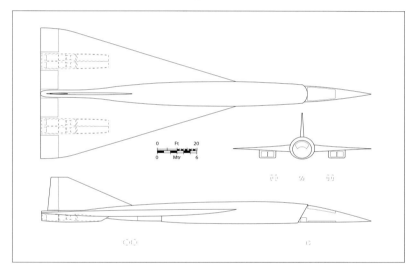

the UK aerospace industry. Perhaps in these days of rocketing fuel costs and with engine efficiencies reaching a plateau, the laminar flow technology that Lachmann investigated might be dusted off and applied to projects that Lachmann couldn't have imagined.

Handley Page ploughed a lonely furrow with LFC while the rest of the British aviation became obsessed with the supersonic transport. Not to be outdone, Handley Page drew up this Mach 2 laminarised passenger transport in August 1963. The entire surface was laminarised apart from the nose, leading edges and control surfaces.

Skybolt and alternative ALBMs

Type	Length	Diameter	Weight	Propulsion	Range
GAM-47 Skybolt	38ft 3in	2ft 11in	11,000lb	Two-stage solid booster	1,000nm
Avro Z.72	22ft 3in	4ft	16,000lb	Two-stage solid booster	1,000nm
Avro Z.89	40ft	2ft	12,000lb	Solid boost / liquid sustainer	765nm
BAC X.12B	26ft	2ft 7in	n/a	Two-stage solid booster	1,000nm
HH Hatchet	24ft 6in	1ft 6in	3,050lb	Rook solid rocket*	350nm
HH RG.17	19ft	2ft 4in	4,600lb	Single-stage rocket	150nm

A 17in motor with Skybolt-style swivelling nozzle and four thrust-reversal ports was under development at RPE.

7 Insurance
Pandora, Stopgap and yet more Blue Steels

'If a new weapon system is not available before, say, 1969, one would have to think very hard indeed about the wisdom of embarking on the project.'
Solly Zuckerman, 4th January 1961

From early 1960 the Skybolt programme was held up as the saviour of the V-Force. As a result, no-one in the Air Staff or Ministry of Aviation would entertain an alternative. Wiser heads prevailed, for example Duncan Sandys, who were prepared to accept that Skybolt was vulnerable to the vagaries of US policy. As an insurance against Skybolt's non-appearance OR.1182 was worked up. When Skybolt was scrapped, the Air Staff needed a gap-filler to replace Blue Steel and arm the V-Force until such time as Polaris entered service. The range and variety of project studies to meet OR.1182 and the Stop-gap/Gap-fillers show the diversity of thinking in the UK's aerospace companies.

In the summer of 1960 Blue Steel was still a long way from service and had yet to become the subject of serial discussions over lunch at Sir Roy Dobson's club. The Skybolt deal was in the bag and the RAF was preparing to send teams to the States to begin integration of the missile with the Vulcan.

Another positive development was that more information was becoming available on potential targets in the Soviet Union through the CIA's U-2 flights and the early Corona reconnaissance satellites. While welcome, this new information revealed that many of the targets of most interest lay 1,300nm (2,408km) beyond the borders of Soviet Russia and as noted earlier, attrition of the attacking force was directly proportional to the distance penetrated. In the face of the burgeoning Soviet air defences the short-range weapon, Blue Steel, was virtually useless against these distant targets while Skybolt, despite its 1,000nm

TSR.2 in the strategic strike role. Air-launched Blue Water was one weapon suggested as a Skybolt replacement. BAC intended using TSR.2 in the Poffler role supported by HP Victor tankers. *Adrian Mann*

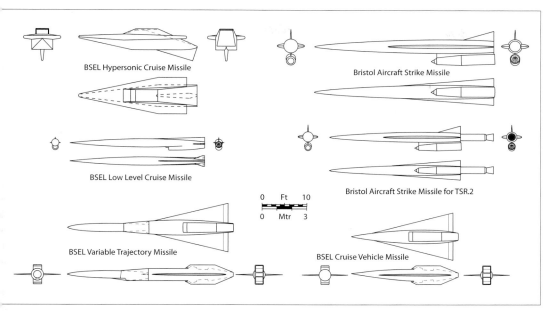

BSEL Hypersonic Cruise Missile

Bristol Aircraft Strike Missile

BSEL Low Level Cruise Missile

Bristol Aircraft Strike Missile for TSR.2

0 Ft 10
0 Mtr 3

BSEL Variable Trajectory Missile

BSEL Cruise Vehicle Missile

Bristol Siddeley Engines Advanced Propulsion Group drew up a variety of studies for the Mixed Trajectory missile. Bristol Aircraft also came up with studies for the Vulcan and TSR.2, which went on to become Pandora.

1,852km) range, still would not be viable without deeper penetration of enemy air space by the pofflers.

There was also a nagging suspicion amongst the Air Staff and Ministries of Defence and Aviation that the Americans were none too serious about Skybolt. Added to that was the fact that 1960 was presidential election year in the United States and changes in administrations lead to changes in policy, particularly in defence procurement. John F. Kennedy, the Democrat candidate, was sceptical of US/UK nuclear co-operation and concerned that an independent deterrent could lead to a repetition of ventures along the lines of Anthony Eden's Suez operation of 1956. Ultimately, as described in Chapter Six, Skybolt was cancelled by President Kennedy, thus proving the Air Staff's suspicions to be correct. In the summer of 1960 that event was still two years away.

Meanwhile at Bristol Siddeley Engines Limited (BSEL) Ramjet Department, R J Lane was examining the problem of long-range missiles. John Lane was in charge of BSEL's Advanced Propulsion Research Group and, working with Roy Hawkins, conducted some of the most sophisticated engine research in the world. In conjunction with Avro's Weapons Research Division and Bristol Aircraft, Lane had by the end of October 1960 drawn up a series of proposals that would use BSEL propulsion systems.

John Lane described these in BSEL Report No. 3168 and he explored a variety of configurations for a long-range stand-off missile. The first, Cruise Vehicle Missile, was a delta-winged missile with dorsal and ventral integrated BSEL ramjets. This weapon was 35ft (10.7m) long with a span

of 15ft (4.6m) and with an AUW of 15,000lb (6,804kg), was to be capable of a Mach 4.5 cruise at 100,000ft (30,480m) over an estimated range of 2,000nm (3,704km). At the end of the cruise the engines were to be jettisoned before the missile entered its terminal dive. One interesting aspect of this study was that the engine exhausts filled the entire base area of the missile for maximum efficiency by removing base drag.

The second of Lane's designs was the Low Level Cruise Missile, a slender, wingless design with an integrated ramjet that was good for 1,000nm (1,852km) at Mach 2 at 1,000ft (305m). The missile weighed 21,000lb (9,525kg) at launch and was 40ft (12.2m) long with a diameter of 3ft 6in (1.1m). The range quoted is odd, as the BSEL report states that the missile would have a range of 720nm (1,333km) using kerosene or 940nm (1,741km) when fuelled with 'HEF III' a high-energy fuel using borane additives (See Chapter Eight). In his report to Avro, Lane described how 'to get the largest ranges slender, almost wingless, vehicles with ramjets integrated with the rear of the airframe must be used.'

The Variable Trajectory Missile was a two-stage ramjet-powered weapon that was intended to cruise at 90,000ft (27,432m) at a speed of Mach 4.5 for 1,700nm (3,148km) before the second stage separated and dived to 500ft (152m) to cruise at Mach 2 for the last 300nm (556km). This proposal combined aspects of the two missiles described above in a vehicle with an AUW of 21,000lb (9,525kg) including boosts. The first stage was based on the earlier Cruise Vehicle Missile while the second stage based on a much smaller Low Level

133

Cruise Missile that weighed 5,000 lb (2,267kg).

The fourth study, the Hypersonic Cruise Missile, represented the cutting edge of high-speed propulsion as it was to use a detonation wave combustion engine that was completely integrated with the airframe and its delta wing. This missile was intended to have a range in the order of 2,000nm (3,704km) at speeds between Mach 7 and Mach 10. The propulsion system was a ramjet 'to use the principle of detonation wave combustion to burn fuel at hypersonic speeds.' The vehicle weighed 12,500 lb (5,670kg) at launch, with 7,500 lb (3,402kg) taken up by boost motors to accelerate the missile from Mach 0.8 at separation from the Vulcan to the Mach 5+ required to start the ramjet. The missile would then have climbed from 70,000ft (21,336m) to end the cruise at Mach 7 at an altitude of 110,000ft (33,528m). A further development was to be capable of Mach 10 and the supersonic combustion ramjet fuelled with hydrogen.

These four proposals were very much paper studies by an engine developer and so could be expected to be highly speculative. The fifth missile in the report was drawn up by Bristol Aircraft and called the Strike Missile. Intended for launch from Avro's Vulcan, the Strike Missile had an AUW of 7,500 lb (3,402kg), was 33ft (10.1m) long and its narrow delta wings had a span of 5ft (1.5m) and a leading edge sweep of 85°. It was to be powered by a podded BRJ.824 ramjet fitted under the rear fuselage. Boost to a Mach 3 cruise speed was to be by a quartet of Gosling IV motors in a wraparound configuration as used on Bloodhound. The missile had a range of 1,300nm (2,408km) with the last 50nm (93km) at low altitude.

A second, 80% scaled, version of the Strike Missile for use by the TSR.2 was also described and would have used the Thor BT.3 ramjet from Bloodhound and be boosted by a single Goldfinch rocket motor in a tandem configuration. This weapon would be for low-level use only and possessed a range of 200nm (370km) at Mach 2.2. If launched at high altitude such as 30,000ft (9,144m) a range of 500nm (926km) could have been achieved. A variant of this weapon was to dispense with the warhead and carry a reconnaissance pack, probably IR linescan.

A more conservative weapon, the Strike Missile used existing components, could be developed quickly and looked feasible. So much so that Bristol Aircraft decided to use this as the basis for a weapon to arm the V-Force and called it Pandora.

Bristol Aircraft was now part of the British Aircraft Corporation (BAC) and therefore had access to technology from other members of the BAC group that included English Electric Aviation and Vickers. Using the experience gained in high-speed structures and propulsion while the Blue Envoy Mach 3 SAM was under development Bristol Aircraft (it took time for all parties involved to get used to the title BAC forgot about the version for TSR.2 and drew up Pandora as a Mach 3 cruise missile with a range of 1,000nm (1,852km). While the airframe and propulsion system were to be developed in house by Bristol Aircraft, the electronics had to be brought in from elsewhere in the BAC group. The guidance system, for example, was to be the same as the English Electric Blue Water tactical ballistic missile and could provide a CEP of 2.5nm (4.6km) at maximum range.

Pandora's advantage as a deterrent weapon was that the last 50nm (93km) of its trajectory was to be flown at low altitude and Mach 2.2. Unfortunately the RAE's Working Party on OR.1182 was concerned that the high level of vibration generated by the ramjet would have a detrimental effect on the gyros and this would be compounded by the low-level flight regime which also required a sophisticated terrain following radar and control system. That equipment was to come from TSR.2 and was under development by Ferranti as the Forward Looking Radar (FLR). BSEL also modified the BRJ.824 pilot and secondary burners to accommodate the diverse operating environment of high and low altitude and thus avoid development of a variable intake. Bristol Aircraft advised that they could have Pandora in service by 1966 by using off-the-shelf equipment, if a development contract was placed soon.

Bristol's rationale for Pandora was that a ballistic missile, such as Skybolt, had a fairly predictable trajectory and was thus vulnerable to any anti-ballistic missile (ABM) system the Soviets developed. Since the Soviets were developing such a nuclear-armed defensive missile in the shape of the A-35 system (NATO reporting name ABM-1 *Galosh*), the Air Staff were interested in what Bristol Aircraft were proposing. Bristol's also pointed out that the longer-range missile would cut the 50% attrition rate the V-Force would have faced on a penetration of Soviet airspace and therefore the V-bombers carrying four Pandora missiles would mean that fewer V-bombers would be required.

It had been a timely proposal and the Air Staff and the Ministries saw Pandora as insurance against Skybolt failing rather than its can

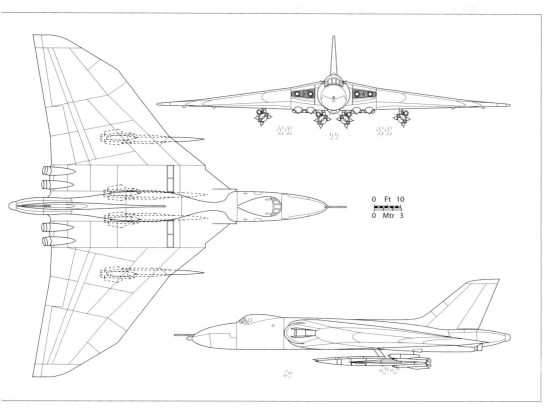

0 Ft 10
0 Mtr 3

Bristol's Pandora became X.12 once official attention had been gained. The Vulcan could carry four rounds, although at the expense of carry range.

cellation, no doubt influenced by the ongoing saga of Blue Steel. Pandora also gave the Air Staff the diversity of deterrence they craved, presenting the Soviets with two threats to defend against. So, satisfied that there was a missile that could fill it, the Air Staff drew up OR.1182, issued on 18th November 1960. Unfortunately they included in the requirement a range of 1,300nm (2,408km), reflecting the realisation that penetration of Soviet air space was fraught with danger.

By the end of 1960 Pandora had undergone another name change and was renamed as the X.12. In its basic form X.12 was to be carried by the Vulcan, with two mounted under the fuselage and a single round under each wing. TSR.2 was to carry a single X.12 under each wing. Interestingly, the X.12 was to be carried inverted and canted on the pylons to maximise ground clearance. On launch it rolled upright as soon as it had cleared the aircraft.

At launch the X.12 weighed in at 15,000 lb (6,804kg) and was 40ft 6in (12.3m) complete with its four boost motors. The original Pandora had a small 85° delta, but the definitive X.12 turned the wing into a long strake along two-thirds of the fuselage length that formed a fuel tank. Directional control was twist-and-steer via elevons on the 'wing' trailing edge for pitch and roll and a rudder on the small dorsal fin for yaw damping.

Launched from a Vulcan at 40,000ft (12,192m) the X.12 was to climb to 70,000ft (21,336m) under the power of the boost motors until the ramjets achieved full thrust at around Mach 2. Once the cruise altitude had been reached, the missile accelerated to Mach 3 for the cruise to a distance of 850nm (1,574km) before descending to 200ft (61m) for the last 50nm (93km) at Mach 2.2. If the low-level portion of the flight were not required, the X.12 could have cruised to 1,250nm (2,315km) before plunging onto its target. The X.12 would have been launched from TSR.2 at low altitude and was good for a sea-level dash at Mach 2.2 to attack a target 120nm (222km) from release point.

A further version of X.12 was the X.12B, proposed in a letter by L H Bedford of English Electric Aviation Guided Weapons Division to the Director General Guided Weapons, J E Serby in March 1961. This was an air-launched ballistic missile and appears to be one of those 'under the counter' projects such as those mentioned earlier in connection with Blue Steel. Bedford wrote 'I understand that there is some doubt as to the actual authorisation of this study, but a small amount of preliminary work has been done…' suggesting it had been worked on 'off the books'. Bedford's letter continued, asking for '…as much information as possible on the corresponding American project', which was of course, Skybolt.

X.12B was to be 26ft (7.9m) long (not including the tail fairing) and had a maximum diameter of 33in (83.8cm). The re-entry vehicle was based on that of Polaris, weighed 840 lb (381kg) and could have delivered this to a target 1,000nm (1,852km) away.

Woodford and the W.140

Avro's response to OR.1182 was to propose a version of their W.130, a weapon designed for the Dassault Mirage IV and subsequently for TSR.2. The W.130 was derived from the W.120 (developed under the WRD designation Z.61) that was intended to be an alternative to the Bullpup on the Mirage IV. This was initially drawn up as Z.58, a half-scale W.100 Blue Steel, in May 1959 and had a launch weight of 4,500 lb (2,041kg) and a range of 50nm (93km).

W.120 was a much tidier canard delta affair, 16ft 6in (5m) long and a span of 5ft 6in (1.7m) with increased wing area and, when powered by a 3,000 lbf (13.3kN) solid rocket motor, the 2,750 lb (1,247kg) missile had a range of 90nm (167km). From this was developed the larger W.130 that dispensed with the canard and sported a large delta wing with a leading edge sweep of 80° that extended almost the full length of the fuselage.

For OR.1182 Avro (or as they were now called, Hawker Siddeley Dynamics, HSD) proposed the Z.89, developed as the W.130B by adding a large tandem booster plus a liquid-fuelled rocket engine in the missile itself to provide a range of 765nm (1,417km) at an altitude of 100,000ft (30,480m) and a speed of Mach 5.5. The booster was described as a 'double thrust-level solid rocket' which suggests it had

a boost/sustain capability along the lines of the Phoenix 24in (61cm) motor intended for Blue Water. This proposal and the related ground-launched Z.82 (See Chapter Eight) were immediately dismissed by the joint Air Ministry/Ministry of Aviation working party, with L Nicholson, head of the RAE's Aerodynamic Department saying that 'W.130 can be discounted as it lacks range and has no low-level capability.'

The DG/GW's thinking on the matter was no doubt a sign of the growing rift between the Ministries and Avro over the much delayed Blue Steel. However, such comments had not put Avro off (assuming they had seen them) and by the turn of the year had drawn up a new proposal to meet OR.1182. This new missile carried the designation Z.98 and by March 1961 had become known as the W.140.

Avro WRD produced a rather handsome missile with a slender fuselage, mid-set narrow delta wings with 85° leading edge sweep and cropped delta vertical stabilisers on each wingtip. A Rolls-Royce RB.153 turbofan was installed in a pod under the rear fuselage. Avro's brochure describes the RB.153 as a 'turbojet' while Rolls-Royce's own documentation describes it as a turbofan, albeit with a very low bypass ratio of 0.7. The early Z.98 was powered by a RB.153-22 engine fed by a simple rectangular intake, soon replaced by a circular intake with a conical centre-body when the missile's high-altitude performance was criticised.

The definitive W.140 of May 1961 was 37ft 4in (11.4m) long and had a wingspan of 6ft 6in (2m). The fuselage had a maximum diameter 2ft 10in (0.8m), much of it containing fuel with terrain-following radar, navigator and warhead in the forward section of the fuselage. A

When France came looking for a missile to arm the Mirage IV, Avro proposed the Z.58, W.120 and W.130. The W.130 was dismissed immediately by the Air Staff when Avro proposed it for OR.1182.

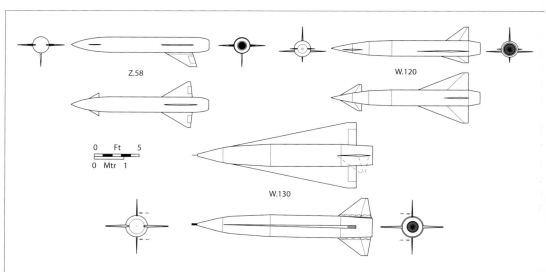

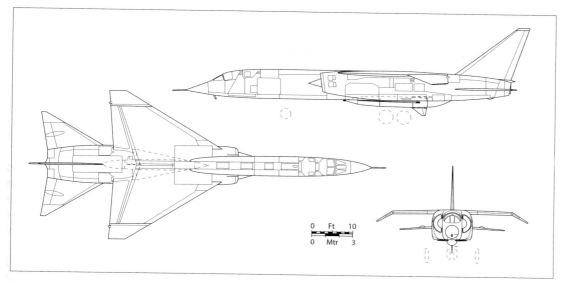

As a weapon for TSR.2, W.130 was a far better option than the Z.122 compact Blue Steel as it benefited from advances in miniaturisation of components, particularly the nuclear warhead.

launch the W.140 weighed 8,550 lb (3,878kg), half of which was fuel. Being powered by a turbofan, the W.140 required no additional boost, nor did it require an external power supply for pre-launch checks as the engine could be fired up with the missile on the pylon.

After launch from a Vulcan the W.140 would climb to 70,000ft and commence its cruise at Mach 3 for 950nm (1,759km) before descending to 300ft for the last 100nm (185km) at Mach 1.5 to the target.

These two proposals were examined in Whitehall and the pros and cons of each weighed up. On a general basis the Ministry of Aviation was concerned that OR.1182 would be a burden on BAC and HSD and would force them to re-allocate technical personnel from existing high-priority projects such as Blue Steel, Blue Water and the PT.428 low-level SAM. Indeed the ministers stated that '...the project might involve the abandonment of some other important project.'

The most bizarre statement that emanated from Whitehall was even more ominous: On 31st January 1961, J Roberts, Permanent Secretary to Julian Amery, the Secretary Of State for the Air, wrote a memo to the Permanent Secretary to the Chief of the Air Staff and stated that '...it was important that the Americans don't find out about this as it would weaken our position on Skybolt.' Please note that the Permanent Secretary is a senior civil servant in charge of the day-to-day running of a British Government department and has considerable clout. They do not take shorthand.

Meantime, the RAE Guided Weapons Department assessed the proposals and declared that neither weapon met the range requirement and was particularly critical of the

W.140. It did not meet the speed or altitude specified and its low-level speed of Mach 1.5 made it vulnerable to air defences. Avro's response to this was that 'terrain following is extremely difficult at higher speed.'

The X.12 was criticised for its higher all-up-weight and the drag penalty that was incurred on the Vulcan loaded with four missiles, something that severely affected the Vulcan's carry range. Such was the drag penalty that to achieve the carry radius requirement would mean a reduction in rounds carried to two, which more or less demolished Bristol's argument for the X.12 needing fewer V-bombers. Only the Vickers VC10 could carry the full complement of four X.12s to the required range. Bristol's were keen to show that X.12 was suitable for carriage in the cargo bay of the Shorts Belfast and the transport aircraft to meet OR.351. Not only were these aircraft capable of

Avro's W.140 was proposed as an alternative to Bristol's X.12 but lacked the range and speed of its ramjet-powered competitor. Avro considered Mach 2 too fast for successful terrain-following flight. The size of the X.12 is also apparent, something that impacted on the carrying aircraft's range.

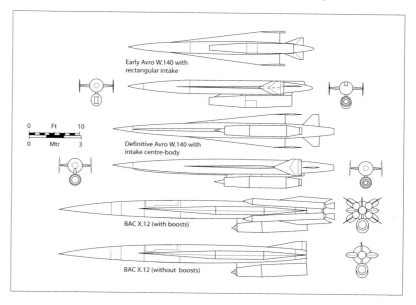

Early Avro W.140 with rectangular intake

Definitive Avro W.140 with intake centre-body

BAC X.12 (with boosts)

BAC X.12 (without boosts)

carrying the missile, they could launch it 'out the back' in flight in a similar manner to that suggested for launching Skybolt from Belfast and the HP.117. (See Chapter Six)

Bristol and Avro said that both their missiles could be in service within five years if existing equipment was used. The RAE had different ideas and was of the opinion that the terrain following system being developed for TSR.2 was unsuitable for OR.1182, and that at least seven years was a more likely time-scale to meet OR.1182 in full. The Chief Scientific Advisor, Solly Zuckerman, weighed in with 'If a new weapon system is not available before, say, 1969, one would have to think very hard indeed about the wisdom of embarking on the project.'

The MoA and Air Ministry pointed out that by specifying 1,300nm (2,408km), the Air Staff had pushed the boat out on the range requirement yet again and almost immediately (10th January 1961) issued an amended OR.1182 that allowed for incremental increases in range over time. This now stated that the initial version in service by 1966 should have a high-altitude cruise range of 600nm (1,111km) increasing to 800nm (1,482km) by 1968 and by 1970 this should be 1,000nm 1,852km). The low-level phase was to be in the order of 100nm (185km) initially, rising to 300nm (556km) by 1970. Full contour-following in the low-level phase was not required, only terrain avoidance, which sim-

plified matters somewhat. This issue of OR.1182 also stated that TSR.2 should be able to carry the weapons with minimal change to either.

In the end the Ministry of Aviation decided that an insurance policy against Skybolt failure was tantamount to defeatist talk. The Air Staff were keen to show 100% support for Skybolt and anything that might threaten its acquisition was to be positively discouraged. This explains the '…don't tell the Yanks' memo between the various ministries described above. By the end of 1961 OR.1182 had withered away and Skybolt became the only option for the British deterrent. Until December 1962.

Stop-gaps

To the British Civil Service, 'Panic' was something that happened elsewhere, usually in newspaper reports from abroad. When the news came though at the beginning of January 1963 that Skybolt had been cancelled, panic was what ran through the Ministries of Aviation and Defence. Within a month the Nassau Agreement was clarified and it became clear that Polaris was to be the future of British deterrence. There was the small matter of fielding a credible deterrent until Polaris reached service in 1970, Blue Steel being viewed as unviable as such after 1965, if not before.

Back in December 1962, when the writing was on the wall for Skybolt, a couple of possi-

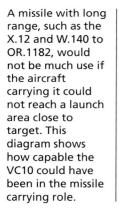
A missile with long range, such as the X.12 and W.140 to OR.1182, would not be much use if the aircraft carrying it could not reach a launch area close to target. This diagram shows how capable the VC10 could have been in the missile carrying role.

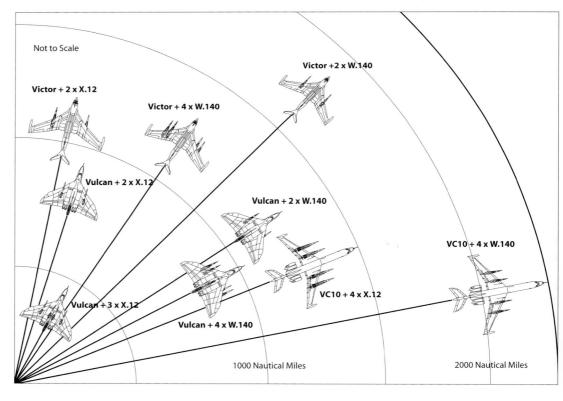

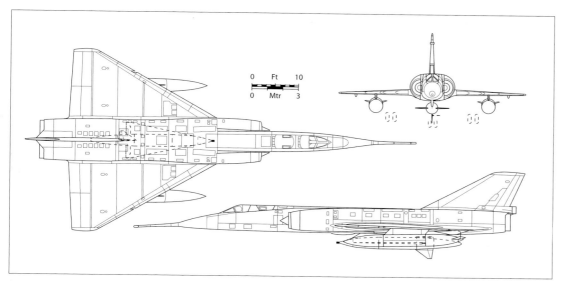

Had l'Armée de l'Air adopted the Avro W.130 for its Mirage IV bombers it would no doubt have been acquired by the RAF for the BAC/Dassault Spey Mirage had it been adopted in the strategic role. The Air Ministry were keen to have a low/slow and high/fast mixed deterrent in the shape of Vulcan and Mirage IV.

bilities for a continued RAF deterrent were discussed. The first was to use the GAM-77 Hound Dog (re-designated AGM-28 in June 1963) on the V-bombers but that plan was a non-starter as the weapon could not be fitted to Victor or Vulcan without radical modification to missile and aircraft. The second proposal was to co-operate with the French on their ballistic missile programme or buy the Dassault Mirage IV, re-engined with Rolls-Royce Speys, from France to provide a high-altitude supersonic threat '…to diversify the attack.'

Development of a British Skybolt was also seen as a waste of resources as such a weapon '…could not be ready before the Vulcans were almost worn out…' and Polaris would probably be in service before it.

On 2nd January 1963 the Ministry of Aviation outlined possible alternatives to Skybolt in the short term: Improved ECM for the V-Force, low-level use of the V-bombers and Blue Steel, the Lay-Down Megaton Bomb, OR.1168 with megaton warhead, Stretched Blue Steel, a developed Black Knight fired from hardened sites in the UK and finally, stretching the range of TSR.2.

In the longer term were: Polaris (already in hand), a British developed ALBM for carriage on VC10 transports, land-launched ballistic missiles, revival of OR.1182 with increased range and finally a short-range ALBM for TSR.2.

The Weapons Department of the Royal Aircraft Establishment produced on 7th January 1963 the aptly named 'Rush Summary Paper of Possible Deterrent Development – Gap Fillers 1963-70' which expanded on the earlier MoA paper. The speed with which these documents appeared suggests that people had had their Christmas holidays disrupted.

The Lay-Down Bomb (already in development for OR.1177) was described as 'the cheapest and earliest system' and no doubt the simplest. The Air Staff soon pointed out that if used by the V-bombers, a heavy toll would be exacted on the force by the new S-125 Neva/Pechora (NATO reporting name SA-3 *Goa*)

With hindsight the obvious deterrent weapon all along was the submarine-launched ballistic missile. Back in the 1960s the solution was not as straightforward. Polaris was also considered as an air-launched weapon, championed by Peter Masefield. *US Navy*

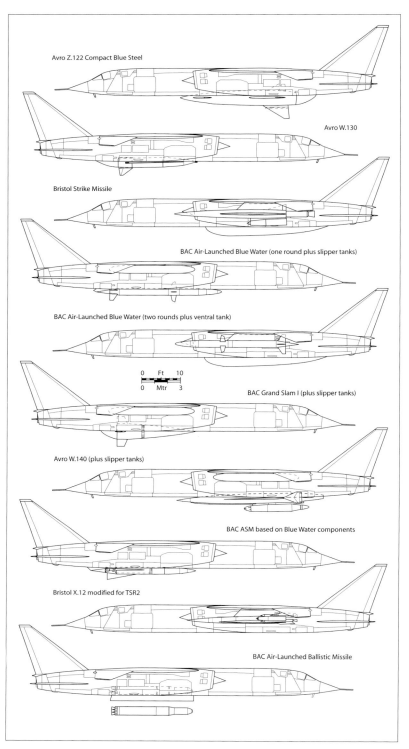

Avro Z.122 Compact Blue Steel

Avro W.130

Bristol Strike Missile

BAC Air-Launched Blue Water (one round plus slipper tanks)

BAC Air-Launched Blue Water (two rounds plus ventral tank)

0 Ft 10
0 Mtr 3

BAC Grand Slam I (plus slipper tanks)

Avro W.140 (plus slipper tanks)

BAC ASM based on Blue Water components

Bristol X.12 modified for TSR2

BAC Air-Launched Ballistic Missile

missiles, so realistically only TSR.2 or Buccaneer could field what would become the WE.177.

The OR.1168 stand-off bomb was what became known as Megaton Martel, based on the AJ.168 missile with a megaton warhead. The RAE suggested that its 50nm (93km) range would be sufficient to attack cities, but would hinge on how vulnerable the V-bombers were to anti-aircraft guns. The Megaton Martel com-

pared favourably with Blue Steel launched from low altitude, on cost and on flexibility. Blue Steel could not be carried by TSR.2 or Buccaneer, both of which could perform low-level penetration much better than the V-bombers. A re-engined Blue Steel designed for low-altitude flight might be attractive, but was the best of a bad bunch 'None of the Blue Steel systems looks attractive overall, the best seems that low-altitude Viper engined version…'. The use of Black Knight as the basis of a silo-deployed two-stage ballistic missile was the costliest, most inflexible and least suitable weapon. Its range of 1,400nm (2,593km) meant that it could only reach targets in European Russia from bases in the UK.

All of these stop-gap solutions to the deterrent needs of the RAF would have taken at least three, if not four, years to produce. Readers can be forgiven if the impression gained from this is that the British Government was scrabbling around for any means to deliver a nuclear weapon to Soviet cities. Essentially this was what was happening; with requests fired out to the various aviation companies for their ideas for delivery systems.

Lord Caldecote, chairman of English Electric Guided Weapons and Deputy Managing Director of BAC, was quick off the mark in mid-January and, seeing an opportunity for BAC, Caldecote enclosed two brochures with his letter to Air Marshal Grundy, Controller of Guided Weapons and Electronics (abbreviated to CGWL, L for electronics obviously). The first brochure was 'Strategic Weapon System: Blue Water on V-Bomber or TSR.2' and described the conversion of the Blue Water tactical missile for air-launch, mainly by extending the motor by 4ft (1.2m) and folding the rear fins for easier ventral carriage of a single missile on TSR.2. An option of a missile on each of the Vulcan's Skybolt pylons was also considered. Lord Caldecote pointed out that the Blue Water proposal '…makes maximum use of past development work and could be ready soonest and at least cost.'

The second brochure was a different beast altogether. 'Project Grand Slam – System of Low Vulnerability for Tactical and Strategic Nuclear Strike from Aircraft' was a Bristol Aircraft rocket-powered toss-bomb with a range of 100nm (185km) intended for the TSR.2. When the aircraft was 100nm (185km) from the target the TSR.2 tossed the re-entry vehicle into a rocket-boosted ballistic trajectory, dispensing its forty decoys as it dived onto the target. The power for the re-entry vehicle came from a 36in (91cm) diameter solid rocket motor.

This motor may have been derived from a shortened RPE Stonechat, a 36in (91cm) motor and the largest solid rocket ever developed in the UK. Stonechat was used in the CQ.941 Falstaff test vehicle that was used for hypersonic research and became the workhorse of the Chevaline development programme in the 1970s. On closer examination the RAE considered Grand Slam to be too complicated for little gain in stand-off range and restricted the freedom of manoeuvre of the launch aircraft during delivery.

Lord Caldecote rounds off his letter to CGWL with the following: 'In addition I have already sent you brief details of a proposal made to us by the Martin Company in my letter of January 14th'. This somewhat mysterious sentence refers to a proposal for the American missile company Martin Marietta to co-operate with BAC in the development of an air-launched ballistic missile based on their MGM-1 Pershing IRBM. The Vulcan-launched Pershing would have had a range of 400nm (741km) and a launch weight and size on a par with Skybolt. A larger version with a range of 1,000nm (1,850km) was also proposed.

Further proposals appeared as January became February, including one listed as 'Modified Polaris (Lockheed-Masefield Proposal) – Polaris type missile for carriage on V-bombers'. This no doubt involved Peter Masefield, who at that point was chairman of Beagle Aircraft! Quite a transformation from chairman of a light-aircraft company to championing a ballistic missile but Masefield was respected in British aviation circles as a hard worker and no doubt his previous employment as Civil Air Attaché in Washington opened many a door in America. He followed that by becoming the managing director of Bristol Aircraft at a time when they were at the cutting edge of engine, airframe and guided weapons development. How he came to be involved with an air-launched Polaris is not documented but the RAE considered the proposal 'Unfavourable due to weight, size, guidance, environment.' and offered little advantage over Skybolt. The air-launched Pershing and Polaris were ultimately discounted as they gave no advantage on time, cost or capability over Skybolt and if such a system was chosen, a resumption of Skybolt under British control was a better option due to sunk-cost and the work completed so far.

By 24th of January, the results of this call to arms were being examined and meeting was held at the RAE Weapons Department at Farnborough. Representatives from the MoA, Rocket Propulsion Establishment and of course the RAE were in attendance, as were senior engineers from Bristol Aircraft and English Electric (under the BAC banner, of course). The meeting concentrated on the short-range weapons and various proposals were discussed and briefing papers drawn up for the ministers. A further outcome from this meeting was the issue on 27th February 1963 of Technical Memorandum WE.1054 written by D J Lyons of the RAE Weapons Department.

With the title 'Stop Gap Deterrent Weapons', WE.1054 contained details of the various weapons that were being proposed 'In this context "Stop Gap" means to fill in the gap between the time when the V-bombers armed with Yellow Sun or Blue Steel become unacceptably vulnerable (assumed to be between now and 1965/60 and the time at which Polaris firing submarines become available, assumed to be 1968/9'. Lyons outlined how Yellow Sun and Blue Steel could be launched at low level in a toss manoeuvre, with Blue Steel entering into its high-altitude cruise. Blue Steel could also be modified to fly at low-altitude after a low-level launch although this might take three years to develop. In this launch mode, Blue Steel's range would be reduced to less than 50nm (93km), something that had been viewed previously as a major limitation. In the new era of stop-gaps, 50nm was deemed just about right as there was about to be a volte face on range requirement if low-altitude launch was possible. Back in the early days of the OR.324 low-level bomber in 1955, Avro proposed a low-level version of Blue Steel that is listed in the WRD projects directory as 'Blue Cat'. This may refer to the warhead involved as Blue Cat was a MoS rainbow code for a 'common-user warhead' for SAMs and tactical missiles, but the reference does show that Avro were considering modifications to Blue Steel to allow low-level delivery.

Lyons next considered the stop-gap weapons themselves. The first item was the Lay-Down Bomb (WE.177) and this is examined in Chapter Three along with other free-fall weapons. This had the advantage of being delivered by high-speed strike aircraft that were less vulnerable than the V-bombers.

The stand-off bomb based on the OR.1168 weapon was based on a feasibility study carried out by de Havilland as part of their work in developing the AJ.168 Martel ASM. This weapon could have been used by the V-bombers, TSR.2 and Buccaneers, with the use of the latter from Royal Navy aircraft carriers adding to its flexibility and mobility. De Havilland stretched the AJ.168 by 13% to accommodate a megaton-class warhead, identified as Warhead D, (possibly from the Lay-Down Bomb) in its 15in (38cm) diameter fuselage. Within the 14ft 7in (4.4m) long fuselage an inertial navigator from the Nord AS.33 replaced the Martel TV system leaving space for a 6ft (1.8m) long rocket motor. With a launch weight of 1,500lb (680kg) the 'Megaton Martel' had an estimated range of 30nm (56km) when launched from a Buccaneer or TSR.2 and a CEP of two nautical miles (3.7km). It soon became apparent that the weapon's initial launch speed of Mach 1.2 diminished rapidly as it approached the target and calculations revealed that the missile would be travelling at Mach 0.4 at the end of its fight, making it vulnerable to just about any ground fire.

Cruise and Toss – the Grand Slams

Bristol Aircraft's main proposal could have easily been a revamped X.12, but what they drew up was much more advanced: a long-range, air-launched, rocket-powered toss-bomb. Called Grand Slam 2, this was a 32,000lb (14,515kg) weapon for the V-bombers with a range of 1,300nm (2,408km). This proposal took the earlier Grand Slam rocket-powered toss-bomb for TSR.2 and added a cruise stage with an integrated BS.1013 ramjet to provide an additional 1,200nm (2,222km) stand-off for the V-bombers. After launch at 40,000ft (12,192m) the Grand Slam 2 cruised at similar altitude for 500nm (926km) at a speed of Mach 3 under inertial guidance before descending to low altitude for Mach 2 terrain-following flight for the next 700nm (1,296km). When the missile was 100nm (185km) from the target, the weapon pitched up to release the re-entry vehicle into a rocket-boosted climb to apogee before dispensing its 40 decoys in its terminal dive. An estimated CEP of 3.5nm (6.5km) was thought probable for the Grand Slam terminal stage.

Grand Slam 2 was to be 50ft (15.2m) long with much of the fuselage between the re-entry vehicle and the propulsion bay full of Shelldyne high-density fuel. The highly-swept (80° on the leading edge) delta wings had a span of 15ft (4.6m) and elevons for roll and pitch control.

Bristol Aircraft had stated that Grand Slam 2 would have taken seven years to reach service, which was beyond the timescale required for the Stop-Gap/Gap-Filler weapon and so was dismissed from the running.

The next project under consideration was a de Havilland proposal for an air-launched, short-range ballistic missile outlined in DH Report RG.17. This weapon was also intended for the V-bombers, Buccaneer and TSR.2 and from a low-level launch DH stated that its range was in the order of 120nm (222km) or 200nm (370km) if a low-level toss delivery was used and a CEP of 2nm (3.7km) was expected. The missile itself was 19ft (5.6m) long, a diameter of 28in (71cm) and an AUW of 4,600lb (2,087kg) of which 700lb (318kg) was the warhead. De Havilland also proposed a smaller unguided ALBM called Hatchet, with a range of 55nm (102km), the warhead from the Lay-Down Bomb and powered by a Rook solid motor or a Foxhound from the Sea Slug naval SAM. Hatchet would have been carried by TSR.2 and launched in a toss manoeuvre. The Air Staff was of the opinion that '…a stand-off range of even

BAC's Grand Slam 2 added a second cruise stage to the Grand Slam (not to be confused with the Second World War earthquake bomb) to produce a long-range mixed-trajectory missile.

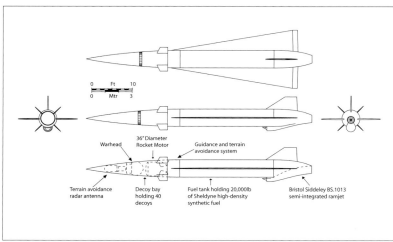

200nm does not provide significantly greater effectiveness than 50-70nm.' The RAE stated that if the DH weapon's range could be increased to 350nm (648km) it would be much improved but as it stood it could not be considered as a gap-filler or a longer term prospect.

In his conclusions, D J Lyons agreed with the Air Staff and considered a weapon with a stand-off range of 50nm (93km) and a launch weight of 2,000 lb (907kg) ideal as it avoided entering the low-level air defence zones around Soviet cities and could be carried by a greater variety of strike aircraft. Grand Slam 2, Blue Water and the RG.17 were too big and would take too long to develop. The RAE and the Ministries wanted small, cheap and soon.

The Gap-Filler

In the light of this, Bristol Aircraft went back to their project office and drew up the 'One Club' series. One Club A: a basic, unguided ballistic missile, that weighed 1,510 lb (685kg) at launch and comprised a Lay-Down Bomb forward section with the tail section replaced by a Raven solid rocket. One Club B used a stretched A model but added four Linnet III boost rocket motors to cope with the launch weight of 2,700 lb (1,225kg). Its re-entry vehicle was described as a lifting body that would behave like a glide bomb. The Air Staff's comments on this are not recorded. Both were intended for internal and external carriage on TSR.2 and Buccaneer and it was suggested that a few dummy rounds with concrete warheads be launched as decoys. What the Air Staff thought of their pilots endangering their lives carrying 'Blue Circle' missiles was not recorded.

The third member of the One Club was the C model: a Bristol Bloodhound SAM fitted with a nuclear warhead and modified for air-launch with a potential 25nm (46km) stand-off. Obviously such a missile could only be carried by the V-bombers; in fact only the Vulcan was intended for these stop-gap weapons.

Avro's TSR.2 Weapons

Avro WRD had also become involved in the small weapon for low-level delivery and tendered a number of missiles for use by TSR.2 and Buccaneer. In 1958 WRD had drawn up a study, Z.34, that they hoped could arm Avro's tender for OR.339 Canberra replacement, the Type 739. The Z.34 was intended to replace Red Beard/TMB on the Type 739 and was to be carried semi-recessed on a pallet in the weapons bay. Powered by a Smokey Joe rocket motor, Z.34 weighed 3,000 lb (1,361kg) at launch and used the same physics package as Red Beard. Dimensionally the Z34 was not much bigger than Red Beard, 14ft 6in (4.4m) long compared with Red Beard's 12ft (4m) and with a diameter of 32in (81cm) while Red Beard was 28in (71cm). The usual canard configuration was used, with the wings spanning 5ft 6in (1.7m). The Smokey Joe motor boosted the Z.34 to a maximum speed of Mach 1.5 and the missile had a range of up to 25nm (46km) under inertial navigation. The odd thing about fitting stand-off weapons to strike aircraft to meet OR.339 was that since these types were designed for low-level penetration, a stand-off weapon made them redundant. The Air Staff were well aware of this and were becoming very keen on the Lay-Down Bomb, which became WE.177.

When the Skybolt cancellation happened, WRD drew up a new small weapon, the Z.128A. By taking the 19/15 test vehicle and stretching it from 14ft 9in (4.5m) to 20ft (6.1m) Avro added a bay for a RE.179 warhead.

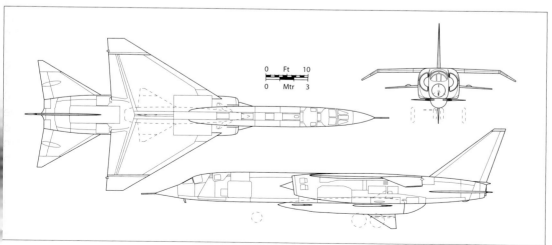

Seen here carried by a BAC TSR.2, the Z.122 was a Blue Steel shortened by 5ft (1.5m) to avoid fouling the aircraft's undercarriage and Doppler antenna.

Tactical strike weapons with strategic pretensions included the Z.34 that Avro had studied for the Type 739 aircraft to meet the same OR.339 that led to TSR.2. The Z.130A went on to become the Avro W.170.

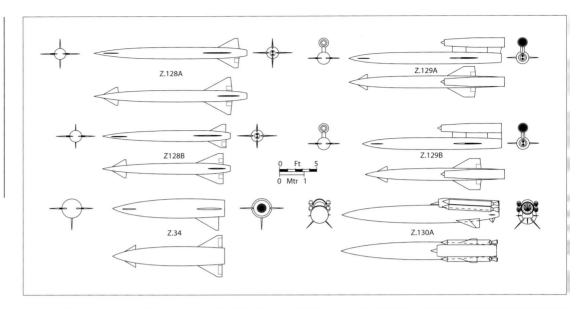

Avro's W.170 as fitted to the Avro Vulcan. The W.170B had the potential to provide a deterrent while the shorter W.170A was for tactical use. *BAE Systems/ RAF Museum*

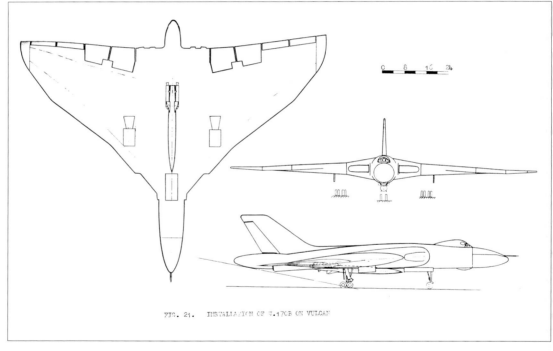

FIG. 21. INSTALLATION OF W.170B ON VULCAN

Avro WRD drew up the W.170 for TSR.2 and Buccaneer. Powered by an integrated BS1014 ramjet and boosted by solid rockets, the W.170 needed imaginative loading methods for the Buccaneer. *BAE Systems/ RAF Museum*

Z.128A was to have a range of 70nm (130km) and a maximum speed of Mach 3 for a launch weight of 2,050lb (930kg). The 70nm range was more than the Air Staff really required in this new era of low, short and small so WRD drafted the Z.128B, by shortening the airframe by 3ft (0.9m) and reducing the length of the motor. As a result the Z.128B had a range of 50nm (93km) in a smaller missile that was 100lb (45kg) lighter, something that aircraft designers always approve of.

With the interest in ramjet-powered missiles, WRD examined fitting the Z.128 with a Bristol BT.3 Thor ramjet from the Bloodhound and called the result the Z.129A. At 20ft 6in (6.2m) this proved too long for the Buccaneer to carry in its weapons bay, so WRD removed the inertial guidance system and replaced it with a basic autopilot that allowed the fuselage

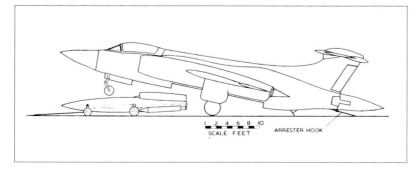

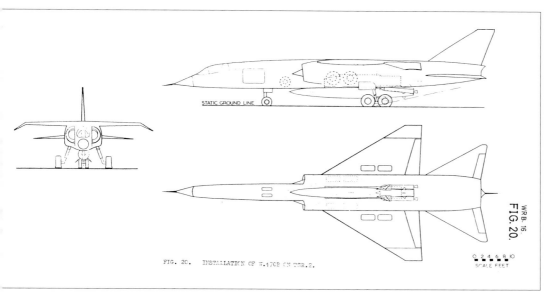

STATIC GROUND LINE

WRB. 16.
FIG. 20.

FIG. 20.   INSTALLATION OF W.170B ON TSR.2.

0 2 4 6 8 10
SCALE FEET

The W.170 came in two versions: long and short. The short A could be fitted to Buccaneer while the long B was for TSR.2 and the Vulcan. This drawing shows the installation of the B on TSR.2. *BAE Systems/ RAF Museum.*

o be shortened by 2ft 6in (0.7m) to produce he Z.129B. Both models had a range of 50nm 93km) and a launch weight of less than ,000 lb (903kg).

Ever since OR.339 (and the subsequent JR.343 that became TSR.2) had been issued, veapons to suit this aircraft had been under onsideration by Avro. This project was called he W.170 that had its origins in the Z.126, a 5ft (7.6m) long, ramjet-powered vehicle based n the Blue Steel fuselage with a range of 20nm (222km) at low-level while cruising at Mach 2.2, aided by a forward-looking radar. Avro hoped the Fleet Air Arm would be inter- sted in such a weapon and since the Z.126 was oo long for the Buccaneer, shortened it to 20ft 6.1m) to allow semi-recessed carriage on the Buccaneer's rotary bomb door as well as on the TSR.2. This weapon became in May 1963 the W.170A, propelled by a BSEL BS.1014 ramjet ntegrated into the rear of the airframe with a Jorsal inlet that was a 'half' Thor intake. The ini- ial boost to ramjet light up speed was provided y a two pairs of solid rocket motors, one each ide of the intake trunking. The W.170A was a 1andsome design that looked the part, and the obvious step was to stretch it to 34ft (10.4m) or use on the V-bombers as the W.170B.

The W.170A had an estimated launch veight of 4,300 lb (1,950kg) while the W.170B Joubled that to 9,900 lb (4,490kg) by adding xtra fuel and replacing the four boost motors vith two larger rockets. One further difference between them was that the 2ft 6in (0.8m) diameter of the W.170A was increased to 2ft 1in (0.9m) in the longer W.170B to preserve ineness ratio. Range-wise the A model's 40nm (259km) was increased to 450nm

(833km) by the extra fuel, while the cruise speed at the 200ft (61m) altitude WRD had been designed for was Mach 2.4. The Vulcan and the TSR.2 could carry a single W.170B semi- recessed, with the Vulcan using a pallet that replaced the bomb bay doors in a similar man- ner to that used for Blue Steel.

Avro WRD may have had an inkling of how the wind would blow on this low-level missile affair and focussed their efforts on a new ver- sion of Blue Steel. They had been working on an alternative to the W.170 and since this would be based on the W.100 Blue Steel, could be ready for service sooner than the W.170. Initial stud- ies by WRD produced the Z.125 by replacing the Stentor rocket engine with a Bristol Siddeley Viper 24 turbojet, rated at 4,000 lbf (17.8kN). As the design was firmed up, the designation W.160 was applied and WRD issued a substan- tial brochure, WRB15, outlining how the

Comparison drawing of the Avro W.160 low- level Blue Steel and the standard W.100/105. The most obvious change was the Bristol Siddeley Viper turbojet in its tail and the intakes to feed it. *BAE Systems/ RAF Museum*

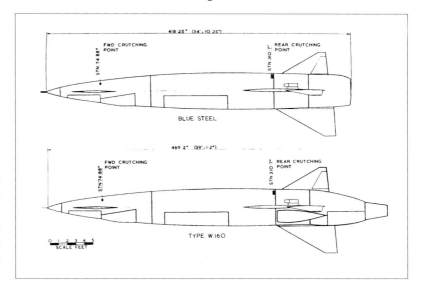

418.25" (34'-10.25")

FWD CRUTCHING POINT
STN 74.88"

REAR CRUTCHING POINT
STN 310.75"

BLUE STEEL

469.2" (39'-1.2")

FWD CRUTCHING POINT
STN 74.88"

REAR CRUTCHING POINT
STN 310.75"

0 1 2 3 4 5
SCALE FEET

TYPE W.160

While Blue Steel construction is under way in the background this example was being modified to became a W.160 with a Bristol Siddeley Viper turbojet in the tail.
BAE Systems/ RAF Museum

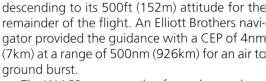

Close up of the W.160 with its Viper in the tail and scoop-type intakes under the wings. W.160 was intended to fly at low-level using terrain-avoidance radar after low-altitude launch from suitably-modified Victors and Vulcans.
BAE Systems/ RAF Museum

weapon would work. The Viper was fed by a pair of semi-circular intakes positioned under the wings and optimised for flight at Mach 0.9 at an altitude of 500ft (152m). With a full load of kerosene the W.160 had a range of 600nm (1,111km) when launched from a V-bomber at 40,000ft (12,192m), which Avro claimed would keep the V-bombers out of harm's way and allow poffling operations. If the RE.179 warhead replaced Red Snow, additional fuel space would be available to provide a range of 850nm (1,574km). The guidance system was modified for a new trajectory whereby, with engine idling to power the systems, the missile descended to 1,300ft (396m) where it flared and increased the engine power to commence its cruise, reaching Mach 0.9 after 35nm (65km),

descending to its 500ft (152m) attitude for the remainder of the flight. An Elliott Brothers navigator provided the guidance with a CEP of 4nm (7km) at a range of 500nm (926km) for an air to ground burst.

The W.160 progressed as far as the mock-up stage, showing how serious WRD were about it; however the Air Staff and Ministries were somewhat inured to Avro's advances after almost a decade. Avro did propose yet another weapon for the Vulcan in the shape of the Z.127 in February 1963. This used the long-awaited Rolls-Royce RB.145 turbojet that had been the powerplant of choice for the W.114 to meet OR.1159 five years previously. The Z.127 was 37ft long and used the standard canard delta configuration, this time to allow the fuselage to be almost entirely filled with fuel, a terrain-avoidance radar in the nose and a RE.179 warhead behind that. The RB.145 turbojet, rated at 2,750lbf (12.2kN) and 3,650lbf (16.2kN) with reheat, would have propelled the Z.127 at Mach 2 on a low-level trajectory for 730nm (1,352km).

At the same time Elliott Brothers, Shorts and Rolls-Royce decided to try their hand at stand-off weapons and proposed SLAM – supersonic low altitude missile – that used an RB.153 engine and Elliotts navigator in a canard delta missile. On submission to the Air staff and ministries, SLAM received a cool response, and was considered to be a '...souped-up low-level Blue Steel' by Air Cdr J H Hunter-Tod of the Ministry of Aviation. SLAM soldiered on until late 1964 possibly to arm TSR.2.

The Last Blue Steel: W.200

What did emerge from all the Gap-Filler and OR.1182 studies was that the RAF had the right weapon from the start in the shape of Blue Steel. Its optimum range was 50nm (93km) and W.160 had shown that its guidance system could be could be modified to fly at a relatively low altitude.

Avro's last throw of the Blue Steel die actually came to pass. With Skybolt cancelled, Polaris on order and the Gap-Fillers pretty much dismissed on timescale grounds, the Air Staff returned to Blue Steel. After all the goings-on with Stop-Gaps and Gap-Fillers, the realisation that the solution had been under their noses all the time was not lost on Avro or the Ministries. In September 1962 WRD had proposed a variant of the W.100, called Z.122, for carriage by TSR.2 by reducing its length by 5ft (1.4m) and replacing the dorsal fin with a much smaller item. This allowed the Z.122 to be carried semi-recessed in the TSR.2's weapons bay and with the reduced propellant volume and Red Snow warhead the missile had a launch weight of 14,360lb (6,164kg). No performance data for the Z.122 was listed in Avro's documents although a range of 50nm (93km) was no doubt expected.

Since Avro appeared to have no problem in modifying a Blue Steel for a low-level strike aircraft, there was a good chance that the existing W.100 Blue Steel Mk.I could be modified in the same manner. The Air staff issued OR.1132 (Issue 4) to cover low-altitude launch of Blue Steel from V-bombers and in August 1963 awarded Contract KF/G/41/CB_23(B) to Avro (or more accurately, Hawker Siddeley Dynamics) to carry out design studies to examine modification of existing Blue Steels for low-altitude launch from Victor and Vulcan B.2s. The greatest drawback to the low-altitude launch of Blue Steel was the effect on target choice. Low level penetration consumed more fuel and reduced the range of the aircraft, so much so that Moscow was off the target list for the Victor.

The requirement stated that the missile must be available for service by the end of 1964. An unmodified Blue Steel was tested first on 19th November 1963 and despite oft-repeated tales of this capability being available 'at the flick of a switch' this revealed that a number of modifications were required. Firstly the control system had to be made less powerful due to the control surfaces being more effective at low altitude. The flight rules com-

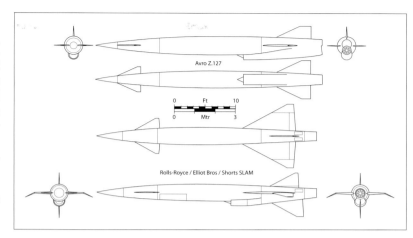

Avro Z.127

Rolls-Royce / Elliot Bros / Shorts SLAM

puter and autopilot required modification for the new trajectory and lastly, the HTP tank exit valves had to be moved to avoid oxidiser starvation at a point 35 seconds into the flight when the HTP level fell below the tank exit. All these changes meant that initially the modified Blue Steel, called W.200 by Avro/HSD, could not be used for conventional high-altitude launch until a further modification allowed the 'flick of a switch' role change.

The W.200's trajectory involved the Vulcan or Victor flying at a speed of 350kts (648kph) at an altitude of 1,000ft (305m). After release, the Blue Steel fell 300ft (94m) in 10 seconds, before both Stentor rocket chambers fired. After 20 seconds, the missile had reached supersonic speed and began to climb until at 59,000ft (17,983m) and Mach 2.3, the main chamber was cut. The Blue Steel continued to climb until it reached 70,000ft (21,336m) after 124 seconds, then cruised to a target up to 60nm (111km) distant before performing a bunt and

'A souped-up low-altitude Blue Steel' was how a member of the Air Staff described the SLAM from Rolls-Royce, Shorts and Elliott Brothers. Avro's Z.127 was very similar and marked the tailing off of the WRD's weapons work.

Low-level operation forced a change to Blue Steel's trajectory. With launch at low-level, use of both Stentor chambers was needed to boost the missile to altitude. The reduction in the missile's range was significant.

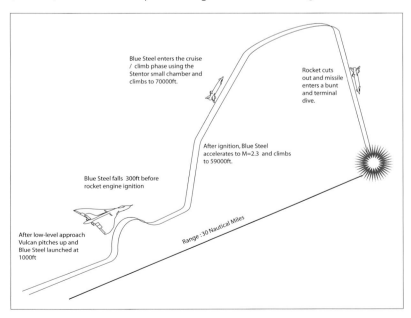

Blue Steel enters the cruise / climb phase using the Stentor small chamber and climbs to 70000ft.

Rocket cuts out and missile enters a bunt and terminal dive.

After ignition, Blue Steel accelerates to M=2.3 and climbs to 59000ft.

Blue Steel falls 300ft before rocket engine ignition

After low-level approach Vulcan pitches up and Blue Steel launched at 1000ft

Range : 30 Nautical Miles

Vulcan XL427 of the Scampton Wing complete with camouflaged upper surfaces is seen carrying Blue Steel at the end of its career as the UK's deterrent. The Vulcan's transition to low-level operation was aided by a terrain-following radar in the nose thimble. *Via Terry Panopalis*

diving onto the target. For ranges up to 20nm (37km) the bunt was entered during the climb.

One feature of the change to low-altitude launch was a two-second delay in the engine firing due to decomposition of the HTP in the pipe work. A quick calculation revealed that this caused a reduction of 0.1 in Mach Number at burn out and a decrease of 1,000ft (305m) in cruise altitude and 2nm (3.7km) in range. A bleed system was proposed and in the event the HTP decomposition was not deemed a major problem. No structural changes were required and the modified W.200 was taken into services as low-level 'ASGW 16,000lb HC No.1 (Blue Steel)'.

After years of angst and much expenditure of time and effort, a weapon designed to meet a requirement from a decade before had finally entered service to meet a requirement that had changed quite a lot over the development period. This would be a constant theme in the field of British weapons systems. Only the costs would change. A system that looked cheap at the outset ended up costing a king's ransom. The prescience of Richard Chilver has to be admired.

Insurance

Type	Length	Span	Diameter	Weight	Propulsion	Speed	Range
Bristol X.12	40ft 6in	7ft	3ft	15,000lb	Bristol BRJ.824 ramjet	Mach 3 Mach 2 low-level	900nm
Avro W.130	20ft	7ft 6in	n/a	4,500lb	Solid rocket	Mach 5.5	300nm
Avro W.140	37ft 4in	6ft 6in	2ft 10in	8,550lb	Rolls-Royce RB.153 turbofan	Mach 3 Mach1.5 low-level	1,050nm
Avro W.170A	20ft	3ft 3in	2ft 6in	4,300lb	BS.1014 ramjet	Mach 2.5	140nm
Avro W.170B	34ft	4ft 3in	2ft 10in	9,900lb	BS.1014 ramjet	Mach 2.4	450nm
Air-Launched Blue Water	29ft	7ft	2ft	3,500lb (estimate)	Phoenix solid rocket	n/a	55nm
BAC Strike Missile	33ft	5ft	n/a	7,500lb	Bristol BRJ.824 ramjet	Mach 3	1,300nm
Avro Z.122	30ft	13ft	4ft	14,360lb	ASM Stentor rocket	Mach 3.5	n/a
Martin Pershing I	10ft 6in	n/a	3ft 4in	10,200lb	Solid rocket	n/a	400nm
Lockheed Polaris (A3)	32ft 3in	n/a	4ft 6in	35,000lb	Solid rocket	n/a	2,500nm

8 Exotica
Space and Research Projects

'Now Solly comes up with a paper giving a totally different account of what Black Arrow is. How can Cabinet come to a sensible decision when none of us have the vaguest idea what these things really are?'
Richard Crossman, *The Crossman Diaries*, 1979

As the delays to Blue Steel mounted, Avro were accused of lacking focus and expending too much effort on distractions. Many of these diversions were aimed at improving the stand-off missile by extending its range and performance. Others were aimed at filling new requirements, furthering knowledge of high-speed flight and expanding the activities of the Weapons Research Division in general. Ultimately these studies were to take Avro into space.

The TV monitors in the control centre wobbled momentarily. 'Track is live', stated the Tannoy in the matter-of-fact manner associated with a well-drilled operation. The displays showed a sleek vehicle that lifted a fraction of an inch and started to move forwards and accelerated until, after ten seconds, it flashed past the mile marker and a double boom announced it had attained supersonic speed. A fraction of a second later an impressive flame and smoke trail, followed by a roar, confirmed that the ramjets had lit. The vehicle rose from the track and climbed into the blue sky above Woomera, as the thunderous roar of the ramjets died away in the distance. Avro's Weapons Research Division's Z.133 was on its way to launch another satellite into low Earth orbit.

Accompanied by its EECo P.10 chase planes, an Avro Z.133 re-usable satellite launcher climbs away from its maglev track to place a payload into low Earth orbit. *Adrian Mann*

Consider the state of the country in the mid-Fifties: Britain had just come through the hardest peace-time decade in modern history. The economy was virtually on its knees, with worn-out infrastructure and heavy borrowing to finance the new Welfare State, and piled upon that was the cost of what amounted to a complete re-equipment of the armed services in the political climate that followed the Korean War.

Compounding this was a major shortfall in the country's power generation capacity due to falling coal production and ageing thermal power stations. The postwar Attlee Government had embarked on an ambitious rearmament programme in 1951 and this re-equipment included the development of nuclear weapons. To address the power generation requirement and as a by-product of the atomic weapons plan, a civil nuclear power programme that included development of Fast Breeder Reactors was going ahead. All this expenditure had to be financed and various loans were taken out and devaluations made to Sterling to fund the whole shooting-match. When Churchill took over from Attlee in 1951, he was somewhat surprised at the steps his predecessor had taken in the armament field, particularly in guided weapons and the atomic bomb. By 1955 Churchill had retired and his place was taken by Anthony Eden who appointed Harold Macmillan as his Chancellor of the Exchequer (Britain's finance minister).

So, as postwar Britain lurched from one fiscal crisis to another, manufacturing and exports offered the sole prospect of salvation. Eden and Macmillan sought the means to boost the economy and build on the 'Set the people free' ideas that saw Churchill elected in 1951. The basic assumption was that abolishing rationing and improving the standard of living required increased output from the workshops of Britain. This needed an increase in manpower and technically-literate manpower in particular. Military establishments and weapons manufacturers, principally the aircraft industry, tied up much of the country's engineering and scientific expertise. These were exactly the people required to set the country back on its feet by developing goods that would provide manufacturing jobs and lucrative exports. They were also the people to design, build and operate the new generation of power stations.

By 1955 the power of the hydrogen bomb (H-bomb) had been demonstrated by the Americans and it was obvious that a) Britain would come under attack by such weapons b) Britain should embark on an H-bomb programme and

c) there was no defence against the H-bomb carried by a ballistic missile. This resulted in further demands on money and technocrats.

What followed has become infamous with anyone with an interest in British aviation. The seeds of the 1957 Defence White Paper were sown two years earlier by none other than Harold 'Supermac' Macmillan himself. As Eden's Chancellor, Macmillan's job was to look after the British economy and after a brief spell as Minister of Defence from 1954-55, was well aware of the defence aspects of this. Faced with the prospect of more technical experts being sucked into weapons work to develop Britain's H-bomb, he proposed some startling actions in his spending proposals in January 1956. The first was to reduce the British Army On the Rhine (BAOR) by a division and the second was the complete disbanding of Fighter Command and the termination of all development of fighter aircraft. The role of air defence of the UK (that is, defence of the deterrent) could be handled by guided weapons such as Red Duster (Bloodhound I) and Blue Envoy that were in full development at this time and showing promise. The third was to stop construction of hardened facilities and cut civil defence spending. The fourth option for saving money was the ending of subsidies on bread and milk, something Eden would not entertain, so the armed forces were lined up for cuts. However as these proposals were being firmed up, these same armed forces were called upon by Eden for his abortive campaign to seize the Suez Canal back from Egypt.

The fallout from the Suez adventure saw Eden resign and Macmillan installed as Prime Minister with the economy as his primary worry. Suez and the resulting sanctions threatened by the United States further compounded the pressures on the British economy, so something had to be done. With Macmillan now in charge and still with an eye on moving engineers and scientists into Civvie Street, the scene was set for the armed forces and aircraft industry to take a fall. Duncan Sandys, Churchill's son-in-law, was appointed Secretary of State for Defence by Macmillan. Seen as a safe pair of hands, his brief was to ensure that Britain's sole means of defence would be deterrence. That deterrent was to be carried by ballistic missiles and these would be defended by surface-to-air missiles. This was the Sandys Plan and would free up the manpower required to sort out the economy. Sandys had a reputation for ruthlessness, alloyed with an arrogance that ensured he would carry a job through no matter how unpalatable. He was also one of the few Cabinet appointees not related to Macmillan and generally acknowledged as Macmillan's hatchet-man, so perhaps Macmillan intended some dirty work for Sandys from the start.

Sandys delivered his White Paper (a statement of the Government's intentions and forthcoming laws). The most obvious result of the Sandys' paper was the ending of National Service that resulted in financial savings and freed up manpower for industry, but not the technocrats that would be instrumental to economic recovery. Such people would come from the aviation industry.

Essentially Sandys knocked out aircraft and missile types whose role had been superseded by 'under the radar' strike aircraft and the deployment of ballistic missiles by the Soviets. Remember that this was the era of the 'Trip Wire' whereby any aggression by the Soviets would be met by massive nuclear retaliation by NATO forces. Such a policy had no need for high-altitude interceptors, especially when the country could not afford to have both conventional and nuclear weapons. From the standpoint of early 1957 and particularly after the Soviets launched Sputnik, it certainly looked like ballistic missiles were the only way ahead. The next war would be all-out and witness thermonuclear warheads on long-range missiles lobbed between the combatants therefore conventional forces would be of little use, particularly in the light of the ongoing withdrawal from Empire. Britain would go ballistic.

Sandys' White Paper appeared at a bad time. The aircraft industry was changing and was being pushed in a technological direction whilst the industry and RAF wished to maintain the status quo. Sandys did his master's bidding to the letter and produced the monetary savings but these were gobbled up immediately by the nuclear weapons programme. Sandys had also consolidated the need for what would become TSR.2 and Blue Streak. His paper forced the aviation companies to take a hard look at their activities and initiated the painful series of amalgamations that would produce two large aerospace companies, but as we have seen, it all started with Macmillan and a desire to put the country back on its feet.

Bombardment Weapons

Of what relevance is the Sandys paper to the development of WRD's weapons? Blue Steel survived the Sandys axe, no doubt because it presented the best prospect of a credible deterrent. Without question, had the Sandys proposals been issued two years later and despite it being the only show in town, its continuation might have been doubtful. Sandys' paper

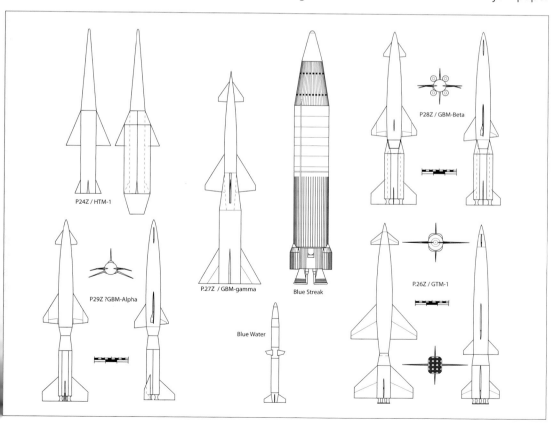

P.24Z / HTM-1

P.29Z ?GBM-Alpha

P.27Z / GBM-gamma

Blue Streak

Blue Water

P.28Z / GBM-Beta

P.26Z / GTM-1

Avro produced many design studies for ballistic and boost/glide weapons. They are shown in this diagram with Blue Streak and Blue Water, the weapons they were to supplement or replace.

emphasised the ballistic missile and Blue Streak was being developed by de Havilland Propellers (soon to become, like WRD, a member of Hawker Siddeley Dynamics) so WRD also examined ballistic weapons. Then in October 1957 a gleaming, beeping metallic ball heralded the start of the Space Age. Sputnik changed the way people viewed space, especially in the aviation business: it became the Aerospace Industry.

Since October 1955 the engineers at Woodford had been looking into ways to expand the uses of the Blue Steel missile, much to the annoyance of the Ministries and Air Staff who considered such effort as diverting from the main task of developing Blue Steel. WRD proposed the P.29Z, also called the GBM-α, to be launched from a ramp, boosted by a tandem boost comprising three solid rocket motors rated at 50,000 lbf (222.4kN) thrust apiece to Mach 2.5 and a cruising altitude of 75,000ft (22,860m). The P.29Z's launch weight was 20,000 lb (9,070kg) and it had a range of 170nm (315km) with the AWRE Orange Herald 2,000 lb (907kg) warhead and the standard Elliott Brothers inertial navigator. In the same month WRD drew up a more ambitious weapon, P.28Z also known as the GBM-β, a three-stage missile to provide a range of 300nm (556km). This was more of an aero-ballistic weapon, vertically launched like a ballistic missile, but its trajectory included a cruise phase and terminal dive like the existing Blue Steel. With a launch weight of 30,550 lb (13,857kg) the three stages comprised, in order of firing: four of the 50,000 lbf (222.4kN) boost motors wrapped around a 34,000 lbf (151kN) solid rocket second-stage booster. The third stage was a Blue Steel, using a 4,000 lbf (17.8kN) rocket engine, the small chamber of what would become the Armstrong Siddeley Stentor. Again the Orange Herald warhead was to be carried, with the missile cruising at Mach 5 at 80,000ft (24,384m).

Avro's Blue Streak

WRD's first foray into vertically-launched ballistic missiles was P.27Z (or GBM γ) a two-stage missile that featured a Blue Steel stretched by 3ft (0.9m), fitted with a larger 14ft 6in (4.4m) span wing and powered by a liquid-fuelled engine rated at 18,000 lbf (80kN). Boosted by what was described as a 'RR/NAA liquid rocket motor' rated at 12,000 lbf (533.8kN) this may allude to an early version of the Rolls-Royce RZ.1, a much modified Rocketdyne S3D engine, North American Aviation (NAA) being the parent company of Rocketdyne.

Intended to carry the 2,000 lb (907kg) Orange Herald warhead to a target 2,000nm (3,704km) from launch point, the second stage was to reach an altitude of 90,000ft (27,432m) and a cruise speed of Mach 8. The P.27Z was not far short of meeting the range requirement of OR.1139 – Blue Streak – that specified carrying Orange Herald a distance of 2,500nm (4,630km).

As is fairly obvious from the descriptions of their trajectories, these weapons were not ballistic missiles per se, more of a means to loft the Blue Steel to high altitude and high Mach Numbers prior to completing its flight in the usual manner, albeit with a faster dive from higher altitude that probably presented a greater interception headache than air-launched Blue Steel. WRD called these weapons 'boost-cruise bombardment missiles' and strove to improve and develop this unusual approach to long-range nuclear strike. This tack had also been taken by North American Aviation with the SM-64 Navaho in the immediate postwar period based initially on captured V-2 technology, although refined beyond recognition by the late 1950s.

By January 1956 WRD had worked on the P.27Z and drawn up the P.24Z (the HBM-1) a much improved model with uprated liquid-fuelled boosts. The P.24Z was smaller than its predecessor, and that missile's simple tandem boost was changed to a trio of the RR/NAA engines giving a boost rating of 360,000 lbf (1,601kN). These engines were housed in a rear-mounted bay with the propellant tanks arranged around the missile's fuselage. Boosted to 60,000ft (18,288m) and Mach 5, the booster stage and its tanks would have fallen away leaving the 35,100 lb (15,921kg) missile to continue in a cruise climb to 108,000ft (32,918m) before diving onto its target, to detonate the Orange Herald as an air burst.

The range, as with the P.27Z was 2,000nm (3,704km) and despite the Mach 5 cruise speed the inertial navigator would not provide sufficient accuracy, so an automatic astro-navigator would have provided updates to the inertial system. Such systems, called Orange Tartan and Blue Sapphire, had been developed by the Radio and Radar Establishment (RRE) for use on the Blue Moon expendable bomber.

Alongside the P.24Z and P.27Z long-range missiles, a tactical missile with a range of 500nm (926km) was being examined in March 1956. The P.26Z (alternatively GTM-1) weighed 29,500 lb (13,381kg) at launch and was to be boosted from a 'pogo-stick' launcher by nine Bulldog solid rocket motors (as used in the Blue Envoy long-range SAM) arranged in tandem as the boost stage. The missile itself was 40ft (12.2m) long with a wingspan of 19ft 5in (5.9m) and shared the Blue Steel's canard configuration. The fuselage had an elliptical cross-section to the rear that became more circular ahead of the wings. The cross-section change was to accommodate the two superimposed DH Spectre rocket engines. The warhead was to weigh 1,000 lb (454kg) and was possibly the same as that used in the Red Beard 'Target Marker Bomb' that AWRE was developing as a tactical weapon.

On reaching Mach 1.5 the boost stage would have separated and the 18,875 lb (8,562kg) missile would have accelerated on under the power of the two DH Spectre HTP/Kerosene engines rated at 8,000 lbf (35.6kN) apiece to reach Mach 2.5 at 86,000ft (26,213m) where one Spectre was cut and the missile continued on a single Spectre to the end of its cruise. Since the P.26Z would be launched from ostensibly friendly territory its range of 500nm (926km) fell between two stools: too far for accuracy with inertial alone, but not inaccurate enough to warrant the additional weight of an automatic-astro system. The solution was to use the Blue Study automatic bombing system that used external radio beacons on the same principle as the Gee-H system and could be considered as an update of the earlier Oboe.

Avro examined ways to attain greater range with less weight and complexity so took the P.26Z and added Rolls-Royce RB.121 turbojets to the tips of the trapezoidal wings to produce the P.25Z (GTM-2). Again, a 1,000 lb (454kg) warhead was to be carried and with a launch weight of 12,500 lb (5,670kg), less than half

that of the P.26Z, a range of 600nm (1,111km) would be achievable. The missile itself weighed 8,000 lb (3,629kg) with the wraparound boost motors making up the balance. The change to turbojets meant that the range would have increased by 100nm (160km), a 20% increase for a 58% weight reduction. The missile was to be 31ft 6in (9.6m) long with a span between engine shaft centres of 13ft 6in (4.1m). In operation the P.25Z would have been launched from a zero-length launcher and entered a rapid climb immediately. The Bulldog boosts would have been jettisoned at Mach 1.3, with the turbojets taking over to continue the climb to 60,000ft (18,288m) and acceleration to Mach 2.5. At the end of the cruise the missile would bunt and enter a terminal dive. Guidance was the same as the P.26Z, inertial with Blue Study.

So far the missile studies described have been for the RAF or the British Army, but the Royal Navy was keen to have a surface-launched bombardment weapon that could be operated from surface ships, particularly aircraft carriers. Avro also hoped to fit RN submarines with deck containers along the lines of the Chance Vought Regulus that was operated from US Navy submarines between 1955 and 1959. WRD drew up the P.2Z (NB-2) in February 1957 that used the Blue Steel forebody and wing (minus the outboard anhedral) mated to a new rear fuselage with a DH Gyron Junior turbojet rated at 10,000 lbf (445kN) fed from a ventral variable shock intake. In this respect the P.2Z was had more in common with the Chance Vought SSM-N-9 Regulus II, a supersonic development of the Regulus I.

A US Navy submarine crew prepares to launch a Chance Vought Regulus II cruise missile. Avro produced a number surface-launched missiles based on the W.112 amongst others. These were intended for use on submarines, aircraft carriers, destroyers and mobile trailers. *US Navy*

The P.2Z carried a pair of Armstrong Siddeley Gamma rocket engines for the acceleration and cruise phases. The Gamma was normally used in quartets to propel British research vehicles such as Black Knight and Black Arrow. Whether this twin-chamber Gamma is the same as the Gamma 2, later known as the Bristol Siddeley BS.606, used for the second stage of Black Arrow is not clear in the WRD document. The P.2Z was more or less a simplified W.110 stand-off bomb, as proposed for OR.1149, modified for surface launch by the addition of a pair of Aerojet-General solid rocket boost motors rated at 130,000 lbf (580kN) thrust. The Gamma rocket engines would continue the boost and accelerate the missile to enter its cruise phase at 75,000ft (22,860m) and Mach 3. At a predetermined time the missile would dive to low level and continue its flight on the power of the Gyron Junior. The P.2Z was described as having a range of 1,000nm (1,852km) carrying a Green Bamboo warhead weighing 4,500lb (2,041kg). It was 45ft (13.7m) long with a wing span of 16ft 2in (4.9m) and weighed 30,000lb (13,608kg) at launch.

Continuing the Regulus theme, the Z.17 from August 1957 was to provide a range of 2,000nm (3,704km) while carrying a 5,000lb (2,268kg) warhead. The Z.17 was much larger than the previous Avro bombardment missiles and was not dissimilar to the TRM-3 reconnaissance drone. Powered by a pair of 44in (112cm) diameter ramjets on the tips of the delta wings and boosted off a ramp at an angle of 40°, the Z.17 weighed 60,000lb (27,216kg) at launch and once the ramjets lit at just over Mach 1, accelerated to Mach 3. As with the other long-range missiles, navigation was to be inertial with automatic astro updates.

Blue Steel Phase 2 gave plenty of scope for surface-launch variants such as the Z.38 from December 1957; that was a W.112 fitted with four wraparound Raven boost motors to boost the missile to the supersonic speed required to light the Bristol Siddeley BRJ.851 18in (46cm) ramjets. With an intended range of 1,400nm (2,593km) when carrying an Orange Herald warhead, it was to be capable of Mach 3 at 75,000ft (22,860m). The Z.38 came in two variants: The W.112N for the Royal Navy to launch from its ships while the W.112G was for the Army. The brochure on the surface-launched W.112 also mentions the possibility of using a lighter US warhead, weighing 1,700lb (771kg)

In addition to air-launch, the W.112 Long Range Guided Bomb was earmarked for surface launch from a variety of platforms. BAE Systems/ RAF Museum

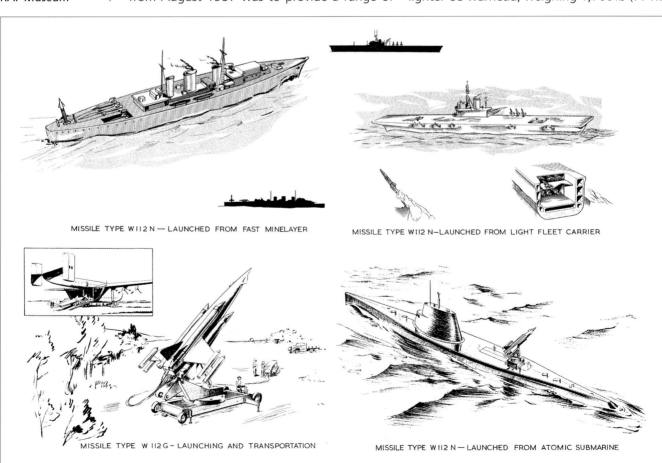

MISSILE TYPE W112N — LAUNCHED FROM FAST MINELAYER

MISSILE TYPE W112N—LAUNCHED FROM LIGHT FLEET CARRIER

MISSILE TYPE W112G – LAUNCHING AND TRANSPORTATION

MISSILE TYPE W112N — LAUNCHED FROM ATOMIC SUBMARINE

which would confer an increase in range to 1,500nm (2,778km). This suggests that the repeal of the McMahon Act was trickling down to the missile developers by making US warheads available for British weapons.

In February 1960 the Martin-Marietta company launched the first of what became the MGM-31 Pershing tactical ballistic missile. This was to have a range of 500nm, be fully mobile on a transporter/erector/launcher (TEL) and enter service with the US Army in Western Europe. By the 1980s the Pershing II and its Soviet counterpart the RSD-10 Pioneer (NATO reporting name SS-20 *Saber*) were seen as destabilising and had the potential to escalate the Cold war. These weapons exemplified the arms race that was such a financial burden on the Soviets and this, combined with political changes in Eastern Europe, brought the Cold War to an end. A further indication of this newfound thaw in the Cold War was the Intermediate-Range Nuclear Forces Treaty signed in 1987 to remove these weapons from the armoury of East and West. Weapons such as the SS-20, Pershing II and cruise missiles were seen as altering the balance of forces due to being longer-ranged, highly accurate and more mobile than their predecessors.

Avro WRD proposed in October 1960 a ground-launched variant of its W.130 airlaunched missile for the TSR.2 and Mirage IV. Called the Z.82 the weapon was intended to be a '…winged equivalent of the Martin Pershing tactical ballistic missile.' Z.82 used a solid rocket tandem first stage of the dual thrust type motor similar to that used in the BAC Blue Water, such as the Saluki or Phoenix whereby the high-thrust boost motor for launch and a lower-thrust sustainer motor are housed within the same casing. The two are separated by a series of petal valves held closed by the thrust of the boost motor acting upon it and only opening when its thrust decreased enough to allow the sustainer's thrust to open the valve at a point where a pressure differential of 150psi (1,034kPa) was achieved. The Z.82 had a range of 400nm (741km) for a launch weight of 10,900 lb (4,944kg) and was to possess a cruising speed of Mach 6.3, more than enough, in Avro's opinion, to provide immunity from interception.

Another bombardment missile project based on the W.130 was the Z.97, possibly the oddest arrangement for extending the range of a weapon. The Z.97 comprised a W.130 fitted to the nose of a pilotless carrier aircraft, which in turn was launched from a rocket-propelled

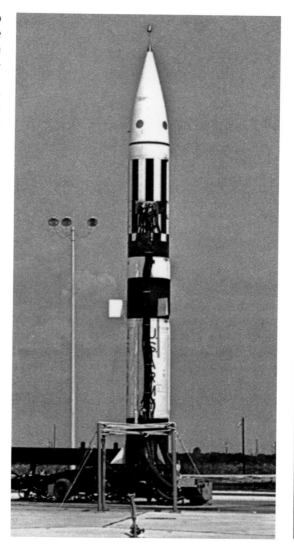

The Martin Pershing tactical ballistic missile was one weapon that Avro WRD hoped to emulate with some of its surface-launched projects. Unfortunately the General Staff thought otherwise. *US Army*

Filling a similar role to Blue Moon from a decade earlier, Avro's Z.97 was to be powered by a DH Gyron Junior and carry a W.130 weapon into hostile territory. No details of performance or guidance systems were available but high subsonic performance with a range of around 1,500nm would be expected.

wheeled trolley. The Z.97 carrier aircraft consisted of a cylindrical fuselage fitted with a 24ft (7.3m) span low-aspect ratio mid wing and a conventional tail. An unreheated Gyron Junior was installed atop the rear fuselage just above

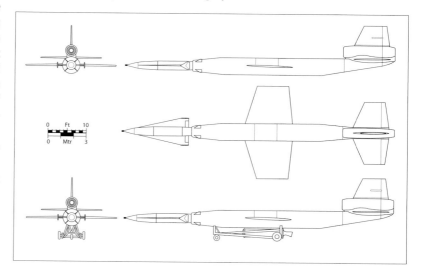

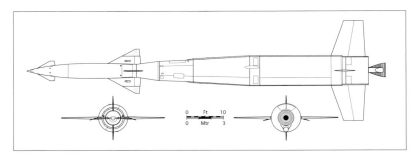

Avro hoped to capitalise on the recent retirement from RAF service of the Douglas Thor IRBM. WRD intended adding Blue Steel as a second stage for a boost/glide strategic weapon. Parametric studies soon revealed that the range of the combination would be less than Thor on its own.

Another weapon whose demise Avro hoped to capitalise on was BAC's Blue Water. By adding two Cuckoo boosts from the Skylark sounding rocket, Avro produced the Z.121 tactical ballistic missile based on Blue Steel. How they proposed transporting it around the battlefield was not discussed.

the tailplanes with the single fin mounted on the engine nacelle. The Z.97 carrier was expendable and optimised for high-subsonic cruise so lacked the high-lift devices, such as wing flaps and slats that a conventional aircraft used for low-speed phases such as take-off and landing. A rocket-propelled trolley launch circumvented the need for such low-speed equipment on the flight vehicle. Z.97 was to use a tricycle-wheeled trolley fitted with a large solid rocket motor, no doubt similar in performance to the Aerojet General motor used on the Snark, to boost the 36,000 lb (16,329kg) combination to flying speed.

By mid-1962 the RAF had been operational with the Thor intermediate ballistic missile (IRBM) for four years. Very much a means to an emergency capability, the Thor was then being phased out in US service in favour of the ICBMs that could be based in the continental United States. Since support for the Thor system would be removed once it had left US service, the British also retired theirs. Avro saw this as an opportunity to expand the roles available for Blue Steel. By replacing the re-entry vehicle of the Thor with a Blue Steel, WRD hoped to increase the range and reduce the vulnerability of Blue Steel by lofting it to higher altitudes and velocities. The intention was to create a strategic weapon that could use existing equipment already familiar to the RAF. To this end WRD drew up the Z.115. The main modifications to the Thor booster were the addition of large fins

at the base of the missile's fuselage to maintain stability in the initial phases of the flight. Avro's parametric studies soon disclosed there was very little to be gained from the exercise. Rather than produce a longer-ranged weapon than the basic Thor, the additional weight of the Blue Steel had a major impact on the Thor's performance. The Z.115 did soldier on as one of Avro's space-related Blue Steel studies in the role of anti-satellite weapon.

Avro's last bombardment missile project was the Z.121, initiated in an attempt to fill the role of Blue Water, a BAC battlefield missile to meet British Army requirement E5077. Blue Water was cancelled by the Defence Minister Peter Thorneycroft in August 1962 with little or no consultation with the Staffs or his advisors. Avro's WRD saw an opportunity to replace Blue Water with a surface-launched Blue Steel, modified to use a ramp inclined at 45° by strapping on a pair of jettisonable Cuckoo solid rocket motors rated at 3,750 lbf (16.7kN) each. On burn-out the Cuckoos would be jettisoned and the Blue Steel operated as normal. With a launch weight of 15,338 lb (6,957kg), of which 500 lb (227kg) was the warhead, probably the same RO.106 warhead from Blue Water, the Z.121 had a range of 66nm (122km). Having opted for a smaller, lighter warhead in the payload bay, extra propellant could have been carried in the newly-available space provided to give a range of 130nm (241km).

The prospect of a missile weighing five times that of Blue Water being carried cross-country on a transporter/erector/launcher must have filled the General Staff with dread. Earlier experience with a tactical missile called Red Rose, a forerunner of Blue Water, showed that a large missile could be carried by an AEC Militant 10-ton 6x6 truck. Perhaps AEC's experience of producing Mandator, the Blue Steel transporter, may have helped produce such a vehicle. Even the larger Militant used for Red Rose would have had stability problems while carrying such a top-heavy load. Nor were the practicalities of fuelling Blue Steel in a forest clearing considered.

The Soviets were the masters of the massive off-roading TEL, with numerous multi-wheeled vehicles such as the RT-2PM – (NATO reporting name SS-25 Sickle) a 14-wheel vehicle carrying an ICBM in a launch canister on its back. No doubt the 18 tons (16.3 tonnes) of Blue Steel would have merited a tracked TEL possibly based on the Centurion tank chassis. So the next time you see a multi-wheeled mobile crane on the road, imagine the jib replaced by a Blue Steel. It must be suspected that in the litany of

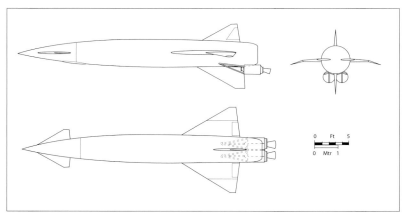

Blue Steel projects that caused such angst amongst the Ministries and Staff, the Z.121 would probably have elicited the most strident opposition. Undoubtedly, despite the well-known inter-service rivalries, a quiet discussion between Army and RAF officers in the Army and Navy Club would have served to warn the General Staff off any notion of a tactical Blue Steel.

Research vehicles

Another factor that, while not directly triggered by the Sandys paper, came to influence the direction of Avro WRD's studies was the advent of the Space Age. In developing the ballistic missile the Super Powers saw the prospect of space becoming a new frontier in the military and technological battlefield. Even before Sputnik, the aerospace companies (with government support) had been investigating the means to access space with the view to putting a man in orbit.

American efforts in what would become the Space Race are well documented, the Soviet Union's less so. Britain's efforts may have lacked the funding and political support of the United States and Russia, but one commodity they had in abundance was vision. Science fiction author Arthur C. Clarke had in 1948 postulated the use of orbiting platforms – artificial satellites – as communications relays and it soon became clear that satellites had a myriad of uses. The problem was placing them in orbit.

The obvious method was to go 'straight up' by replacing the warhead of a ballistic missile with a satellite and launching into a trajectory to carry it to a speed, the so-called escape velocity, and altitude whereby the payload entered orbit rather than returned to Earth. Such a launch vehicle was under development by Saunders-Roe under the name 'Black Arrow' and is the item under discussion at Cabinet in the quote that heads this chapter. Black Arrow used Kerosene and HTP to fuel its Gamma engines and the culmination of its four launches was its successful placing of the satellite 'Prospero' in orbit on 28th October 1971.

Another method was to use a carrier aircraft as a first stage to lift a rocket-powered vehicle to a high-altitude start point from which the rocket vehicle could accelerate and climb to orbit. The carrier can be either a conventional aircraft or a rocket booster. The benefit of using an aircraft as the first stage is that it can be re-used, unlike the expendable rocket boosters of the Fifties and Sixties. Rocket boosters were seen as an expedient; a quick means to access

space in the short term, while in the longer term a re-usable, air-breathing, hypersonic spaceplane would be the future. The first steps towards this goal were to investigate the physical environment that such a spaceplane would inhabit. Fly too slow and the aircraft would not generate sufficient lift to reach the required altitude, fly too fast at insufficient altitude and the high temperature generated from kinetic heating of the airframe would require a heavier structure. The conclusion was that there was a flight corridor within which, by balancing speed and altitude, flight without the aforementioned problems becoming insurmountable was possible and to investigate this Avro WRD proposed a number of research vehicles.

Blue Steel Research Vehicles

Missile test vehicles were intended to assess the various systems and technologies that would lead to a functioning missile. A research vehicle could be used to expand the knowledge of, and develop technologies for, specific goals. In short, to borrow an expression from Tom Wolfe's *The Right Stuff*, research vehicles push the envelope. Avro's WRD were keen to exploit this interest in hypersonic aircraft, spaceplanes and spaceflight in general as this was seen as the future for the aviation business. The earliest such research vehicles were the Z.51 series from April 1959 whose goal was the investigation of advanced fuels for stand-off weapons. This was to explore the use of hydrazine/fluorine propellant, the same fuels that caused much annoyance amongst the Air Staff when suggested for Blue Steel improvements. The aero-engine manufacturer D. Napier and Son had been working on methods of improving the performance of rocket engines, such as the in Scorpion that had helped capture a World Altitude Record in August 1957 when fitted to a Canberra B.2, and more potent propellants were the answer. Rocket engine power is generally expressed as a thrust force but changes depending on altitude and atmospheric pressure. A more relevant unit of measurement where different fuels are involved is specific impulse, Isp, which can be used to compare the efficiency of rocket engines. Specific impulse is the change of momentum per second per unit of fuel consumed. If momentum and fuel mass are expressed in pounds, the pounds cancel each other out leaving seconds as the unit of specific impulse, Isp, which allows various fuels to be compared.

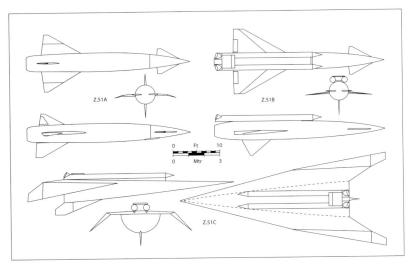

Z.51A

Z.51B

Z.51C

0 Ft 10
0 Mtr 3

To maximise the range of its missiles, Avro investigated a number of different propellants. The Z.51 series was intended to use hydrazine and fluorine, fuels that they hoped to use for a Blue Steel variant.

Hydrazine (N_2H_4) with fluorine (F_2) possesses a high Specific Impulse of 338 seconds, close to that of liquid hydrogen (H_2) with oxygen (O_2), 381 seconds, making it ideal for applications where high thrust from compact, non-cryogenic storage was required. Hydrazine and fluorine are not only extremely reactive, but highly poisonous to humans, making their handling during operations such as fuelling a hazardous affair.

Parametric studies suggested that very useful improvements to range and speed were attainable with these propellants so Avro drew up a study to convert a Blue Steel airframe as the Z.51A vehicle for hydrazine/fluorine propellant research. A pair of modified Napier Scorpion engines were to power the Z.51A, with solid rocket motors for initial boost. Despite the increase in launch weight to 17,060 lb (7,737kg), range would increase to 435nm (806km), almost four times that of the HTP/Kerosene-fuelled Blue Steel, while cruise speed and altitude increased to 100,000ft (30,480m) and Mach 5 respectively. Selection of the Scorpion may have been down to its ability to cope with the higher combustion temperatures of hydrazine/fluorine and those higher temperatures may have been the keys to better performance.

An improved Z.51B had a new, larger wing, with a similar planform but a non-tapered trailing edge and anhedral from root to tip, rather than just the outboard third. A revised ventral fin was fitted farther forward and the dorsal fin deleted, allowing a pair of Raven solid boost motors from OR.1159's W.114 to be fitted atop the fuselage. These changes increased weight to 21,150 lb (9,593kg) but this additional boost in the initial phase of flight increased the calculated range to 512nm (948km). This is an example of how critical a powerful solid-rocket boost motor was to the development of guided weapons.

The initial results of these propulsion system studies were applied in April 1959 to Z.51C. This was a stand-off bomb whose 75° sweep delta wing was optimised for the Mach 5 cruise by having the outboard 50% of the span canted downwards at 45°, a configuration that survives to this day in hypersonic flight regimes. With the Raven boosts, this 21,750 lb (9,864kg) missile could carry a 750 lb (340kg) warhead, cruise at 100,000ft (30,480m) and Mach 5 and attain a range of 582nm (1,078km). The final applications for hydrazine propellant were in Blue Steel Mk.1* and Mk.1*E where it was used with 90% HTP to fuel the Bristol Siddeley PR.41/1, a four-chamber rocket engine rated at 2800-5,400 lbf (12.5-24kN). These were the proposals that so upset the Ministry of Aviation and Air Staff when Sir William Farren proposed Blue Steel Mk.II.

Exotic, that is unconventional fuels, left Avro's WRD unfazed. The hydrazine/fluorine-fuelled Z.51C was actually based on an earlier research vehicle drawn up as a performance exercise in March 1959 called the Z.55. This is a remarkable vehicle in being described in Avro's documentation as a 'Hypersonic vehicle using liquid hydrogen as coolant/propellant'. The Z.55 was 66ft (20.1m) long and therefore approximately 35% larger than the later Z.51C and the description includes an interesting comment appended to the drawing: 'Performance exercise – too big'.

The 75° sweep delta wing spanned 28ft (8.5m) and with the outer panels canted downwards at 45°, the Z.55 was 66ft (20.1m) long and weighed 29,350 lb (13,313kg). The fuselage was a half-cone along the same lines as the earlier W.108 stand-off bomb for OR.1149 and housed the tanks for the liquid hydrogen and oxygen propellant used by the sustainer rocket. One of the innovative aspects of the Z.55 was the proposed use of regenerative cooling whereby the cryogenic fuel is pumped around the airframe to reduce the thermal effects from kinetic heating. In addition to cooling the structure, this allows the fuel to be warmed prior to entering the combustion chamber reducing the thermal shock on the engine. Therefore less energy was required to burn the fuel and more thrust was produced by the engine. The intended cruise speed of the Z.55 was Mach 10 at an altitude of 100,000ft (30,480m) and the range with a 2,500 lb (1,134kg) payload was to be 2,000nm (3,704km). Since the aim of this design exercise was to assess performance, it must be noted that even in the second decade of the 21st Century such performance is still difficult to achieve in a winged vehicle. Regenerative cooling with liquid hydrogen is still to be made a practicality.

One other fuel that Avro looked at in 1960 was boron-based 'zip fuel' for a study called Z.75, a low-level Mach 2 missile. Zip fuels based on hydro-boranes offered higher power output from gas turbine and ramjets, typically an increase in specific energy in the order of 40% over the various conventional kerosene blends that were in use in the 1950s. This extra power was to be translated into additional range and higher speed for jet-propelled aircraft and missiles, the most famous proposed user of zip fuel being the North American XB-70 Valkyrie.

Used on their own boranes proved hazardous, being prone to spontaneous combustion if handled improperly, although if blended with standard jet fuels they became more stable. Unfortunately they were still hazardous as both the fuels and their combustion products were poisonous. A further problem was their propensity to coat the turbomachinery of gas turbines with toxic residue that made maintenance very difficult and reduced the efficiency of the turbine blades and stators. The cure for this was to only use zip fuels in reheat or in ramjets where no such problems occurred. Unfortunately this required a separate fuel system for the zip fuel, adding weight and complexity. Added to the tale of woe was the dense black exhaust smoke generated by the engines that increased the visual signature of any aircraft using zip fuels. Despite this, Avro's WRD examined using zip fuels in a study for a variant of the W.170B called Z.75. The standard W.170B possessed a range of 360nm (667km) when using

kerosene or 450nm (833km) if a high-density jet fuel such as Shelldyne was used. With a fuselage stretch of 2ft (0.6m) and a boron fuel, the estimated range for the Z.75 was to be in the region of 1,000nm (1,852km) despite a lower cruise speed of Mach 2.

Nuclear option

The recurring theme throughout this book has been the extent of Soviet territory and the efforts made to produce a missile or bomber aircraft with sufficient range to reach the targets therein. One remarkable solution to this was nuclear propulsion. With unlimited range and endurance this had been the answer to the development of the true submarine, capable of staying submerged for months on end as opposed to the submersibles of the Second World War that had to surface to charge their batteries or refuel their diesel engines.

Submarine nuclear propulsion was a scaled-down version of the power generation plants that had sprung up in the postwar era to provide electricity for the public and fissile material for the bomb builders. Aircraft designers looked on, waiting for the nuclear reactor to shrink to a size at which they were feasible for installation in an aircraft.

The Americans and the Russians both carried out trials with airborne nuclear reactors, but neither ever took the concept to the stage where an aircraft was propelled by nuclear power. As a technology-demonstrator for the nuclear-powered aircraft the Americans planned to convert two Convair B-36 bombers to carry a reactor in the bomb bay under a project called Nuclear Energy for the Propulsion of Aircraft (NEPA) that dated from 1946. This programme became known as the Aircraft Nuclear

The Convair NB-36 proved that a nuclear reactor could be carried in an aircraft. The X-6, a much modified B-36, was to carry its nuclear engines under the rear fuselage. *USAF*

Propulsion Program (ANP) in 1951. Designated NB-36H or the Nuclear Test Aircraft, the first modified B-36 carried a 3MW air-cooled reactor and served as a development aircraft for the shielding that would be necessary to protect the crew from radiation. The second B-36, possibly based on the swept wing YB-60, was to be called the X-6 and would be a test bed for the nuclear engines.

These engines were to be developed by General Electric and designated X-39. This was based on GE's J47 turbojet with the combustion chamber removed and air from the compressor passed through a General Electric P-1 reactor that provided the heat addition that forms the 'bang' component of the gas turbine's suck/squeeze/bang/blow continuous cycle. As it passed through the reactor the air attained temperatures of 1,100°C (2,000°F), that were comparable with the turbine entry temperatures of turbojets and on exiting the jet pipe, generated thrust. Four X-39s were to be mounted under the aircraft's rear fuselage and when combined with the P-1 reactor, would provide more than the equivalent thrust of the eight J57 turbojets on the YB-60. A number of ground-based test beds were built and operated until it soon became obvious that nuclear power in the air could be problematic. The nuclear-powered aircraft foundered due to safety concerns for the crew and support staff on the ground plus the prospect of a very dangerous crash involving the spread of radioactive material over a large area. Another factor was that the air passing through the reactor picked up radioactive particles and these were transferred to the atmosphere in the exhaust. This so-called open or direct cycle

was considered undesirable even in the 1950s. Therefore an indirect, closed cycle system, similar to that on submarines, was used with coolant circulated through separate heat exchangers to transfer heat from the reactor to the gas turbines.

Russian attempts included the Tupolev Tu-95LAL, a modified Tu-95 *Bear* bomber, which used two modified NK.12 turboprops powered by the direct-cycle with minimal shielding. Then, in December 1957, *Aviation Week* magazine stated that the Soviets had made great progress in the nuclear-powered aircraft field and were flight-testing a supersonic bomber. An aircraft answering the descriptions had been observed in flight by a variety of observers. The aircraft eventually turned out to be a conventionally-powered bomber prototype called the Myasishchev M-50, NATO reporting name *Bounder* and the whole story was generally held to have been an elaborate hoax by the Soviets to get some return on an unsuccessful design.

By 1961 the nuclear aircraft was dead in the USA, but the prospect of putting the nuclear aircraft's hazards to 'good' use was under consideration. To avoid the need for shielding, the crew could be removed and to avoid the need for a dual-cycle engine, the engine need only operate over enemy territory. Thus was born SLAM, the Supersonic Low Altitude Missile. Since 1957 the USAF and the Lawrence Radiation Laboratory had been working on a development project called Pluto that was intended to use a reactor as a source of heat for a ramjet. This was to be a direct-cycle engine for use in a long-range cruise missile that could carry multiple warheads that were dispensed as Pluto

This familiar layout formed the basis of a nuclear-powered aircraft drawn up by E P Hawthorn from the nuclear arm of de Havilland. It used the closed cycle system to avoid the 'dirty' exhaust plume of the direct gas-cooled reactor engine.

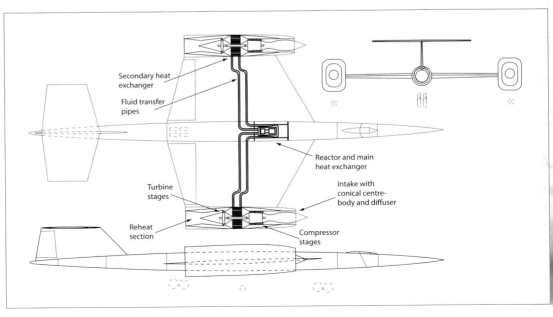

flew along and leave a trail of radioactive fall-out along its route. Its final act would be to plunge to Earth, its reactor becoming a very dirty bomb that could contaminate a large area. It could be described as a Doomsday weapon whose conception was very much in line with the Mutually Assured Destruction doctrine of the late 1950s and early 1960s. After launch from a site in the USA, the missile was accelerated to a speed at which the ramjet had enough compression to operate. The ramjet was to be fed from a ventral intake and was capable of reaching speeds in excess of Mach 4 before descending to low altitude for its attack phase.

Having described briefly the US and Soviet developments in the nuclear aircraft field, how does this relate to British deterrent weapons? In March 1958 the in-house magazine of the de Havilland group published the first information on British work towards a nuclear-powered aircraft. The de Havilland Engine Co. had set up a Nuclear Power Group for production of power-generation plants to replace Britain's ageing coal-burning power stations. As a business with its roots in the aircraft world the application of such technology was an obvious adjunct to the power stations. The initial work focused on liquid-metal-cooled reactors but soon de Havilland become more interested in gas-cooled reactors. Working with the United Kingdom Atomic Energy Authority, de Havilland developed lightweight ceramic fuel elements for a gas-cooled reactor that could be light enough for airborne application.

By 1957 de Havilland was part of the Hawker Siddeley Nuclear Power Company Limited and had its nuclear power development projects under way. One project of interest was a nuclear-powered aircraft that bore a resemblance to some of the submissions to OR.330. Drawn up by E P Hawthorne, the aircraft carried a shielded nuclear reactor and heat exchangers in the fuselage with the nuclear turbojets at the wingtips. This type used the secondary cooling system with recirculating fluid being used to transfer the reactor's heat to the engines.

A British Pluto

In late 1959 the nuclear power company joined forces with Avro WRD to develop a nuclear powered ramjet and apply it to a stand-off missile. The result was Z.59 that mated a Blue Steel with a dorsal nuclear ramjet. This used a reactor/engine combination of the primary type with the air passing through the reactor but no secondary heat exchanger. The reactor material

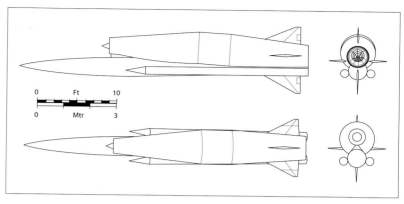

was listed as uranium 235 and the moderator was 'beryllia' – beryllium oxide, a refractory compound with very high thermal conductivity, almost on a par with diamond. This would have been ideal as a conductor of heat from the uranium fuel-pellets to the air as it passed through the ramjet 'heat addition' chamber, producing an exhaust temperature of 2,240°F (1,227°C) and a thrust of 17,000 lbf (75.6kN). As noted above, the exhaust from such a ramjet picked up fallout, leaving a radioactive plume behind it, with a sprinkling of carcinogenic beryllia to boot. The Z.59 had a launch weight of 14,500 lb (6,577kg) including a pair of solid rocket boosters to propel it to sufficient speed to 'light' the ramjet. Operating at Mach 2 the Z.59 flew at low-level, leaving its noxious trail but that would pale into insignificance once its warhead had detonated and added the reactor components to the fallout of a very dirty bomb.

Hypersonic Research

In the 1950s the future was hypersonic; Australia in two hours looked achievable rather than being the stock story of 'silly season' newspaper articles. The advanced projects offices of all the major aircraft manufacturers carried out many a design study on ramjet and scramjet-powered hypersonic vehicles. Avro's WRD was no different and, using their experience on Blue Steel, proposed a number of vehicles to explore the high Mach regime.

The established thinking on hypersonic flight in the Fifties was the flight corridor, a balance of speed and altitude where propulsion systems, structures and kinetic heating trod a fine line between too hot and too heavy. To explore the flight corridor Avro used their guided weapons experience and as the work progressed, intended putting the knowledge they gained to good use in further missile developments. WRD drew up their initial flight corridor research vehicle, Z.47, based on Blue Steel

Avro's Z.59 was a Blue Steel forebody mated to a nuclear ramjet. The solid boosts would have propelled the Z.59 to a speed high enough to run the ramjet. The ramjet used the direct-cycle system with air passing through the berylia matrix.

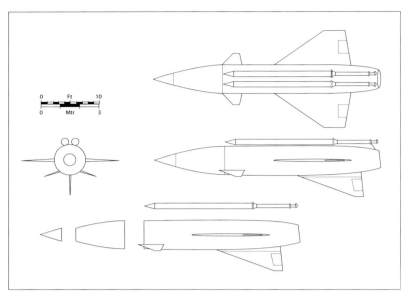

0 Ft 10
0 Mtr 3

The four-stage Z.47 flight corridor research vehicle was to use as many Blue Steel Phase II/W.114 components as possible. If the Vulcan that carried it aloft is included, Z.47 would be a five stage vehicle.

Mk.I and Phase II experience. This weighed 40,000 lb (18,144kg) and was a four-stage vehicle, five if you include the Vulcan that could carry the vehicle above the densest regions of the atmosphere to around 50,000ft (15,240m). On launch, the first stage propulsion comprising two modified Raven boosts fired and the Z.47 accelerated in a dive in the familiar Blue Steel trajectory, and on pulling up, the main engine on the second stage boosted the Z.47 into its climb. The second stage engine was a Rocketdyne A-6, a liquid oxygen/alcohol engine rated at 82,595 lbf (367.4kN) used on the Redstone ballistic missile and developed from the XLR-43-NA-1 used on the booster for the Navaho cruise missile. The A-6 could trace its roots directly to Von Braun's rocket engine on the V-2. On burn-out the third stage separated and continued to climb under the power of an Armstrong Siddeley Snarler rated at 2,000 lbf (8.9kN) until the fourth stage separated at 400,000ft (121,920m). This represented the vehicle's payload and weighed 300 lb (136kg) and according to WRD's documents flew at 20,000ft/sec, which at 40,000ft, relates to Mach 22!

The next attempt at a flight corridor research aircraft included manned versions and a version with the potential to place a payload in orbit. John Allen, Head of Aerodynamics, Projects and Assessment Department at WRD outlined such a vehicle at a lecture to the Manchester branch of the Royal Aeronautical Society in January 1958. Allen displayed a model of a vehicle that could have four stages, five if the Vulcan carrier was included, and was to have a number of uses including boosting of test vehicles and aerodynamic research. After launch

from a Vulcan, the vehicle was to be boosted to a speed of Mach 2 by a quartet of solid rocket motors that were jettisoned at burn-out. The second stage was a large liquid-fuelled booster that was to accelerate the vehicle to Mach 10 and 200,000ft (60,960m) before burning out and, depending on the mission, separating from the third stage that continued the climb under the power of its liquid fuelled engine. The fourth stage, the payload could then be released to carry out its tests. The vehicle was fitted with trapezoidal mainplanes with rectangular canard foreplanes at the forward end of the main cylindrical portion of the fuselage. Dorsal and ventral trapezoidal fins were fitted for directional control.

In the manned role the vehicle dispensed with the third and fourth stages and the vehicle remained intact throughout the flight. The pilot was housed in an ejection capsule that displaced some of the propellant, reducing the volume of the tanks in the fuselage. As might be expected for a manned version, the performance would be much lower than the unmanned variants. The space formerly taken up by the third-stage engine and its fuel now housed life support equipment and control systems. The pilot's capsule had no glazing, so he viewed the outside world via a periscope that deployed once speed had reduced for landing. The undercarriage comprised a nosewheel and a pair of skids at the rear. The vehicle's planform remained the same, with additional fin area à la Blue Steel fitted. The ventral fin was no doubt jettisonable for landing.

Re-entry vehicles

Another area of WRD's high-speed research was re-entry vehicles, RVs. Much of the work for Blue Streak's re-entry vehicles was carried out using the Black Knight rocket and, since these were scaled to that booster, may not have been truly representative of the full size RV. Avro proposed using some of the surplus Thor missiles for such research and in August 1959 drew up the Z.56 series. With wings, or rather strakes, along the centreline, these were winged cones that differed in their fineness ratio. The Z.56A was a blunt-nosed cone 4ft (1.2m) long with the narrow wings extending aft of the base. One half of the cone comprised a fairing that jettisoned when the RV separated. The Z.56B was 7ft (2.1m) long with a more acute angle to the cone. Both weighed 300 lb (136kg) and were to be boosted to 300,000ft (91,440m) and Mach 15 to 20. Rather than using a Thor missile, the B-model was boosted on a large ballistic vehicle powered by four solid rocket motors and the whole vehicle and booster was 29ft (8.8m) long.

In February 1960 WRD examined boost/glide vehicles with a view to developing such a vehicle for advanced hypersonic missiles. The initial study, Z.69 was a glider with a blunt wedge-shape and a ventral fin. The glider was 10ft (3m) long and 6ft (1.8m) wide and boosted on a two-stage boost system with a total length at launch of 24ft 3in (7.4m) and as such could be carried internally on a Vulcan. The whole system weighed 16,000lb (7,257kg) of which the glider comprised 3,300lb (1,497kg). The Z.69 vehicle proved unstable during its boost phase and the glider itself was difficult to control in its cruise.

By March 1960 the Z.70 boost/glide vehicle had been drawn up and this used a convex cone body with wings along its entire length and was stabilised by ventral and dorsal fins. Powered by a solid rocket booster, the glider weighed 7,000lb (3,175kg) and was 16ft (4.9m) long with a wingspan of 10ft (3m). To launch it to its cruise altitude of 110,000ft (33,528m) required a 'Blue Steel booster' powered by a Stentor and weighing 12,700lb (5,760kg).

The outcome of this boost/glide research was the Z.71, an advanced stand-off bomb to be carried in the Vulcan's bomb bay. This took the Z.69, lengthened and widened it to 15ft (4.6m) by 7ft (2.1m) and added a pair of Bristol Siddeley ramjets. As with the Z.69, a tandem-boost (smaller than the Z.69's) was used to propel the Z.71 to the ramjet light-up speed that would power the Z.71 to Mach 4 for a cruise at 100,000ft (30,480m) over a range of 1,000nm (1,852km). The whole vehicle was 23ft (7m) long and weighed 12,000lb (5,443kg) at launch, 7,750lb (3,515kg) of which was the missile itself. The Z.71 could carry a 1,000lb (454kg) warhead and does not appear to be aimed at any particular requirement.

A year after the Z.55 with its liquid hydrogen coolant and propellant was studied, WRD returned to that fuel with the Z.73. With its booster the Z.73 weighed 20,100lb (9,117kg) of which the vehicle itself made up 6,080lb (2,758lb). The vehicle was 36ft (11m) long and had a wingspan of 17ft (5.2m). The wing was interesting as it was a double delta, à la SAAB Draken (or a Blue Envoy SAM minus the forward strakes) and under each wing was a fairing containing a 'hypersonic ramjet' to give a cruise speed of Mach 7 at 130,000ft (39,624m).

The Toblerone Missile

The culmination of this hypersonic boost/glide and ramjet research was the Z.76 from March 1960. A Mach 7 long-range missile that could carry a 1,000lb (454kg) warhead to a target 2,000nm (3,704km) distant, the Z.76 had a very odd configuration indeed. So odd in fact that the designers called it 'The Toblerone Missile' and its planform did match the shape of the Swiss confectionery. In plan view it was a delta wing with 80° sweep on the leading edge with the apex of the delta as bluff, rounded shape. The side elevation revealed its flat top, large fin and a fuselage that deepened to the rear with the intakes for the Bristol Siddeley hypersonic ramjets faired into the fuselage. The front elevation shows that the fuselage was a deep, slab-sided V-shape with a rounded underside. Unlike the Z.73, the Z.76's ramjets were integrated into the airframe with large box intakes projecting from the fuselage. Unfortunately no rear view was available in Avro's documents, nor was this described, so the configuration of the exhaust is unknown. The Z.76 was 21ft (6.4m) long and 9ft (2.7m) wide (describing it as wingspan seems unsuitable) and with a weight of 9,500lb (4,309kg) without boosts,

Avro's WRD became quite imaginative in its hypersonic test vehicle designs in the early 1960s. Z.55 used a liquid hydrogen rocket with regenerative cooling and a solid boost. The Z.69 was a boost/glide vehicle with a two-stage rocket booster. Powered by a 'hypersonic ramjet' the Z.73 used liquid hydrogen for fuel and cooling. The Z.76 'Toblerone' was to be a Mach 7 cruise missile powered by Bristol Siddeley ramjets.

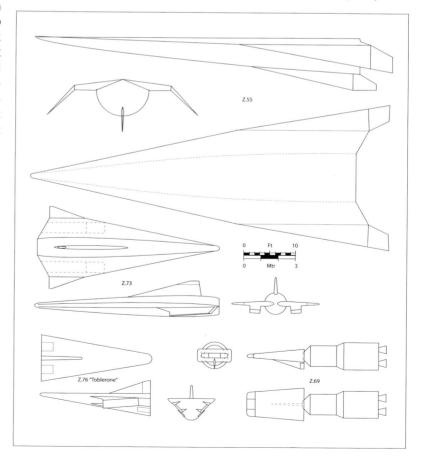

22,000 lb (9,979kg) with boosts, the Z.76 could cruise at 100,000ft (30,480m) at Mach 7. The Z.76 was intended as a cruise missile and could carry its warhead for 2,000nm (3,704km). It was a very interesting exercise.

Into Orbit

As noted above, Sputnik had a tremendous effect on the defence policies of Great Britain and the United States. Sputnik also prompted an increase in the pace of development involving vehicles to place payloads in Earth orbit.

In October 1961 Avro decided to create a 'versatile high-speed research vehicle' based on Blue Steel for use in a variety of roles. The Z.100 was to be used at extreme altitudes and speeds to allow testing of materials and aerodynamics in these regimes and as a carrier for small rockets to reach space. At the other end of the spectrum it could have been used for low-altitude development of terrain clearance radar and ramjet development. Versatility was its goal. The

Z.100 was a W.100 airframe with no anhedral on the wingtips and vertical fins added at three-quarter span. A variety of recovery system were examined including parachutes and a paraglider although a skid undercarriage turned out to be most efficient as it used less space, even with the radio control landing system installed. With the basic Z.100 designed, it could be put to use. The Z.102 was a two-stage research vehicle, essentially a Z.100 fitted with a ventral pylon to carry a small solid rocket powered payload.

WRD's initial study for placing a payload into orbit was the Z.103 and that involved a modified Z.100 recoverable research vehicle fitted with a larger pylon than the Z.102 to carry a launch vehicle. Having been lifted to 45,000ft (13,716m) on a Vulcan (the first stage) the Z.100 second stage was released and performed a standard Blue Steel-style boost manoeuvre to 70,000ft (21,336m). At this point the launch vehicle was to be released, the third stage fired and boosted the vehicle higher and faster, followed by the fourth stage that took the 10 lb (4.5kg) payload to a final velocity of 26,000ft/sec (7,925m/sec) and into low Earth orbit. Avro discovered that British solid rocket motors lacked the power to place the payload into orbit so opted to use American motors.

The chosen motors came from the Scout satellite launcher (Scout stood for Solid Controlled Orbital Utility Test system) and was for a long time the only satellite launcher that used solid rocket motors. The motors involved in Z.103 were the Antares for the third stage and Altair for the fourth stage. Essentially Avro WRD substituted a Vulcan and a Z.100 for the first two expendable stages of the Scout. If this appears to be an awful lot of effort to place 10 lb into orbit, consider this – the massive R.7 launcher used to place the tiny Sputnik in orbit was completely expendable and that was how satellites would be launched until 1981. The Z.103 represented the first step towards a reusable launch system. By October 1962 Avro had become involved with Eurospace, an association of European aerospace companies that was set up in 1961 to examine satellites and their launch systems. Avro carried out a couple of design studies on launchers and re-entry vehicles for Eurospace. In the field of expendable launchers, Avro's Z.124 was a four-stage launch system that used the Vulcan as the first stage. The booster itself was a three-stage rocket that weighed 40,000 lb (18,144kg) and used 'hypothetical solid-propellant rocket motors' to deliver a 400 lb (181kg) payload to an altitude of 300nm (556km).

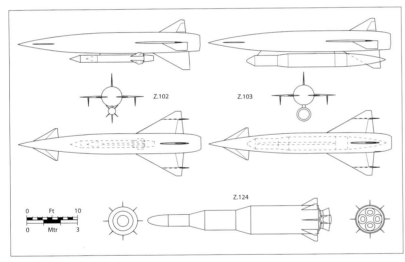

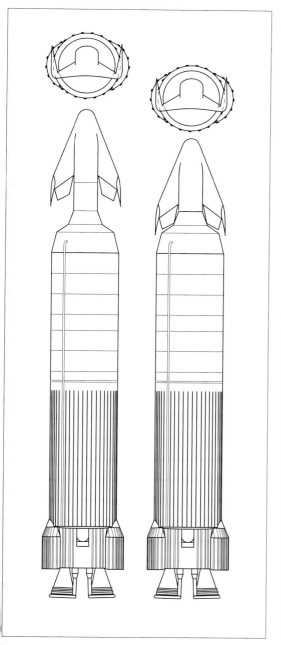

Above: As part of the Hawker Siddeley Group, Avro's WRD had access to equipment from around the Group. As part of a Eurospace project, WRD used de Havilland's Blue Streak as a booster for its Z.123 re-entry research vehicle, with the three-stage version capable of climbing to a peak altitude of 49 miles (79km). Its similarity to the X-20 DynaSoar is readily apparent.

Above right: Boeings X-20 DynaSoar was a re-useable spaceplane the USAF planned to use for routine space access. *Via Bill Rose*

Right: Avro WRD's first manned aircraft was the Z.101, a manned version of the Z.100 research vehicle that formed the basis of many of WRD's test vehicles. It would have been carried by a Vulcan and used many Blue Steel components.

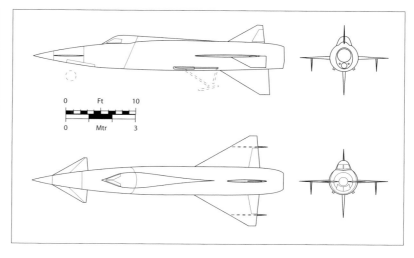

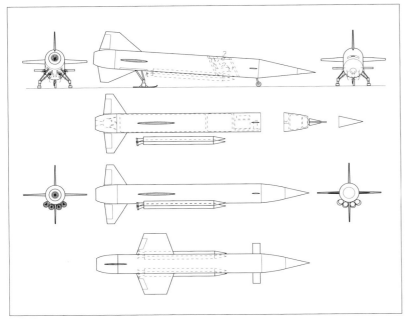

This more advanced and flexible test vehicle outlined by John Allen came in a variety of versions including manned. The basic type would have had a payload in the nosecone, while the manned variant carried the pilot in the modified control equipment bay.

A Thor Able satellite launcher on the pad. On its retirement from RAF service, Avro hoped to use the Thor missile as a first stage for its Z.115 strategic weapon and anti-satellite weapon with Blue Steel and Z.109 as the second stage. Unfortunately the Blue Steel's weight reduced the range to below that of the original Thor. *USAF*

Of much more interest was the Z.123 re-entry research vehicle. This was a test bed for a re-usable (possibly manned) spaceplane that used Blue Streak as its first stage, with an optional second stage to increase re-entry velocity and height. The 4,000 lb (1,814 kg) test vehicle shared a configuration with Boeing X-20 Dyna-Soar; a flat-bottomed wing/fuselage with the wingtips upturned into fins. The optional second stage fitted between the booster and the test vehicle and if used, would have increased the velocity at burn-out from 20,000 ft/sec to 22,000 ft/sec (6,096-6,705 m/sec) to assess re-entry behaviour at higher velocity.

All this re-entry and high-speed research was aimed at providing useful information on development of manned hypersonic aircraft and aerospaceplanes. The North American Aviation X-15 had been flying since September 1959 and Avro were keen to utilise what they had learned and apply it to a similar vehicle.

In September 1961, WRD drew up a proposal for a manned version of the Z.100. The entire forward fuselage of the Z.100 was replaced by a cockpit for a pilot in a pressure suit, autopilot system and a nosewheel. Called the Z.101/35 the aircraft was intended to reach a speed of Mach 3.6 under the power of the Stentor engine before gliding back to land. The 35 ft (10.7 m) long Z.101/35 was to weigh 16,480 lb (7,475 kg) at launch and 8,550 lb (3,878 kg) at engine burn-out. A version stretched by 3 ft (0.9 m) was called the Z.101/38 and was to be capable of Mach 5 at an altitude of 300,000 ft (91,440 m).

Blue Steel ASAT

As well as launching satellites, Avro WRD examined the means of intercepting them; after all they were the Weapons Research Division. In 1962 the Air Staff issued ASR.9001, 9002 and 9003. These were respectively a space-fighter, a counter-satellite system and a reconnaissance satellite. The space-fighter underwent studies at other members of the Hawker Siddeley group while the counter-satellite system was examined by WRD at Woodford. Using the Blue Steel as a basis for an interception system, WRD drafted a pair of proposals for an anti-satellite (ASAT) system, one ground-launched and another for air launch from a Vulcan.

The air-launched version, Z.116, used a Z.109, the droop-snoot stretched Blue Steel, as a carrier for a small solid rocket powered interceptor. The interceptor would have been carried on a ventral pylon along the same lines as the Z.102 described above. For an interception to take place the Vulcan with its ASAT had to fly in the same orbital plane as the target satellite. The ASAT launch had to lie in a time period of 100 seconds for a successful interception. Positioning and launch of the ASAT was under the

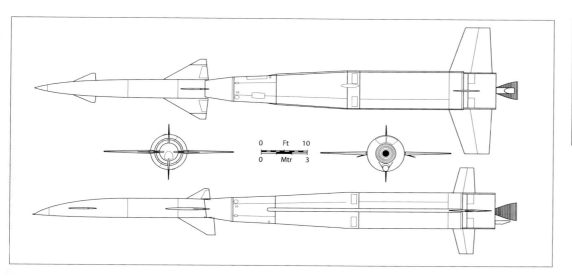

0   Ft   10
0   Mtr   3

The Z.115-based ASAT system used the Z.109 stretched Blue Steel to carry an interceptor in its nose. A Vulcan-based system called Z.116 was also under consideration.

control of a ground computer, using radar to track target and interceptor. On launch at 30,000ft (9,144m), the Z.116 dived under the power of its Stentor to reach Mach 1.4 before pitching up until the point of burn-out. WRD advised that the missile could enter a vertical climb until burn out at 200,000ft (60,960m) and Mach 5. The interceptor would then fire its rocket motor to boost the warhead on a collision course. At motor burn-out the interceptor continued to coast until it intercepted the target at the interceptor's apogee at an altitude between 250 and 400nm (463 and 741km).

The Vulcan could carry a maximum payload of 24,000 lb (10,886kg) so with a fully-fuelled Z.116 weighing 21,400 lb (9,707kg) that left 2,600 lb (1,179kg) available for the interceptor. Since the ventral carriage of the interceptor added drag to the missile, WRD suggested that the Z.109 stage carried less fuel and could be shortened to accommodate the ASAT vehicle on the front of the Z.109, making for a cleaner, less draggy installation. The report into the Z.116 by J B Caress concluded that the system's development was not particularly worthwhile as '…an unmodified Skybolt has sufficient performance and apparently sufficient guidance accuracy.' The ground-launch system was based on the Z.115 – a Thor missile with a Blue Steel proposed as a strategic ballistic missile. The W.100 second stage was replaced by the Z.109/ASAT and flew a similar trajectory as the Z.116 after the Thor burn-out at 125,000ft (38,100m).

All of the systems proposed in ASR.9001 to 9003 foundered for lack of an indigenous launcher: Blue Streak having been cancelled as a military system and the RAF and MoD did not want to rely on the French or Americans for their military payload launches.

Maglev Launcher

Magnetic levitation, maglev, is one of those technologies on a par with hypersonic airliners – a great idea, but horrendously expensive. The first commercial maglev railway opened at Birmingham Airport in 1984 and continued to operate until 1995. To gain the full maglev railway experience in 2011 requires a trip to Shanghai where the Shanghai Maglev Train whisks passengers along in silent rapidity between Shanghai and its Pudong airport.

In the Sixties, maglev was the future: silent, frictionless and clean. When combined with Prof. Eric Laithwaite's linear induction motors there would be a transportation revolution. Indeed that's what WRD intended doing with the maglev track except that their revolution would head into space. In September 1963 WRD produced what was its last project. Z.133 would combine just about everything that WRD had learned since its inception in 1954: advanced aerodynamics, materials, propulsion and innovation. The Z.133 was a track-launched, air-breathing booster to place a 5,600 lb (2,540kg) payload into a 150nm (278km) orbit. As a satellite launcher, Z.133 was a three-stage affair, with the first stage an air-breathing hypersonic aircraft powered by four underwing ramjets. The ramjets were to be fuelled with kerosene, which suggests they utilised subsonic combustion, which in an aircraft flying at Mach 7 at 62,000ft (18,898m) would generate a great deal of stagnation heating within the intake diffuser. The air-breather was an all-wing anhedral delta affair, with a 75° sweep on the leading edge with the anhedral on the upper surface of 22.5° and endplate fins at the tips. The ramjets were installed under the wings, while above the wings on the centreline was a cockpit for a single pilot.

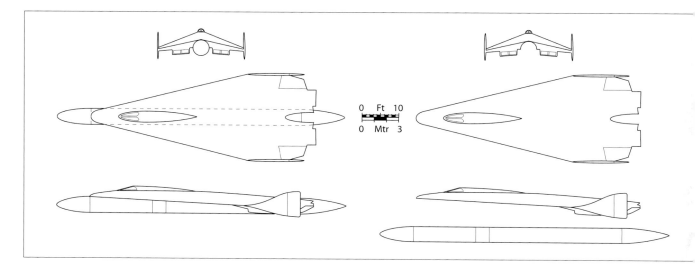

Avro Weapons Research Division's swan-song was the Z.133 satellite launcher. It combined much of the technology that made Britain a leader in the engineering field. Accelerated on a maglev track to ramjet light-up speed the re-usable piloted vehicle was to carry a two-stage launch vehicle to high altitude before releasing it.

The aircraft weighed 41,300 lb (18,733kg) fully-fuelled with kerosene.

The second and third stages were each powered by liquid-fuelled rocket engines using liquid oxygen and liquid hydrogen and the rocket boosters plus payload weighed 28,700 lb (13,018kg) at launch. The entire Z.133 vehicle would have weighed 70,000 lb (31,751kg) in total when fully loaded and ready for launch. For the launch itself the Z.133 was to be mounted on a sled that was to be propelled by six Rolls-Royce RZ.2 liquid oxygen/kerosene engines as used on the Blue Streak. The sled weighed 63,750 lb (28,916kg) fully fuelled with 23,750 lb (10,773kg) of liquid oxygen and kerosene.

An alternative means of propelling the sled was a linear induction motor. These work by taking the stator of an electric motor and unrolling

it along a surface. Rather than producing rotational torque and movement, the movement is linear along the 'stator'; they are suitable for applications that require high acceleration, while other types can be used for slower steady speed applications. For the Z.133, a rapid acceleration was required, in fact the sled and launcher were to have reached Mach 1.5 in 10 seconds over a distance of 1nm (1.85km) by which time the ramjets would have lit and be producing thrust.

Avro WRD's space and research vehicles are an exceedingly interesting set of projects that require further investigation. From the brute force of adding a re-entry vehicle to a Thor missile and blasting it into the air to the sophisticated multi-stage launchers aimed at re-usable launchers, WRD's engineers and scientists deserve recognition for their advanced thinking.

Exotica

Type	Length	Span	Diameter	Weight	Propulsion	Range
Blue Streak	60ft	n/a	10ft	210,000 lb	RZ1 rocket engine	2,000nm
Blue Water	25ft	7ft	2ft	3,000 lb	Solid rocket	55nm
Avro Z.115	99ft	30ft	8ft	122,500 lb	Liquid rocket	2,000nm
Regulus II	57ft 6in	20ft 1in	n/a	24,250 lb	GE J79 turbojet Solid rocket boost	1,200nm
Avro P.2Z	45ft	16ft 2in	n/a	30,000 lb	DH Gyron Jnr. 2 x ASM Gamma	1,000nm
Avro Z.101/35	35ft	13ft	n/a	16,480 lb	ASM Stentor	n/a
Avro Z.101/38	38ft	13ft	n/a	18,180 lb	ASM Stentor	n/a
Avro Z.124	37ft	n/a	5ft	40,000 lb	3-stage solid rocket	n/a
North American X-15	50ft 9in	22ft 4in	n/a	34,000 lb	Thiokol XLR99 rocket	n/a
Avro Z.133	65ft	26ft	n/a	70,000 lb	Ramjet	n/a
Avro Z.73	36ft	17ft	n/a	20,100 lb	2 x 'Supersonic ramjet'	1,000nm
Avro Z.59	35ft	7ft 6in	n/a	14,500 lb	Nuclear ramjet	n/a
Avro Z.55	66ft	28ft	n/a	29,300 lb	Liquid hydrogen rocket	2,000nm

9 Post Polaris

With Blue Steel retired and Polaris in the deterrent role, the V-Force changed markedly. The Victors became tankers and the Vulcan carried free-fall weapons such as the WE.177. Post-1970 new weapons for the Vulcan would be events-driven. On the deterrent front, the rise of the cruise missile led to its consideration as a Polaris replacement. The large weapons of the 1960s were gone, replaced by the small weapons that allowed the Vulcan to adopt diverse roles that included air defence and suppression of enemy air defences.

The weapons of the V-Force were, in general, somewhat large. This was driven by the size of the nuclear warheads and the technology that went into the guidance system combined with the range and therefore fuel requirements. None of these reached any level of miniaturisation until the mid to late 1960s so the weapons from the V-Force days, being state of the art, were necessarily large.

In the post V-Force era weapons became smaller and reflected the change in role from strategic deterrent to tactical strike, saw the Victors converted to tankers and the Vulcan take on roles that would have surprised designer Roy Chadwick. Interceptor and 'Wild Weasel' were two such roles that cropped up in the face of changing threats and in the Seventies and Eighties, the threat changed direction.

Red Barrel – *Foxbat*, *Backfire* and the Vulcan Interceptor

Foxbat and *Backfire* – these odd names filled the hearts of the Air Staff with dread in the early 1970s and that anxiety was due to the RAF's impotence at countering them. *Foxbat*, the NATO reporting name of the Mikoyan-Gurevich MiG-25, was considered a major threat to NATO air operations, with its Mach 3 performance and air-to-air missiles while *Backfire*, NATO reporting name for the Tupolev Tu-26 (now known to be designated Tupolev Tu-22M), was seen as a major threat to NATO

Vulcan's Hammers: Blue Steel, Shrike, Martel, iron bombs and Paveways. Conspicuous by their absence are the WE.177 and Yellow Sun.
Via Kev Darling

Foxbat! The formidable MiG-25 had yet to reveal its secrets when the ADV versions of the Vulcan were proposed in 1976. *Via Terry Panopalis*

shipping and land targets in the United Kingdom. The mystery of these aircraft and their perceived potential continued for many years with the puzzle of their true capability only solved after the Cold War ended in 1989.

To readers under forty years old, the mysterious nature of Soviet aircraft in the Cold War might be difficult to understand. Such was the mystique around Soviet aircraft that in the 1980s this author took a job in Angola just to see Russian aircraft and was not disappointed. Despite the application of what the Americans called 'national technical means' to the task, the closed nature of Soviet society made the analysis and performance estimation of their aircraft very much an art rather than a science. One pundit concluded that much of the *Backfire* airframe was empty space and that its formidable range was a myth.

The *Foxbat* revealed most of its secrets on 6th September 1976 when Lt Viktor Belenko landed his brand-new MiG-25P (NATO reporting name *Foxbat A*) at Hakodate Airport in Japan, claimed political asylum and handed his aircraft over to the Japanese authorities. The Japanese allowed the USAF's Foreign Technology Division to analyse the *Foxbat* for more than two months at Wright-Patterson Air Base before the aircraft was returned to the Soviets in crates. *Backfire* on the other hand, until the 1990s when Russian aircraft began to appear at Western air shows and the Soviet Union collapsed allowing greater access to information, gave nothing away and it still remained the subject of massive speculation. It was only in the post-Cold War era that the type's true designation was discovered: Tu-22M, a ruse by the Tupolev design bureau that ensured continued funding as the work was ostensibly done on a variant of an existing type, the Tu-22 *Blinder*. It was not only the Western aerospace companies

that had funding troubles caused by politicians.

Prior to this and the resultant revelations, the *Foxbat* and *Backfire* were the bogey-men of the NATO air forces whose equipment was rendered impotent by the *Foxbat's* estimated Mach 3+ speed and service ceiling in excess of 90,000ft (27,432m). Backfire was also seen as a high-performance anti-ship missile carrier that had to be intercepted before it launched its warload. Both types formed the basis of threat to be countered when the NATO air planners and requirement branches drew up their specifications.

The only aircraft deemed capable of dealing with such threats were the McDonnell Douglas F-15 Eagle and the Grumman F-14 Tomcat of the USAF and USN respectively but for budgetary reasons neither of these was available to the RAF. The RAF was stuck with its English Electric Lightning carrying two 1950s-vintage de Havilland Red Top IR homing missiles with a range of less than 8nm (13km) or the McDonnell Douglas F-4 Phantom and its semi-active Hawker Siddeley Dynamics XJ.521 Skyflash that had a range of 24nm (45km). Neither aircraft carried radar capable of detecting a *Foxbat* or *Backfire* at a distance that would allow an interception to take place. Both types were to be replaced by the Panavia Tornado air defence variant (ADV) that along with its Foxhunter AI.24 radar would provide a limited capability against the *Foxbat*, but was tailored specifically to dealing with *Backfire*. Realistically, Tornado ADV was not expected to enter service with the RAF until the mid 1980s, so an alternative was sought in the interim.

In early 1976 development of the Tornado ADV had yet to be sanctioned and the *Foxbat's* secrets were still secure. The *Backfire* fleet was seen as a menace to the Atlantic convoys that would carry reinforcements to West Germany in the event of the Cold War turning hot, an event that was simulated by the annual REFORGER (REturn of FORces to GERmany exercise). Flying from Soviet bases in the Kola Peninsula, the *Backfires* would have flown at supersonic speeds to attack the convoys in the North Atlantic. This problem would spark some radical ideas from the Air Staff in Whitehall and see an obscure engineering study from the 1960s resurrected.

RAF Henlow was until 1980 the home of the RAF's Technical College where engineering officers received their training, its most famous alumnus being Sir Frank Whittle. Part of an engineering officer's assessment was a technical exercise in solving some engineering problem and to produce a report outlining their solutions. The students could also examine technical aspects of a problem associated with a specific type or carry out studies into solving particular tactical or strategic quandaries. One example of this was an airborne anti-ballistic missiles system, but another project of interest was known as Red Barrel and produced what was essentially a flying surface-to-air missile site. Such a proposal had been considered as far back as November 1957 in a letter from a Mr Wilkins of the RAE Guided Weapons Department to Reuben Aspinall, Director of Guided Weapons Research at the Royal Radar Establishment. Wilkins suggested the creation of a 'Flying Battleship' by fitting V-bombers with modified SAGWs: 'It seems to me that a possible solution may exist in a V-bomber carrying your long-range CWAI and a few Green Flax missiles'. Green Flax was the English Electric Thunderbird II that used continuous-wave radar, hence the reference to CWAI, continuous-wave airborne interception, radar. The idea found its way into an article in *Flight* magazine in August 1958, complete with an artist's impression of a Victor launching a large missile. The article explained that a large, long-endurance aircraft such as a V-bomber, Bristol Britannia or Canadair Argus could carry a much more powerful AI radar antenna that provided much longer operating range than that in a fighter and also considered that the number of missiles that could be carried was much greater.

Red Barrel comprised a version of the Vickers VC10 fitted with a large airborne interception (AI) radar and a formidable armoury of eighteen air-to-air missiles. Red Barrel could be seen as a British version of the American Project AERIE that proposed fitting KC-135 tankers with radar and 24 Bendix AAM-N-10 Eagle missiles or the Lockheed CL-520 variant of the P-3 Orion with a dorsal rotodome and ten Eagle missiles. Capable of Mach 4.5, the Eagle missile possessed a range of 96nm (177km) and was launched into a climb before diving onto its target once the missile's active-homing radar was within range.

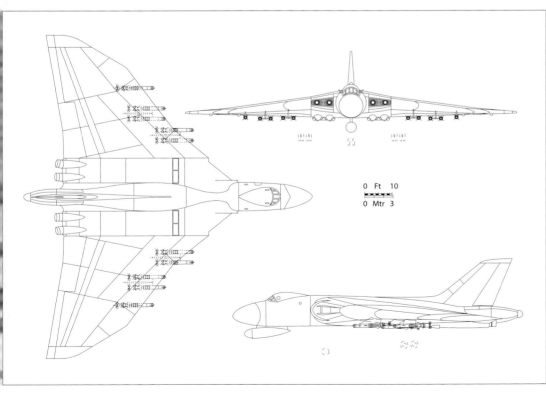

The Sea Dart Vulcan required a second radar pod and a reprofiled nose. The Sea Dart was heavier, with ten to be fitted, and no doubt less suitable for the role than the Phoenix. The entire Sea Dart installation would have generated more drag and required much more work, assuming the AWG-9 radar from the Tomcat was used.

The Texas Instruments AGM-45 Shrike was developed by the US Navy for use against Soviet radars. It became operational in the Vietnam War and was used to attack Argentinian radars by RAF Vulcans during the Falkands War of 1982. *USAF*

This Hawker Siddeley Woodford drawing shows the radar installation for the Sea Dart Vulcan. The difference in size of the two radars is obvious, with the illuminator radar transmitting at high power over long range for the semi-active Sea Dart. *BAE Systems/ Avro Heritage*

British guided weapons companies had no active-homing air-to-air missiles, never mind one with sufficient range, on the drawing board in the early 1960s, so the Red Barrel VC10 was shown with somewhat idealised guided weapons under the wings. Fortunately Hawker Siddeley Dynamics did have in 1962 a long-range surface-to-air missile that could be modified for air-launch in the shape of the CF.299 naval SAM. Later called Sea Dart, the CF.299 was powered by a Bristol Siddeley BS.1003 Odin ramjet and, after launch from a rail, was boosted to the Odin's light-up speed by a Chow solid rocket booster. This booster, unlike previous British SAMs, was in a low-drag tandem configuration that, along with its launch rail mounting, made it ideal for conversion to aircraft launch and so was submitted to meet the joint requirement OR.1193/GDA.103.

The original air-launched CF.299 was intended to arm the Fleet Air Arm's fighters such as the de Havilland Sea Vixen or the new generation of aircraft such as the Hawker P.1154 to meet AW.406/OR.356. The air-launched CF.299 would have a range of 45nm (83km), a figure that the Admiralty viewed with great glee. Unfortunately it soon became apparent that the missile's range was beyond the illumination

range of the fighter's radar and being a semi-active homing missile, CF.299 needed a radar return from its target to home in on. Another problem was the CF.299's seeker itself that comprised a polyrod system with four antennae arranged around the intake lip that limited sensitivity to the returned signal. The simple expedient of fitting a larger antenna to CF.299 was not possible and that, combined with the drag associated with external carriage of a ramjet missile, prompted the Admiralty and Air Staff to scrap the air-launched CF.299 in late 1963.

That is possibly where the story of air-launched Sea Dart might have ended had the RAF in 1976 not been looking for a counter to the *Foxbat* and *Backfire*. The radar sensitivity problem was never an issue for the Navy as their warships carried the Type 909 tracking and illumination radar with an 8ft (2.5m) diameter Cassegrain antenna under a hemispherical dome. Unlike a ship, a radar installation on an aircraft requires much more consideration of size and weight, not to mention electrical power, especially for a radar such as the Type 909 that was regarded as heavy even for naval applications. The only aircraft with radar antenna dimensions in the same league as the Type 909 was the Hawker Siddeley HS.801 AEW aircraft with 8ft (2.5m) diameter antennae that would eventually become the Nimrod AEW.3, although this type would not enter development until the late 1970s. One type that was available and could carry such a radar antenna plus the required missile load was the Avro Vulcan B.2. The Vulcan fleet was being reduced in strength, so many airframes were available for conversion to an air defence variant. The modifications included the fitting of a 6ft (1.8m) radar antenna in a new radome that replaced the entire nose forward of the cockpit. This antenna for the Sea Dart illuminator would provide the radar power required to allow the Sea Dart to home in on a target up to 60nm (111km) away. Finding the targets required a search and tracking radar with a 3ft (0.9m) diameter antenna housed in a teardrop-shaped nacelle mounted on the centreline under the nose. The new nose radome, profiled for optimum radar performance, was blunter and 3ft 6in (1.1m) shorter than the Vulcan B.2 nose.

Ten Sea Dart missiles were mounted on under-wing pylons, with double rails at stations 252 and 350 and a single rail at station 446 on each wing. Why ten missiles? A Soviet attack on a naval fleet would invariably be a two-phase affair. The initial wave of missile carriers such as Tu-95 *Bear* and Tu-16 *Badger* would be tackled

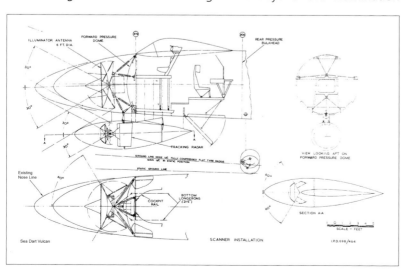

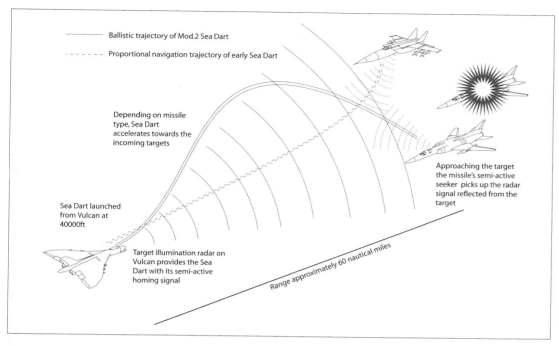

The Hawker Siddeley Dynamics Sea Dart was proposed as the Armament for the Vulcan in a reprise of the 1960s Red Barrel studies. This diagram shows the missile's two modes of operation.

Diagram labels:

—— Ballistic trajectory of Mod.2 Sea Dart

- - - Proportional navigation trajectory of early Sea Dart

Depending on missile type, Sea Dart accelerates towards the incoming targets

Approaching the target the missile's semi-active seeker picks up the radar signal reflected from the target

Sea Dart launched from Vulcan at 40000ft

Target illumination radar on Vulcan provides the Sea Dart with its semi-active homing signal

Range approximately 60 nautical miles

by air defence fighters flying combat air patrols, but these would soon run short of fuel and weapons. A second wave, that no doubt comprised *Backfires*, could attack unhindered by the fighters. A flight of Sea Dart-armed Vulcan air defence variants on patrol over the north east Atlantic or the Barents Sea would have possessed the endurance and weapons load to provide the fleet with extended protection from *Backfires*. Combined with an AEW platform such as the Nimrod AEW as intended, the Vulcan fighters would have provided a formidable barrier to the Soviet attackers. The Sea Dart possessed the range and the Mach 3.5 performance to tackle the *Foxbat* in a head-on attack.

Hawker Siddeley's documentation for the Sea Dart/Vulcan combination shows that the combination was capable of interception of high-speed targets such as the *Foxbat* at ranges in excess of 60nm (111km) and altitudes in excess of 80,000ft (24,384m). This range capability may have been achievable in part by the missile following a ballistic trajectory on the early part of its flight and was in turn made possible by the reduction in size of the electronics replacing 1960s-era valve based systems with solid-state equipment. This allowed an autopilot to be added, as in the later Mod 2 version of Sea Dart that could also be used against multiple targets, a useful addition for an air-defence weapon tackling massed attacks.

The 6ft (1.8m) diameter of the tracking and illumination radar's antenna listed in the documents suggests a system similar to the Type 805 proposed for HSD's Lightweight Sea Dart in the late 1970s. Radar coverage was 30° above and below and 60° either side of the aircraft centreline. This allowed the radar to cover a vast volume of airspace, particularly from the 40,000ft (12,192m) patrol altitude at which the Vulcan would cruise.

All these changes, and the need to carry two radars, made the Sea Dart/Vulcan complex and draggy. As well as the weight of the radars, the Sea Dart weighed in at 1,213lb (550kg) and while its aerodynamics were optimised for Mach 2+, carriage of ten at Mach 0.8 created a lot of drag for the Vulcan to overcome.

The ideal solution was to fit a dedicated air-to-air missile and in the mid-1970s there was only one missile with the required capability: the Hughes AIM-54 Phoenix as used by the US Navy Grumman F-14 Tomcat. Phoenix was

The Grumman F-14 Tomcat and its AIM-54 Phoenix proved a formidable air defence platform for US Navy carriers. The Phoenix Vulcan could have filled a similar niche defending the 'Unsinkable Aircraft Carrier'. *US Navy*

Vulcan ADV with Hughes AIM-54 Phoenix air-to-air missiles. With a load-out of 12 Phoenix AAMs, the Phoenix Vulcan would have made a formidable barrier air defence system. The AIM-7 Sparrow was also considered but lacked the Phoenix's long-range clout.
Via David Fildes

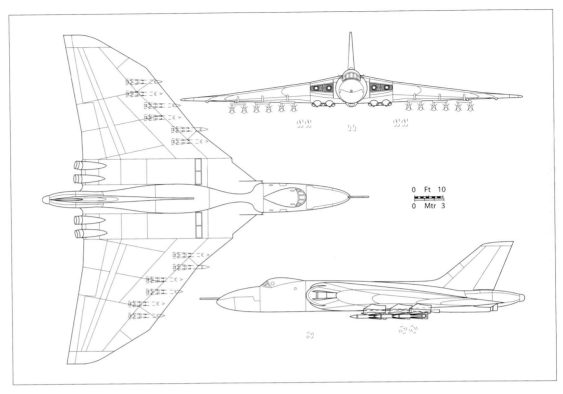

Probably the only type that approached the 'flying SAM site' concept of Red Barrel and the Vulcan ADV was the Tu-128 *Fiddler* with its four long-range Bisnovat R-4 air-to-air missiles, NATO reporting name AA-5 '*Ash*'.
Via Terry Panopalis

lighter at 1,040 lb (470kg), carried a much larger warhead, had a range of more than 100nm (185km). It also used a single radar, the Hughes AWG-9, for target detection and tracking, with the missile using an active seeker. Although the Grumman F-14 was not available on cost grounds, there was a possibility of acquiring the Phoenix. Hawker Siddeley's studies showed that the Vulcan could carry up to 12 Phoenix on six pylons and dispensed with the need for the undernose pod for a tracking radar.

Ultimately the only country that fielded such a flying missile base was the Soviet Union who used the Tupolev Tu-128 (NATO reporting name *Fiddler*) to patrol the vast tracts of territory that would have been extremely costly to defend with SAMs.

Wild Weasel Vulcan – Anti-radiation weapons

The Air Staff had by 1962 issued OR.1168 for an air-to-surface weapon with TV guidance and anti-radiation capability. This became the Anglo-French MARTel, (Missile, Anti-Radiation, Television), developed from a series of missiles that had their origins in a Franco-German missile called AS.30, with conventional and nuclear variants proposed. The French took the AS.30 and fitted it with a Dassault AD.37 passive radar seeker to produce the AS.37 as an anti-radiation missile (ARM) to attack air defence radars.

The British Air Staff were keen to have a new air-to-surface missile to replace the Bullpup and also had a requirement for an anti-radar missile. Seeing an opportunity to save some money on OR.1168 and foster Anglo-French relations, the UK embarked on a joint project with France. While the French company Matra took charge of the anti-radar weapon, de Havilland Propellers (soon to become Hawker Siddeley Dynamics) took over the design and develop-

ment of the replacement for the Martin AGM-12 Bullpup under the Ministry of Aviation reference number AJ.168. This became the TV Martel, which the RAF were never really happy with, particularly its need for a guidance pod on one of the carrying aircraft's pylons.

Hawker Siddeley at Woodford did ponder fitting the AJ.168 to Vulcan with six rounds carried on wing pylons. The datalink pod was to be fitted in the tail-cone, replacing the Red Steer rear-warning radar which was moved to a new pod at the top of the fin. The most difficult aspect of using the TV-guided AJ.168 Martel on the Vulcan was that it allowed the aircraft to launch it and escape on a reciprocal bearing. As a result, the datalink antenna faced aft and the operator had to acquire the datalink signal after the escape manoeuvre had been performed, with the aircraft departing the target area at speed. The Buccaneer carried three Martels and the expectation (or perhaps hope) was that at least one attempt would be successful. How a Vulcan crew would react to having to enter and egress the target area up to six times is not documented, but the mission profile would be more like the 'hokey-cokey' than an attack.

A better bet for attacking surface targets, albeit with less stand-off, was the Paveway laser-guided bomb. Precision Avionics Vectoring Equipment refers to any US system that uses a laser for targeting or guidance and had its origins in the Vietnam War. Paveway equipment, a seeker head with control fins and larger tail

kit, could be attached to a standard free-fall bomb such as the US 2,000 lb (907kg) Mk.84 and in the case of British weapons, the standard 1,000 lb (454kg) bomb. On the Vulcan, four Paveway bombs could be carried in the bomb bay, with the laser designator being operated by one of the crew in the bomb-aimer's position under the nose. There is a certain irony in this throwback to the 1940s being used to aim a high-technology weapon in the 1980s.

Attacks on surface targets with guided weapons brings the story back to Martel, specifically the anti-radiation AS.37 Martel, which being a passive homing weapon, did not need a datalink pod. Fitted with a Basilie boost rocket and a Cassandra sustainer, the AS.37 was guided to the target radar at high subsonic speed by its passive seeker, to destroy it with a 150kg (331 lb) blast/fragmentation warhead. The AS.37 Martel's Dassault-developed seeker had two modes: pre-programmed with a particular radar's signature or in an environment where no friendly radars were operating, scan a range of frequencies for hostile radars. In the first mode, the missile seeker had to be tuned before the mission. Martel was slow, heavy and non-programmable after take-off. Bear in mind that this system was designed in the days of the thermionic valve, long before the advances in digital electronics and computing made in-flight retuning possible.

So, in May 1982 when British forces were in the process of retaking the Falkland Islands from

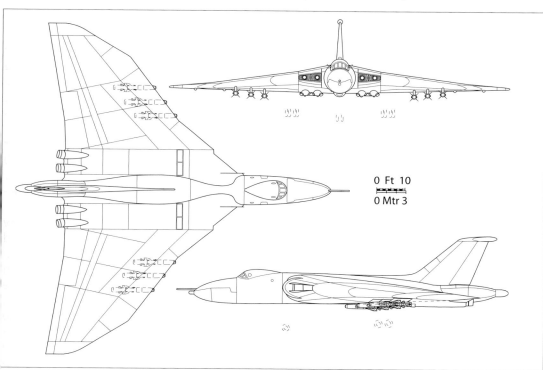

0 Ft 10
0 Mtr 3

The TV-guided AJ.168 required a datalink pod for the guidance system. This took up a stores pylon on aircraft like the Buccaneer, thus reducing the weapons load. This design study from Woodford saw the Vulcan fitted with six AJ.168 TV Martel and the datalink pod replacing the Red Steer rear-warning radar. Red Steer was relocated to the top of the tail fin. *Via David Fildes*

175

the Argentinians there was a need, before any amphibious assault could take place, to render inoperable the air defence radars that had been installed on the islands. These radars included AN/TPS.43F and AN/TPS-44 3-D air surveillance radars with a useful detection range of up to 275nm (443km), giving a measure of early warning of approaching aircraft and allowed the direction of attacking Argentinian aircraft. Other radars were associated with the Roland SAM system, which used an X-band frequency-agile fire-control radar, and the Contraves Skyguard 30mm anti-aircraft gun. Another problem was that the Argentinian kit was of Western origin, while the British forces' electronic warfare equipment was tailored to counter Soviet equipment.

The Air Staff and planners were of the opinion that these radar-directed anti-aircraft systems posed a threat to any air operations carried out over the Falkland Islands. Therefore the air defences had to be suppressed, but the British did not have the luxury of a dedicated SEAD (Suppression of Enemy Air Defences) unit like the USAF's 'Wild Weasels'. Even if they had such a unit it would have been equipped with modified strike aircraft that lacked the range for the Falklands missions. So the burden of SEAD passed to the Vulcan B.2, which as luck would have it, had wing hard points and wiring fitted for the putative Skybolt role which was used later for air-sampling pods on the Vulcan B.2MRR. These hard points could carry pylons and the wiring was put to use for the firing systems for an anti-radiation missile.

The RAF had but one anti-radiation missile in its armoury, the Martel AS.37. Unfortunately this was only cleared for use on the Blackburn Buccaneer S.2B, which lacked the range for the round trip from the British base at Ascension Island to the Falklands. The HS Nimrod was capable of carrying Martel and could make the mission with in-flight refuelling, but was deemed more useful in its anti-submarine and airborne search and rescue co-ordination roles. So, the Vulcan had the range, the fittings and the radar-warning systems that would allow it to become the SEAD platform for Operation Corporate.

Vulcan B.2s XM597 and XM612 were fitted out to carry Martel on a pylon fitted to the hard points that were originally intended to carry the Skybolt. XM597 made a sortie over the Cardigan Bay missile range on 6th May, launching an AS.37 Martel successfully; thus the Vulcan was cleared for Martel. Although fitted with two pylons carrying a single Martel, the port pylon was removed later as it was considered to generate excessive drag. An interesting observation

given that, as noted throughout this book, missiles for the Vulcan were usually large, heavy and drag-inducing. Perhaps this was an indication of how close to operational margins the missions to the Falklands were.

This sterling effort came to nought as the Martel was thought to be better used on the Nimrod and a long flight at high-altitude was considered too arduous for the notoriously unreliable Martel. Meantime an offer of AGM-45A Shrike anti-radiation missiles was made by the Americans and the offer was snapped up immediately.

From its inception in 1958 as a means to attack naval air defence radars, Shrike was developed for the US Navy by a consortium of Texas Instruments and Sperry-Univac. Its seeker came in a variety of types, each tuned to a particular class of radar, so the relevant seeker had to be selected and fitted before the mission. Sharing the configuration of the AIM-7 Sparrow AAM, Shrike was 10ft (3.1m) long with a diameter of 8in (20cm) and carrying a 145lb (66kg) blast fragmentation, proximity-fuzed warhead it could reach Mach 2 and was effective over a range of 22nm (40km). One feature of the Shrike was that it depended on a constant signal from the target radar to home in on which limited its effectiveness and meant it could be defeated by the simple expedient of turning off the transmitter. Its first use in combat was against Soviet radars in Vietnam where, along with the larger and longer ranged AGM-78 Standard ARM, it provided the main armoury of the 'Wild Weasel' operations against North Vietnamese air defences. In the October War of 1973, the Israeli Defence Force (Air Force) used the Shrike against the Soviet SA-6 *Gainful* mobile SAM system, but lacking the relevant seeker head, the *Gainfuls* soon had the upper hand, forcing the Israeli strike aircraft to fly low, into the effective range of Egyptian AA guns.

In British service, the Shrike came and went within a few short weeks during May and June 1982. Two Vulcans, XM598 and XM597 were fitted for Shrike capability, a twin rail launcher on each pylon allowed four Shrikes to be carried, a great improvement on the single Martel. The Vulcan crews were trained by personnel from the USAF's 52nd Tactical Fighter Wing, a Wild Weasel unit equipped with F-4G and E Phantoms at Spangdahlem in West Germany. What they thought of the Vulcan as a Wild Weasel has not been recorded, although in later years the idea of the Boeing B-52 in a SEAD role has been discussed. The operations of the Shrike-equipped Vulcans are beyond the scope of this book, but suffice to say the Shrikes did their job against the Argentine radars on the Falklands.

The RAF's experience with the Shrike provided additional information in the development of a new anti-radiation missile to meet AST.1228, issued in 1978. Developed by British Aerospace Dynamics, the result was the Air-Launched Anti-Radiation Missile (ALARM) and included a simple method to counter the radar-operator's favoured defence. After identifying and locking on to a radar, and if the radar switched off, ALARM climbed immediately after launch. After the first stage of the Nuthatch motor burned-out, a parachute deployed and the missile loitered while waiting for the radar to be turned on again. On detecting the radar, ALARM fired the second stage of its motor and attacked the radar. ALARM entered RAF service in 1990 and it remains the SEAD weapon of choice for the RAF.

Shrike was the last weapon to be developed for the Vulcan, with the last weapon used in anger by the V-bomber being the 1,000 lb (454kg) free-fall bombs dropped on Port Stanley airfield. However it must be remembered that the Vulcan operations against the Falkland Islands could not have been carried out without the support of the Victor tankers that plied their trade from Wideawake. It took a minimum of eleven Victor K.2 tanker sorties to put one Vulcan B.2 over Port Stanley, so at the end of the Vulcan's operational career it was only made possible by the Victor. Long seen as rivals in V-Force days, the two surviving V-bombers, their flight and ground crews, development teams and support personnel all worked together to perform the task the V-Force had been designed for: drop bombs on targets at great range. Their like will never be seen again.

Cruise missiles in the 1980s and beyond

Britain's deterrent in the shape of the Lockheed UGM-27 Polaris was by 1969 gliding quietly along under the sea in HMS *Resolution,* followed in the next few years by her sister boats. As with all complicated weapon systems, its replacement was being planned.

In addition to a full replacement, HMG investigated an upgrade of Polaris submarine-launched ballistic missile (SLBM) to defeat the Soviet anti-ballistic missile (ABM) systems such as the A-35 *Aldan* and its Fakel 5V61 (NATO reporting name ABM-1 *Galosh*) missiles deployed around Moscow. This upgrade had been initiated shortly after the Wilson Government took office in October 1964 and the project remained secret until its existence was disclosed by the incoming Thatcher Government in 1979. Chevaline, as the British Polaris Improvement was called, would extend the life of the SLBM into the 1980s, but after that a new system was required to replace the Resolution-class submarines and the Polaris A3TK missiles. There was also a need to replace the Vought MGM-52 Lance tactical nuclear missiles employed by the British Army in West Germany. In response to this, the Defence Operational Analysis Establishment (DOAE) in 1978 set in train Quick Study 122 to examine the various possibilities for replacement of the UK's nuclear capability. These included the American Trident SLBM and air-launched cruise missiles.

The modern cruise missile had become a reality in the mid-1970s with the development of small turbofans, compact computer guidance systems, miniaturised warheads and high-density fuels. These advances, particularly in

A Boeing AGM-86 air-launched cruise missile in flight. The small size and folding aerodynamic surfaces allowed many ALCMs to be carried within aircraft designed to carry the massive weapons of the 1950s such as the B-52. The VC10 could have carried up to 15 cruise missiles of this type had it been converted to the role. *USAF*

guidance systems, allowed an aircraft to carry a number of small missiles that could penetrate Soviet territory at low altitude and either saturate the defences or have immunity from interception due to their low-level flight and small radar cross-section. The cruise missile was not new; the Miles Hoop-La and the German V-1 were early examples as were the American Snark and Matador, but the difference with the new cruise missiles was accuracy.

The biggest breakthrough came in the form of their guidance system: TERrain COntour Matching (TERCOM). Using TERCOM a cruise missile could find its target with an accuracy of a couple of hundred yards or metres after a four-hour flight whereas an inertially-guided missile's navigator would drift in the region of 600 yards or metres for every hour of flight. This drift was what forced the necessity of short-range and high-speed for Blue Steel in the 1950s and made the Skybolt's short flight time so attractive in the early 1960s. An accuracy of a couple of hundred yards was more than adequate for nuclear warhead delivery and allowed attacks on command centres and weapons sites. With TERCOM, an aircraft or missile used its radar altimeter to read the height of the terrain over which it was flying and compare the land profile with a 'height map' stored in the guidance system memory. Rather than storing an entire landmass in its memory, the system held the data as a series of heights in a strip that equated to the route along which the missile would fly. The TERCOM system allowed the missile to fly very low, in the ground clutter that, along with a very small radar cross-section (RCS), would obscure it from the radars of higher-flying interceptors. The low altitude and minimal RCS would also serve to prevent detection by air defence radars and therefore interception by SAMs. In short, cruise missiles had accuracy, range and reduced vulnerability which, combined with their use in great numbers, would allow their use in the deterrent role. They also appeared to be relatively cheap, requiring neither the submarine to carry them nor the maintenance needs of ballistic missiles.

At first glance the air-launched cruise missile deterrent looked very attractive financially. It didn't need a flotilla of submarines to lurk menacingly in the depths as a number of ALCMs can be loaded on a variety of aircraft, whose day job can be anything from strategic bomber to airliner, and in a short time, these can be converted to provide a credible deterrent. Cruise missiles sounded ideal but upon close examination of the finances of nuclear deterrence, something rather alarming was revealed.

The SLBM's raison d'être is that it had more or less 100% certainty of warheads arriving on target if launched successfully. In a submarine, the launch site is pretty much immune from destruction and this combination made SLBMs very attractive as a deterrent. Cruise missiles on the other hand were subsonic and vulnerable to SAMs and anti-aircraft artillery. In reality an attrition rate of more that 50% would be expected so the obvious solution was to increase the number of missiles launched to put the same number of warheads on target. That increase in missiles was where economics reared its much-maligned head. In comparison to submarines and ballistic missiles, ALCMs were cheap. Very cheap. Unfortunately, while the airframes are comparatively cheap, the warheads were not. The warheads may have been small and they may have been compact but their manufacture and maintenance were decidedly costly, particularly the fissile material for the physics package. In balance the ostensibly cheap cruise missile was nothing of the kind, with the greater number of warheads requiring much more fissile material than three Vanguard-class boats and their complement of Trident SLBMs.

As a strategic weapon, the cruise missile needed considerable range to hit targets deep inside Russia even when launched as close to the edge of enemy territory as possible. One technology that contributed to this was the development of special fuels. Shell and Bristol Siddeley Engines Ltd had developed a high-density jet fuel called Shelldyne for high-speed ramjets. Similar fuel technology was used to produce JP-10, a fuel with a volumetric energy content more than 10% higher than standard aviation fuels such a Jet-A. Combined with a much improved low-temperature performance, which is important when a missile is carried externally at high-altitude, such fuels would allow either a larger warhead or more range for the same volume of fuel.

In support of the DOAE studies, the Royal Aircraft Establishment (RAE) set in train a series of paper exercises to examine the possibilities for a British cruise missile and, supplementary to the American Boeing AGM-86 and General Dynamics AGM-109 Tomahawk, came up with four configurations: A through D. In addition to being air-launched, all proposals were required to be either surface-launched, from land or ship, by the addition of a boost system.

Configuration A was more or less a British copy of the AGM-109 Tomahawk complete with folding tail surfaces and flip-out wings.

The main difference was a more pointed nose and a longer, retractable air intake for the TRI-60 turbofan. For a 1,200km (648nm) range the missile was 8.8m (28ft 10in) long and with a fuselage diameter of 0.4m (1ft 4in) possessed a RCS of 0.1m². The length of this variant may have precluded its use in some launch modes, particularly in submarine and carriage on certain aircraft, so a shorter, fatter version 5.5m (18ft) long with a diameter of 0.5m (1.6ft) was also considered, whose RCS was 0.15m². In an effort to reduce the RCS of the cruise missile to minimum, the RAE proposed a somewhat radical design, Configuration B that used a flat-topped, boat-shaped fuselage with flush intakes, S-shaped jet pipe plus fixed wings and tail surfaces. Faired-in to reduce corner reflections, the aerodynamic surfaces were fixed and could not be folded for carriage. All these changes produced a significant reduction in RCS to less than 0.01m² but at the expense of warhead weight. Configurations A and B were subsonic low-level designs and intended to be powered by a Lucas Aerospace GG.220 turbofan or, more likely the Microturbo TRI.60-1, rated at 790 lbf (3.5kN) as used in the BAe Dynamics Sea Eagle anti-ship missile.

The next pair of studies examined the supersonic high-altitude mission profile that had prevailed in the Fifties and Sixties. As noted above, this had been forced upon designers of that era in an attempt to reduce the flight time, which in turn was governed by drift in inertial navigators. Configuration C came in two lengths; 7.8m and 9.7m (25ft 7in and 31ft 10in) depending on the range requirement and/or carriage method and was 0.5m (1ft 7in) in diameter. A pair of wings of very low aspect-ratio, more like strakes than wings, were set in the mid-fuselage. A Rolls-Royce RB.247 turbo-jet rated at 4,200 lbf (19kN) was installed in the rear of the fuselage and fed by a ventral intake. The ventral intake contributed to the greater RCS of 0.2m², but with cruising speed of Mach 2 at an altitude of 18,000m (59,000ft) RCS was secondary. At high altitude the C version possessed a calculated range of 2,400km (1,296nm) whereas at sea-level a range of around 500km (270nm) was more likely. For surface-launch this model required rocket motors to accelerate it to the speed that the intake was optimised for before accelerating to the cruise phase on turbojet power. Powered by a Rolls-Royce BS.1003 Odin ramjet as used in the CF.299 Sea Dart SAM, Configuration D had the shortest range, 200km (107nm) and smallest payload (250kg as opposed to 500kg) in the low-level mission profile. At high altitude, 24,000m (78,739ft), the missile had a speed of Mach 3.5. This weapon saw a return to the high-speed cruise phase followed by low-level dash to target much loved by the tacticians of the 1960s. With a 100km (54nm) final approach to the target at low-level, a total range of 1,500km (810nm) could be achieved.

As with all ramjet-powered missiles, boost rocket motors were required to accelerate the vehicle to ramjet light-up speed. In this case, four solid rocket boosters were wrapped around the fuselage. These boosts were required whatever the launch mode as ramjet intakes have limited speed range and it was

The Duff-Mason studies into a Polaris replacement outlined a number of possibilities including air-launched cruise missiles. As ever the RAE was heavily involved, producing a number of design studies. The logical choice would have been to buy American, but that would be contrary to HM Government's train of thought.

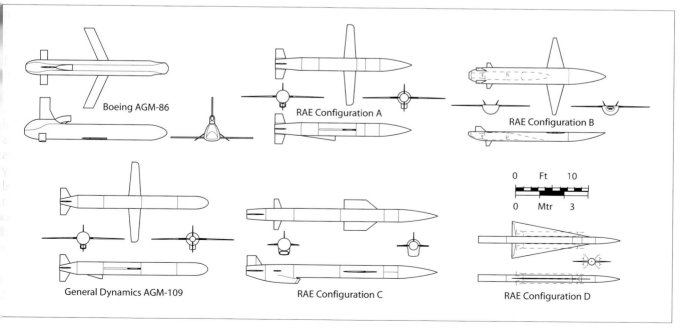

Boeing AGM-86

RAE Configuration A

RAE Configuration B

General Dynamics AGM-109

RAE Configuration C

RAE Configuration D

intended to use the existing Sea Dart intake. One aspect that was not made clear was how that configuration would work. The BS.1003 was an axi-symetric ramjet and Sea Dart SAM was a miracle of packaging with components fitted around the ramjet and intake system. Configuration D came with the classic high-speed delta wing and would no doubt have a nose cone that covered the intake and could be blown off at launch. At 1,650kg (3,638 lb), more than three times the mass of the Sea Dart, the wraparound boosts on Configuration D would have been necessary to boost the missile, and well beyond the capability of Sea Dart's original Chow tandem boost-motor.

When launch and carriage were considered, Quick Study 122 showed that the size and performance characteristics of the cruise missiles affected the load carried by various aircraft. When the Tomahawk was considered for air-launch from the Panavia Tornado, the study revealed that two of the longer variants could be carried on the ventral stations with a shorter Tomahawk on each of the inboard wing pylons. Presumably this situation would be applicable to the Configuration A missile while the B, C and D missiles were limited to two rounds on ventral pylons. The other strike aircraft considered for the Configuration A missile was the Buccaneer, but it soon became apparent that the Buccaneer could not carry a weapon that was longer than 5m (16ft 5in) which ruled out Tomahawk and all

of the configurations apart from the shorter Configuration A. One aircraft that was considered was the VC10, which at this time, the late 1970s, was in service with a few airlines around the world as well as the RAF. The VC10 would have been capable of carrying twenty Tomahawks/Configuration A types or up to fifteen of the B, C or D types. The limiting factor on the carriage these types on aircraft were dimensions of the fixed wings and or boost motors.

Ultimately the development of TERCOM guidance systems made the high-speed/high-altitude missile, and associated higher costs in materials and engines redundant. It would be the low/slow cruise missile that would promote dissent in Britain and Europe in the Eighties and 'shock and awe' in the Middle East in the Nineties and Noughties. The above studies were exactly that: the paper exercises that are the first stage of any weapon's development and in the grand scheme of things for every piece of hardware that enters service, a thousand paper studies were conducted.

There was one UK project that had potential to produce a cruise missile: the BAe Dynamics Sea Eagle anti-ship missile. Called P3T during its development in the late 1970s, Sea Eagle already possessed many of the features applicable to a cruise missile, specifically a turbojet propulsion system, a large warhead and sophisticated guidance system. The transformation from P3T to a missile to attack land targets called P4T involved modifying the guidance system and extending the fuselage to carry more fuel. While not strictly a cruise missile P4T, being based on existing technology may have made it an attractive option. By the early 1980s, US cruise missile technology had shown the way ahead and P4T was quietly dropped. Had P4T been developed as a cruise missile it would no doubt have entered service with the RAF as its stand-off weapon, sharing much of its technology with the Sea Eagle that entered service on the RAF's Buccaneer and Tornado. What made cruise missiles attractive was that their size allowed many weapons to be carried on a large aircraft, either externally or internally. The drag penalty of external carriage of any store always made internal carriage an attractive option and, as shown in Chapter Six, that had been explored for the Skybolt ALBM.

The USAF developed a rotary magazine for the AGM-86 cruise missiles and installed these in the bomb bays of B-52 and B-1. The AGM-86 had a trapezoidal cross-section and thus was particularly suitable for such an installation. Whether such a rotary magazine could have fit-

Rotary launchers were developed for the AGM-86 cruise missiles to maximise the load on Boeing B-52 and B-1 bombers. Rumours that such launchers were considered for the HP Victor or Avro Vulcan have not been substantiated. *USAF*

ted the bomb bays of the Victor or Vulcan has no doubt been investigated and although there were rumours of a study that involved such a system on the Victor, no evidence of this has been found.

BAe Woodford carried out design studies to examine the possibilities for internal carriage and launch of the P3T Sea Eagle from large aircraft. As noted above the P4T was a stretched Sea Eagle so the launch equipment could have been used for the P4T as well. These studies involved Nimrod and the Future Large Aircraft, an early name for what became the Airbus A400 transport aircraft. The Nimrod study dates from 1987 and was a consequence of the cancellation of the Nimrod AEW.3.

Never one for scrapping an old airframe when it could be used for something else, the British MoD had re-used old aircraft for various 'new' roles on a number of occasions: the DH Comet into Nimrod MR.1/2, former VC10 airliners into tankers and transports. In the airborne early warning field the MoD had converted old piston-era Shackletons into the AEW.2 and of course, redundant Nimrod MR.1 airframes into the Nimrod AEW.3. The Comet, designed in the late Forties was a firm favourite as the airframe of choice. The choice was usually the MoD's on a 'like it or lump it basis' whatever the manufacturers thought. Nimrod AEW.3 was the classic example of this 'customer's always right' policy and in the fallout from the AEW project, the Comet would become a bomber.

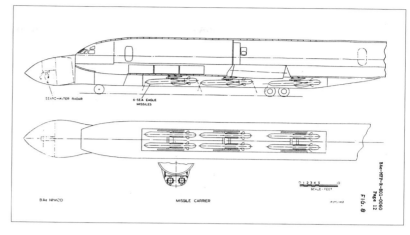

By 1987 the Nimrod AEW project had run its course and the airframes were in storage around the country. BAe at Woodford had been the lead contractor for the AEW.3 aircraft and had converted the maritime reconnaissance aircraft to the radar role with great success. The Nimrod MR.1's capacious weapons bay had been filled with fuel tanks and cooling systems for the AEW role. By removing these, the weapons bay was available again and could carry missiles. BAe Woodford carried out a number of studies that re-used the Nimrod AEW airframes that included electronic warfare, tanker and anti-ship missile carrier.

For the latter role the front radar scanner was replaced by Searchwater maritime surveillance radar and the weapons bay fitted out to carry six BAe Sea Eagle missiles. Presumably the fitting of cruise missiles was also considered to

British Aerospace proposed using redundant Nimrod AEW.3 airframes as missile platforms. Seen here with a six-round load of Sea Eagles, the P4T cruise missile version of Sea Eagle would been easily substituted. *BAE Systems/ Avro Heritage*

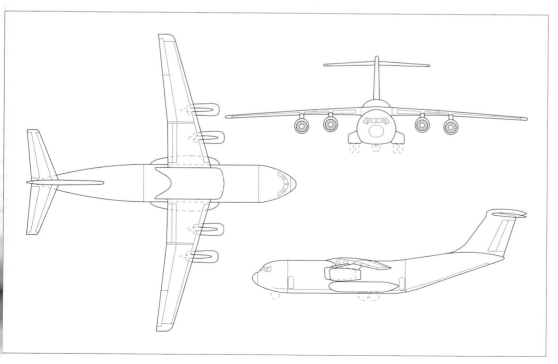

The Future Large Aircraft, a transport aircraft that eventually became the Airbus A400M transport. The 26 year gestation period from conception to first flight must be a record, being a quarter of the time that powered flight has been possible. BAe studied its use as a missile carrier for up to 27 Sea Eagles.

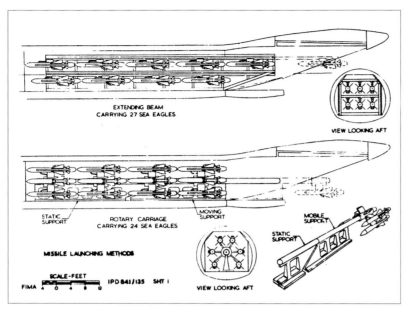

EXTENDING BEAM
CARRYING 27 SEA EAGLES

VIEW LOOKING AFT

STATIC
SUPPORT

ROTARY CARRIAGE
CARRYING 24 SEA EAGLES

MOVING
SUPPORT

MOBILE
SUPPORT

STATIC
SUPPORT

MISSILE LAUNCHING METHODS

SCALE-FEET

FIMA   IPD 841/135   SHT I

VIEW LOOKING AFT

The reason for loading and launching up to 27 Sea Eagles from a transport aircraft is unclear but the obvious answer is to use the type as a cruise missile carrier. This BAe Woodford study was based on the Future Large Aircraft, ultimately developed as the Airbus A400M.
BAE Systems/ Avro Heritage

turn the Nimrod into a strategic weapon platform.

In 1982 Aérospatiale, BAe, Lockheed and MBB co-operated on a replacement for the Lockheed C-130 Hercules and the C-160 Transall airlifters. The organisation charged with development was the Future International Military Airlifter (FIMA). Lockheed left the group in 1989 to develop the C-130J and were replaced by Alenia and CASA, creating a pan-European project that became Euroflag, European Future Large Aircraft Group. The aircraft itself was designated FLA, Future Large Aircraft and went through a number of configurations with a variety of powerplant options. BAe at Woodford became involved and drew up design studies for a high-wing, turbofan-powered transport aircraft capable of tactical and strategic airlift. As ever the usual variants such as tanker were examined and one study was for a missile carrier, with Sea Eagle shown on the drawings. As noted above, if Sea Eagle could be accommodated, there is little doubt that the P4T or another cruise missile could be carried and launched.

The missile carrier version of the FLA came in two versions. The first carried 27 missiles on a frame in the cargo hold. The frame held the missiles in two layers with 15 on top and 12 on the bottom. To launch the missiles the cargo bay door opened, the upper section of the door swinging up into the cabin roof. An 'extending beam' was deployed into the open cargo door and the missiles were transferred to the back of the frame and onto the extending beam. This used a similar principle to a gantry crane and moved the missile aft to a position clear of the

cabin floor where the missile was released. The second proposal used a rotary magazine with a central shaft running the length of the cabin. How this worked is pure conjecture based on the available drawings. The 24 missiles were mounted on four shuttles that carried six radial arms. An extending beam similar to that described above was fitted and the shuttles moved onto this beam clear of the cabin. The lowermost missile was released and the shuttle rotated to fire the next. When all six missiles on a shuttle were launched, it must be suspected that the shuttle itself was jettisoned.

No doubt such a system could have been developed; indeed the Americans had proposed similar equipment for their transport aircraft and even for modified airliners. As ever in the UK, paper studies were about as far as the large cruise missile carrier went.

The Americans continued with their cruise missile developments and deployed the AGM-86B on Boeing B-52H carrier aircraft in late 1986. The ground-launched General Dynamics BGM-109 Tomahawk was deployed to Europe in 1983 as a counter to the Soviet deployment of the RSD-10 Pioneer (NATO reporting name SS-20 *Saber*). Ultimately this deployment and that of the Pershing II led to the opening of negotiations that led to arms reduction treaties and eventually the end of the Cold War. NATO and the Warsaw Pact reduced their arsenals under the Intermediate-range Nuclear Forces (INF) Treaty with verification a major factor in the treaty. During the negotiation that led up to this treaty, US President Ronald Reagan picked up on a Russian proverb '*doveryai, no proveryai*' – Trust, but verify – and this became the key phrase of the process.

Return of the Stand-off Bomb

In the light of this the Air Staff re-examined the long-range strike role and, given the controversy surrounding the term 'cruise missile' in the early Eighties, resurrected the term 'stand-off'. Nuclear strike remained the goal so a new Staff Target, NGAST.1236, was drawn up in 1982 as a joint requirement with the USA and West Germany under the designation long-range stand-off weapon (LRSOW). Two years later when Canada, France, Italy and Spain joined it became a full-blown NATO project under the 1986 Nunn Amendment. This allowed US companies and those of its NATO allies to co-operate fully rather than be treated as if they were foreign buyers of US weapons. This new-found zeal for co-operation covered a variety of high-technology systems such as the MBB/Rockwell X-31 Enhanced Fighter Maneuverability Programme and smart munitions. In 1987 the UK/US/FRG LRSOW project was merged with the existing French/Canadian/Italian/Spanish Low-Cost Powered Dispenser (LOCPOD), a low-altitude munitions dispenser project. This prompted a change in name to Modular Stand-Off Weapon (MSOW), an air-launched cruise missile with a range of 600km (373 miles) that could carry a variety of stores such as JP.233 dispensers for anti-runway munitions.

British Aerospace had examined a number of configurations for MSOW and when this project foundered for the usual national differences, BAe picked up the baton. There had always been a suspicion that the Americans were pursuing a 'black' solution and amidst the arguments, promptly withdrew to produce the AGM-154 Joint Stand-Off Weapon (JSOW). BAe sought to continue MSOW work to meet the still extant AST.1236 and BAe Warton's studies were generally based around the Hunting JP.233 dispenser that Warton had much experience of having integrated that weapon with the Tornado. One other project that contributed to the development of technologies for what had become SR(A).1236 was REVISE – REsearch Vehicle for In-flight Sub-munition Ejection. A joint effort with the Royal Aircraft Establishment's (RAE) Attack Weapons Department, this test vehicle was intended to form the

basis of a weapon system called Revise Plus that would fill the SR(A).1236 requirement. Revise Plus was much more advanced than Warton's proposals and as the eighties became the Nineties, British Aerospace Dynamics merged with the guided weapons divisions of aerospace companies in France, Germany and Italy to form MBDA.

Matra in France had meantime been working on the APACHE, a winged dispenser of anti-runway munitions and this formed the basis of what ultimately became known as CASOM, conventionally armed stand-off missile, for the Royal Air Force. By 1997 Matra had become amalgamated into MBDA so a contract to produce CASOM was placed. This involved the APACHE being modified to meet SR(A).1236 and thus became Storm Shadow. From America came two proposals from McDonnell Douglas and Hughes: McDonnell Douglas teamed up with Hunting Engineering Ltd to propose a variant of the Stand-off Land Attack Missile Expanded Response (SLAM-ER) which, with shades of the BAe P.4T, had evolved from the Harpoon anti-ship missile by stretching it to 16ft 7in (5.1m) and adding flip-out wings. Guidance was by INS/GPS with terminal homing by imaging infrared. Hughes proposed a variant of their Tomahawk cruise missile for the CASOM requirement. Called AirHawk, this was 17in (43cm) shorter than AGM.109 but the bespoke, European weapon was preferred.

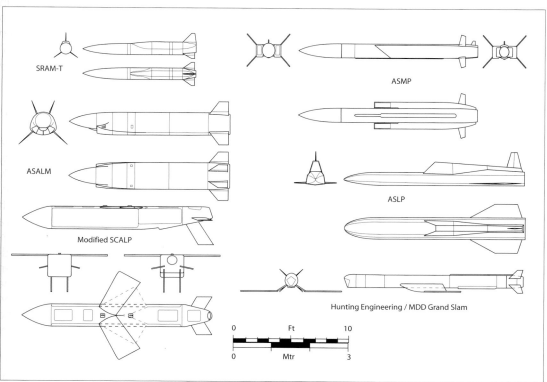

SRAM-T

ASMP

ASALM

ASLP

Modified SCALP

Hunting Engineering / MDD Grand Slam

0   Ft   10

0   Mtr   3

The contenders for SR(A).1244 included French and American missiles. These would have been developed for the RAF with British companies as partners to the US and French firms. Of the types illustrated only the ASMP and the original SLAM-ER, upon which Grand Slam was based, entered service.

Fitted with large drop tanks under each wing and an ASMP on the centreline station, aircraft like this Dassault Mirage 2000N carry the French airborne nuclear deterrent. The Force de Frappe could be described as the French equivalent of the V-Force and still carries out the deterrent role. *Author's Collection*

SR(A).1236 was to provide a weapon for the RAF's Tornado GR.4s in the deep strike role, deep meaning 250km (135nm) rather than the hundreds of miles of earlier years. Storm Shadow flies at low-level under the power of a Microturbo TRI 30-30 turbofan, using GPS and TERPROM guidance. On approaching the target, Storm Shadow climbed and the nose cone was jettisoned to reveal an imaging-IR seeker that searched the scene for a match with an image in its memory.

On finding a target that corresponded to that in the database, the missile dived onto the target, triggering the missile's BROACH warhead on impact. BROACH, (Bomb, Royal Ordnance Augmenting Charge), was a two-stage warhead designed for use against bunkers and hardened aircraft shelters. The first charge penetrated the protective layer and the second charge entered the structure through that hole to detonate inside. Storm Shadow entered service in time for the 2003 invasion of Iraq and continues to be used on Tornado and Typhoons of the RAF.

In the late eighties there was a perceived need to replace the WE.177 free-fall bomb with a long-range cruise weapon to meet SR(A).1244, also known as Future Tactical Nuclear Weapon or latterly, Tactical Air-to-Surface missile, TASM. Intended for launch against targets in Eastern Europe, TASM was to be carried by Tornados. As well as an all-British weapon based on the work for MSOW, the American Short Range Attack Missile-Tactical (SRAM-T) and French *Air-Sol Longue Portée/ Air–Sol Nucléaire* (ASLP/ASN) or *Air-Sol Moyenne Portée* (ASMP) were also considered. Martin Marietta bid for the requirement with its ramjet-powered advanced strategic air-launched missile (ASALM) based on their supersonic low-altitude target (SLAT) target drone. Speculation on the prospect of the UK buying yet another foreign missile system prompted questions in the House of Commons, where Archie Hamilton MP, a junior minister at the MoD confirmed that the ASLP was indeed under consideration, as were American systems.

By 1993 UK defence spending was yet again feeling the pinch of recession and the end of the Cold War in 1989 afforded the opportunity of a peace dividend. There had also been concern, dating back to the issuing of SR(A).1244, that the weapon could infringe the 1987 Intermediate-range Nuclear Forces (INF) Treaty that had seen the withdrawal from Europe of the US cruise missiles from the United Kingdom and Soviet missiles such as the RSD-10 Pioneer (NATO reporting name SS-20 *Saber* (sic). One project that was sacrificed for this was SR(A).1244, replaced by the use of so-called 'sub-strategic' Trident. Another factor may have been that the Pentagon cancelled SRAM-T in September 1991, no doubt depriving the RAF of its preferred choice. The French government scrapped the ASLP/ASN system in 1996, and thereafter relied on the ASMP as its airborne deterrent. In the mid-Nineties the UK government's policy was that the forthcoming

The Aérospatiale ASLP (air-sol longue-portée) was proposed for the SR(A).1244. This artist's impression shows the faceted construction used to reduce radar cross-section. *Aérospatiale*

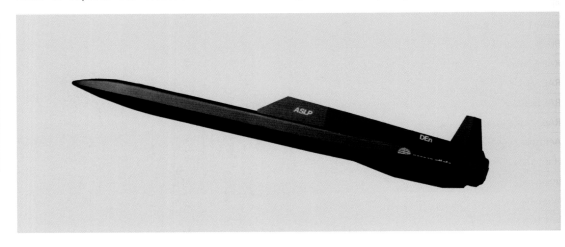

Aérospatiale's ASMP (air-sol moyenne-portée was considered for the SR(A).1244 as a replacement for the WE.177 bomb. This ramjet powered missile has a range of up to 300km (162nm) and is seen here in its ASMP-A guise after release by a Dassault Rafale F3. *Aérospatiale*

MBDA Storm Shadow cruise missile would not be armed with nuclear warheads, leaving the sub-strategic nuclear role to the Trident system. The scrapping of SR(A).1244 and the gradual withdrawal of the WE.177 marked the end of the Royal Air Force's association with nuclear weapons.

By 1998 all WE.177s had been returned to AWE Burghfield and Aldermaston for decommissioning. The last vestiges of Vulcan's Hammer rest upon their handling trolleys in aviation museums, scrutinised by visitors who wonder how an object so small can create such destruction.

The Post-Polaris Weapons

Type	Length	Span	Diameter	Weight	Propulsion	Range
HSD Sea Dart	14ft 5in	3ft	1ft 5in	1,200 lb	Odin Ramjet	80nm
HSD Martel	13ft 8in	4ft	1ft 4in	1,200 lb	Solid rocket	32nm
Shrike	10ft	3ft	10in	390 lb	Solid rocket	24nm
Paveway (GBU-10E)	14ft 2in	5ft 6in	1ft 6in	2,110 lb	n/a	n/a
Phoenix	13ft	3ft	15in	1,040 lb	Solid rocket	100nm
BGM-109 Tomahawk	18ft 2in	8ft 9in	1ft 8in	3,200 lb	Williams turbofan	1350
Boeing AGM-86	20ft 10in	12ft	n/a	3,200 lb	Williams turbofan	1,300nm
RAE Missile A	28ft 10in	n/a	1ft 4in	n/a	TRI-60 turbojet	648nm
RAE Missile B	n/a	n/a	n/a	n/a	TRI-60 turbojet	648nm
RAE Missile C	25ft 7in	n/a	1ft 7in	n/a	RB.247 turbojet	270nm
RAE Missile D	n/a	n/a	n/a	3,638 lb	Odin Ramjet	107nm
Aérospatiale ASMP	17ft 7in	n/a	1ft	1,896 lb	ramjet	162nm
Hunting/MDD Grand Slam	16ft 7in	7ft 11in	1ft 1in	1,600 lb	Teledyne turbojet	150nm
Boeing SRAM-T	14ft	n/a	1ft 6in	2,000 lb	Solid rocket	135nm
Grumman ASALM	14ft	n/a	1ft 9in	2,500 lb	Marquardt ramjet	260nm
BAe Dynamics P4T	14ft	3ft 11in	1ft 4in	1,300 lb	TRI-60 turbojet	110nm+

Conclusion

The challenges to be met in the provision of a viable deterrent for the UK were outlined in the introduction to *Vulcan's Hammer*. Realistically there was only ever one answer to the economic, geographical, political and technological challenges: the ballistic missile, specifically the submarine-launched ballistic missile in the shape of Polaris and later, Trident.

For a decade and a half the V-Force carried the deterrent and even after Polaris took over, the Vulcan carried WE.177 nuclear weapons until replaced by the Tornado in 1981. No-one can answer the question as to the effectiveness of the V-Force in action as it was never used in anger, but as a deterrent it was the fact that it existed that made the difference. That the Cold War never turned into a Hot War is perhaps the V-Force's greatest achievement.

Throughout this period the 'backroom boys' of Britain's aerospace industry attempted to use new technologies to produce viable weapons in the face of economic and political turmoil. Such was the pace of technological advancement that any weapon that took more than five years from conception to deployment was obsolete. One of the main problems in Britain in the decade from 1955 until 1965 was that the economic conditions were changing rapidly, from what was more less a war footing in 1955 to a consumer society in 1965. There was never enough finance in the Treasury to maintain weapons development at the required pace. Only an economy on the scale of that in the United States or a command economy like the Soviet Union could ever hope to compete.

Harold Macmillan appreciated this and instructed Duncan Sandys who, playing Rosa Klebb to Macmillan's Blofeld, attempted to make the necessary changes and has been vilified since. His was the voice of Cassandra in the Skybolt process, perhaps the only member of the Government who saw that the emperor had no clothes. Sandys was wrong about the reason for Skybolt's demise, which had its source across the Atlantic. Macmillan is famous for the phrase: 'Events, dear boy, events' It was events that did for the UK deterrent plans in the first five years of the Sixties. The American cancellation of Skybolt was possibly the best thing that happened to the V-Force. Perhaps it was better to be shot down metaphorically by one's own government than, as a file in the National Archives suggests, slaughtered on a mission to Moscow in a repetition of the Nuremburg Raid of 30th March 1944.

Blue Steel has long been viewed as a less than effective weapon but when it commenced development in 1954 it was the cutting edge of British technology. Apart from the guidance and propulsion systems, the basic function of keeping the various components at the correct temperature was a mammoth task. The fact that it could be launched in mid-air and navigate at high-speed to a target is a triumph of British technology that has gone uncelebrated and it is shameful that it is only remembered for its delays and development problems. The engineers and scientists who worked on Blue Steel deserve better.

Vulcan's Hammer has gone, replaced by Neptune's Trident. In 2011 the country finds itself facing defence decisions as important as any taken in 1947. Hopefully the correct decisions will be taken without the numerous false starts and disappointments that punctuated the era of the V-Force.

Flying at very low altitude and Mach 2, the Avro WRD Z.59's nuclear ramjet gave it unlimited range while the reactor core would add to the fall-out created when its warhead was detonated. *Adrian Mann*

Appendices

APPENDIX A

Avro Weapons Research Division Projects

Avro's Weapons Research Division's project nomenclature appears somewhat confusing at first glance but essentially follows a few basic rules. The W-Series were subject to either development or proposals that were tendered to the Air Staff or Air Ministry/Ministry of Aviation/Ministry of Supply. The 'P.nnZ' series were the earliest and are in reverse order of date, for reasons unknown, from 1954 until 1957. In 1957 new studies were assigned the Z.nnn designations that continued from the Z.1 (W.110) to Z.133 (track-launched satellite booster). In the period from 1954 until 1962, WRD produced 176 different studies. Only one, W.100 and its W.200 variant, reached service.

W-Series

W.100	Basic Blue Steel test vehicle and final designation of operational rounds
W.102	Blue Steel test vehicle
W.103	Light-alloy Blue Steel test vehicle
W.104	Air-launched Blue Steel test vehicle
W.105	Ultimate test vehicle for Blue Steel. Designation was to be used for operational rounds, but W.100 used instead.
W.106	Target drone version of Blue Steel
W.107	Air-launched turbojet missile with arrow wing for OR.1149
W.109	Air-launched rocket missile with drop tanks with arrow wing OR.1149 Study
W.110	Air-launched extended range Blue Steel Phase 2 for OR.1149
W.111	Air-launched ramjet missile for OR.1149
W.112	Air-launched extended range Blue Steel Phase 2
W.113	High-altitude OR.1159 missile
W.114	OR.1159 missile – Blue Steel with four BRJ.821 ramjets
W.120	Tactical weapon for Marcel-Dassault Mirage
W.130	Two-stage narrow delta for TSR.2 and Mirage IV
W.140	Turbojet missile for OR.1182
W.150	Reconnaissance drone
W.160	Blue Steel with Viper engine
W.170	Missile for TSR.2, Buccaneer and Vulcan
W.200	Low-level Blue Steel Mk.1

P-Series

P.43Z	Air-launched missile 38/27/1
P.42Z	Air-launched Blue Steel missile W.100
P.41Z	Ground-launched 1/8th scale Blue Steel
P.40Z	Air-launched 2/5th scale blue Steel test vehicle (19/15)
P.39Z	Air-launched radar reconnaissance vehicle TRM-1
P.38Z	Air-launched radar reconnaissance vehicle TRM-2
P.37Z	Air-launched bombing missile SBM-1 (Supersonic bomber)
P.36Z	Air-launched bombing missile UBM-1 (Utility)
P.35Z	Air-launched glide bombing missile (SBM-2)
P.34Z	Blue Cat – Blue Steel launched from low altitude
P.33Z	Ground-launched radar reconnaissance vehicle (TRM-3)
P.32Z	Air-launched long-range bombing missile (SBM-3)
P.31Z	Air-launched long-range Blue Steel (W.100 Stage 3)
P.30Z	Free-fall bomb for supersonic bomber
P.29Z	Ground-launched Blue Steel missile GBM
P.28Z	Ground-launched Blue Steel missile GBM
P.27Z	Ground-launched two-stage rocket missile GBM
P.26Z	Ground-launched tactical rocket missile GTM-1
P.25Z	Ground-launched turbojet tactical missile GTM-2
P.24Z	Ground-launched long-range missile HBM-1
P.23Z	HBM-2
P.22Z	Blue Steel with two Rolls-Royce RB.121 turbojets
P.21Z	Blue Steel with four Rolls-Royce Soar turbojets
P.20Z	Blue Steel with Bristol Orpheus turbojets
P.19Z	Blue Steel with Gyron
P.18Z	Air-launched supersonic bomber missile SBM-4
P.17Z	Air-launched turbojet missiles G1 – narrow delta
P.16Z	Air-launched turbojet missiles D – narrow delta
P.15Z	Air-launched turbojet missiles H – narrow delta
P.14Z	Air-launched turbojet missiles J – narrow delta

Blue Steel as museum piece. On display at Newark Air Museum, Avro Weapons Research Division's most famous project rests under the wing of a Vulcan. Its size and bulk can only be appreciated at close quarters. *Author*

P.13Z	Air-launched ramjet missile– narrow delta
P.12Z	Air-launched rocket missile with drop tanks (W.109) – Arrow wing
P.11Z	Air-launched turbojet missile W.107 – Arrow wing
P.10Z	Air-launched blended-wing missile
P.9Z	Air-launched delta-wing turbojet missile
P.8Z	Air-launched long-range turbojet missile – TA4
P.7Z	Air-launched rocket missile W.107
P.6Z	Ship-launched long-range missile NB-1
P.5Z	Ground-launched two-stage test vehicle (M.50)
P.4Z	Air-launched Blue Steel test vehicle (W.104)
P.3Z	Free-flight ground-launched test vehicle M.40
P.2Z	Surface-launched naval turbojet missile NB.2
P.1Z	1/8th Scale free-flight model of Z.1

Z- Series

Z.1K	Air-launched extended range Blue Steel Phase 2 (W.110)
Z.2	Air-launched rocket/ramjet missile
Z.3	Air-launched ramjet missile
Z.4B	Air-launched long-range ramjet missile
Z.5	Experimental ramjet vehicle (19/15 modified to take Thor ramjets)
Z.6	Air-launched 45ft Blue Steel missile
Z.7	Air-launched rocket/ramjet missile
Z.8	Ground-launched Blue Steel W.103
Z.9	Two stage Blue Steel – two Gammas in second stage, Stentor in 10ft first stage
Z.10	Air-launched ramjet test vehicle
Z.11	Increased range Z.1 missile
Z.12F	Air-launched ramjet missile W.111
Z.13	OR.1149 Study – W.109
Z.15	Air-launched Blue Steel Phase 2 Test vehicle – W.110 TV
Z.16	Air-launched extended range Blue Steel Phase 2 W.112A
Z.17	Ground-launched long-range missile
Z.18	Air-launched extended range Blue Steel
Z.19	W.111 with scaled-up Rolls-Royce turbojets
Z.20	Air-launched extended-range Blue Steel Phase 2 (W.112C)
Z.21	Long-range air-launched bombing missile 45ft (Z.12)
Z.22	3,500 miles ground-launched air-breathing winged missile
Z.23	2,000 miles ground-launched winged rocket missile
Z.24	W.112 with 500 lb HTP/Kerosene rockets
Z.25	Naval bombardment missile NB-3 (Z.16)
Z.26	Naval bombardment missile NB-4 (1,000 miles)
Z.27	Z.20 with four Bristol BRJ.851 ramjets Mach 3.5
Z.28	Target drone version of Blue Steel W.106
Z.29	Solid rocket target drone
Z.30	Target based on 19/15
Z.31	Blue Steel with two external Raven solid boost motors
Z.32A	Phase 2 Blue Steel with integrated engine installation
Z.32B	Phase 2 Blue Steel with integrated engine installation
Z.33	Ground-launched three-stage hypersonic rocket cruise missile
Z.34	Stand-off bomb for Avro 739
Z.35	Low-wing canard stand-off bomb with four strut-mounted ramjets
Z.36	High-altitude OR.1159 missile (W.113)
Z.37	The 1958 stand-off bomb

Z.38	Surface-launched Phase 2 Blue Steel (W.112N)
Z.39/a	Configuration study for OR.1159 missile
Z.39T/3	OR.1159 turbojet missile for high and low altitude
Z.39/UC	Configuration study for OR.1159 missile
Z.39/UE	Configuration study for OR.1159 missile
Z.40	OR.1159 missile (high-altitude only)
Z.41	OR.1159 missile for high and low altitude
Z.42	One of the OR.1159 missile
Z.43	OR.1159 missile with DH Gyron Junior
Z.44	OR.1159 missile (W.114)
Z.45	OR.1159 missile study with two Gyron Juniors
Z.46	Air-launched supersonic ramjet missile
Z.47	Air-launched four-stage flight corridor research vehicle (Scheme A and Scheme B)
Z.48	Ground attack guided bomb for Avro Type 739
Z.49	Ramjet missile for Avro Arrow
Z.50	Earth Satellite laboratory – recombination ramjet
Z.51a	Hydrazine /Fluorine research vehicle
Z.51b	Hydrazine /Fluorine research vehicle
Z.51c	Hydrazine /Fluorine Stand-off bomb
Z.52	Stand-off bomb and VTOL Carrier
Z.53	W.114 with wingtip turbojets
Z.54	W.105 (small payload) with solid boosts
Z.55	Hypersonic vehicle using liquid hydrogen as coolant/propellant
Z.56	Douglas Thor boosted re-entry test vehicle
Z.57	Air-launched tactical missile
Z.58	Tactical weapons for Marcel Dassault Mirage
Z.59	Low-altitude missile powered by nuclear ramjet
Z.60	Reduced-scale W.114 with two ramjets
Z.61	Air-launched tactical missile
Z.62	Modified W.110 with Gyron Junior turbojet
Z.63	W.100A missile with four internal solid boosters
Z.64	W.100 missile with three small liquid rockets
Z.65	OR.1159 missile suitable for Vulcan only
Z.66	Modified OR.1159 missile with internal solid boosts
Z.67	W.114B Missile with Gyron Junior Turbojet
Z.68	Long range ramjet cruise missile
Z.69	Hypersonic research study boost-glide vehicle
Z.70	Boost glide vehicle
Z.71	Advanced stand-off bomb – ramjet proposal
Z.72	Air-launched ballistic missile proposal
Z.73	Hypersonic ramjet vehicle Liquid H2 propellant
Z.74	Blue Steel Mk.1*
Z.75	Low-level boron fuelled missile (Mach 2)
Z.76	Hypersonic ramjet vehicle (Mach 7)
Z.77	Ramjet Missile (Mach 4.5)
Z.78	Low-level Blue Steel with four Thor ramjets
Z.79	Hypersonic high-level weapons system with low-level approach
Z.80	W.120 variant – W.130
Z.81	Blue Steel Mk.1A
Z.82	Ground-launched W.130
Z.83	W.130 – 'X-15' variant
Z.84	Mark 1B Blue Steel
Z.85	Mark 1C Blue Steel
Z.86	Mark 1D Blue Steel
Z.87	Mark 1*E Blue Steel
Z.88	Mark 1Kg Blue Steel
Z.89	W.130B Vulcan-launched two-stage narrow delta
Z.90	W.130D 1,200nm ground-launched three-stage
Z.91	Ballistic missile for 400nm Ground-launched
Z.92	Blue Steel Mk.1S
Z.93	Ramjet W.130 (See DAJ memo. Aero 7/10g – 26/11/60)
Z.94	3,000 mile ramjet missile base don Z.68

Z.95   Long-range ramjet with low-level approach
Z.96   1,000 mile turbojet – Blue Steel (two Rolls-Royce turbojet engines)
Z.97   Winged launching devices for W.130
Z.98   W.140 turbojet missile
Z.99   Parachute recovered experimental W.100
Z.100 Skid-recovered experimental W.100
Z.101 Manned, skid W.100A
Z.102 Blue Steel two-stage research vehicle
Z.103 Blue Steel Satellite launcher
Z.104 High-altitude W.100 with RB.153 turbojets
Z.105 Skid recovered test vehicle based on W.100
Z.106 Low-level missile with Rolls-Royce Spey turbofan
Z.107 High-altitude, long-range Blue Steel with Stentor and ventral tanks
Z.108 Modified Blue Steel for Vulcan Phase 6
Z.109 Blue Steel with Skybolt warhead in nose, miniaturised equipment and 3ft extension
Z.110 Low-level missile with turbojet
Z.111 Blue Steel with miniaturised equipment and turbojets
Z.112 Recoverable reconnaissance drone – 100nm radius of action
Z.113 Recoverable reconnaissance drone – 15nm radius of action

Z.114 Expendable reconnaissance drone – 15nm radius of action
Z.115 Blue Steel/Thor combination – strategic missile
Z.116 Blue Steel/Vulcan combination – anti-satellite missile
Z.117 Extended range W.100 (200nm)
Z.118 Ramjet version of Z.114 (15nm radius of action)
Z.119 Recoverable Mach 5 to 6 research vehicle based on Blue Steel (Vulcan launch)
Z.120 Recoverable Mach 6 research vehicle based on Blue Steel (Thor launch)
Z.121 Blue Steel tactical bombardment missile
Z.122 Modified Blue Steel for TSR.2
Z.123 Eurospace Blue Streak hypersonic vehicle
Z.124 Vulcan-launched satellite vehicle for Eurospace
Z.125 Blue Steel with Viper turbojet
Z.126 Low-level ramjet vehicle for TSR.2
Z.127 Low-level turbojet vehicle for Vulcan
Z.128 Missile for TSR.2 and Buccaneer
Z.129 Ramjet missile for Buccaneer and TSR.2. B-model 2ft shorter than A
Z.130 W.170 – Type A
Z.131 W.170 – Type B
Z.132 Unknown
Z.133 Track-launched air-breathing booster

APPENDIX B

Project E

With the resumption of nuclear co-operation between the USA and UK in 1958, a number of US nuclear weapons were made available to the RAF and British Army On the Rhine. The intention was to arm the RAF with American weapons until such time that a British-developed weapon became available. These initially involved American Mk.7 variable yield weapons carried by RAF English Electric Canberra bombers committed to NATO in West Germany. As the project progressed, 72 Mk.5 bombs were supplied to the RAF for use on V-Force aircraft until 1962 when the much improved B28 and B43 bombs were carried on Valiants assigned to NATO.

Project E weapons were under American 'guardianship' at all times and held at specific stations. Any RAF aircraft that was to be loaded with Project E weapons had to be flown to these airfields for arming. This was very much against the Air Staff's policy of dispersal. Project E continued until the early 1990s as the RAF still relied on the Americans for nuclear depth charges.

An RAF Canberra XM278 and its weapons on display in a hangar on an airfield in Germany. The large store with the butterfly tail is an American Mk.7 bomb supplied under Project E. *Via Terry Panopalis*

Glossary of terms

A&AEE Aeroplane & Armament Experimental Establishment.

Air burst detonation of a nuclear warhead at height above the target. Inflicts maximum damage by blast on a 'soft' target, such as a city, rather than having the fireball contact the target. Air bursts reduce the amount of material vaporised by the fireball thus minimising the volume of contaminated material thrown up to become fallout.

Bunt Outside loop. In the case of a stand-off bomb the missile moves from wings level flight to a dive.

Canard a configuration whereby the horizontal stabilisers (foreplanes) are to the front of the vehicle and the wings are towards the rear. As old as powered flight; the Wright Flyer had a canard configuration.

CEP Circular Error Probable – a measure of a, usually ballistic, weapon's accuracy and refers to the radius of a circle within which 50% of the rounds will land.

Cruise-climb aircraft or missile gains height as its fuel load is used up during the cruise portion of the mission.

Fineness ratio ratio of length to body diameter. High-speed aircraft generally have a high fineness ratio, for a typical example see Concorde.

Ground burst detonation of a nuclear warhead at ground level. Used against hardened targets such as bunkers. Fireball vaporises a large volume of material and thus creates a great amount of fallout.

INF Intermediate-range Nuclear Forces.

MoD Ministry of Defence.

MoS Ministry of Supply.

NATO North Atlantic Treaty Organisation.

Physics package the components of a bomb that create the nuclear explosion. Includes the fissile material and explosive lenses.

RAE Royal Aircraft Establishment.

RATO Rocket Assisted Take-Off, formerly called Jet Assisted take-off. Strap-on rocket packs that provided extra thrust for take-off of heavily laden aircraft.

Selected bibliography

A great deal of primary material has been consulted for this book. Much of this is held by The National Archives at Kew (AIR 20, AVIA 6, AVIA 28, AVIA 54, AVIA 65, DSIR 23). Further original material is held at the Brooklands Museum and North West Heritage Group at Warton. Access to Prof. John Allen's archive material in the RAF Museum Hendon allowed the story of Avro's Weapons Research Division projects to be compiled.

A Vertical Empire: C N Hill; Imperial College Press,2000.
Aeromilitaria: Air-Britain; various issues.
Anti-Aircraft Artillery: I V Hogg; Crowood Press, 2002.
Avro Vulcan: K Darling; Crowood Press Ltd, 2005
Avro Vulcan: P Butler and T Buttler, Midland Publishing, 2007
Blue Envoy's Peaceful Legacy: C Gibson; Prospero, British Rocketry Oral History Project, 2005.
British Secret Projects – Jet Bombers since 1949: T Buttler; Midland Publishing, 2003.
Cambridge Aerospace Dictionary: B Gunston; Cambridge University Press, 2004.
Cold War: W D Cocroft and R J C Thomas; English Heritage, 2003.
Cold War Hot Science – Applied Research in Britain's Defence Laboratories 1945-1990: ed R Bud and P Gummett; Science Museum, 1999.
Fire Across the Desert: P Morton; AGPS Press, 1989
Flight and Aircraft Engineer: various editions.

Flight International: various editions.
Good Company: A R Adams; British Aircraft Corporation, 1976.
Handley Page Victor: R Brooks; Pen and Sword Aviation, 2007
Handley Page Victor: P Butler and T Buttler; Midland Publishing, 2009
Illustrated Encyclopaedia of Rockets and Missiles: B Gunston; Salamander, 1979.
Jane's All the World's Aircraft: Jane's Publishing; various editions.
Jane's Weapon Systems: Jane's Publishing; various editions.
Journal of the Royal Aeronautical Society: various editions.
Project Cancelled: D Wood; Jane's, 1976.
Rolls-Royce Aero Engines: B Gunston; PSL, 1989.
Spacelists 14 and 19: J Pitfield; Rocket Services, 2001.
The Early Development of Guided Weapons in the UK 1940-1960: S R Twigge; Harwood, 1993.
The Secret World of Vickers Guided Weapons: J Forbat; Tempus, 2006.
Vickers Valiant: E B Morgan; Midland Publishing, 2002
Violet Friend: C Gibson; Air Pictorial, Nov 2001.
World Encyclopaedia of Aero Engines: B Gunston; PSL, 1998.

The following websites were also consulted:
www.secretprojects.co.uk; www.flightglobal.com

Index

AIRCRAFT

Airbus A400 181, 182
B-29 Superfortress, Boeing 36, 56
B-52 Stratofortress, Boeing 68, 109, 110, 111, 113, 114, 117, 120, 176, 177, 180
B-58 Hustler, Convair 37, 44, 110, 117
B-70 Valkyrie, North American 62, 110, 159
Backfire, Tu-22M 169, 170, 172, 173
Badger, Tu-16 172
Bear, Tu-95 160, 172
Belfast, Shorts SC.5 120, 121, 122, 125, 131, 137, 138
Buccaneer, Blackburn 38, 48, 49, 52, 53, 57, 63, 105, 127, 140, 142, 143, 144, 145, 175, 176, 180, 187, 189
C-135, Boeing 113
Canberra, English Electric 19, 27, 28, 29, 30, 31, 38, 39, 46, 48, 49, 52, 53, 56, 58, 63, 122, 143, 157, 189
Cascade 61, 62
F-106 Delta Dart, Convair 34, 35, 44
Farmer, MiG-19 19
Fiddler, Tu-128 90, 174
Foxbat, MiG-25 169, 170, 172, 173
Gannet, Fairey 41
Gloster Javelin 48, 113, 116
Harrier, BAe 60, 66, 101
Hercules, Lockheed C-130 182
HS.125, Hawker Siddeley 117, 128, 130
Jaguar, SEPECAT 52, 53
JetStar, Lockheed 128, 129
Me163, Messerschmitt 69, 108
Mirage IV, Dassault 82, 136, 139, 155, 187
Nimrod, Hawker Siddeley 29, 52, 172, 173, 176, 181, 182
P.10, English Electric 6, 15, 23, 24, 26, 29, 30, 31, 32, 33, 34, 35, 37, 38, 39, 49, 97, 98, 149
P.17, English Electric 49, 63, 64
Phantom, McDonnell Douglas F-4 53, 170, 176
Scimitar, Supermarine 49
SP4, Vickers 22, 23, 24, 44
Swallow, Vickers 61, 62, 64, 92, 100
Tomcat, Grumman F-14 170, 171, 173, 174
Tornado 19, 35, 52, 53, 170, 180, 183, 184, 186
Transall, C-160 182
TSR.2, BAC 27, 46, 47, 49, 52, 62, 63, 64, 71, 81, 83, 87, 122, 123, 132, 133, 134, 135, 136, 137, 138, 139, 140, 141, 142, 143, 144, 145, 146, 147, 151, 155, 187, 189
Type 730 15, 18, 21, 23, 24, 25, 26, 27, 28, 29, 39, 41, 58, 76, 77
U-2R, Lockheed 40
Valiant, Vickers 7, 17, 20, 30, 46, 47, 48, 52, 54, 55, 56, 57, 73,
74, 75, 78, 80, 119, 190
VC10, Vickers 6, 119, 120, 121, 122, 125, 131, 137, 138, 139, 171, 172, 177, 180, 181
Victor, Handley Page 6, 7, 10, 17, 21, 23, 40, 41, 47, 49, 50, 51, 52, 61, 68, 69, 73, 75, 80, 81, 84, 86, 88, 90, 91, 93, 96, 97, 99, 102, 103, 106, 107, 108, 110, 111, 112, 113, 114, 115, 117, 118, 123, 129, 132, 139, 147, 171, 177, 181, 190
Vulcan 5, 6, 7, 8, 10, 13, 17, 18, 21, 22, 39, 40, 41, 44, 45, 47, 49, 50, 52, 53, 59, 60, 61, 65, 68, 69, 72, 73, 74, 75, 80, 81, 83, 84, 85, 86, 88, 89, 90, 96, 97, 99, 102, 103, 106, 108, 110, 111, 112, 113, 114, 115, 116, 117, 118, 119, 123, 132, 133, 134, 135, 137, 139, 140, 141, 143, 144, 145, 146, 147, 148, 162, 163, 164, 165, 166, 167, 169, 170, 171, 172, 173, 174, 175, 176, 177, 181, 185, 186, 187, 188, 189, 190

GENERAL

19/15 76, 78, 79, 88, 143, 187, 188
48/35 76, 77, 79, 88, 102
617 Squadron 6, 85, 86
Air Staff 8, 12, 13, 15, 16, 17, 21, 23, 24, 25, 26, 27, 28, 29, 30, 31, 32, 33, 34, 38, 39, 45, 50, 51, 54, 56, 57, 58, 60, 62, 68, 69, 70, 71, 72, 76, 82, 85, 86, 87, 89, 90, 93, 95, 97, 100, 102, 103, 104, 105, 106, 107, 108, 109, 110, 111, 112, 113, 114, 116, 117, 121, 122, 128, 132, 133, 134, 135, 136, 137, 138, 139, 142, 143, 144, 146, 147, 152, 157, 158, 166, 169, 171, 172, 174, 176, 182, 187, 189
Aldermaston 72, 82, 185
Apple Turnover 62, 63
Armstrong Siddeley 21, 26, 27, 40, 69, 70, 76, 77, 79, 91, 93, 100, 152, 154, 162
Atomic Weapons Research Establishment 8, 47, 72, 74
Avro Aircraft 6, 23, 60
AWRE 36, 38, 47, 50, 51, 52, 60, 72, 74, 114, 152, 153
Black Arrow 149, 154, 157
Black Knight 139, 140, 154, 162
Blue Boar 16, 55, 56, 57, 58, 60, 61, 64, 65, 67, 68, 70, 74, 78, 80, 94
Blue Cat 142, 187
Blue Danube 9, 16, 35, 36, 37, 46, 47, 48, 50, 51, 52, 55, 56, 57, 60, 70
Blue Jacket 105
Blue Ranger 80
Blue Rosette 25, 27, 36, 37
Blue Sugar 15, 16, 19, 57
BNDSG 109, 110
Bomber Command 7, 10, 19, 45, 51, 68, 71, 84
Bristol Engines 12, 24, 34, 59,
60, 95, 102, 105
Bristol Siddeley Engines Ltd 133, 178
British Nuclear Deterrent Study Group 109
Chevaline 53, 141, 177
D-21, Lockheed 41, 44
de Havilland Propellers 152, 174
Douglas Aircraft Company 111
Elliott Brothers Ltd 72
English Electric Aviation 15, 23, 91, 94, 97, 134, 135
Eurospace 164, 165, 189
Ferranti 66, 134
Fleet Air Arm 49, 63, 64, 70, 145, 172
Fritz-X 54, 57
Gamma, Armstrong Siddeley 88, 92, 100, 101, 108, 154, 157, 168
Gap-Filler 132, 142, 143, 147
Green Bamboo 25, 36, 38, 58, 60, 73, 76, 79, 93, 98, 101, 102, 103, 104, 154
Green Grass 47, 50, 51, 52, 60, 82, 106
Gyron, de Havilland 23, 42, 91, 92, 93, 95, 96, 97, 100, 101, 102, 107, 108, 153, 154, 155, 168, 187, 188
Handley Page Aircraft 23
Hawker Siddeley 42, 43, 44, 66, 104, 108, 128, 130, 136, 147, 152, 161, 165, 166, 170, 172, 173, 174, 175
Hawker Siddeley Dynamics 42, 136, 147, 152, 170, 172, 173, 174
High Test Peroxide 69
HTP 69, 70, 76, 86, 87, 88, 92, 98, 108, 120, 147, 148, 153, 157, 158, 188
Improved Kiloton Weapon 52
Interim Megaton Weapon 50, 51
Journey's End 54, 55
Larynx 10
Lay-Down Bomb 114, 122, 139, 142, 143
Low Altitude Bomber 70, 71
Manoeuvring Bomb 63, 64
Minimum Conventional Bomber 10, 16, 17
Ministry of Aviation 53, 81, 83, 84, 108, 109, 114, 116, 122, 123, 124, 128, 132, 136, 137, 138, 139, 146, 158, 175, 187
Momentum Bomb 49, 61, 63, 64
MoS 13, 15, 27, 34, 55, 57, 71, 74, 75, 77, 104, 111, 142, 190
National Gas Turbine Establishment 12, 60
NATO 8, 19, 39, 42, 53, 84, 90, 134, 139, 151, 155, 156, 160, 169, 170, 174, 177, 182, 184, 189, 190
Odin ramjet 172, 179, 185
One Ton Warhead 104, 106, 108
Operation Unthinkable 39
OR.1132 65, 72, 74, 75, 76, 77, 89, 90, 95, 147
OR.1149 27, 87, 88, 89, 90, 91, 92, 93, 94, 95, 97, 98, 99, 100, 101, 102, 103, 104, 105, 106,
107, 108, 110, 154, 158, 187, 188
OR.1159 29, 81, 87, 88, 89, 104, 105, 106, 107, 108, 110, 146, 158, 187, 188
OR.1182 132, 134, 135, 136, 137, 138, 139, 147, 187
OR.330 15, 21, 23, 24, 25, 26, 27, 28, 29, 30, 31, 33, 35, 36, 37, 38, 39, 40, 42, 59, 77, 93, 96, 98, 161
Orange Herald 38, 73, 76, 93, 104, 152, 154
Paveway 175, 185
Poffler 116, 117, 118, 119, 120, 121, 122, 123, 125, 131, 132
Prospero 157, 190
R.156 15, 21, 22, 23, 24, 25, 27, 30, 31, 33, 34, 59, 98
Radar Research Establishment 28, 72
RAE Controlled Weapons Department 74
RAE Controlled Weapons Section 98
RB.156D 27
RE.179 53, 88, 114, 143, 146
Red Angel 54
Red Barrel 169, 171, 172, 173, 174
Red Beard 24, 38, 46, 48, 49, 52, 53, 56, 57, 63, 143, 153
Red Cat 70, 71, 72
Red Drover 21, 22, 23, 25, 27, 31, 33, 34, 37, 39, 41, 42
Red Shrimp 85, 113
Red Snow 51, 52, 82, 84, 86, 104, 146, 147
Royal Aircraft Establishment 10, 11, 12, 24, 25, 29, 36, 37, 55, 58, 62, 66, 68, 70, 71, 72, 73, 74, 75, 77, 80, 91, 92, 94, 95, 96, 97, 98, 99, 134, 136, 137, 138, 139, 140, 141, 143, 171, 178, 179, 183, 185, 190
SCOUT 164
Screamer, Armstrong Siddeley 70
Shelldyne 95, 142, 159, 178
Short Granite 102
Small Subsonic Bomb 70
Soviet Union 7, 8, 13, 14, 15, 16, 18, 20, 23, 39, 42, 44, 45, 54, 57, 61, 66, 90, 132, 157, 170, 174, 186
Special Weapon 12, 25, 36, 47, 55
Spectre, de Havilland 26, 70, 74, 79, 100, 103, 119, 153
Sputnik 29, 42, 151, 152, 157, 164
Stentor 26, 69, 77, 80, 87, 88, 100, 102, 103, 105, 107, 145, 147, 148, 152, 163, 166, 167, 168, 188, 189
Stop-Gap 132, 140, 142, 143
Strategic Air Command 59, 111
Super Sprite, de Havilland 120
Tallboy 36, 54, 55
Target Marker Bomb 48, 49, 53, 63, 153
Thor 134, 144, 145, 188
Tirpitz 54
Tumbling Bomb 36, 37, 38

Having landed on a dry lake-bed on the Woomera range after an unpowered test flight, an Avro Z.101 manned research vehicle is overflown by its Vulcan B.3 mothership and RAE TSR.2 chase plane.
Adrian Mann